THE LOST PARABLE

OF THE CROSS

D. G. Lett, Jr.

Cover Design by Don G. Lett, Jr.
Edited by Rosemary Newton

Published by Agape Press
32432 Robeson
St. Clair Shores, MI   48082
www.agapepressonline.com

Unless otherwise indicated, inline Scripture quotations are from the English
Standard Version, Modern King James Version or the King James Version.

Bold, and underlined words in quotations indicate emphasis by the author.

"I die daily"

– Paul of Tarsus in his first letter to the Corinthians
(approximately 55 A.D.)

TABLE OF CONTENTS

DEDICATION

I wish I could say I came up with the idea for the subject matter for this book. However, I cannot. I wish I could say I uncovered the picturesque symbols of this beautiful parable, but I cannot. I wish I could say that I live such a holy and pure life since I began my walk with Jesus, who caused Him to bless me with these revelations, but once again, I cannot. I wish I could say that He loved me with a greater love because something that is special within me caused this extraordinary love; however, I cannot. His love knows no bounds. His love is greater and higher than anything we can understand in human terms. We attempt to comprehend the level of His love through our temporal, impartial understanding, but all we truly understand is only a small, glittering light that shines over a vast ocean. No, the subject for this book came about as an answer to prayer. When I could not find the answer for some intricacies in this parable through academic research, I turned again, to prayer, and He gave the revelation. When I was befuddled and stopped the work, He woke me from my stupor and told me to be about my Father's business. He is my Father, my friend and the lover of my soul; He is my Jesus – my God.

The Lord of Glory not only speaks to us in His still small voice, but He also works through His servant-vessels. In the course of refining this work, He brought Rosemary Newton into my life. I am so grateful to her, for tirelessly working with me, in order to clarify the message of The Parable of the Cross.

To the Supreme Judge of the Universe, we stand in reverent awe, giving praise and honor to the only true God. To the One who loved me, long before I knew Him, who died the death, I deserved to die. To Him be praise and honor and glory, forever and ever. Amen

ACKNOWLEDGMENTS

First and foremost, I acknowledge the Holy Spirit's leading and guiding influence, both in this work and in my life.

Am I also greatly indebted Rosemary Newton for the extraordinary amount of time and dedication she contributed to the project. She not only helped me with every jot and every tittle within the book, but she was also a tremendous source of inspiration. Many times, I was concerned, I was asking too much from her. Her response was that "She was glad to be part of this work and felt it was a very important message." Authors are not impervious to criticisms of their work. Many times, we expose our heart, thoughts and dreams for to the world to determine if they are worthy of contemplation. In essence, we place ourselves in extremely vulnerable positions. Rosemary was a source of strength, throughout the process. She became the editor for this work. However, if you find some passages within this volume too wordy, or off topic, it is likely that she suggested something I rejected.

I also would like to acknowledge those spiritual leaders in my life that have helped to shape many of the revelations I discuss in this book. Thank you to John Denson, my father-in-law and spiritual father. I am also grateful to my pastor, Dan Stewart and my former pastors, David Eells, Mark Byers and John Terrice for their discipleship and spiritual guidance.

THE LOST REVELATION

Josiah was a godly King that came to the throne of Judah after terribly idolatrous reigns of his father Amon and his grandfather Manasseh; for they both *"did what was evil in the sight of the LORD, according to the despicable practices of the nations"* (2Ki 21:2) and *"shed very much innocent blood."* (2Ki 21:16) Manasseh was so full of wickedness; he *"burned his son as an offering and used fortune-telling and omens and dealt with mediums and with necromancers."* (2Ki 21:6) However, his grandson, King Josiah, began to *"seek the God of David his father."* (2Ch 34:3) He broke all the idols into pieces, pulverized them into dust *"and scattered it over the graves of those who had sacrificed to them."* (2Ch 34:4) Afterwards, He began to restore the temple of God when…

> *Hilkiah the high priest found a copy of The Revelation of Moses. He reported to Shaphan the royal secretary, "I've just found the Book of God's Revelation, instructing us in God's way—found it in The Temple!" He gave it to Shaphan, who then gave it to the king…*

> *Then, Shaphan told the king, "Hilkiah the priest gave me a book." Shaphan proceeded to read it out to the king.*

> *When the king heard what was written in the book, God's Revelation, he ripped his robes in dismay. Then, he called for… [his council and] …ordered them all: "Go and pray to God for me and what's left of Israel and Judah. Find out what we must do in response to what is written in this book that has just been found! God's anger must be burning furiously against us—our ancestors have not obeyed a thing written in this book of God, followed none of the instructions directed to us."*

> *Hilkiah and those picked by the king went straight to Huldah the prophetess. … In response to them she said, "…Tell the man who sent you here, 'God has spoken, I'm on my way to bring the doom*

of judgment on this place and this people. Every word written in the book read by the king of Judah will happen. And why? Because they've deserted me and taken up with other gods; they've made me thoroughly angry by setting up their god-making businesses. My anger is raging white-hot against this place and nobody is going to put it out.'"

"And also tell the king of Judah, since he sent you to ask God for direction, God's comment on what he read in the book: 'Because you took seriously the doom of judgment I spoke against this place and people, and because you responded in humble repentance, tearing your robe in dismay and weeping before me, ... I'll take care of you; you'll have a quiet death and be buried in peace. You won't be around to see the doom that I'm going to bring upon this place and people.'"

The men took her message back to the king.

The king acted immediately, assembling all the elders of Judah and Jerusalem, and then proceeding to The Temple of God bringing everyone in his train—priests and prophets and people ranging from the least to the greatest. Then he read out publicly everything written in the Book of the Covenant that was found in The Temple of God. The king stood by his pillar and before God solemnly committed himself to the covenant: to follow God believingly and obediently; to follow his instructions, heart and soul, on what to believe and do; to confirm with his life the entire covenant, all that was written in the book.

Then he made everyone in Jerusalem and Benjamin commit themselves. And they did it. They committed themselves to the covenant of God, the God of their ancestors.

Josiah did a thorough job of cleaning up the pollution that had spread throughout Israelite territory and got everyone started fresh again, serving and worshiping their God. All through Josiah's life the people kept to the straight and narrow, obediently following God, the God of their ancestors. (2Ch 34:14-33 MSG)

chapter one

WHY DO YOU SPEAK IN PARABLES?

I was lying in bed at about 4:30 AM, meditating on what God would have me teach for our Bible study lesson that evening. When all of the sudden I received a word from God to teach The Parable of the Cross. I continued to dwell on the imagery the Holy Spirit revealed to me in my mind's eye. By the time I got out of bed at 5:00 AM the entire lesson had been unveiled. Quickly, I turned on my computer, made my coffee and the words of the lesson began streaming from my mind onto the computer.

That night I began the lesson explaining we were going to discuss The Parable of the Cross. When I asked, *"We all know that our redemption was accomplished at the cross. Can you think of any other message that God may have wanted us to receive from the events that led to the crucifixion?"*

There was no answer.

Attempting to lead them, I asked, *"Does the picture of Jesus, the cross, the crucifixion, and the death, burial and the resurrection story hold another meaning for us as Christians besides the story of redemption?"*

Everyone continued to look at me with blank stares.

I have asked this question to many other believers since that time and have never received the correct answer. Maybe I am being too vague in the question, but I believe the response is, at least partially, indicative of a much larger problem prevalent within the body of Christ. Actually, I believe this message, for the most part, has been lost over the last century from many modern pulpits.

1

I have heard people in the church ask teachers, *"What does it mean when Jesus tells us to pick up the cross?"* To which, the typical response is something akin to, *"It means we are going to have to go through trials and persecutions."* Although this is correct, it is only partially correct, because it lacks the depth that the question deserves. In fact, this gospel teacher has jettisoned a tremendous teaching opportunity with this carte blanch response. I am afraid, in effect, that the vague answer is due to not having a thorough understanding of what Jesus meant when He said, *"If anyone would come after me, let him deny himself and **take up** his cross and follow me."* (Mat 16:24) According to the teacher's response, we are to bear the cross that is **put on us** by the trials and tribulations of this world. However, that appears to be much less active participation than The King of Glory described in Matthew 16:24. In fact, Jesus appears to describe the assertive action of **taking up** our cross. Combining the teacher's response with Messiah's revelation, we should conclude that we are supposed to actively look for opportunities to bear the cross; either, by denying ourselves for others' good, or by willingly going through trials, tribulations and persecutions. This may be one of the most significant teachings in the New Testament, and yet, so many times, teachers vaguely gloss over the principle. When we grasp the full understanding of this verse, it will fill the believer with spiritual insight, transforming defeated Christians into the image of the Captain of their Salvation, causing us to say, *"…we are more than conquerors through him who loved us"*! (Rom 8:31)

It is precisely the concept of the victorious Christian life that Western Laodicean churches have distorted, fermenting the enormous rise of the *Name-It-and-Claim-It Prosperity* Churches and the *Many-Roads-to-God New Age "Christian"* Churches. Had the laity been made acutely aware of the correct teaching of this verse, then the error of these false doctrines would have been readily apparent. However, since the message is almost entirely lost by many fallen churches, or muddled by many of the churches actually following Christ's teachings, there is a great deal of confusion as to what it means to be a Christian. Barna's surveys, for example, have shown a steady decline of Christians, who maintain the essential doctrines of the faith, citing that less than 10% has a biblical worldview in 2005. Astoundingly, another study found that only about half of the pastors teaching in our churches, hold to the central doctrines of the faith!

Why Do You Speak in Parables?

It is surprising that we are so easily deceived. However, this is why God wrote the Bible. It is also astounding that so many of us do not read the Bible that Christians in the past, true to the faith, fought vigilantly for our right to read. For nearly a thousand years, it was only legal to read the Holy Writ in Latin, which none of the laity understood. Men risked their lives in order to translate and print the scriptures into the common vernacular of the people. Because of this, they were tortured and persecuted in the most heinous ways, many giving up their lives for the cause of the faith. The ruling church of that time burned with white-hot, bitter rage against these reformers. In an example of this spewing hatred, poured out against reformers, they dug up John Wycliffe's bones forty years after his death to burn him as a heretic. Likewise, America held blacks in subjection, not allowing them to read the Bible, fearing that when they read that Moses demanded the Hebrews freedom from slavery, they would make similar demands upon their own oppressors. The slaves also had to fight for their right to read the Bible. Unfortunately, today, if you are lucky enough to walk into a person's house who even owns a Bible, you will probably have to brush the thick dust off it before you can begin to read it.

The message of this book is written in the Bible in plain view for the entire world to see. However, since the American republic has become so averse to reading they have allowed themselves to be deceived by various religious organizations and Christian sects to believe many things that were never taught before in Christianity.

There are also those hidden verses in the Bible that offer the reader a great deal of edification and deeper insight into the message. If you have been a believer for any amount of time, then I am sure that you have had the experience of reading a passage when all of the sudden the Holy Spirit gives you a new, fresh meaning about the verse that you have never seen before. So, why does the Lord hide so much in His Word? I believe there are several reasons for this. First, the King of Glory answered this same question for the disciples:

> *To you it has been given to know the **secrets of the kingdom of heaven**, but to them it has not been given. **For to the one who has, more will be given, and he will have an abundance**, but from the one who has not, even what he has will be taken away. This is why I speak to them in parables, because seeing they do not see, and hearing they do not hear, nor do they understand. Indeed, in their*

*case the prophecy of Isaiah is fulfilled that says: "You will indeed hear but never understand, and you will indeed see but never perceive. For this people's heart has grown dull, and with their ears they can barely hear, and their eyes they have closed, lest they should see with their eyes and hear with their ears and understand with their heart and turn, and I would heal them." **But blessed <u>are your eyes, for they see</u>, and <u>your ears, for they hear</u>.** (Mat 13:11-16 ESV)*

The first point the King makes is that there are secrets in the Kingdom of Heaven. He follows this with the statement that the person who has a great abundance will receive more, but the one who has very little, will have his taken away. This sounds completely upside-down to our modern, progressive mind-set. Furthermore, since God said to help the poor and the widow, I am sure this statement immediately took the disciples aback. Can you imagine a politician running on this proposal today in our society? He steps up to the podium to deliver his speech to the crowd and begins with, *"Today we are going to revise the tax code completely."* The crowd cheers! He goes on to say, *"…by taxing the poor much more and giving that money to the rich, so that he who has an abundance will have more and to those who have very little even that which they have shall be taken away."* Can you imagine the listeners' stunned silence? This suggestion is so preposterous that I am confident these spectators would have to wait for a moment to hear the next sentence, in order to determine if it was a set up for the punch line of a joke.

What is so fascinating about this statement is that it probably had the same effect on the disciples. They may have been passively listening to the King at this time, but after He said this statement, their ears perked up. This is one of the reasons that Christians and non-Christians alike agree that the teachings of Jesus are the greatest of any man in history. He is able to grab your attention with these little phrases like this, so your curiosity now has taken you captive to His speech.

What else is interesting in this teaching is that He essentially is using a parable to explain the parable. This parable, although, is more straightforward and easier for the disciples to decipher than the previous one.

If you were to say something like this to the world, they would look at you as if you are crazy. However, with a little further explanation maybe we can grasp this extremely powerful spiritual truth. Say, for example, you like to golf, so you spend a bunch of money to buy a class set of clubs. Then, you practice every day for a year. Would you expect that your golf game would be better at the end of the year? Of course, you would. What would you expect to happen to your game if you took a couple of years off from playing? It is obvious that you would not perform as well as you did practicing every day. God gave to you a certain amount of natural ability to play golf, and then because you invested your time and effort, you became better at the game. When you did not make this investment, you became worse, so our example validates this spiritual principle. You can apply this to working out and weight lifting. You can apply this to reading and studying. However, the King is applying this law to growing spiritual seed in your heart, which is the parable that He was explaining at the time.

The Word of God speaks to us on many levels. A person can read a bible verse and come away with a prophecy about the future. Another person can read that same portion of scripture and gain a greater understanding about the redeeming work of Christ. Sometimes you can come back to the Holy Writ and see things you never have seen before that speaks to your current circumstances. Does this mean that there are many truths in the scriptures, and therefore, we should not hold to any specific dogmas? The simple answer to that question is no. Jesus said, "*I am the way, and **the truth**, and the life. No one comes to the Father except through me.*" (Joh 14:6) Notice, the King of Glory uses the definite article, "*the*", to say, He is THE TRUTH. This means, He is the embodiment of the truth, and that truth, is definitive. God speaking to us on many different levels should not surprise us, after all, His voice is described "*like the roar of many waters*" (Rev 14:2) and His Word "*is living and active.*" (Heb 4:12) We can understand truth on several levels, but the truth that will be the focus of our discussion, is the life application of its principles, according to scriptures, and applied to the born-again believer.

You will need to see these matters with your spiritual eyes and not your natural eyes. As the King has said of the blinding effect of religious pride, "*seeing they do not see, and hearing they do not hear, nor do they understand.*" He was literally speaking of the scribes and the Pharisees. When we apply this verse to our spiritual lives, then we should comprehend that He is speaking to the Pharisees in us. This part of us is self-righteous, religious and legalistic. This part of us believes that we are living good, wholesome lives, acceptable to God's standards of righteousness. This is spiritual pride. It causes us to look at others and conclude we are better than them. If you listen to this part of yourself, then you will not understand the Word of God, for "*God resists the proud, but He gives grace to the humble.*" (Jas 4:7)

The Pharisee in us is what the Bible calls the flesh, the old man or the natural man. This is also why the world cannot receive these sayings because "***the natural man*** *does not receive the things of the Spirit of God, for they are foolishness to him; neither can he know them, because they are spiritually discerned.*" (1Co 2:14)

Messiah also warns us "*not [to] give **that which is holy** to the dogs; nor [to] cast **your pearls** before swine, lest they trample them under their feet and turn again and tear you.*" (Mat 7:6) The reaction to the truth in these verses is to attack the person delivering the message. We have seen this occur many times in history. However, notice that the King of Glory equates these words-of-truth to pearls. Pearls used to be called the "*Queen of the Gems,*" because they were the most valued jewel of antiquity. Cleopatra had two expensive pearls ground into powder. Then, in order to demonstrate the vast wealth of Egypt, she drank one as she entertained Marc Antony.[1] Pearls value reached their zenith at the height of the Roman Empire's power when General Aulus Vitellius (15-69 AD) financed an entire military campaign by selling one of his mother's pearls. Notice that this period coincides with the dates Messiah equated the truth of the scriptures with the amazing value of this gemstone. Thus, Jesus was not only referring to the value of scriptures, but He was also stating that we should not waste something of such matchless worth on a person who is not demonstrating any inclination to desire the truth. Messiah not only uses this to discuss sharing the truth in scriptures, but He also applies this principle when He speaks in parables to believers. Consider, treasure for example. It is something we search diligently to find. We are highly motivated, as well, to find treasures because of their considerable value. Diamond mines run deep into the earth. The owner of the diamond mine will spend millions of dollars on labor and equipment just for the prospect of finding diamonds. Men who work

---

[1] Pliny writes in "*Natural History*" that the two pearls were worth an estimated 60 million sesterces, which is about $9,375,000 with silver at $5/ounce.

for these mines risk their lives to find these precious gems. Do we assess the wisdom of our Lord's teachings with so great a distinction? Do we freely cast pearls of wisdom, without regard, in front of those who have no desire for truth? For this reason, an evangelist needs to be sensitive to the Holy Spirit, in order to determine if they should cast their pearls before a non-believer.

Many believers are quite happy with their relationship with God. They have no desire to dig deeper into the Word of Truth. They stand outside the mine, not receiving the added benefits of digging deeper into a relationship with the Lord of Glory, because they never seek; they do not find these precious gems of truth. For this reason, the scriptures declare, "*It is the glory of God to conceal things, but the glory of kings is to search things out.*" (Pro 25:2) Scriptures also reveal that Messiah's sacrifice made every believer "*kings and priests.*" (Rev 1:6) Consequently, the Word of Truth hides His precious truth in parables. This also, is the reason I have written this book, because there is a parable in the story of the cross. The most significant message to the non-believer is the good news that God will forgive your sins because of the great work His Son accomplished at the cross, if you simply accept Him as your Lord and Savior. However, there is also a hidden message for the believer in the story of the cross, as a parable, which will enlighten our Christian walk and cause us to contemplate the Lord's sanctifying work in our lives. When a believer grasps this principle and applies it to their life, they will no longer live as defeated Christians, dragging their feet in the dirt, but rather, will become transformed into a potent vanguard of sanctifying power, leading the way for weaker vessels and enlightening a lost world. This powerful message has been lost to our generation. Therefore, let us dig deeper to discover the precious treasure troths of truth the King of the Universe has buried within The Parable of the Cross.

chapter two

RAISING THE DEAD

The first story of the Old Testament begins with life. The first story of the New Testament also begins with life, so that we have a perfect parallel between the creation of the world and the creation of the Savior, or the incarnation. In like manner, the story of Adam moves from life to death, which also is paralleled by Jesus' story from life to death. However, our story begins with death, for we *"were dead in the trespasses and sins."* (Eph 2:1) For this reason, it is only fitting that we should begin our discussion of The Parable of the Cross with, what has become known in some churches, as *Lazarus Saturday.*[2]

This story is recounted for us in John chapter 11. A quick overview of the chapter reveals that a man named Lazarus, living in Bethany, became deathly ill. Jesus was extremely close to Lazarus and his family, as John informs us, *"Jesus loved Martha and her sister and Lazarus."* (Joh 11:5) When Lazarus became ill, Mary and Martha sent word to Jesus to come immediately to Bethany, in order to save his life. However, instead of moving quickly to save Lazarus, Jesus seemingly disregarded the message and remained where He was for two more days. Only after Lazarus died did He finally decide to leave for Bethany. When Messiah came near the town, Martha met Him, and said, *"Lord, if you had been here, my brother would not have died."* (Joh 11:21) Afterwards, Mary fell at His feet and reiterated the same sentiment saying, *"Lord, if you had been here, my brother would not have died."* (Joh 11:32) Although Jesus was deeply grieved in the spirit, He ignored Mary's conclusion and simply asked her to show Him Lazarus' tomb. When He arrived at the cave, He told the people to roll the stone away. Then, Martha cautioned Jesus about the pungent odor of death because Lazarus had been dead for four days. To which,

---

[2] The Bible only states that this event happened close to the Passover (Joh 11:55)

He responded, *"Did I not tell you that if you believed you would see the glory of God?"* (Joh 11:40) At which time, Jesus turned to God Almighty and prayed aloud:

> *"Father, I thank you that you have heard me. I knew that you always hear me, but I said this on account of the people standing around, that they may believe that you sent me." When he had said these things, he cried out with a loud voice, "Lazarus, come out." The man who had died came out, his hands and feet bound with linen strips, and his face wrapped with a cloth. Jesus said to them, "Unbind him, and let him go." (Joh 11:41-44 ESV)*

The subsequent response to this miraculous event is almost as equally remarkable because it gives us a extraordinary insight into the stubbornness of human nature.

> *Many... who had come with Mary and had seen what he did, believed in him, but some of them went to the Pharisees and told them what Jesus had done. So the chief priests and the Pharisees gathered the Council and said, "What are we to do? **For this man performs many signs**. If we let him go on like this, **everyone will believe in him**, and the Romans will come and take away both our place and our nation." But one of them, Caiaphas, who was high priest that year, said to them, "...it is better for you that one man should die for the people, not that the whole nation should perish." ...So from that day on **they made plans to put him to death**. Jesus therefore no longer walked openly among the Jews... (Joh 11:45-54 ESV)*

The Talmud corroborates John's testimony, as well.[3]

> *On the eve of Passover they hanged Yeshu[4] and the herald went before him for forty days, saying, "**[Yeshu] is going forth to be stoned** in that **he hath practiced sorcery and beguiled and led astray Israel**."*[5]

Jesus traveled Bethany and raised a man from the dead, who had been dead for four days. This caused many of the common people to believe that Jesus must be God's promised messiah. The ruling class also

---

[3] Rabbinical teachings produced in the first and second century.
[4] The Hebrew word for Jesus is Yeshu or Yeshua.
[5] Babylonia Sanhedrin 43a

believed that Jesus performed these miracles, but their response was entirely different, saying, *"the Romans will come and take away both our place [that is, status and position] and our nation."* Therefore, instead of falling to their knees and acknowledging this incredible miracle, they plotted to kill the messenger of God, in order to preserve their own place of power and prestige. In fact, they became so obstinate, that within a couple of days *"the chief priests made plans to put Lazarus to death as well, because on account of him many of the Jews were going away and believing in Jesus"*! (Joh 12:10-11)

These are the historical events of the incarnate God-Man Jesus the day before His triumphal entry into Jerusalem. It is intriguing that God can use actual incidents and use them for prophetic pronouncements and life application spiritual principles, while, continuing to remain true to the historicity of the finest details of the events. On the historical level, we see that the Jewish Talmud validated the episode. This compelling testimony considering that the Talmud never acknowledged Jesus as Messiah, but instead, professed that He used *"sorcery"* to *"beguile"* the people and lead them *"astray"*. Thus, the Talmud corroborates Jesus performed miracles, although they believed the source of that power came from *"by Beelzebul, the prince of demons."* (Luk 11:15) This is not the only time the Holy Writ uses a person's life experiences to develop spiritual messages for the believers. In fact, God does this many times through scriptures. The life stories of Abraham, Isaac, Jacob, Joseph, David and all the other patriarchs come into view, validated by the historical record, and yet, their stories are full of spiritual and prophetic revelations. Truly, The Sovereign, Omnipotent, Omniscient, Author of Life is the greatest artist, poet and writer to weave such glorious, divine truths from the actual events, of real people, into the majesty of the Bible.

On the next level, we touch upon the prophetic understandings of this story. Within seven days, God will raise Jesus from the dead, so Lazarus foreshadows the resurrection. It is significant that Lazarus had been dead four days. Many teachers state that Jesus probably allowed this time to elapse, because, according to Jewish tradition, a person was not considered officially dead until at least three days had passed. While this may be true, I believe God may also have hidden a prophetic meaning within the text. Peter explicates *"with the Lord one day is as a thousand years."* (2Pe 3:8) Applying this principle, we have a person in the grave for four thousand years. Lazarus, then, when looked at through the lens of prophecy, is typified as humanity attempting to justify ourselves according to our own righteousness before Holy God. From Adam to Jesus, God gave man 4,000 years to find a way to justify himself according to His perfect law. We could not do it. Even when God gave the law by the prophet, Moses, it was apparent that man could never completely follow the law. In James' epistle, we are told that if you break even the smallest portion of God's perfect law, then you are a transgressor, and not considered justified before Him. (Jam 2:10) Prophetically, we comprehend from Lazarus that man cannot raise himself from a dead spirit. When Lazarus became ill his sisters sent word to Jesus stating, "*Lord, he whom you love is ill*" (Joh 11:3), signifying that Jesus had a particularly strong love for Lazarus. We know, as well, Jesus had stated, "*you are my friends if you do what I command you.*" (Joh 15:14) Again, He said, "*Who is my mother, and who are my brothers? ...whoever does the will of my Father in heaven is my brother and sister and mother.*" (Mat 12:48-50) Thus, Jesus clarified that love and faithful dedication are inherently tied to one another. Love being internal emotion, and faithful obedience being the outward expression of that love. Considering Lazarus is the one whom Jesus loved, then, it is also safe to assume, he was faithfully obedient to Christ and did the Will of His Father. Lazarus, therefore, is an ideal representation of a man who was as righteous as he could be before God, and yet, he was not able to free himself from the law of sin and death. Although he was faithfully obedient to Messiah, he could not overcome the sickness of sin, and he died. He remained dead for four days to underscore that not one person in history had the ability to be justified before God, not Abraham, not Moses, or any of His other faithful prophets. If Moses was not justified before God by the law; then, what hope do any of us have?

Even the faithful prophet, Isaiah, comprehended his unworthiness before God, when he was lifted up to heaven, and stated:

> *I saw the Lord sitting upon a throne, high and lifted up; and the train of his robe filled the temple. Above him stood the seraphim. Each had six wings: with two he covered his face, and with two he covered his feet, and with two he flew. And one called to another and said: "Holy, holy, holy is the LORD of hosts; the whole earth is full of his glory!" And the foundations of the thresholds shook at the voice of him who called, and the house was filled with smoke. And I said: "**Woe is me! For I am lost; for I am a man of unclean lips, and I dwell in the midst of a people of unclean lips;***

for my eyes have seen the King, the LORD of hosts!" (Isa 6:1-5 ESV)

What an incredible scene of the power and holiness of God! Even His righteous angels cover their faces and feet out of respect for His Shekinah glory. They are so overwhelmed by His splendor that they call to one another, *"Holy, holy, holy is the Lord."* Is your righteousness greater than the sacred angels of God?

For this reason, Isaiah also makes it clear that *"we are __ALL__ as an unclean thing, and __ALL our righteousnesses are as filthy rags__; and we all do fade as a leaf; and our iniquities, like the wind, have taken us away."* (Isa 64:6)

No matter how hard you try, you cannot save yourself! You are Lazarus. You cannot raise yourself from the dead. The most committed Protestant cannot justify himself by his works. The most devout Catholic will not be vindicated by adherence to the liturgical rites of the church. The most dedicated Hindu will not be deemed righteous through daily veneration. The most devoted Muslim will not be acceptable in obedience to the Islamic law, and the list of unacceptable religious works goes on and on. Indeed, there is not a religion on earth, which can justify you before this Holy God! Every religion attempts to build a tower of Babel, by their works, up to God. However, this is an impossible feat! It cannot be done! God utterly scorns and severely judges those who attempt to bridge the enormous gap between God and man by building a tower of works. (Gen 11)

The apostle Paul speaks to our utterly lost condition in Romans chapter seven; expounding upon justifying ourselves through righteous works for several verses, and concluding our absolute inability to save ourselves, he cries out in despair, *"O wretched man that I am! __Who shall deliver me__ from the body of this death?"* (Rom 7:24)

Lazarus was deathly ill and not able to save himself from his disease. Later, he was dead four days and completely unable to save himself from that condition. Likewise, mankind had four thousand years to have someone live a sinless life and demonstrate that it was possible to save ourselves, yet not one person through all those centuries was able to live a perfect, sinless life. If anyone could have risen to this challenge, it would have been the apostle Paul, who stated that,

If anyone else thinks he has reason for confidence in the flesh, I have more: circumcised on the eighth day, of the people of Israel, of the tribe of Benjamin, a Hebrew of Hebrews; as to the law, a Pharisee; as to zeal, a persecutor of the church; as to righteousness under the law, blameless. (Php 3:4-6 ESV)

Yet, it is this same Paul, who desperately cries out, "*O wretched man that I am!* ***Who shall deliver me*** *from the body of this death?*" (Rom 7:24) Notice, he is not asking what else he can do, or what religion can he follow or what sacrifice can he offer, but "***WHO*** *shall deliver me?*" No matter how hard you try, you cannot save yourself.

Many people think this is a New Testament doctrine, which did not exist until Christ became the propitiation for our sins on the cross. However, that is problematic, because the Immutable God has said; "*I the LORD do not change*". (Mal 3:6) The Supreme Judge made this statement to the people of Malachi's time, explaining that His righteous judgments do not change. If God had a different standard of righteousness for His pre-Christian believers, and now has different criteria, since the sacrifice of Christ, then, would that not constitute a change? I know many strong believing Christians are now reading this and pulling out their dispensationalist doctrines, to announce that I am not rightly dividing the truth. Even so, bear with me for one moment. Take note, the Old Testament prophet, Hosea, understood that God "*desired mercy and not sacrifice, and the knowledge of God more than burnt offerings.*" (Hos 6:6) King David, likewise, acknowledged this sentiment stating, "*You do not desire sacrifice; or else I would give it; You do not delight in burnt offering. The sacrifices of God are a broken spirit; a broken and a contrite heart.*" (Psa 51:16-17) The prophet Samuel, said, as well, "*Does Jehovah delight in burnt offerings and sacrifices as in obeying the voice of Jehovah? Behold,* ***to obey is better than sacrifice****! To listen is better than the fat of rams!*" (1Sa 15:22)

Most Christians believe that justification by faith is a New Testament doctrine. They will readily quote, "*For by grace you have been saved through faith. And this is not your own doing; it is the gift of God, not a result of works, so that no one may boast.*" (Eph 2:8-9) However, most have not considered that was God's plan of justification from the beginning. The New Testament witnesses to this fact, stating, "*Abraham believed God, and it was counted unto him for righteousness.*" (Rom 4:3) In addition, in an earlier epistle to the

Galatians, Paul was quotes the Old Testament prophet Habakkuk stating, *"that no one is justified before God by the law, for '**The righteous shall live by faith**.'"* (Gal 3:11)

The very first reference in the Bible to the remedy for the fall of man from grace is written in the third chapter of Genesis.

> *The LORD God said to the serpent, "Because you have done this, cursed are you above all livestock and above all beasts of the field; on your belly you shall go, and dust you shall eat all the days of your life. I will put enmity between you and the woman, and between your offspring and her offspring; **he shall bruise your head, and you shall bruise his heel**." (Gen 3:14-15 ESV)*

Reflect upon, that the Lord did not speak to Adam or Eve, saying you shall prepare burnt offerings, or go to church once a week, or that you shall pray five times a day facing a temple. In other words, the remedy was not in religious rituals at all. In truth, the Lord made no reference to any sort of religious worship, needed to be performed by man, during His discourse of the curses, and the solution that He would provide for the fall. When we read the last line of the Genesis excerpt above, we notice the Lord did not assign a methodology for man to save himself, but rather, he promised a Deliverer. The Jewish people began to call this deliverer the *"Meshiach,"* from which we derive from the Greek, *"Christ"*. Thus, from the outset of man's fall, we see the answer for sin was never wrapped in the garb of religious rituals, but in the personhood, and the promise of a deliverer, the Christ.

For this reason, I can confidently say, there is no religion on earth, which can justify a person before this Holy God, because the justification is in the personhood of Christ alone. Consider all that we have discussed up to this point. The Old Testament prophets understood the real absolution for their sins was never dependent on burnt offerings. They understood it was faith in God's deliverer from the beginning. In addition, God never mentions religious rites during His discourse at the fall of man. Thus, we understand that justification is not due to religious practice, but inherent in our relationship with the Savior. Because of this, although the expression has become somewhat trite, Christianity is not a religion but a relationship with Messiah. Therefore, Jesus states, *"My sheep hear my voice, and I know them, and they follow me."* (Joh 10:27) Lazarus, as well, is a perfect representation of the sheep, who will be raised on the last day. Lazarus loved Jesus. He was the one whom Jesus loved. Is it not magnificent that Messiah states in the very next verse, He will *"give them eternal life, and they shall never perish"*? (Joh 10:28)

Imagine what may have occurred if Lazarus was an entirely religious man of works with no personal faith relationship with our Lord and Savior. Jesus would have shouted, *"Lazarus come forth."* He would not have listened to His voice; choosing rather to remain in the cave of his dead religious works. To punctuate this crucial point; Christianity is a faith relationship with our Sovereign Lord and Savior. It is not a works religion.

Does this mean that Christians do not need to go to church? God forbid! In the book of Revelations, our Lord Almighty begins by addressing the seven churches. Paul wrote most of the epistles after his conversion, spending his life addressing the churches through his letters. The book of Hebrews was written to admonish Christians in the Judean area to continue to assemble as believers.

> *Let us hold fast the profession of our faith without wavering... And let us consider one another to provoke unto love and to good works:* ***Not forsaking the assembling of ourselves together****, as the manner of some is; but exhorting one another... (Heb 10:23-25 KJV)*

Now that we have completed our exercise in examining the previous passages on the historical and the prophetic levels, let us view how we may apply them to our lives. Do not imagine that believers should not read their Bible and gain understanding on how to conduct their lives. After all, a man must crawl before he can walk, and in due time, he will be able to run. As you learn to walk, the Holy Spirit should lead you in your daily studies, so even a mature believer can return to a passage and gain a new perspective, speaking to their present life circumstances.

To summarize the events thus far, Lazarus was deathly ill. Next, Mary and Martha sent a messenger to Jesus to let Him know to come and save Lazarus. However, Jesus decided to stay where He was for two additional days. When He said He needed to go to Bethany, His disciples were shocked, because they knew the Jewish leaders wanted to stone Him. When He arrived, Martha and Mary both complain to the Lord Almighty that if He had been there Lazarus would not have died. Jesus responded that He was going to raise Lazarus from the dead, but both sisters spiritualize the message. Messiah then asked them to bring Him to Lazarus' grave and for them to remove the stone. Even at this time, the sisters had no comprehension that Jesus was going to bring Lazarus back to life. Finally, He performed this extraordinary miracle; causing many to believe that He was Messiah. Nevertheless, others, who were hard of heart, took word back to the religious leaders, who believed the miracle, but responded by plotting not only Jesus' death, but Lazarus' death, as well.

On the life application level, there are many lessons that can be harvested from this story. First, we must trust in God. Jesus' disciples, Lazarus' sisters, and those present had no knowledge of what Jesus was doing. They did not comprehend Lazarus death four days earlier as necessary for Jesus to demonstrate the power of God. Mary, Martha, and their friends went through a terrible time of suffering, in order for the Lord to demonstrate that he carries the keys to life. Although it appears the Lord took this occasion lightly, He did not. Take note, for example, when Mary saw Jesus, she came to Him and

> *...fell down at His feet, saying to Him, "Lord, if You had been here, my brother would not have died." Then when He saw her weeping, and also the Jews who came with her weeping, Jesus* **groaned** *in the spirit and troubled Himself. (Joh 11:32-33 MKJV)*

What incredible compassion the Lord has for His creation. Other gods, from other religions, would most likely look upon such a fiasco of events and become indignant, that they did not trust the gods, or that mortals could be so foolish. They may have been upset that these humans would bother them in the first place. Though Messiah knew all the grief, they experienced during Lazarus' death was temporary, He genuinely felt their pain. However, the translation of the word *groaning* in the text does not quite capture its full meaning. The word used in the Greek is, *"embrimaomai,"* which means to *"snort with anger."* It is intriguing that this word is only used two other times in the entire New Testament, one of those being, in this same story:

> *Then Jesus,* **groaning** *in Himself again, came to the tomb. (Joh 11:38 MKJV)*

When we contemplate the severe agony of emotions that overcame our Savior, we gain a new appreciation for the shortest verse in the Bible, *"Jesus wept."* (Joh 11:35) I used to read this verse, believing Jesus had a few tears well up in His eyes that needed to be wiped away. Now, after comprehending His extraordinary level of emotion, I believe His face became flooded with tears. What an incredibly moving portrayal of the empathy of our Sovereign Lord! How much He loves us! How He *"sympathize[s] with our weaknesses"*! (Heb 4:15) If I was God, I would have become impatient, knowing in a few minutes that Lazarus would be walking around and all these tears of sorrow would have been turned to joy; but not our Savior. Instead, He experienced the intense pain caused by sin and death, and He must have thought, it never had to be this way. Despite knowing the eventual outcome, He deeply sympathized with Martha and Mary's grief; and *"HE WEPT"*! Selah! In the Hebrew, this means pause and consider this! If God loves us this much, then, is He not worthy of all of our love? His love for us is both personal and eternal.

I recall visiting a church in the Chicago area. The pastor made some announcements and then preached for about 5-10 minutes. Afterwards, he released the congregation. I was a little confused, so I asked the person beside me if the service was already over. He said to me, *"Yeah, isn't this great, now we have the rest of the day to ourselves."* What! Are you kidding me? Why even bother going to church if this is your attitude towards our amazing, loving Savior, who died on the cross for your sins!

Jesus lived the Christian life as an example. Then, following in His footsteps, we should demonstrate patience and compassion for unbelievers and carnal Christians. Ironically, we fervently desire God's patience and love for us, yet it is rare to find that same compassion for others expressed in ourselves.

Other lessons we can carve out of this story are; we should trust in Jesus, even when we may not understand why He allows things to occur as they do. We should not harden our hearts when God works on our behalf. We should know that our time to depart from this world would not come until we have fulfilled all our purposes in the Lord, as long as we walk in His ways

In addition, consider the incredible picture of prayer and the Trinity in this story. Mary and Martha send, *prayer*, a messenger, *the **Holy Spirit***, to ask Jesus to save Lazarus. **Jesus** arrives, interceding for them praying,

> ***Father***, *I thank You that You have heard Me. And I know that You hear Me always… (Joh 11:41-42 MKJV)*

17

This is an ideal model representing our relationship with the Almighty. It illustrates that we should begin with prayer, which is exactly how this story begins.

Now, let us begin to expound upon how the parable depicts our sanctifying walk with Jesus. We have already demonstrated that adherents from every other religion, besides true Christianity, attempts to justify themselves before God by their works, many times through religious rites. We also discovered that even before Christ's payment on the cross, no one was justified by the law. Instead, they were justified by their obedience, which demonstrated their true faith walk in God Almighty. This may now cause you to ask, "*What does the law have to do with me?*" After all, one of the most fundamental teachings in Christianity today is, we are saved by grace through faith, and it is not of works. We all know, as well, we are constantly battling our old nature. This is precisely what Paul described in Romans 7, when he stated that his higher nature knows what he should do, yet his lower nature is so powerful and demanding, that he ultimately is destined to fail. Because he cannot live a perfect life, and because he acknowledges that obedience to the law is good, and yet unattainable, by his own conscience, he stands convicted before God. It is that old nature; within us, that is the focus of our parable, The Parable of the Cross.

It is fascinating that you do not have to be a Christian to believe man has a dual nature. It is obvious Robert Louis Stevenson was representing the universal truth of our own self-struggle between good and evil in his famous story "*Dr. Jekyll and Mr. Hyde.*" Modern pop culture depicts this conflict, as well. One of Star Trek's most well known episodes, for instance, was the battle between the good and the evil Kirk. This struggle is so obvious that even children comprehend the duality of our natures and the battles they wage. When I asked my six-year-old son why he continued to make the wrong choice, he told me that the bad in him told him to do it, while the good in him told him not to. In like manner, Sigmund Freud divided the psyche into three parts, the ego, super-ego and the id. The id is your lower nature. The super-ego is your higher nature, and the ego is the battlefield of the mind, forced to choose between the impulses of the id or the morality of the super-ego. Frankly, he could easily have arrived at these very same conclusions directly from Bible passages like Romans chapter seven. Long before our modern era, Plato recorded Socrates (469 - 399 BC), speaking of this dual nature in "*The Republic.*" His argument was, if we all agree people use self-discipline, then we agree there are two natures in man; since to be disciplined requires at least two parties; one to enforce the discipline and the other who is under the discipline. This also means that self should control the lower nature, from which derive the word "*self-discipline*," the word itself implicating our agreement with Socrates' syllogism.

It is intriguing, as well, that Plato uses a cave in "*The Republic*" as an analogy to describe our impaired understanding of the truth. Consider the following summary of the "*Analogy of the Cave.*" Several prisoners are chained in the bottom of a cave for their entire lives. They are immobile, only able to view the wall in front of them. Behind the prisoners is a large fire. Between the fire and the prisoners is a raised walkway, along which "*figures of men and animals made of wood, stone and other materials*" appear. Since the only things the prisoners can see are the shadows cast on the wall, they believed the shadows are reality. Eventually, one of them breaks free and finds his way out of the cave. Now, for the first time, he sees the world as it truly is, realizing what he thought was reality his entire life were actually only shadows of that reality. He is extremely excited to share this newfound truth, so he returns to the bottom of the cave to tell his fellow prisoners. The prisoners' reaction is the exact opposite of what he had expected; instead of receiving the truth and being set free, they become so angry that "*if they were somehow able to get their hands on and kill the man who attempts to release [them]… they [would] kill him*".

Notice how closely this allegory parallels the parable God orchestrated for us in the historical details of Jesus raising Lazarus from the cave. It is fascinating, pagan philosophers, Plato and Socrates, were able to discern so much truth without the Bible. This underscores the primary message in Romans 1, in which Paul states that God has given all men some light; thus, they are able to come to knowledge of the truth of God. Because of these premises, he concludes in Romans 2, "*Therefore, you are without excuse, O man*" (Rom 2:1) for "*They show that the work of the law is written on their hearts.*" (Rom 2:15)

The cave represents utter darkness. It is a state, as in Socrates' allegory, most people do not realize they are in until they somehow see the light. Coming to the light is where Christianity departs from Socrates, because in Lazarus' case, he is in an utterly helpless condition, until the Resurrection and the Life calls him to come forth. The Almighty uses this pattern of historical events to demonstrate our need for spiritual restoration, also known as the born-again experience. Now, let us compare the fundamentals of this supernatural birth God painted for us by raising Lazarus with Messiah's conversation with the Pharisee Nicodemus several years earlier.

> *Jesus answered him, "Truly, truly, I say to you, unless one is **born-again he cannot see the kingdom of God**." Nicodemus said to him, "How can a man be born when he is old? Can he enter a second time into his mother's womb and be born?" Jesus answered, "Truly, truly, I say to you, unless one is born of water and the Spirit, he cannot enter the kingdom of God. That which is born of the flesh is flesh, and that which is born of the Spirit is spirit. ...The wind blows where it wishes, and you hear its sound, but you do not know where it comes from or where it goes. So it is with everyone who is born of the Spirit." (Joh 3:3-8 ESV)*

After Messiah makes these statements Nicodemus seems even more puzzled so Jesus goes on to explain.

> *Truly, truly, I say to you, we speak of what we know, and bear witness to what we have seen, but you do not receive our testimony. If I have told you earthly things and you do not believe, how can you believe if I tell you heavenly things? No one has ascended into heaven except he who descended from heaven, the Son of Man. (Joh 3:11-13 ESV)*

It is striking how similar this explanation is to Socrates' understanding of the truth. However, there is one prominent, fundamental difference. Socrates believed the philosophers have seen the light, but Jesus clarified, He is the only one who has ever seen the light, stating, *"No one has ascended into heaven except he who descended from heaven, the Son of Man."* (Joh 3:13) This distinction is extremely significant since most people believe they can come to the light through their own effort, partially due to the pervasive influence of New Age thought on our mindset. The New Age movement is actually nothing new at all, but rather, something that is very old; namely, this type of philosophy garbed in Christian idioms. This error was taught as early as the first century, to which the Apostle John vehemently warned of in his epistles to the church. According to modern Neo-Gnostic teachings, YOU are the *"light of the world."* This is extracted from Matthew 5:14. The implication from the New-Age-Neo-Gnostic perspective is YOU are YOUR own savior. YOU are able to come to the knowledge of the truth through YOUR introspection and meditation. Notice the catalyst of your salvation, YOU. As a result, Jesus is nothing more than a normal human being who has shown the world how to achieve salvation through a state of mind, which New Age calls *"Christ consciousness."*

How prevalent has this thought become on our society? Consider that books that teach these types of errors are always among the best-selling books in the country. *"The Secret"* is a perfect example of this phenomenon. Consider, as well, that Oprah Winfrey's spiritual advisor is the best-selling New Age author and speaker Marian Williamson. Furthermore, reflect upon the impact of Oprah's influence now that she has begun to teach *"The Secret"* to millions of listeners, in what has been called the largest online church in America. Contemplate the effect of Dan Brown's best-selling, Neo-Gnostic novels, many of which have become movies, whose plots explicitly hold Neo-Gnostic teachings and hold to conspiracies against orthodox Christianity. Think about the influence of best-selling movies, undergird with these philosophical contexts, such as; *"The Matrix," "Star Wars"* and *"The Lion King."* Since most Americans no longer look to scriptures for truth, the entertainment industry has been quite happy to fill the void of their philosophical frameworks with New Age fundamentals.

In summation, Socrates understanding of the truth is similar to Christian understanding, but it is not the same. He has correctly identified the problem, but the solution is a counterfeit, built from a false foundational premise, and therefore, entirely incorrect. C. S. Lewis, in the preface to his book *"Pilgrim's Regress,"* succinctly addressed the matter.

> *The books and music in which we thought the beauty was located will betray us if we trust them. It was not in them, it only came through them and what came through them was a longing, for they are not the thing itself. They are only the scent of a flower we have not found, the echo of a tune we have not heard, news from a country we have never yet visited.*

Most people believe this new ideology is superior in its understanding of spirituality, the interpretation of Jesus and the revelation of God. The foundations of these assessments are supported by the following premises. You are essentially good. You have the ability to come to, or find, the light through introspection, and finally, Jesus was an example of how to achieve this mindset and not the only redeeming work of God. However, these premises stand in stark opposition to Messiah's conversation with Nicodemus. They also contradict the picture God painted for us by raising Lazarus from the grave. For example, Lazarus was completely dead and his body was decaying. This is symbolic of our decaying, sinful, unredeemable nature without God's active intervention. Furthermore, Lazarus was completely dead. He had no ability **in himself** to modify that state. Finally, Jesus stood outside the cave and called Lazarus to come forth. If God never resurrected Jesus, then, not one believer would be able to enter the Kingdom of Heaven.

The first apostles fought these same battles. Consider what Paul had to say about Gnostic teachers coming into the church, who attempted to re-interpret the meaning of these events, in order to fit them into Socrates' philosopher-redeemer insights. These teachers taught Christ was not the Incarnate God. Because of this, they also taught the resurrection never occurred. Instead, God made it appear that Christ walked the earth, was crucified and resurrected. Thus, Christ was an example of how to come to the light. However, Paul severely rebuked this deviant doctrine.

> *...how do some among you say that there is no resurrection of the dead? But if there is no resurrection of the dead, neither has Christ been raised. And if Christ has not been raised, then our proclamation is worthless, and your faith is also worthless. And we are also found to be false witnesses of God, because we testified of God that He raised Christ; whom He did not raise if the dead are not raised. For if the dead are not raised, then Christ is not raised.* ***And if Christ is not raised, your faith is foolish; you are yet in your sins. Then also those that fell asleep in Christ were lost.*** *If in this life only we have hope in Christ,* ***we are of all men most miserable.*** *(1Co 15:12-19 MKJV)*

In our born-again experience, if Christ does not stand outside the cave and call for us to come forth, because he has not resurrected, then we are the most miserable human beings in the world, having placed our faith upon a false hope.

> *But now Christ has risen from the dead, and has become the firstfruit of those who slept. For since death is through man, the resurrection of the dead also is through a Man. For as in Adam all die, even so in Christ all will be made alive. But each in his own*

order: Christ the first-fruit, and afterward they who are Christ's at His coming; (1Co 15:20-23 MKJV)

The Pharisees were like the people who were chained to the bottom of the cave, sitting in darkness, refusing to believe the shadows cast on the wall were mere representations of reality. In like manner, before we came to Christ and received the born-again experience, we all were Pharisees. Nicodemus, as well, was a Pharisee, who came to Jesus, the *"light of the world"* (Joh 8:12), in the middle of the night to receive the revelation about the necessity of the born-again experience. This is the fundamental point of The Parable of the Cross. This parable is not a picture of how to discern our world, but rather, a picture of how to discern ourselves. We are all like Nicodemus, walking in darkness until we are ready to come to Jesus and receive the light. This is God's promise in one of the most prominent Messianic chapters in the entire Bible, stating,

The people who walked in darkness have seen a great light; they who dwell in the land of the shadow of death, on them the light has shined. (Isa 9:2 MKJV)

Continuing to explicate on the nature, character and authority of Messiah, God Almighty states,

For to us a Child is born, to us a Son is given; and the government shall be on His shoulder, and His name shall be called Wonderful, Counselor, The mighty God, The everlasting Father, The Prince of Peace. (Isa 9:6 MKJV)

What an astonishing verse, written 650 years prior to the incarnation!

Nicodemus, which means *"innocent blood"* in Hebrew, immediately became justified after he received Jesus as his Lord and his Savior. Likewise, the Supreme Judge also declares us justified, or *"innocent"* of the crimes we know we committed, when we come to Jesus and receive His truly innocent blood for our tainted blood.

Now, let us return to the time when Messiah arrived at Bethany to raise Lazarus from the dead. The name Bethany has two fascinating meanings that fit perfectly into our story. The first meaning is the *"house of affliction or house of the poor,"* and the second, shortened meaning is *"Yah has intervened."* The first illustrates our utterly hopeless state prior to Jesus coming into our lives. Could Lazarus raise himself from the dead? Can you? The answer is simply no. However, thank the Lord, *"Yah has intervened,"* by the incarnation, and then, by coming to our place of darkness and calling us to come forth into the light of His love.

Digging a little deeper into the meaning of the names in this story offers additional fascinating insights. The story begins with the sisters sending word to Jesus to come and save Lazarus. The first sister mentioned is Mary, whose name means *"rebellion."* This is fitting since our terminal condition is caused by our rebellion, driven by our fallen state. Most people do not care for the concept that Adam's sin got us into this mess; yet, it is not his sin that separated us from God, as much as it was our own sin. Even so, because Adam's sin nature was passed on to his posterity, we never stood a chance to measure up to God's Holiness. Nevertheless, that is part of the package of being human.

The second sister mentioned in this story is Martha, whose name means, *"who becomes bitter."* This is exactly what we see in this story. The story begins with Lazarus becoming ill, then the sisters know exactly what to do; they call for Jesus to save him. They were doing everything correct up to that moment, but when God had a different method in answering their prayer, they both became bitter, as did many of their friends. Like Martha and Mary, we also find that our impatience and low vantage point causes us, at times, to become bitter with God. The unredeemed are also bitter with God's plan of salvation. The secular world constantly complains, *"If we are born as sinners, then why doesn't God just make us so we cannot sin?"* Or, as I have previously alluded, *"Why should I have to pay for Adam's sin?"* These demonstrate that we have better plan of salvation than God, but as Jesus does in this story, God is groaning in the spirit that His plan to redeem man, through the sacrifice of His son, is not good enough for most of the human race. Moreover, because we do not like His plan, or His timing, we become bitter with God.

We see this perfectly in Martha's dialog with Jesus.

> *So when Martha heard that Jesus was coming, she went and met him, but Mary remained seated in the house. Martha said to Jesus, **"Lord, if you had been here, my brother would not have died..."** (Joh 11:20-21 ESV)*

This is a fascinating portion of the story, because we can almost hear the oldest, most responsible sister, Martha, speaking in a tone of some bitterness to Jesus that He should have come quickly and saved her little brother. However, it is easy to read past the subtle hint in these scriptures that Mary was also so upset with the Lord that she continued to remain in the house, in rebellion, despite Messiah's arrival. She eventually did come out to meet Jesus, but only after He called for her to come. This is exactly how the plan of salvation works. Scriptures plainly state, no one would come to God, because of our rebellious nature, if God did not draw us first. (Joh 6:44) Therefore, Martha sends word to Mary that Jesus is calling her out of her rebellion.

> *Now when Mary came to where Jesus was and saw him, she fell at his feet, saying to him, "**Lord, if you had been here, my brother would not have died.**" (Joh 11:32 ESV)*

Now Jesus becomes very emotional, which is expressed by the shortest verse in the Bible as, "*Jesus wept.*" Afterwards, again, scriptures inform, He groaned in the spirit. Perhaps this reaction was due to sorrow over those who have no understanding, or trust, in God's plan of salvation for Lazarus. Subsequently, the town's discontent is reiterated a third time by several bystanders.

> *So the Jews said, "See how he loved him!" But some of them said, "**Could not he who opened the eyes of the blind man also have kept this man from dying?**" (Joh 11:20-37 ESV)*

Allow me, for a moment, the presumption to fill in the gaps of this story. Martha and Mary send the fastest messenger to Jesus to tell Him to come quickly, because their little brother Lazarus is deathly ill. After the messenger arrives, Messiah does nothing, except to say, "*This illness does not lead to death. It is for the glory of God, so that the Son of God may be glorified through it.*" (Joh 11:4) Then, the runner quickly returns to Bethany. They ask, "*Is Jesus coming?*" The messenger responds that the Savior was not worried about the sickness, repeating Messiah's words, "*This illness does not lead to death.*" Mary and Martha feel more secure, but that does not last very long as they watch their younger brother becoming sicker. Eventually, Lazarus dies and is buried in the tomb. Confusion and discontent lead to bitterness and rebellion, filling the house with the sentiment, "*If only Jesus had been here. How could He have allowed this to happen?*" For two days, Lazarus' loved ones fomented in grief, displeasure and disappointment.

Then, Jesus arrived. Too little, too late, was the feeling, *"How could Messiah have reacted so callously to this emergency affecting the one whom He claimed to love so dearly?"*

This illustrates our feeling about God's plan of salvation, when viewed through our fleshly secular eyes. We are in sinful rebellion with God, which has caused our separation from Him. We do not understand His plan, and the parts we do understand, we do not like; as a result, we become bitter with God. Nevertheless, thankfully, God cares so much for us, that He weeps over us, and calls us to come to Him.

The final name in this story is Lazarus, which means, *"God has helped."* How fitting. We are separated from God, dead in our sins, fomenting in bitter rebellion, and yet, God has helped! Glory to the King!

Now let us combine all of these names together to see what scriptures may reveal. We were dead in our *"rebellion"* that grew into *"bitterness,"* because we were living in the *"house of affliction,"* until God *"intervened,"* and *"helped"* with our terminally ill condition, to redeem us by His *"innocent blood."*

Lazarus emerged from the cave with *"his hands and feet bound with linen strips, and his face wrapped with a cloth."* To which the Captain of our Salvation, leading captivity captive, commanded, *"Unbind him, and let him go."* (Joh 11:44)

Consider that the robes of the Old Testament Hebrew priests consisted of four linen garments. (Exo 28) Thus, when Lazarus emerged from the cave wrapped from head to toe in linen strips, this was symbolic of our new position as priests of God, for scripture declares Christ has *"made us kings and priests to God"*. (Rev 1:6)

The next sequence of events in this story parallels that of every person who has become a believer in Christ. It also undergirds the concept that no matter how much proof you show an unbeliever they will remain steadfast against your witness, unless the Holy Spirit softens their heart. Think about it; Jesus just raised Lazarus from the dead, and yet, there were still some people so loyal to the rulers of their day, they went to tell them about this event; not out of a heart of repentance, but out of a disturbed heart, saying, people were beginning to believe that Jesus truly was Meshiach.

The rulers' response is equally disturbing. They not only decided they need to kill Jesus, but they also decide to get rid of the evidence, Lazarus. This is a perfect representation of people quickened by the Holy Spirit, and raised to new life into the Kingdom of God. Straight away, old friends and family desire to kill the regenerative spirit and coax the believer back to his former life. This is a common tactic of Satan, having lost his grip over your soul, to use loved-ones to pressure you to leave the newness of the spirit and return to the darkness of the cave.

A careful reading of this chapter will reveal there are three other names we have not yet discussed. One of which is Caiaphas, the high priest, whose name means *"comely or attractive."* Jesus, on the other hand, means, *"Jehovah is salvation,"* *"salvation,"* or *"savior."* Scriptures declare that Jesus had *"no form nor comeliness ... [and] no beauty that we should desire him."* (Isa 53:2) Notice, there is a true priest and a false priest. The one the world acknowledges is *"comely and attractive"* to the eyes, the one the world rejects has *"no beauty that the world would desire Him."* This also serves as a metaphor to us, the people of the spirit; for in the flesh, we desire outward beauty, the appearance of righteousness and the acceptance of men, but in the spirit, we desire only to follow God. The priest who desires the world's honor has usurped Christ's place of honor. We do this, as well, when we choose the physical man over the spiritual man.

Finally, we have Thomas, whose name evangelist John defined for us in the following verse.

> *Thomas, called the Twin, said to his fellow disciples, "Let us also go, that we may die with him." (Joh 11:16 ESV)*

How fitting it is to close this chapter on Thomas' forthright comment. His name means *"twin."* This has a special significance to our discussion, for the moment you are born-again, you become a twin, having both the born-again spirit and the old sin nature indwelling you at the same time. Returning to Freud's concept of the psyche, there is the id, which the Bible calls the *"flesh"* or the *"old man"* and there is the super-ego, which the Bible calls the *"spirit"* or the *"new man."* Then there is the mind, which Freud calls the *"ego,"* that decides between the two of them, to which the bible refers to as the battlefield of the mind. For this reason, God calls us to

...present your bodies [as] a living sacrifice, holy, pleasing to God, which is your reasonable service. And do not be conformed to this world, but be transformed by the renewing of your mind, in order to prove by you what is that good and pleasing and perfect will of God. (Rom 12:1-2 MKJV)

I love Thomas' candidness when he states, *"Let us also go, that we may die with him."* He was making this statement out of his usual blunt cynicism, but what a profound lesson we can draw from these words when we compare it with other verses like...

...if we died with Christ, we believe that we shall also live with Him, (Rom 6:8 MKJV)

This is The Parable of the Cross.

chapter three

THE ANOINTING

A few days later, the Apostle John describes the following incident:

Six days before the Passover, Jesus therefore came to Bethany, where Lazarus was, whom Jesus had raised from the dead. (Joh 12:1-8 ESV)

In one short sentence, John sets the stage for this entire story and recaps the previous events by answering the following questions, when, where, who and what? It is remarkable how densely packed the Word of God is. This is a whole chapter for most authors, called the introduction. Let us begin to unpack the first verse of this amazing story. When? It was *"Six days before the Passover"* feast. Where? Jesus returns to Bethany. Who? Lazarus. What? *"...whom Jesus had raised from the dead."*

Notice, the Lord of Creation begins this story with the number six. Since the King has said, *"not one jot or one tittle shall in any way pass from the Law until all is fulfilled"* (Mat 5:18), then, we also know, the Lord did not just arbitrarily add this detail; for a jot is the smallest letter of the Hebrew alphabet and a tittle is like a dot on the English *"i"*. Thus, what do we know about the number six from the Bible?

In Revelations, we find the antichrist's number is from *"the number of a man. And its number is six hundred and sixty-six."* (Rev 13:18) Notice, as well, the Almighty created man on the sixth day. Therefore, the number six is explicitly tied to man. When the number is repeated three times, as in Revelation 13:18, it represents the most supreme form of man's rebellion against God, and more specifically, man standing in the place of our Savior Jesus as the antichrist. The antichrist, also known as the son of perdition, *"opposes and exalts himself above all that is called God, or that is worshiped, so that he sits as God in the temple of God, setting himself forth, that he is God."* (2Th 2:4)

These verses seem to add an ominous foreboding to the story. Nevertheless, consider, our El Shaddai created the entire material universe in six days, at which time, scriptures declare, *"behold, it was very good"*. Gen (1:31) Therefore, the number six also speaks of God's creation. In summation, then, the number six appears to signify a paradoxical dichotomy of good and evil things.

It may be helpful to our understanding to consider the following: In addition to Man, the serpent was also created on the sixth day. The serpent and the lion each have six Hebrew names in the Old Testament. The sixth commandment is murder. The number six is representative of a government ruled by man's wisdom; Solomon's throne had six steps (1Ki 10:19) and his kingdom was soon divided.[6]

Finally, scripturally, the number six appears to indicate falling short or imperfection, especially in comparison to the completion seven appears to represent. In the story of creation, for example, we observe the Lord worked six days and rested on the seventh day. The Lord also told the Israelites when He gave them the law, *"You shall work six days, but on the seventh day you shall rest"* (Exo 34:21), which is a particularly notable concept, considering *"the Son of Man is also Lord of the Sabbath."* (Mar 2:28) Now, since Jesus is our Lord as well, then we should learn to abide in the Sabbath rest of His finished work.

Jesus came to the house of Bethany *"Six days before the Passover."* The Passover feast was a celebration commemorating God deliverance of the Israelites out of the bondage of slavery by miraculous signs and wonders. The Israelites were powerless in their own ability to free themselves from the terrible oppression of the most powerful government in the world. It was the Lord's power, and His might, and His works that freed them from the bondage of the Egyptians.

The Almighty used Moses to bring nine terrible judgments on Egypt to force them to free the slaves. Pharaoh, however, continued to harden his heart against setting the captives free. Finally, the Lord brought one final judgment, allowing the Death Angel to kill the first-born son of every living creature in Egypt, except those whose house was marked with the blood of the lamb. The Israelites were told to choose a male lamb without blemish to sacrifice and eat. Then, they were instructed

---

[6] These examples were taken from E. W. Bullinger's website: http://www.Biblestudy.org/Bibleref/meaning-of-numbers-in-Bible/6.html

to mark their doors with his blood. This story is related to us in Exodus chapter 12. Entire books have been written, which demonstrate the symbolic meanings of Jesus as the Lamb of God, however, for the sake of brevity, we will just accept John the Baptist's testimony when he saw the Only Begotten, stating, *"Behold the Lamb of God who takes away the sin of the world!"* (Joh 1:29)

Any Israelite who did not partake in the sacrifice of the lamb, a prefiguring symbolism of the born-again experience, was under the same judgment as the Egyptians. Those who obediently remained in their house marked by the blood of the lamb were passed-over, because they had entered into the rest of the Lord's finished work. Psalm 91 exhibits this same spiritual abiding.

> *He who **dwells in the secret place of the Most High** shall rest under the shadow of the Almighty. I will say of Jehovah, my refuge and my fortress; my God, in Him I will trust. Surely He will deliver you from the fowler's trap **and from the destroying plague**. He shall cover you with His feathers, and under His wings you shall trust. His truth shall be your shield, and buckler. **You shall not fear the terror by night**; nor because of the arrow that flies by day; **nor for the plague that walks in darkness**, of the destruction laying waste at noonday. **A thousand shall fall at your side, and ten thousand at your right hand; it shall not come near you. Only with your eyes you shall look and see the reward of the wicked.** Because You, O Jehovah, are My refuge; **<u>if You have made the Most High Your dwelling-place</u>, no evil shall befall You, nor shall any plague come near Your dwelling.** For He shall give His angels charge over You, to keep You in all Your ways. (Psa 91:1-11 MKJV)*

Immediately after that night of judgment, the Lord separated His people from the Egyptians. This common theme throughout scriptures demonstrates the spiritual concept of consecration and sanctification. Consider, for example, that the first thing the Lord does after He creates the heavens and the earth is to create the light. Then God *"saw that the light was good. And God **separated the light from the darkness**."* (Gen 1:4) Likewise, the first thing that occurs after Messiah raises Lazarus from the dead, being born-again, is to separate him from the darkness of the cave of worldly sin and bring him into the light of His love. If the Israelites had not separated themselves from the worldly Egyptians, then they would have been under the same

31

judgment. Instead, they accepted God's grace, believed His Word about the forthcoming judgment; and therefore, acted upon that faith and followed God's plan of salvation. That is saving grace!

This is exactly what James, the brother of Jesus, advocates in his epistle "*to the twelve tribes in the Dispersion*" (Jas 1:1):

> *You believe that there is one God, you do well; even the demons believe and tremble. But will you know, O vain man, that **faith without works is dead**? (Jas 2:19-20 MKJV)*

The Lord told the Israelites after He had brought them out of the land of Egypt that "*you shall be to Me a kingdom of priests and a **holy** nation.*" (Exo 19:6) Elsewhere Adonai states,

> *For I am Jehovah your God, and you shall **sanctify yourselves**, and **you shall be holy**, for I am holy. ...For I am Jehovah who brought you up out of the land of Egypt, to be your God. **You shall therefore be holy**, for I am holy. (Lev 11:44-45 MKJV)*

What exactly does it mean to be holy? Webster's Dictionary explains that it means, "*to be set apart and consecrated for the sole use by God*". Examples of this include the holy Sabbath, the holy oil, the holy vessels, a holy nation, the holy temple, and a holy priesthood. "*Sanctify*" has a similar meaning, except that it is in cooperation with the spirit that works to attain our holiness. These Hebrew words offer great insight into this understanding: "*You shall sanctify yourselves*" [qâdash] and you shall be "*holy*" [qâdôsh]. The first is the act of becoming. The second is a promise of a state of being. Therefore, the Lord is promising that if we will allow His spirit to work through us to *separate* and *consecrate* ourselves to Him, we will become separate and consecrated to Him, not by our power but by His! Read in the English, this verse appears to make a demand, but the Hebraic undertone suggests more the tenor of a promise. The Lord tells us to set ourselves apart and He will set us apart, or as the Lord of Glory has stated, "*sanctify yourselves and **you shall be holy***." How do we transform from wholly depraved, irreparable beings, to become holy, consecrated, set apart beings for the sole use of our God? In the next phrase, our God gives us the answer, "*for I am holy*." Praise God! The promise is that if we separate ourselves for God's service, then we will be set apart, because He is set apart, therefore He will set us apart. In other words, He will lift us from the dirt and the filth of our low estate into the holy cleanliness of His hallowed sanctuary simply because of who He is!

We are dead. We cannot make ourselves alive. We cannot bring ourselves back to life and walk out of the cave. How in the world are we able to *"sanctify ourselves"* if we are dead and so lost in our darkened understanding that we do not even want anyone to help us to become free from the bondage of sin? Our reality is the shadows that are cast upon the cave's wall and we cling to them with every fiber of being that is within us in order to save ourselves. All the while the Spirit of God continues to pull at our heart strings beckoning us to come out of the darkness and into the light of His Love. When we finally submit to this call from the Spirit of God then we are able to walk out of this dark bondage and into the freedom of His light that the Lord of Glory desires so desperately for us.

This same scene is painted so clearly for us in the story of creation.

> *In the beginning God created the heavens and the earth. And the earth was without form and empty. And darkness was on the face of the deep.* ***And the*** <u>***Spirit of God***</u> ***moved on the face of the waters****. And God said, Let there be light. And there was light. And God saw the light that it was good. And God divided between the light and the darkness. And God called the light, Day. And He called the darkness, Night. And the evening and the morning were the first day. (Gen 1:1-5 MKJV)*

Notice that the story of creation also begins with darkness. It is the Spirit of the Lord that moves over the face of the waters. Waters in the Bible tend to symbolize great multitudes for Revelations tells us that *"The waters which you saw ...are peoples and multitudes and nations and tongues."* (Rev 17:15) It is the Spirit of the Lord that moves over people that allows them to become born-again. Next, the Lord separated the light from the darkness. Jesus followed this same pattern when He told Lazarus to come forth out of the darkness of the cave into the light of His world. After Lazarus was separated from the darkness of the cave the Lord said, *"Unbind him"* (Joh 11:44), which represented freedom from the bondage of our sin. Likewise, notice that this event echoes what occurred in the first Passover story. First there was the dark bondage of Israel's slavery to the worldly Egyptians. Next, the Lord moved in a miraculous way and called upon the Israelites to come forth. Finally, the Lord separated them from the

Egyptians. They did have to walk; the Lord did not just transpose them into the Promised Land. They had to sanctify themselves in order to become separate and therefore holy, but this could only have been accomplished if they had cooperated with the Lord; for He had to set them free and called them to come forth.

Now that we have laid a foundational backdrop for the Spirit is message to us, let us return to the events of the dinner at Bethany.

> *Six days before the Passover, Jesus **therefore** came to Bethany, where Lazarus was, whom Jesus had raised from the dead. (Joh 12:1 ESV)*

Many pastors and Bible study teachers will say when you see the word therefore to go back and ask yourself, "*What is it there for?*" Therefore, here is a brief moment to summarize the pictures of the previous pages and the depth of meaning hidden within this sentence. Six days represents the work of creation. We also know that the number six has many more significant meanings that relate to this work, for example; the number of man, the number of the serpent, the days of work, and etc. The seventh day represents entering into His rest, which was provided seven days later on the Passover. The Passover was the ultimate image of both freedom from the bondage of slavery and the sacrifice of the lamb, so let us now re-read this sentence with our full understanding. It was six days (God's work of creation for the man born of the spirit) before the Passover (God's redemption of those who are held in bondage of the slavery to sin by offering His perfect sacrifice, a lamb without blemish), **therefore** Jesus (salvation) came to Bethany (the house of affliction) where Lazarus (God is my help) was, whom Jesus (salvation) raised from the dead.

Notice God's wonderful plan and perfect timing. Also, notice how perfectly Son's walk is with the Father. The verse appears to allude to the crucifixion of Jesus Messiah as a foregone conclusion. Other synonyms for the word therefore are; "*consequently, as a result of, or for that reason*". John states because it was six days before the Passover therefore, or for that reason, Jesus came to the house of affliction. Jesus' understanding and His perfect walk with the Father kept Him in God's perfect will and because of this He had no fear, stating in the previous chapter that if "*anyone walks in the day, he does not stumble, because he sees the light of this world. But if anyone walks in the night, he stumbles, because the light is not in him."* (Joh 11:9-10)

There were so many times that the people desired Jesus to step into what they expected of Him to be His glory. He consistently stated, *"My hour has not yet come."* (Joh 2:4) There were also the times when Satan had stirred up the hearts and minds of the people's religious zeal and they either wanted to stone Him (Joh 8:59) or throw Him off a cliff (Luk 4:29) but in both of these instances He was able to completely walk directly through the midst of the people unharmed! This was because His hour had not come and because He was walking in the light of God rather than the darkness of this world. He never had to fear anything that was happening to Him. He was walking perfectly in God's sovereign will.

> *So they gave a dinner for him there. Martha served, and Lazarus was one of those reclining with him at table. (Joh 12:2 ESV)*

What a lovely picture. The guest of honor was our beloved Jesus. The Savior came to the house of affliction to free the bound, and they honored Him with a magnificent dinner. It is not just beautiful because they created a wonderful dinner, that included all of the disciples, but it is beautiful because the King of the Universe actually came to have dinner with them. It is remarkable that even today the Lord of Glory has promised us *"if any man hear my voice, and open the door, I will come in to him, and will sup with him, and he with me."* (Rev 3:20) How can we not stand in awe that our Glorious Creator would stoop to our level to sup with us?

> *For by him all things were created, in heaven and on earth, visible and invisible, whether thrones or dominions or rulers or authorities--all things were created through him and for him. And he is before all things, and in him all things hold together. (Col 1:16-17 ESV)*

Job understood His power and might when he stated that it is God

> *...who removes mountains ...who shakes the earth out of its place, and its pillars tremble; who commands the sun, and it does not rise; who seals up the stars; who alone stretched out the heavens and trampled the waves of the sea; who made the Bear and Orion, the Pleiades and the chambers of the south; who does great things*

beyond searching out, and marvelous things beyond number. (Job 9:5-10 ESV)

The book of Job clearly illustrates our low estate when compared to the Almighty Creator of the Universe, who by the power of His Word created all things and continues to hold them together in their ordinances.

How then can man be in the right before God? How can he who is born of woman be pure? Behold, even the moon is not bright, and the stars are not pure in his eyes; how much less man, who is a maggot, and the son of man, who is a worm! (Job 25:4-6 ESV)

Can you imagine the joyous atmosphere that accompanied this dinner celebration? Lazarus was alive! Heavy grief-stricken hearts were now filled with sublime delight. Jesus, the King of All Kings, the miracle worker who called Lazarus from the dead, was the guest of honor and He was coming to sup with them! Martha, *"who becomes bitter"*, is now serving the Lord with newness of heart. The first time that we met Martha in the scriptures, she was very upset with her sister Mary and with Jesus, almost scolding the King for not telling her sister to help her serve. *"But the Lord answered her, 'Martha, Martha, you are anxious and troubled about many things, **but one thing is necessary**. Mary has chosen the good portion, which will not be taken away from her. '"* (Luk 10:40-42) In the previous chapter Martha was probably upset that the Lord did not come immediately in order to save her beloved younger brother; however, now Martha appears to be serving with gladness of heart. She once again is serving, which appears to be her ministry, but now she also realizes that it is more important to listen to Messiah.

Meanwhile, supping with the Lord is Lazarus, who needed God's help in order to be revived from his desperate and mortally fatal condition. Lazarus continues to rely on the Spirit of the Lord as his help as he sups with the Bread of Heaven (Joh 6:41) and listens to His Words of Life. (Joh 6:68) Remember that this is also a parable for us today. Likewise, let us continually remember that it was not by our own power that we were raised from the dead and became a new creation but by the power of God, therefore, let us continue to nourish this new life with *"the bread of life."* (Joh 6:48) For it was Jesus has told us that *"It is the Spirit who gives life; the flesh is no help at all. The words that I have spoken to you are spirit and life."* (Joh 6:63)

Matthew and Mark inform us that this dinner was held at Simon the Leper's house. According to Levitical law lepers were completely isolated from society. Their disease was repulsive to view and completely incurable. If you were to touch a leper then you would have been considered ceremonially unclean, even if you hadn't contracted the disease. Because of this, most lepers lived outside of the city, many times near the dump, in order to find food. Obviously Simon the Leper is no longer diseased and since there was no cure for leprosy we have to assume that he was healed by Jesus. This makes the meal that much more celebratory.

The name Simon means, *"to hear."* He is also like Lazarus who was dying from a completely incurable disease. When Jesus came into his life, Simon heard His voice and came forth from the darkness of his repulsive sin into the light of the righteous Son of God. Once again, we see in a picture how devastating our sin is to us and how repulsive it is before the pure eyes of a Holy God.

Then comes Mary who

> *...took a pound of expensive ointment made from pure nard, and anointed the feet of Jesus and wiped his feet with her hair. The house was filled with the fragrance of the perfume. (Joh 12:3 ESV)*

If you will recall, Mary's name means *"rebellion"*, and yet every time we see Mary from Bethany she is falling at the feet of Jesus. If she was rebellious, it may have been so indirect and subtle that most people do not recognize. The first time that we see Mary she is rebellious against the authority of her sister Martha, allowing her to do all the work, while she sat at the feet of Jesus. However, Jesus did not rebuke her but He did rebuke Martha. This lesson was not an affirmation Mary's lack of help, but rather, to affirm her value on the importance of His words. The rebuke was primarily directed at Martha who had placed a higher value on serving out of her own strength than resting in the Word of God. The next time we see Mary she is falling at Jesus' feet again and saying to Him that if He had come earlier He could have saved her brother. When she first heard about Jesus coming to Bethany she remained in the house mourning over the death of Lazarus, while everyone else went out to meet Jesus. When Jesus finally arrived at Bethany He was first met by the bitterness of Martha and then by the passive rebellion of Mary.

Now the events that transpired during this dinner are similar one described in Luke 7:36-50 that many expositors have assumed are the same event. It is easy to see how this could occur since the names of many of the participants and the events that immerge are very similar. For example, the feast is given at Simon the Pharisee's house for Jesus as the honored guest, which the disciples are also invited. A woman then burst into the scene; broke open a jar of expensive perfume, kissed Jesus' feet and then wiped them with her hair and her tears. However the time frame in Luke's account does not fit into the time frame of the dinner hosted at Simon the Leper's house, and there are other clues that these were separate events. The first of which is the indignation of Simon the Pharisee when he saw the woman kissing Yeshua's feet.

> *Now when the Pharisee who had invited him saw this, he said to himself, "If this man were a prophet, he would have known who and what sort of woman this is who is touching him, for she is a sinner." (Luk 7:39 ESV)*

The second clue is also held within the verse above. The Pharisee describes this woman as a sinner. That may not sound so bad to us because we know that we are all sinners. What is being communicated in this verse is that this woman was such an especially wicked and notorious sinner that her lifestyle was one that was considered reproachable even in the eyes of the lost secular world. Although Mary from Bethany may have been passively rebellious, prior to her conversion, I have never insinuated that she was living a life even close to the one described by Simon the Pharisee. Nevertheless, notice that the outcome was the same and that God had forgiven her sins.

> *And he said to her, "Your sins are forgiven. ...Your faith has saved you; go in peace." (Luk 7:48-50 ESV)*

Why would the Lord in His omniscient providence place two stories so similar in His Holy Writ that many would mistake for the same event? I can only assume so that our Sovereign Lord desired for us to juxtapose these two very similar events in order to demonstrate the vast contrast between the two Simons' responses to Jesus. Simon the Leper, for example, could easily see his need and his utterly helpless condition. Simon the Pharisee, on the other hand, thought his morality made him righteous before God and better than the sinners. Therein lies the difference and the lesson that is gleaned. If we do not recognize our utterly lost condition then we have no appreciation for how grateful we should be that the Holy King of the Universe has come to heal our wounds and sup with us. Jesus concludes the conversation with Simon the Pharisee by relating to him the following parable.

> *A certain moneylender had two debtors. One owed five hundred denarii, and the other fifty. When they could not pay, he cancelled the debt of both. Now which of them will love him more? (Luk 7:41-42 ESV)*

Jesus then affirms Simon's response that the one who owed the moneylender more would love him more. Then He ends the dinner with a stunning rebuke directed at His host:

> *Then turning toward the woman he said to Simon, "Do you see this woman? I entered your house; you gave me no water for my feet, but she has wet my feet with her tears and wiped them with her hair. You gave me no kiss, but from the time I came in she has not ceased to kiss my feet. You did not anoint my head with oil, but she has anointed my feet with ointment. Therefore, I tell you, her sins, which are many, are forgiven--for she loved much. But he who is forgiven little, loves little." (Luk 7:44-47 ESV)*

Do not misunderstand this story; we have all been forgiven very much. We are all the same unabashed spiritual adulterers and notorious sinners is symbolized by this woman; for we have all "*sinned and fall[en] short of the glory of God.*" (Rom 3:23)

When these two dinners are held side by side, they seem similar to another parable that the Lord imparted to his disciples.

> *And He spoke this parable to certain ones __who trusted in themselves, that they were righteous__, and despised others: Two men went up into the temple to pray; the one a Pharisee, and the other a tax-collector. The Pharisee stood and prayed within himself in this way: God, I thank You that I am not as other men are, extortioners, unjust, adulterers, or even like this tax-collector. I fast twice on the Sabbath, I give tithes of all that I possess. And standing afar off, the tax-collector would not even lift up his eyes to Heaven, but struck on his breast, saying, God be merciful to me a sinner! I tell you, this man went down to his house justified rather than the other. For everyone who exalts himself shall be*

abased, and he who humbles himself shall be exalted. (Luk 18:9-14 MKJV)

Now consider the different personalities depicted at Simon the Leper's feast. First, there is Martha, the diligent caretaker, driven by duties and responsibilities. Then there is Lazarus, the obedient and beloved follower of Jesus. The host is Simon the Leper, the immensely grateful leper who has been cleansed from his incurable disease and his sins. Finally, there is the heart of Mary, driven by her impulsive love for Jesus was unrestrained from the social mores of her culture. They all loved Jesus, but they all were different personalities and had different ways of demonstrating that love for him; for Martha it was to serve, for Lazarus it was faithful obedience, for Simon the Leper it was to honor Him and for Mary it was to give her most important possession; herself.

It is very easy to appreciate and yet still utterly under value Mary's great love offering to Jesus from our perspective twenty centuries later. In order to gain the fullest understanding of this great sacrifice it is necessary to discuss the culture of that time. Thankfully, Judas affixed an estimated value to her love offering. *"Why was this ointment not sold for three hundred denarii and given to the poor?"* (Joh 12:5) Judas Iscariot stated with indignation. Because of Judas's contemptible outrage we are able to surmise that the fragrance was equal to about an entire year's worth of wages. At that time, the most precious ointments were carried in alabaster flasks. These flasks were so highly esteemed that they were often times handed down as inheritances or family heirlooms. Many times the women wore small alabaster flasks of perfume tied around their necks. Various expositors have assumed the gift was a family inheritance. Others have supposed that Mary may have purchased this huge amount of pure nard in order to anoint Lazarus's dead body, since the Jewish burial practice was to wash the body and then anoint it with perfumes. Still other expositors have assumed that Mary had spent her entire life amassing this great amount of expensive perfume for her wedding day, which makes this offering all the greater considering the time and effort that would have been involved in this accumulation. Whether Mary's original purpose for acquiring the perfume was through years of gathering or from a one-time purchase out of her life-long savings really does not matter since Jesus informs us that her motivation was to anoint His *"body beforehand for burial."* (Mar 14:8)

If the flask was originally intended for her wedding day this would be a fitting image since the church is called the bride of Christ.

> *Let us rejoice and exult and give him the glory, for the marriage of the Lamb has come, and his Bride has made herself ready; (Rev 19:7 ESV)*

In the parable of the ten virgins, Jesus tells us that

> *...the kingdom of heaven will be like ten virgins who took their lamps and went to meet the bridegroom. Five of them were foolish, and five were wise. For when the foolish took their lamps,* ***they took no oil with them, but*** ***the wise took flasks of oil*** *with their lamps. (Mat 25:1-4 ESV)*

Elsewhere Jesus also admonishes us to "*Stay dressed for action and keep your lamps burning*" (Luk 12:35) just after He states "*where your treasure is, there will your heart be also.*" (Luk 12:34)

This picturesque scene is an outward demonstration of what Paul described in his letter to the Corinthians when he stated, "*I betrothed you to one husband, to present you as a pure virgin to Christ.*" (2Co 11:2)

What is the meaning of marriage anyways? Is it not the dying of one's self so that the two may "*become one flesh*"? (Gen 2:24) In the Jewish marriage tradition, a young woman would spend her entire life accumulating this very costly perfume in a beautifully crafted alabaster jar and then surprise her husband by breaking the flask and pouring this lovely scent on her husband. This was symbolic of her now giving herself completely to her husband. O' that the church would pour out our lives for the bridegroom in this manner!

Many expositors note that it was considered shameful for a woman to let down her hair in public. When Mary "*wiped his feet with her hair*" (Joh 12:3) her display of love was of a very personal nature and in defiance of the social mores of that culture. However this is the manner of worship the King seeks from all of his children; one that is drawn from our personal relationship, unrestrained by society, and out of our unadulterated love for Him. To further elaborate on this subject a woman would only let her hair down in the privacy of her own home and in the intimacy with her husband. Furthermore scriptures tell us that "*if a woman has long hair, it is her glory*" (1Co 11:15 ESV); so this was not only a very personal display of worship, but one in which Mary was willing to give her greatest treasures; both of herself and her greatest possessions.

Many see these four different personalities and decide that since Mary's display of love was the greatest they should model their lives in this way. I suggest, however, that all of these traits should make up the complex personality of a Christ follower. Like Martha, we should be diligent, dedicated and look for ways to serve our Lord. Like Lazarus, we should lean on our Savior's breast in faithful obedience. Like Simon the Leper we should be grateful and give honor to our King who has freed us from the repulsive curse of our sins and like Mary we should be in such a close personal relationship with our Jesus that we are driven by this extravagant love and completely surrendered. This then is not one of the compartments of a personality trait that we should wish to espouse but rather an umbrella under which all of these ministries ought to abide. Therefore, like Martha – serve Him, like Lazarus - spend time with Him, like Simon the Leper - honor Him; but like Mary - completely surrender to Him.

It is at the height of this beautiful act of worship that the story takes a more ominous turn, as the dark heart of Judas pretentiously condemnations Mary.

> *But Judas Iscariot, one of his disciples (he who was about to betray him), said, "Why was this ointment not sold for three hundred denarii and given to the poor? He said this, not because he cared about the poor, but because he was a thief, and having charge of the moneybag he used to help himself to what was put into it." (Joh 12:4-6 ESV)*

Judas represents the world's reaction to true heart-felt worship of God's grateful children, which they also regard with utter condemnation. They mock, *"You are a fool for giving your money to the church."* They quip, *"Why do not you take a day off from going to Bible study and church service?"* They sneer, *"Why do you believe all of this superstitious nonsense that is in the Bible; do not you know that it is full of contradictions?"*

Judas is also representative of unsaved church-goers who have not been changed by the Spirit of God but are living in secret sin; they appear to be the most upstanding and righteous believers in the sanctuary. Even the disciples, who lived with him for three years, were not able to discern this man's heart. In fact it appears that they thought he was the most respectable and trustworthy disciple, who they entrusted with the money bag. They were so convinced that he was a true disciple that when Jesus told them that he was the one that would betray Him they did not believe it.

> *"It is he to whom I will give this morsel of bread when I have dipped it." So when he had dipped the morsel, he gave it to Judas... Then after he had taken the morsel... Jesus said to him, "What you are going to do, do quickly." (Joh 13:26-27 ESV)*

Notice that despite Jesus' statement that Judas would betray Him, the disciples were so blinded by his outward appearance of righteousness that they still believed Jesus must be saying something else; so *"Some thought that, because Judas had the moneybag, Jesus was telling him, 'Buy what we need for the feast,' or that he should give something to the poor."* (Joh 13:29)

Jesus is the image of the Living God and Judas is the image of Satan. Outwardly Satan appears to be *"an angel of light"* (2Co 11:14) but inwardly he is a ravenous wolf. (Mat 7:15) He is *"more subtle than any beast of the field"* (Gen 3:1) and his passion and purpose in life is to destroy you; for he came to *"steal, and kill, and destroy"* (Joh 10:10)

> *He was a murderer from the beginning, and has nothing to do with the truth, because there is no truth in him. When he lies, he speaks out of his own character, for he is a liar and the father of lies. (Joh 8:44 ESV)*

He wanted God's glory so he said in his heart that

> *I will ascend to heaven; above the stars of God I will set my throne on high; I will sit on the mount of assembly in the far reaches of the north; I will ascend above the heights of the clouds; I will make myself like the Most High. (Isa 14:13-14 ESV)*

Pride was Lucifer's downfall. He was the *"signet of perfection, full of wisdom and perfect in beauty."* (Eze 28:12) God, therefore, reproached him saying, *"Your heart was proud because of your beauty; you corrupted your wisdom for the sake of your splendor."* (Eze 28:17)

Considering his beauty and craftiness, and how Satan used Judas, it is easier to appreciate just how beautiful this apostle must have appeared. It is also easy to see why Judas would cast such condemnation at

Mary's beautiful act of worship, as John informs us that he was a thief. He also may have had enough of Christ's talk about death and submission; that was not a king he wanted to follow. Instead, the king that appealed to him was the one that would conquer the oppressors, deliver Israel and establish the earthly kingdom. He wanted the glory and riches that accompany that glory. This is descriptive of so many preachers, televangelists and churches that we must question whether *"certain people have crept in unnoticed... who pervert the grace of our God into sensuality and deny our only Master and Lord, Jesus Christ."* (Jud 1:4) Or is it possible that *"as the serpent deceived Eve by his cunning, your thoughts"* we have been *"led astray from a sincere and pure devotion to Christ"* because *"someone comes and proclaims another Jesus than the one [the apostles] proclaimed"*? (2Co 11:3-4)

Judas' name means *"the praised one."* He appeared beautiful and was extremely beloved but in reality he was really nothing more than *"a white sepulcher, which outwardly appeared beautiful, but inwardly was full of dead men's bones and all uncleanness."* (Mat 23:27)

Judas chastises Mary and because he is so respected, the other disciples follow his lead, having *"indignation, saying, 'To what purpose is this waste?'"* (Mat 26:8) How fickle human emotions can be. I am confident the disciples highly esteemed Martha and Mary's hospitality and probably looked forward to staying with these loved ones after one of their long journeys towards Jerusalem. Jesus seemed to make Bethany a respite prior to facing confrontations that awaited Him in Jerusalem. Yet the disciples' affections for Mary were so easily swayed by Judas' impure motivations. This is why the Bible counsels, *"It is better to take refuge in the LORD than to trust in man."* (Psa 118:8)

Take a moment and imagine how this scene being played itself out. The dinner feast is rich and festive. Everything is going exactly according to plan. The food is perfectly prepared and Jesus is being greatly honored by His loved ones. The dinner was at Simon the Leper's house, who used to be an outcast from society, but now he is not only a part of society but able to entertain at his home. Lazarus who was dead a couple of days ago is also sitting at the table. Martha has been on an incredible rollercoaster ride of emotions from the turmoil of watching her brother's sickness increase daily, to the despondency of watching him die, to the bitterness of waiting for the Savior to come and finally to the joy of regaining her brother when

Messiah called him to come forth from the grave. The dinner feast was extremely festive, joyous and the evening was turning out just as planned.

Then Mary, who we may speculate is in her room at her own home, hears all this joyous noise coming from Simon's house. This seems to go on for some time as she sits brushing her long hair thinking about how wonderful it is to have her Jesus here in Bethany. Like Martha, she also has been on an incredible rollercoaster of emotions, but unlike Martha she is driven almost completely by her heart. She recalls all of the times that Jesus visited with them and how spellbound she was by the words of life coming from her Jesus that she literally just sat at His feet for hours. She is at the height of her joy reminiscing about all of this and hearing celebratory sounds emanating from Simon's house. However, then, of the sudden a terrible thought crashes into her mind. Jesus is going to Jerusalem for the Passover feast and the Pharisees have put out word that He is to be stoned because they believed that He was practicing sorcery and has led Israel astray. She has also heard that

> *Jesus began to show his disciples that he must go to Jerusalem and suffer many things from the elders and chief priests and scribes, **<u>and be killed</u>**, and on the third day be raised. (Mat 16:21 ESV)*

Nobody really believed that these things were going to happen to the Son of David. Somehow Jesus must be alluding to some spiritual meaning as He was when He told the disciples to "*beware of the leaven of the Pharisees and Sadducees*" (Mat 16:6), which they mistook to literally mean they should have brought bread but were later ashamed to find that He meant "*the teaching of the Pharisees and Sadducees.*" (Mat 16:12)

Mary now sitting in the quietness of her home has a revelation that none of the other disciples probably completely understood at the time; Jesus is literally going to die at this feast! Her peaceful solitude has now been completely turned upside down. Just a few days ago, the sorrowful tears that were continually streaming down her face were wiped away by her Jesus. Now she was going to lose her Jesus! Who was going to raise Him from the dead? He was the only one that could perform such a miracle! This may be the very last time that she will ever see Him! What can she do to show Him how much He means to her? She does not have anything that she can think of that would be worthy of her love for the King of Kings!

Her eyes fall on the alabaster jar full of expensive nard that she has been saving for that very special occasion. There is not going to be another time like this in her whole life. She makes the impulsive decision to give this to her Jesus and immediately runs out of her house with the alabaster jar in hand, heart pounding, as she bursts into the dinner celebration. The guests immediately notice Mary's hair is down and wonder why she would be so shameful to show herself in public in this manner. Immediately Mary breaks open the bottle of spikenard and pours some of this on Jesus' head and then the rest of it on His feet. She falls at the feet of her beloved Raboni and begins to wipe His feet with her hair. None of this was premeditated by Mary's impulsive heart. She is acting out of pure love and the revelation that she may never see her beloved Jesus!

Then the scornful chastisement of Judas is berates her. Almost immediately, most of the other disciples begin to murmur in agreement with his pretentious reproach. She continues to worship at the feet of Messiah, but inwardly she begins to doubt herself. Maybe this act of loving worship is inappropriate. After all, all these men of God are lashing out at her in condemnation. Dumbstruck, she does not speak a word. She is mortified! Was this extravagant expression of love as stupid as Judas' has portrayed?

Most of us Christians would have lashed back at Judas. We would have defended our motives as pure and would have defended our actions in the court of public opinion. Most of us in the course of defending ourselves would have attacked Judas' character in the process. This is, however, the exact opposite of Messiah's teachings.

> *Do not resist the one who is evil. But if anyone slaps you on the right cheek, turn to him the other also. (Mat 5:39 ESV)*

This was Mary's response. She never said a word; and in fact that *"woman of the city, who was a sinner,"* in the similar story that Luke describes, also reacted in the proper manner. She said nothing. In both cases, however, because they did not defend themselves, Jesus came to their defense.

This is precisely what Paul was explaining when he told us:

> *Beloved, never avenge yourselves, but leave it to the wrath of God, for it is written, "Vengeance is mine, I will repay, says the Lord." (Rom 12:19 ESV)*

The reason we are to act in this manner is two-fold. First, we are not the judge of the world. We are told to make the discerning judgments of the jury but not to issue the condemning judgments of the judge. Second, it is God who will repay, as the Apostle Paul is quotes God speaking in the Old Testament.

> *In due time their feet will slip. Their day of disaster will arrive, and their destiny will overtake them.' (Deu 32:35 NLT)*

It was because Jesus understood this that He said, "*Father, forgive them, for they know not what they do.*" (Luk 23:34) Likewise, notice that Stephan reacts in the exact same manner:

> *And as they were stoning Stephen, he called out, "Lord Jesus, receive my spirit." And falling to his knees he cried out with a loud voice, "Lord, do not hold this sin against them" And when he had said this, he fell asleep. (Act 7:59-60 ESV)*

Jesus, our Lord and our example, tells us:

> *Blessed are you when others revile you and persecute you and utter all kinds of evil against you falsely on my account. Rejoice and be glad, for your reward is great in heaven, for so they persecuted the prophets who were before you. (Mat 5:11-12 ESV)*

It because of our spiritual blindness that our Lord encourages us to have His heart:

> **Love your enemies and pray for those who persecute you**, *so that* <u>**you may be sons of your Father who is in heaven**</u>. *For he makes his sun rise on the evil and on the good, and sends rain on the just and on the unjust. For if you love those who love you, what reward do you have? Do not even the tax collectors do the same? And if you greet only your brothers, what more are you doing than others? Do not even the Gentiles do the same?* **You therefore must be perfect, as your heavenly Father is perfect**. *(Mat 5:44-48 ESV)*

This is perfect love. It is not a love that asks "*What has this person done for me?*" but rather, "*What can I do for this poor soul, who in most cases is not living according to the Spirit of God, and is likely under a much harsher judgment?*"

Jesus teaches us not to defend ourselves because when

He was oppressed, and he was afflicted, yet he opened not his mouth; like a lamb that is led to the slaughter, and like a sheep that before its shearers is silent, so he opened not his mouth. (Isa 53:7 ESV)

We are taught that when someone who is weak is being attacked that it is our responsibility to defend that poor soul; as is the case with Mary in this story.

This is a principle that is central to the message of The Parable of the Cross.

What was Judas' reaction to Jesus' rebuke of his condemnations? In the book of Mark we shown an example of how we should not react. Immediately after Judas' condemnation of Mary and the disciples agreement with his denunciation Jesus tells them all to *"Leave her alone."* (Mar 14:6) Then He went on further to exult her immediately afterwards and admonished them stating that *"wherever the gospel is proclaimed in the whole world, what she has done will be told in memory of her."* (Mar 14:9) What a huge slap in the face this must have been to Judas, the praised one. In that culture women were considered inferior to men in almost every respect. For example, a woman's testimony was not allowed to be admitted in court; *"though the woman is subject to the commandments, she is disqualified from giving evidence."* (Jewish Talmud, Baba Kamma 88a) The Jewish Mishnah also stated *"may the words of Torah be burned, than that they should be handed over to women."* (Sota, 10a) This attitude had become so extreme during Jesus' time that in some segments of the Jewish culture it was considered perfectly reasonable to divorce your wife just for burning your food! You can imagine Judas' utter disdain when he was publicly reprimanded, which was followed immediately by Jesus' praise of Mary's simple act of worship, proclaiming that her story would be told throughout the ages! Judas had such a high estimation of himself that he was immediately offended. *"How could Jesus have done such a thing? Does not he know that I am the most respected disciple?"* he may have thought to himself. It is easy to surmise that bitterness and anger burned within his heart, as Mark tells us in the next verse:

Then Judas Iscariot ...went to the chief priests in order to betray him to them. And when they heard it, they were glad and promised to give him money. And he sought an opportunity to betray him. (Mar 14:10-11 ESV)

Let us contrast Mary with Judas in this story. Consider justice and motive. Was Judas justified in criticizing Mary's act of worship? No. Was Jesus justified in criticizing Judas' pretentious indignation of Mary? Yes. Was Mary's motive completely pure in heart? Yes. Was Judas' motive pure? No. Therefore, Jesus was justified to criticize Judas and Judas was completely unjustified to criticize Mary. Now let us consider the reactions of Mary and Judas. Mary, who is completely justified, says nothing. Judas, who is not only wrong in his actions but also his motives, is completely unjustified and yet he speaks against Mary and then so driven by vengeance that he betrays Jesus to the Pharisees. This is a perfect picture of how a Christ-follower should react to condemnation and how the world reacts to condemnation. The Christ-follower is told to turn the other cheek, while the world says, *"I do not get angry, I get even."*

Please take these two examples to heart because entirely too many Christians act out with what they call righteous indignation; preferring to hold on to their anger like a wounded badge of honor. In the example above we have one person following Satan and the other is following Jesus. Which example displays how you react to condemnations, insults and slander? Mary would have been perfectly justified by the world to defend herself, but she would not have been justified by God. Who do you want to be justified by: God or man?

In The Parable of the Cross this story represents receiving the Holy Spirit immediately after being called to come forth from the bondage of sin and death to walk in the light of His love; this is symbolized by the anointing of Jesus with the oil. This is fitting since Jesus Christ literally means Jesus *"the anointed one."* Notice also that Jesus is remarking that this is a celebration of death, *"she has done a beautiful thing to me. ...In pouring this ointment on my body, she has done it to prepare me for burial."* (Mat 26:10-12) The death is the death of the flesh. The enchanting aroma that filled house was symbolic of Jesus' sacrifice on the cross that Paul describes as *"a fragrant offering and sacrifice to God."* (Eph 5:2)

Mary breaks what the world considers to be a very beautiful alabaster jar in order for the fragrant oil to be able to be poured all over Jesus, from His head to His feet. The breaking of this vessel is the symbolic gesture that Christ referred to when He stated, "*And he who falls on this Stone shall be broken, but on whomever it shall fall, it will grind him to powder.*" (Mat 21:44) Stop and consider the ramifications of this part of the parable. If the vessel is never broken the fragrance will never be released. We must realize that we are "*poor in spirit*" (Mat 5:3) and then repent in order for the fragrant aroma of the spirit to be released. Then and only then is our spirit able to commune with Christ. This is why Paul pleads with you "*to present **your bodies** a living sacrifice, holy, pleasing to God, which is your reasonable service.*" (Rom 12:1) Notice that the Lord wants our body. Our spirit is now alive and the spirit is already subservient to the spirit of the Lord but it is your body that is needed to be given to the Lord in order for you to not be "*conformed to this world, but be transformed by the **renewing of your mind**.*" Remember that we spoke of the battlefield of the mind in the last chapter. Therefore, if you offer your body as a living sacrifice then the spirit or the super-ego is ruling your life instead of the flesh or the id and this is allowed by the Lord "*in order to **prove by you** what is that good and pleasing and [the] perfect will of God.*" (Rom 12:2) That last sentence is a lot to grasp. To "*prove by you*" means "*to test, examine, or scrutinize*". Yet why does the Almighty need to test you? Does not He already know if you are a spirit filled Christian? Absolutely! However, it is we who need to know and we need to have this confirmation. This is why the Lord has stated "*You shall know them by their fruits*" (Mat 7:16) and elsewhere He implores us to "*therefore bring forth fruits worthy of repentance.*" (Luk 3:8)

> *When we reach this stage of brokenness and offer our bodies as living sacrifices, then we are offering the true worship of a believing Christ-follower that is a sweet smelling savor to the Lord. This is what Jesus is seeks in our lives. When we do this, He says our act of worship is* "a beautiful thing to Me." *(Mat 26:10) Therefore,* "let us continually offer up a sacrifice of praise" *(Heb 13:15) that is* "a fragrant offering, [and] a sacrifice acceptable and pleasing to God." *(Php 4:18)*

chapter four

CORONATION OF BAPTISM

The next day was Jesus' Triumphal Entry into Jerusalem. For many years, He was somewhat ambiguous about His mission and who He was, but now He enters Jerusalem openly and publicly proclaimed as the long awaited Messiah and the King of Kings.

At that time conquering kings entered fallen cities either on the back of a white horse or a young donkey. The white horse signified that the conqueror would mercilessly exact retribution. However, riding into the city on a donkey indicated the king would show mercy and peace. How wonderful it is for us that our God Most High chose to present Himself humble and full of grace!

> *When he drew near to Bethphage and Bethany, at the mount that is called Olivet, he sent two of the disciples, saying, "Go into the village in front of you, where on entering you will find a colt tied, on which no one has ever yet sat. Untie it and bring it here. If anyone asks you, 'Why are you untying it?' you shall say this: 'The Lord has need of it.'" So those who were sent went away and found it just as he had told them. And as they were untying the colt, its owners said to them, "Why are you untying the colt?" And they said, "The Lord has need of it." (Luk 19:29-34 ESV)*

Matthew also informs us that this fulfilled Zechariah's Messianic vision.

> *This took place to fulfill what was spoken by the prophet, saying, "Say to the daughter of Zion, '**Behold, your king** is coming to you, humble, and mounted on a donkey, and on a colt, the foal of a beast of burden.'" (Mat 21:4-5 ESV)*

Notice that Messiah is called the King, to which Zachariah also adds that He is *"righteous and having salvation."* (Zec 9:9) Now consider the following Messianic passage in Isaiah:

*So says Jehovah, the **King of Israel**, and **His redeemer, Jehovah of Hosts**; I am the first, and I am the last; and besides Me there is no God. (Isa 44:6 MKJV)*

Did you notice that there appears to be two Jehovah's speaking to Isaiah; for the verse says, *"So SAYS" "Jehovah, the King of Israel"* and *"His redeemer, Jehovah of Hosts"*? Consider that the King of Israel riding on the colt spoken of in Matthew is Jesus the redeemer, which Zechariah also testifies to His redemptive mission saying *"He is righteous and **having salvation.**"* Therefore, we are able to extrapolate that; the King is Jehovah, Jehovah is the redeemer, the redeemer is Jesus and Jesus is Jehovah. Yet they are separate. In other words we now find ourselves contemplating the first and second persons of the mystery of the Trinity and the incarnation of God. Compare Jehovah words to Isaiah *"**I am the first, and I am the last; and besides Me there is no God**"*; with Jesus Messiah words to the Apostle John in Revelations, saying *"I am the Alpha and the Omega, **the first and the last**, the beginning and the end."* (Rev 22:13) What a tremendous mystery to contemplate; Jehovah left His Holy place to come to this sinful world to save lowly man!

Moreover, all persons of the Trinity are symbolically represented in the Triumphal Entry picture of grace. The owner of the colt is God the Father. The colt, having never been ridden, is symbolic of being free of corruption and set apart for God. The colt, a *"beast of burden"*, does the work bearing heavy loads. It is, therefore, quite apparent that the colt is symbolic of Jesus' ministry in the Godhead. Finally, we have two unnamed disciples who act as the messengers by bringing back the colt to Jesus and set Him upon it. This is representative of the ministry of the Holy Spirit who came upon Mary and brought Jesus into this world.

Whom does Jesus symbolize in this scenario? The answer is you. Now do not think for a second that I am saying that you are Jesus. However, I am saying that Jesus is our example and we are admonished *"to walk in the same way in which he walked."* (1Jn 2:6) It is God's purpose that we are to *"not be conformed to this world but be transformed"* (Rom 12:2) *"to the image of his Son"* (Rom 8:29) *"by the renewing of your mind."* (Rom 12:2)

What a glorious picture this is of our salvation. Once again, we are reminded that we have not done anything to earn so great a prize.

*For **by grace you are saved through faith, and that <u>not of</u> <u>yourselves, it is the gift of God</u>, not of works**, lest anyone should boast. (Eph 2:8-9 MKJV)*

In summation, the disciples, representative of the Holy Spirit, get the colt. The owner, representative of the Father, freely gives up the colt. The uncorrupted colt, representative of Jesus and His work, is brought to you, and you are set upon it and He carries you into Jerusalem, the City of Peace.

The journey into the City of Peace began at the towns of Bethpage and Bethany, which Luke tells us are part of the mountain range called Olivet. Bethpage means *"the house of unripe figs."* This is symbolic of the fact that we will never be able to produce fruit worthy of our King. We are a house of unripe figs until Jesus transforms us by the renewing of our minds. Furthermore, notice that Jesus is also leaving Bethany, which we know means *"the house of affliction."* The mountain range is called the *"mount of Olivet,"* which means *"olive garden."* Later Jewish writings gave this mountain the name the *"Mount of Oil"*, bringing to our attention once again the great depth of meanings in the names of these places.

Now pulling all of this together, we observe that Jesus leaves the *"house of unripe figs"* and the *"house of affliction"* in the *"Mount of Oil"*, or the *"olive garden"*, to go to the *"city of peace."* Everything seems to fit, except that the corrupt *"house of unripe figs"* and the *"house of affliction"* are part of what seems to be the pureness that is symbolized in the name the *"Mount of Oil"*. However reviewing the scriptures we discover that the purity of this mountain was defiled when Solomon *"desecrated the high places that were east of Jerusalem"*; (1Ki 11:7, 2Ki 23:13) so that it became known as the *"Mount of Corruption"* or the *"Mount of Offence."*

This is an ideal metaphor, not only of the salvation that Jesus would attain for us, but also of the story of the entire Bible! Adam began in the perfect garden full of ripe olives and flowing with oil. He became an *"offense"* to God when he rebelled against His commandment and brought *"corruption"* into the world. He was banished from the Garden of Eden and exiled to the *"house of affliction"* and *"unripe figs."* This is not only symbolic of our worldly state, but is also represented in our tabernacle, the body, which also became a *"house of affliction"* and "*unripe figs.*" As a result of this Jesus, the uncorrupted colt, came into the world as our salvation and take us to the "*City of Peace.*"

Notice also that the colt continues to remain separate from the earth as "*most of the crowd spread their cloaks on the road, and others cut branches from the trees and spread them on the road.*" (Mat 21:8) They realized that this moment was holy and therefore the colt should not be contaminated by the world. It brings to memory the time when Moses first talked to God at the burning bush and God said, "*Take your sandals off your feet, for the place on which you are standing is holy ground.*" (Exo 3:5)

Therefore, it was fitting that

> *...the crowds that went before him and that followed him were shouting, "Hosanna to the Son of David! Blessed is he who comes in the name of the Lord! Hosanna in the highest!" (Mat 21:9 ESV)*

Nevertheless, notice that once again the world, controlled by Satan, cannot stand to see God Almighty praised and worshipped.

> *And some of the Pharisees in the crowd said to him, "Teacher, rebuke your disciples." (Luk 19:39 ESV)*

Jesus, however, refuses the world's demand and gladly accepts the loving praise of His followers, saying, "*I tell you, if these were silent, the very stones would cry out.*" (Luk 19:40)

Notice also that the crowd grew in large part because of the testimony that He was the one who raised Lazarus from the grave; therefore, the crowd increased because "*they heard he had done this sign.*" (Joh 12:18) The Pharisees once again despaired stating, "*Look, the world has gone after him.*" (Joh 12:19)

There are three very important lessons we can learn from this story. First, if we will separate ourselves onto God and allow Jesus to do the work we will draw people to Him. Secondly, when we draw people to God the world will resist us and possibly even some people in the church. Thirdly, we should have evidence of changed lives. This is what the world truly desires to witness. Every other religion on the planet promises a better life, but none of them promises to raise people from the dead. We need to allow the world to see how our changed lives and attest to this wonder; that we have been called out of the cave of sin and death and into life. If we walk in this manner then many will follow and those watching will say *"Look, the world has gone after him."* (Joh 12:19)

Jesus finally allowed His followers to acknowledge that He was the prophesized Messiah three and a half years into His ministry. For example, earlier in His ministry, a man with an unclean spirit in the synagogue asked, *"What have you to do with us, Jesus of Nazareth? Have you come to destroy us? I know who you are--the Holy One of God."* To which, His reply was *"**Be silent**, and come out of him!"* (Mar 1:25) Elsewhere scriptures state,

> *...whenever the unclean spirits saw him, they fell down before him and cried out, "You are the Son of God." **And He strictly ordered them not to make Him known.** (Mar 3:11-12 ESV)*

He also told many of the people that He healed, *"See that you say nothing to anyone."* (Mar 1:44) Likewise, John relates a similar reaction from Jesus after He performs the miracle of the feeding of the 5,000.

> *When the people saw the sign that he had done, they said, "This is indeed the Prophet who is to come into the world!" Perceiving then that they were about to come and take him by force **to make him king, Jesus withdrew again** to the mountain by himself. (Joh 6:14-15 ESV)*

Later that evening Jesus asked the disciples, *"Who do you say that I am?"* To which *"Simon Peter replied, 'You are the Christ, the Son of the living God.'"* (Mat 16:15-16) Then, *"He strictly charged and **commanded them to tell this to no one**."* (Luk 9:21)

Why did Jesus teach the Word of God *"as one who had authority"* (Mat 7:29) and yet not claim His kingship? I think His very first miracle written about in the gospels offers some insight into the answer. Jesus, His disciples, and His mother were attending *"a wedding at Cana in Galilee"* (Joh 2:1) when they ran out of wine. Then Mary said to Jesus *"They have no wine."* (Joh 2:3) I believe that she must have seen some of miracles or prayers of faith that were answered as Jesus was growing up in order to have so much faith that her son could do something to remedy the problem. Jesus then said to her, *"Woman, what does this have to do with me"*, which in today's vernacular means *"Ma'am this is none of my business."* What He said after that is of even greater importance to our study, which was *"My hour has not yet come"* (Joh 2:4), which clarifies why Jesus continued to preach the Word of God *"as one who had authority"* and yet not claim His kingship.

The day after the Triumphal Entry, Andrew and Phillip told Jesus that some Gentiles asked about Him, to which He now responds, ***"The hour has come*** *for the Son of Man to be glorified."* This is also in complete accord with *"six days before the Passover, Jesus therefore"* knowing His time had come to save His people through His redemptive work, traveled to Bethany, *"the house of affliction."* (Joh 12:1)

Jesus' first public appearance was when John the Baptizer baptized Him. *"And all the country of Judea and all Jerusalem were going out to him [John the Baptist] and were being baptized by him in the river Jordan, confessing their sins."* (Mar 1:5). All the people watched the Baptizer with great anticipation, quite literally from the day he was born, because of the miraculous events that surrounded his birth. Elizabeth was barren and since she was also well advanced in years, she had no natural ability to conceive a child. They also knew that Zechariah was struck mute by the angel Gabriel because of his unbelief until the baby was born. They also knew that that the Holy Spirit inspired his parents to name him John. Although God's miracles occurred often throughout Israel's past, for 400 years, there were none and the prophets became silent. For this reasons the people watched John with great anticipation that God was once again going to speak to Israel. Therefore, when this very rough looking prophet, seemingly appeared out of nowhere, to cry out in the Judean wilderness, *"Repent, for the kingdom of heaven is near"* (Mat 3:2), a great multitude naturally began to make their way out to see him. He was so highly esteemed by the people that even King Herod feared him *"because they revered John"* (Mat 14:5) *"for all consider[ed] John as a prophet."* (Mat 21:26) Therefore, it was no small matter when he saw *"Jesus coming toward him, and said, 'Behold, the Lamb of God, who takes away the sin of the world!'"* (Joh 1:29) That testimony alone would have been enough to make Jesus a very recognizable public figure; and yet, can you imagine the impact the following event had on the on the God's chosen people, when our Father in Heaven spoke to them for the first time in 400 years?

*And when **JESUS** was baptized, immediately he went <u>up from the water</u>, and behold, the heavens were opened to him, and he saw* the **SPIRIT OF GOD** *descending like a dove and coming to rest on him; and behold, a* **VOICE FROM HEAVEN** *said,* **"This is my beloved Son, with whom I am well pleased."** *(Mat 3:16-17 ESV)*

What a marvelous scene! It is the family of God in celebration of the baptism of the Son; for notice the **Holy Spirit** descending upon the **Son** with the testimony of the **Father**. This is a beautifully intimate picture of the Father and the Son at baptism. Likewise, our Father in Heaven captured my feelings precisely when my sons were baptized, when He said *"This is my beloved Son, with whom I am well pleased."* Clearly we observe the close intimate relationship of the family of God; the love of the Father for the Son and the rejoicing of the Holy Spirit. Moreover, when we are baptized it is not just our father on earth that is very well please, but also our Father in Heaven; it is not just our family that rejoices but the Jesus and the Holy Spirit. What a marvelous scene! The intimate family of God in the as seen in the Trinity to which we also now belong!

Jesus came *"up from the water."* It is my desire to avoid polemical arguments, since our goal is to gain a greater understanding of the Christian walk regardless of our sectarian differences. However, this is a very important element of The Parable of the Cross; therefore the matter needs to be expounded upon. Reviewing the New Testament, we find that when baptism is spoken of the believer is referred to coming UP out of the water. The Greek word for baptism, *"baptizo"*, also agrees with this understanding, which means *"...cover wholly with a fluid"* according to *"Strong's Hebrew and Greek Dictionaries."* Therefore, it is clear that biblical obedience of baptism is to also follow this same pattern. Moreover, we are instructed to participate in this public declaration AFTER we have repented of our sins and accepted Jesus as our Lord and Savior. (Act 10:44-48)

After Jesus was baptized, He was immediately driven into the wilderness by the Spirit and then He ministered for roughly three and a half years. Then finally, He revealed Himself to the Jews as Messiah King by allowing the procession and praise to be heaped upon Him; and by sending His disciples to acquire the donkey He became an active participant in the coronation ceremony. People were ecstatic to receive their King, and yet within a few days, their praise and adoration was replaced by a scorn and a crown of thorns.

We must remember that even though Jesus is our example and we are being conformed into His image; His objectives were very distinct from ours. He had a twofold mission to be accomplished at the cross. The first was to pay for our sins, the redemption, and the second was to set the example of our need to die to sin in our daily walk, our sanctification. Therefore, His baptism was followed by three and a half years of teaching before He went to the cross. It was precisely this obscurity that allowed Him to that inspire billons of people with His teachings and speak words that changed the world.

Our mission, on the other hand, is to be the recipients of redemption and sanctification. Then by participating with God's plan of sanctification, and laying down our lives as a living sacrifice, He will use us in His plan of redeeming others. So that we follow after Christ in like manner allowing God to use us to bring people to saving grace and faith in Jesus.

When we are baptized, we make a public declaration that we are

> *...putting off the body of the sins of the flesh by the circumcision of Christ, **buried with Him in baptism**, in whom **also you were raised through the faith of the working of God**, raising Him from the dead. And you, being dead in your sins and the uncircumcision of your flesh, He has made alive together with Him, having forgiven you all trespasses. (Col 2:11-13 MKJV)*

Notice that we are "*buried with Him in baptism*" and that we are "*raised through the faith*". This is a beautifully rich picture of full immersion baptism is designed to represent. When we are baptized we take a symbolic stand with Jesus that we have died to our sins and were raised to a new life. This also seems to have some very important spiritual significance that is beyond the scope of our discussion. Therefore, we will just suffice it to say that being obedient in the Lord's precepts will always afford the blessings and protection of God. When we go under the water we testify to God and the world that we have died to our sins. When we come up out of the water we are testify that we have been raised in the newness of life. Jesus died, was buried and resurrected to become the first born of a new creation. That new creation is us. In the spirit we were in Christ Jesus when He died, was buried and resurrected. In the body we now proclaim our death, burial and resurrection in the ceremony of full immersion baptism. By descending into the water we proclaim our death, by going under the water we proclaim our burial and then by coming up out of the water we proclaim our resurrected life in Christ.

When we come up out of the water there is the joyous celebration of our church brothers and sisters and of course our family, as we also witness in the celebration at Jesus' baptism.

Tying the coronation celebration together with the baptismal ceremony we are made kings and given the crown of life.

> *...Jesus Christ the faithful Witness,* **the First-born from the dead** *and* **the Ruler of the kings of the earth***. To Him who loved us and* **washed us from our sins** *in His own blood,* **and made us kings and priests** *to God and His Father (Rev 1:5-6 MKJV)*

Jesus made us kings and He is our Lord and King, therefore, He *"has on His garment and on His thigh a name written,* **KING OF KINGS AND LORD OF LORDS***."* (Rev 19:16)

What did we do to deserve this great honor? Nothing! In fact *"while we were yet sinners Christ died for us."* (Rom 5:8) Remember in this parable that we are Lazarus. We cannot raise ourselves from the dead. Jesus had to bring us back to life. We are so dead in our sins that without the voice of Jesus calling us to come forth, we would not even realize that we are dead. It is because we have done nothing to earn this great reward that we will throw our

> *...crowns before the throne, saying, O Lord, You are worthy to receive glory and honor and power, because You created all things, and* **for Your will** *they are and were created. (Rev 4:10-11 MKJV)*

Remember that Jesus' mission was slightly different from ours. Our mission is to make the public statement that *"you are not your own, for you are bought with a price."* Therefore, you *"glorify God in your body and in your spirit, which are God's."* (1Co 6:19-20) Then you begin your ministry of making His glory known to the world. Then, if you have truly died to yourself then you will be like Lazarus who drew people because Jesus had raised him from the dead and was with Him.

> *When the large crowd of the Jews learned that Jesus was there, they came, not only on account of him but also to see Lazarus, whom he had raised from the dead. (Joh 12:9 ESV)*

As a final note, notice that the transition from death to life is also symbolized in the path Jesus takes into Jerusalem. He begins the journey on the mountain range called Olivet. Remember that that mountain range at one time was pure but it became defiled by Solomon's false worship and rebellion, like the fall of man. This is followed by His descent into the Kidron valley and then an ascent into the City of Peace. Therefore, we see the parallels in His death, burial and resurrection and His baptism, descending into the water, going under the water and ascending out of the water. Our baptism, descending into the water, going under the water and ascending out of the water; our death to ourselves, burying the old man's sin nature and ascending out of the water to new life that was bought, paid for and won by our KING OF KINGS AND LORD OF LORDS!

chapter five

CLEANSING THE TEMPLE

On the following day, when they came from Bethany, he was
hungry. And seeing in the distance a fig tree in leaf, he went to see
if he could find anything on it. When he came to it, he found
nothing but leaves, for it was not the season for figs. And he said to
it, "May no one ever eat fruit from you again." And his disciples
heard it. (Mar 11:12-14 ESV)

It is difficult at first blush to understand why Jesus would curse the fig
tree considering it was not the *"season for figs"*. However, the key to
this particular story is the fact that the *"fig tree was in leaf"*. Most trees
will first produce their leaves and then produce their fruit, but this
particular type of fig tree produced its fruit at the same time that it
sprouted its leaves. Therefore, this tree was offensive in two respects;
first, it did not bear fruit and yet secondly, it appeared to profess from a
distance that it would bear fruit.

It appears to be a ridiculous and even childish reaction of our
temperate Raboni, *"full of grace and truth."* (Joh 1:14) It seems to
contradict His life and teachings. For example, when the Tempter
suggested turning stones into bread after fasting forty days, He
responded that He would wait upon the Word of the Lord rather than
fulfill the instantaneous gratification of the flesh. (Mat 4) After He met
with the woman at the well, the disciples, knowing He was hungry,
asked if He wanted to eat, and yet, He refused the food and went into
town to preach the gospel. (Joh 4) In addition, consider His extreme
sufferings on the cross, and yet, He does not curse those people.
Reflect on the many taunts of the Pharisees and the Sadducees. Jesus
never pronounced a curse against them, although He observed the
sufferings, woes, they caused from their choices in Matthew 23.
Hence, these woes were not active curses, in the manner that He
decreed against this poor fig tree that did not bear fruit, although it was
not the season to bear fruit.

Furthermore, this appears to be the only time Jesus ever cursed anything. During His entire ministry, He never produced such a negative miracle. For this reason, and because the reaction was so atypical when compared to other, more extremely difficult circumstances, it stands out in significance. For example, consider Our Grace's reply to James and John's request to bring down fire upon the Samaritans in the following verses:

> *...he sent messengers ahead of him, who went and entered a village of the Samaritans, to make preparations for him. But the people did not receive him, because his face was set toward Jerusalem. And when his disciples James and John saw it, they said, "Lord, do you want us to tell fire to come down from heaven and consume them?" But he turned and rebuked them. (Luk 9:51-55 ESV)*

Do you see our ongoing struggle with understanding sin? We cannot know right from wrong without the Word of God and the effectual working of the Holy Spirit in our lives. We could easily have read how Jesus brought down fire and brimstone on Samaria and said it was justified. How was this circumstance different from Sodom and Gomorrah? We certainly could have read that the Bread of Life turned the stones into bread and gloried in His demonstration of power; and yet, the bible implies that this would have been a sin. However, our heart would condemn Him for cursing a defenseless fig tree. In many respects, this is the lesson of Job; we do not always understand God's purposes and our human reaction is to hold Him accountable to us. This is also the lesson of Jonah; we believe our plan is better than God's plan. We cannot create the heavens, or the earth, or for that matter, even a single, solitary atom. Many of our most renowned scientists, after many years of education, spend their lives attempting to uncover the secrets of the atom and its sub-atomic parts; and yet, they only have the smallest fraction of knowledge of these basic building blocks of matter. Despite all of this, our pride is so great; we have the audacity to call God to our courtroom and to stand as judge of Him!

Should we then not assess Our Grace's seemingly uncharacteristic reaction? On the contrary, we absolutely should! If this were our response to the hidden things of the Bible, then we would never grow in spirit and truth. However, we do need to attend to this quandary with the correct heart. Therefore, let us respectfully enter the Judge of the

Earth's courtroom and make our discernment as members of the jury. After all, we may boldly stand upon His promise to inquire of Him because He has assured us:

> *...if any of you lacks wisdom, let him ask of God, who gives to all liberally and with no reproach, and it shall be given to him. (Jas 1:5 MKJV)*

The Creator has created all things, and so it is reasonable to acknowledge He is also the owner of all things. It is, therefore, a faithful saying that the Lord giveth and the Lord taketh away, since *"The earth is the Lord's and all that dwell within it"* (Psa 24:1); *"for thou hast created all things, and for thy pleasure they are and were created."* (Rev 4:11) Since the Creator is the owner of that property, then He also has the right to destroy it. However, we do recognize cursing the fig tree was entirely inconsistent with the Lord's reaction to other more pressing, and difficult situations. Finally, we also acknowledge this is the only time Jesus ever pronounced a curse. Therefore, this seemingly inane story about Jesus cursing a fig tree may contain a tremendously significant message to unveil.

Thus far, we have made three particularly significant determinations. First, we cannot always trust our own human judgment. It is for this reason that God has given us the light of the Gospel to reveal the truth about our darkened reasoning and completely staggering spiritual pride. Secondly, we determined that it is allowable, and reasonable, to ask God for the wisdom to uncover veiled metaphors. Finally, because of the story's uniqueness, we concluded this story might be especially valuable. So let us hold that final thought for now, as we continue to walk with Jesus through the events of that day.

> *And they came to Jerusalem. And he entered the temple and began to drive out those who sold and those who bought in the temple, and he overturned the tables of the money-changers and the seats of those who sold pigeons. And he would not allow anyone to carry anything through the temple. And he was teaching them and saying to them, "Is it not written, 'My house shall be called a house of prayer for all the nations?' But you have made it a den of robbers." (Mar 11:15-17 ESV)*

The man portrayed in this story certainly does not sound like the amiable, conciliatory Jesus emphasized by the modern church. Therefore, let us take a moment to contemplate the magnitude of the commotion Jesus caused when He entered the temple and began to drive out the moneychangers. Suppose you are a merchant in an exceptionally large flea market, when all of the sudden a wild zealot enters the market and begins overturning tables, breaking open the animal cages, demanding that everyone leave. Subsequently, he does not permit you or anyone else to take their goods. Moreover, this man is completely unarmed, and he has no legal authority from the owners of the flea market. To make matters worse, once a year this city has a huge event, in which you will make more money during this time then you will make for the rest of the entire year. You paid a premium for one of the most traveled spots. Everything seems to be going perfectly. You are making more money this year than you have ever made. Then, all of the sudden a crazy, religious fanatic walks in and begins overturning tables. This is not a small flea market. The dealers set up hundreds of booths and tables. The enormity of the market is only overshadowed by the magnitude of the merchants' investments. It was excessively expensive to rent space. It took years to develop the contacts just to have the opportunity to rent the space, considering it was so highly sought after and extremely limited.

How would you react to this religious fanatic? How do you suppose the mob would react? If he did shut down all the booths, would you leave your merchandise, because this man would not allow you to carry it through the building?

Models of the temple reveal its enormity. It was comprised of three parts. In the center was the Holy of Holies, where once a year the high priest entered to offer sacrifice for the nation. The surrounding region was the inner court, where the law forbade Gentiles to assemble.

However, the area surrounding this, the outer court, was the area set aside for devout Gentiles to worship and pray to God.

Now let us consider why Jesus may have taken such extreme actions against the moneychangers. When a believer came to Jerusalem, they were required to offer a sin sacrifice. This had to be a perfect lamb, approved by the priests. Many scholars believe the priests purposely rejected the pilgrim's lamb, as an unworthy sacrifice, so they could sell them a priestly-approved lamb at inflated prices. Afterwards, scholars believe, they offered to buy the defective lamb from the pilgrim under the pretense to ease their burden of travel, and then later sold it to some other traveler.

Additionally, every Jewish male had to pay a temple tax in the currency of the temple. Therefore, they had to convert their form of money into temple currency, most likely exchanged at exorbitant rates.

Imagine the immense sums of money generated from this corrupt relationship. This was not just an attack against the moneychangers, but also an attack against the entire system. The moneychangers had to pay for their spots in the temple in order to obtain this filthy lucre. The priests made a fortune cheating the people by selling their priestly-approved lambs. Meanwhile, the chief priests and rulers completely turned a blind eye towards all this activity, because they were knee-deep in the racket, choosing instead to become corrupt cohorts in these crimes.

The rulers' rampant corruption was so blatant that it was obvious to most secular people. The church's involvement with this type of political, economic and religious corruption causes the Lord to decree, *"you have given great occasion to the enemies of Jehovah to blaspheme."* (2Sa 12:14) Even those who were of the Lord's fold easily observed the priest's self-proclaimed piety did not match the reality of their lives. They had become foul hypocrites and *"whitewashed tombs"* (Mat 23:27), rather than church leaders without spot or wrinkle, holy and without blemish. (Eph 5:27)

Jesus was livid for three legitimate reasons. First, the conspirators set up the racket in His Father's house, causing Him to call it a *"den of robbers."* Second, the leaders were preying upon the flock, having become wolves in sheep's clothing, merchandising God's people. Third, they transformed the only place Gentiles could commune with God in prayer, the Holy Outer Court, into a debased flea market.

Now let us juxtapose the cleansing of the temple with the cursing of the fig tree. Jesus was hungry. From a distance, He noticed a leaf-bearing fig tree; therefore, He fully expected to fulfill that hunger with fruit. Likewise, as people walked toward Jerusalem, driven by their hunger for God, they would have seen the brilliant, gold plated temple glistening in the sun, causing expectation to grow they would soon be in the presence of the Holy One of Israel, who would nourish their hungry souls on fruits of purity and righteousness. When Jesus arrived at the fig tree, advertising fruit, He was disappointed to find it was nothing more than a pretense. As the pilgrims arrived at the temple, the symbol of purity and holiness, they were disheartened to discover the polluted corruption in the Outer Court and the collusion of their highly esteemed leaders. Both cases created great expectations, but neither promise lived up to actual experience. Therefore, God's response was judgment. In the case of the fig tree, Jesus cursed it. In the case of the temple, He drove out the racketeers.

Imagine how hotly the moneychangers' disputed with the Pharisees. They surely demanded that the Pharisees remove this man or return the vast sum of their investment. What do you suppose was the Pharisees' reaction? Would they harden their hearts and serve unrighteous mammon, or submit to the Righteousness of God, and the pliable heart of repentance?

> *And the chief priests and the scribes heard it and were seeking a way to destroy him, for they feared him, because all the crowd was astonished at his teaching. (Mar 11:18 ESV)*

Consider the utter amazement of the crowd. Most dedicated pilgrims devoutly made this journey many times in the past. The radiant beauty of the temple's exterior no longer disillusioned them with the promise of holiness. The pollution that infected its interior had become an accepted way of life. However, when the Meshiach arrived at His temple He immediately began the work of cleansing, fiercely extricating the infectious disease with the brute force of a Civil War surgeon hastily removing a gangrenous limb. O' to have seen the Lion of the Tribe of Judah violently eradicating the crime syndicate with a rod of iron, and fearlessly confronting the corrupt leaders with the sword of His mouth, freeing the oppressed! Of course, they were astonished! Would not we also be astonished if someone actually began to weed corruption out of Washington?

Cleansing the Temple

The Word will not abide in an unclean temple. Therefore, notice the pattern, first He cleanses the temple then He teaches in the temple. For that reason, He then spent the rest of that day teaching the doctrines of God.

Let us summarize what we have learned thus far in The Parable of the Cross. After being raised from the dead by the Creator, we are then anointed by the baptismal fire of the Holy Spirit. Afterwards, we make a public profession of our death, burial and resurrection, symbolized by water baptism. In the meantime, Jesus comes to the infected temple of our flesh as the King of our heart and drives out the polluted strongholds of the racketeers.

The only occasion in which we do any work is our public profession of faith at our water baptism. However, God's work is not dependent on our work. In other words, after we have been awakened from the dead and Jesus has become our Lord; He is coming to cleanse the temple of our flesh, regardless of whether we have been baptized or not. Nevertheless, do not despise the ordinance of your King; He said be baptized, therefore, do it as soon as possible after having been awakened from the slumber of sin.

This part of the parable is very easy for any born-again Christian to embrace. We believe it because we experienced it. I personally love to hear testimonies of how Jesus called believers from the dead. They are like the billions of snowflakes that have fallen to the earth, in which none is alike in their unique details; and yet, all are alike in that they all are snowflakes. What an expression of God's personal love and affection for our individual souls! Every one of us has a love story about how the Shepherd so desired us that He left the other ninety-nine sheep to search for our lost souls and lead us back into the sheepfold. In addition, it is also extremely exciting to hear how the Sanctifier of our Souls then drove out the moneychangers, cleansing the temple of our flesh.

Jesus cleansed several characteristics in me after calling me out of the world of sin and darkness and into His light. Among the first, He delivered me from a profane tongue, which is also the one that most of my acquaintances noticed, who knew me in my formally sorry condition. At the time of my salvation, I owned a construction company, which meant I was always around extremely rough living and speaking individuals. Every sentence I spoke contained at least two profane words. I am sickened to consider my former manner of speech. Nevertheless, about three weeks after being translated into His light and meditating upon the Word of God, the Holy Spirit spoke to my spirit saying, *"Have you noticed that you have not said a profane word in the last few weeks?"* I was amazed. So many times in the past I attempted to stop swearing, but it was more than just a task, it was who I was and it was my habit; thus, it was an impossible feat, always doomed to failure. However, now after being born-again and spending time with His Holiness, the Lover of my Soul, I no longer had the disposition to swear. The words had just disappeared. He had removed the old *"heart made of stone"*, darkened by sin, and replaced it with *"a new heart and a new spirit."* (Eze 36:26)

As a babe in Christ, I personally had no doctrinal understanding how serious my words were to my Savior. I began to contemplate that scriptures must have some guidance about our language considering the miracle Christ wrought in me. I was shocked, after researching the matter, to discover the vast quantity of material in the Holy Writ that addressed this particular topic.

For example, consider James' admonition,

> *It takes only a spark to start a forest fire!* ***The tongue is like a spark. It is an evil power that dirties the rest of the body*** *and sets a person's entire life on fire with flames that come from hell itself. (Jas 3:5-6 CEV)*

Moreover, in the following parable, the Author of our Faith compares the health of our heart to the health of a tree. Notice also that a person's words, what we can see, will reveal what we cannot see, the hidden condition of their heart.

> *For **a good tree does not bring forth corrupt fruit**, neither does a corrupt tree bring forth good fruit. For every tree is known by its own fruit. ... **A good man out of the good treasure of his heart brings forth the good**. And an evil man out of the evil treasure of his heart brings forth the evil. For **out of the abundance of the heart his mouth speaks**. (Luk 6:43-45 MKJV)*

The fruit of our life will indicate the cleansing of our heart, which our Sovereign Lord performed at the time of our salvation. He is also working every day, sanctifying our heart, and continuing to drive out the moneychangers; for *"He who began a good work in you will bring it to completion at the day of Jesus Christ.*" (Phi 1:6) Because of this, a newborn believer may appear unchanged. However, there is a crucially important difference between the carnal Christian, who has never grown in the faith, and the professing believer, who has never been born-again into the faith. Thus, we are soberly warned not to be deceived, "***Except a man be born again, he cannot see the kingdom of God.***" (Joh 3:3) Therefore, if we are His then we are now **NEW** Creations in Him, as confirmed by many other testimonies in the New Testament.

Do you have a problem with profanity? Do you covet material possessions? Does the fire of lust burn in your heart? Are you controlled by the passion of anger and revenge in disputes? Does gluttony overpower you with its desire? Are you driven by the lust of your eyes? We cannot win these battles in ourselves. It is a desperately precarious state of affairs. We cannot rehabilitate the old man! The infection is so pervasive that it has contaminated every cell in our body. It has entangled itself right into the DNA that makes us who we are. Therefore, God Almighty, the God of the New Creation, has given us one solitary, radical choice: we must die! We must realize we cannot win this battle. If we allow the Lord to open our prideful eyes, it will become apparent to us that Pharaoh's army is far too mighty for us. We need God's help to fight the battle, but even more importantly, we need God's help to remove the scales of pride from our eyes that have blinded us to this truth for so long. Thus, if we look to Him then He will be our victory. Therefore, the only way to win these battles is to stop fighting the battles in our own strength. We must release this life and let it die, because we are not fighting the sin within us, but rather we are fighting against who we are at the very core of our nature. Therefore, we lay our lives down so that Christ may pick it up again and renew our souls. He drives the moneychangers out of our hearts. Our obligation is only to claim this position, by faith, and then the Lord of Armies will drive out the racketeers. All the work, all the glory, belongs to Him, the Lord of Glory, the King of the New Creation.

Several years ago, I spoke with a young Christian woman about her profanity. I informed her that the Lord wanted her speech tempered with grace. She responded that she was ashamed to use those words, but it was her habit and she was unable to stop. Despite this defect, she was a exceptionally strong Christian in many respects. She had been president of the Campus Crusade for Christ in college, and we prayed together often. I am confident that she was a true believer because God always answered our prayers. I asked her if she spent time reading the Bible, and she replied that she was too busy. I told her that if she truly wanted to stop swearing all she had to do was begin reading scriptures daily, and those vulgar words would soon disappear. She did not heed my advice for several months, although I did plant a tiny mustard seed of truth. Eventually, I saw her again, and she was ecstatic to inform me that she now devotes her mornings to the Word of God, and that she was no longer under the bondage of a profane tongue. Glory to God!

Your words and your walk in this world indicate your actual spiritual condition. Have you been truly regenerated by the Spirit of Life? We are instructed to *"judge ourselves, [so that] we would not be judged"* (1Co 11:31); for judgment begins at the house of the Lord. (1Pe 4:17) However, there are two types of judgment; one is the discipline of the Lord's children and the other is the judgment of the lost. Neither is enjoyable, and at times, they are indistinguishable from each other. The discipline of the Lord's children is our punishment for making wrong choices. If the sheep leaves the shepherd's pasture the wolf is waiting to *"steal, kill and destroy"* (Joh 10:10), but he is still one of the Lord's sheep. However, there are many others, and I say many because our Raboni cautions:

> *"Enter by the narrow gate.* **For the gate is wide and the way is easy that leads to destruction, and those who enter by it <u>are many</u>**. *For the gate is narrow and the way is hard that leads to life, and those who find it are few. (Mat 7:13-14 ESV)*

Many people claim they have accepted Jesus as their Savior and their Sovereign King of their heart. However, their life walk consistently contradicts their testimony. Their actions constantly bear witness against His image in their minds. Jesus offers so many solemn warnings to those people who think that they can have it both ways. To the unfruitful trees of professing Christians, He says,

> *You hypocrites! Well did Isaiah prophesy of you, when he said: "This people honors me with their lips, but their heart is far from me; in vain do they worship me." (Mat 15:7-9 ESV)*

The Judge of the Earth also admonishes us that "**<u>every idle word</u>**, *whatever men may speak, they shall give account of it in the Day of Judgment. For* **<u>by your words</u> you shall be justified, and <u>by your words</u> you shall be condemned.**" (Mat 12:34-37)

Consider also the following admonition from the Sanctifier of your Heart and the Lover of your Soul.

> *Not everyone who says to Me, Lord! Lord! shall enter the kingdom of Heaven, but **he who <u>does the will</u> of My Father in Heaven**. Many will say to Me in that day, Lord! Lord! Did we not prophesy in Your name, and through Your name throw out demons, and through Your name do many wonderful works? Then, I will say to them **<u>I never knew you</u>**! Depart from Me, those working lawlessness! (Mat 7:21-23 MKJV)*

However, to those who do know Him and have given their lives to Him the Lord of Glory says,

> *Who shall ascend the hill of the LORD? And who shall stand in his holy place? He who has clean hands and a pure heart, who does not lift up his soul to what is false and does not swear deceitfully. He will receive blessing from the LORD and righteousness from the God of his salvation. Such is the generation of those who seek him, who seek the face of the God of Jacob. Selah*

> *Lift up your heads, O gates! And be lifted up, O ancient doors, that the King of glory may come in. Who is this King of glory? The LORD, strong and mighty, the LORD, mighty in battle! Lift up your heads, O gates! And lift them up, O ancient doors, that the King of glory may come in. Who is this King of glory? The LORD of hosts, he is the King of glory! Selah (Psa 24:3-10 ESV)*

Therefore, O Lord, King of Glory, come in and cleanse our hands and purify our heart. Let your perfect Will be done, on earth as in heaven. Sanctify us O Lord so that our old nature will die and we may be born-again to the newness of your spirit.

> *This is The Parable of the Cross.*

71

chapter six

BEARING THE FRUIT OF FAITH

The next day,

> *As they passed by in the morning, they saw the fig tree withered
> away to its roots. And Peter remembered and said to him, "Rabbi,
> look! The fig tree that you cursed has withered." And Jesus
> answered them, "**Have faith in God**. Truly, I say to you, whoever
> says to this mountain, 'Be taken up and thrown into the sea,' and
> does not doubt in his heart, but believes that what he says will
> come to pass, it will be done for him. Therefore, I tell you,
> whatever you ask in prayer, believe that you have received it, and
> it will be yours." (Mar 11:20-24 ESV)*

The central message above is "*Have faith in God.*" If we have a REAL
faith in God, then we KNOW He is able. Do you truly believe the
Almighty spoke this incalculable collection of celestial bodies that
comprise this vast universe into existence simply by uttering "*Let there
be...*"? Do you honestly think the Creator formed every trillion-cell
living creature with just the word of His mouth? Did not He carefully
craft the most minuscule detail of every cell in those trillion cell
organisms with hundreds of millions of strands of DNA coding? Did
not He precisely order trillions of chemical reactions to occur every
second in order for each life form to exist? Is He not so concerned over
you that He has counted all the hairs on your head? In the vastness of
this universe, we stand in awe of His power; in its splendor, His glory;
in its details, His care; in its precision, His immaculate love. Do you
honestly believe these things and "*Have faith in God*"? If so, then do
you not believe this All-Powerful, Loving God is able to help you with
your seemingly insurmountable mountain of problems?

Something appears to be amiss. Is it possible we have taken all the
extraordinary things our God is able to do and has done for granted?

Maybe we acknowledged these things from Bible studies and sermons without sincerely reflecting how marvelous our God must be in order for all these things to be true. This is the power and the sovereignty of God. We truly need to grasp His astonishing power and our relationship to Him through Jesus Christ; then we will begin to fathom the riches of His power and His grace. Then we will grasp that if we have laid down our life of sin and accepted His call on our lives, that we are sons of the Most High God, whereby we "*come boldly to the throne of grace*" (Heb 4:16) and cry out to the Holy King of the Universe, "*Abba! Father!*" (Rom 8:15)

Do you not know troubling over the mountain of your problem is an insult to your Father in Heaven, the Sovereign King of the Universe? Do you honestly believe in the God of Wonders portrayed in scriptures; or is the mountain of your problems so great and the God you believe in so small that He cannot remove it? Is He so uncaring that He will not remove it? In the first case, you have diminished the power of the Omnipotent God. In the second case, you have diminished the concern of a Loving Father. In the latter case, you may not have considered that you are a prince to the Most High King of the Universe in Christ Jesus.

If the Sovereign King is completely in control, and you are an adopted son of the Father by the blood of Jesus; do you actually have to worry? Has He not promised us "*that **all things** work together **for good** to those who love God*"? (Rom 8:28) O ye of little faith, if your son asks for a fish do you give him a snake? How much more will your Father in Heaven give good things to those who ask Him? (Mat 7:10-11) Does this mean that we now have a license to feed our immediate gratifications and licentious desires of the flesh? God forbid!

> *[Live] as free people, [yet] without **employing your freedom as a pretext for wickedness**; but [live at all times] as servants of God. (1Pe 2:16 AMP)*

The pure water of this word has been so muddied by "*certain people [who] have crept in unnoticed*" into the church and "*who pervert the grace of our God into sensuality*" as a license to feed the sins of the flesh. (Jud 1:4), with televangelists assert that donating to their ministries will force God to return thirty, sixty or one-hundred fold. They have taken a verse out of context in order to seduce and deceive you. It is quite apparent that they have made the servant the master and the God of the bible the servant. This is so obvious and loathsome that even the blind world of the lost can see that they are "*making merchandise of you.*" (2Pe 2:3)

> ***They give the way of truth a bad name.*** *They're only out for themselves. They'll say anything, anything, that sounds good to exploit you. They won't, of course, get by with it. They'll come to a bad end, for God has never just stood by and let that kind of thing go on. (2Pe 2:3 MSG)*

They are the lowest snakes preying on the more needful segments of society. However, if they are preying on you then it is because you gave the materialism of this world much too high a place in your own heart. God's promises are not for your wealth in this world. He was not manifest as a servant in the flesh in order to make us wealthy in materialistic possessions. He came to make us right with God. The Apostle Peter exhorts us as sojourners and "*pilgrims to **abstain from fleshly lusts which war** against the soul.*" (1Pe 2:11) To sow a seed in order to create greater material wealth is not sowing a seed with the correct heart. God may bless us, but our primary concern should be about His Kingdom and His Righteousness, not our physical comfort. When you sow a seed out of a covetous heart with the expectation of a materialistic payback then you have placed mammon above the God Most High; not to serve Him but to have Him serve you in order to feed the gratifications of the flesh. Do not play God the way you play the stock market! It is for this reason the scriptures warn us that "*the carnal mind is enmity against God, for it is not subject to the Law of God, neither indeed can it be.*" (Rom 8:7)

If this has been your heart when you have sown the seeds of your faith standing on promises like "*whatever you ask in prayer, believe that you have received it, and it will be yours,*" (Mar 11:24) and yet it has not been given to you; do not think that God's Word is untrustworthy. Instead, acknowledge that you have been completely misled by these "*false prophets, which come to you in sheep's clothing, but inwardly they are ravening wolves*" (Mat 7:15), who have prayed upon your evil desires. Would you call God's character into question? God forbid! "*But let God be true, and every man a liar.*" (Rom 3:4) I am sure that you would never call God a liar, but perhaps His Word is untrustworthy. However, the Lord tells us "*All scripture is God-breathed.*" (2Ti 3:16) David also affirms this of God saying, "*You have magnified Your Word **above all Your name**.*" (Psa 138:2) The implications of this statement are immense. To the ancients, a name was much more than just a word we called a person by, but rather it was an accurate representation of their *nature*, *character* and *authority*. Therefore, David is making the astounding statement that God's Word is even more important to Him than His very being! Can we trust God? If so, then we can trust His Word.

How then do we reconcile unfulfilled prayers with His assurance that He answers all our prayers as long as we *"have faith in God"*? We must look at the promises of the scriptures in their entirety rather than as bits and pieces as we have become accustomed to doing. I would strongly urge the reader to read the Bible all the way through from cover to cover and not to stop for explanations, except for possibly a very brief time. After this, then return to the Bible and *"rightly divide the Word of Truth."* (2Ti 2:15) Most Christians have never read the entire Bible, so they have taken the exact opposite approach. They arrived at the church with little or no biblical knowledge and then had short passages exposited to them by the pastor. If this was your course then you also were easy prey for the deceptions of the enemy. Bear in mind that when Satan tested Jesus in the wilderness he extracted small portions of scripture and reinterpreted them in order to cause the Son of Man to sin. It was only Jesus' complete understanding of the Holy Writ that allowed Him to withstand these heresies.

If our Advocate does not hear your prayers then it is possibly because you have been praying with the wrong heart.

> ***You ask and receive not, <u>because you ask amiss</u>***, *that you may spend it upon your lusts. Adulterers and adulteresses! Do you not know that the friendship of the world is enmity with God? Therefore, whoever desires to be a friend of the world is the enemy of God. (Jas 4:3-4 MKJV)*

Remember that your *"kingdom is not of this world"* (Joh 18:36) and therefore you should not be laying

> *...up treasures on earth for yourselves, where moth and rust corrupt, and where thieves break through and steal. But lay up treasures in Heaven for yourselves, where neither moth nor rust corrupt, and where thieves do not break through nor steal. **For where your treasure is, <u>there will your heart be also</u>**. (Mat 6:19-21 MKJV)*

Therefore, we need to seek the heart and the mind of Jesus when we pray. Then we will be praying in His name; nature, character and authority and then He will honor His promise that "*If you ask anything in My name, I will do it.*" (Joh 14:14) This is no small matter. Recall that He has magnified His Word above His name. (Psa 138:2)

This is a little troubling, is not it? On the one hand, is the positive message of faith, on the other hand, the Prince of Life is standing beside a fig tree that died because He cursed it. This is quite a dichotomy of extremes and in many respects just does not sit well within our earthly hearts. It appears almost evil that Our Salvation would be standing beside a dead fig tree, boasting that He killed it, and imploring His disciples to "*have faith in God*", so they could accomplish the similar exploits. However, this imagery is so vivid and meaningful that it is needful for our edification. I feel sorry for the tree, but the earth is the Lord's and all that dwell within it. Thus, if God deemed that the life of this tree held such little importance in comparison to the lesson for our souls then who are we to disagree.

Do you recall that the leaves in bloom of this particular tree gave the impression there would be fruit? This is symbolic of seemingly pious or externally upstanding-appearing people whose lives bear little or no fruit. God's Suffering Servant displayed extraordinary patience for all, except for unrepentant, self-righteous individuals that claimed to be the children of God, and yet they were not producing good fruit for the kingdom. This only stands to reason. Imagine for a moment that you were the CEO of a company. In this company, you had a group of salespeople that was lying, cheating and stealing from your customers. If you did nothing then people would begin to believe that the company itself was dishonest. Thus, the observed character of individuals will define the perceived character of the group. Therefore, you would not tolerate it. Neither will Jesus. He is so repulsed by these charlatans' behavior that He begins each rebuke in Matthew 23 with "*But woe to you, scribes and Pharisees, hypocrites!*" They were not producing good fruit. Notice also that the Judge of All the Earth sternly admonishes us that if "*you are lukewarm, and neither cold nor hot, I will vomit you out of My mouth.*" (Rev 3:16) These are very strong words for non-fruit producing Christians. Jesus is saying get hot for the kingdom or stop pretending!

Therefore, we have concluded that Vinedresser desires good fruit. Thus, we should do all we can to produce good fruit for the kingdom, right? Wrong. However, I cannot produce good fruit, because "*nothing good dwells in me.*" (Rom 7:18) The task is impossible. How can I produce good fruit with a corrupt tree? You probably do not believe me when I attest to these things because humanism has privily crept into the hearts and minds of the laity. However, the One with Eyes like a Flame of Fire has informed us "*we are all as an unclean thing, and all our righteousnesses are as filthy rags.*" (Isa 64:6)

> *There is **none** righteous, no, **not one**: There is **none** that understandeth, there is **none** that seeketh after God. They are **all** gone out of the way, **they are together** become unprofitable; there is **none** that doeth good, no, **not one**. (Rom 3:10-12 KJV)*

Eight times in two verses, the Seven Eyes of the Lord pierces the windows of our souls, attempting to beat into our self-righteous, dull minds the fact that we are not justified in ourselves. This is counterintuitive to our psyche, so it is exceedingly difficult for us to accept this appraisal about our utterly degenerate condition. It is almost funny that no one considers themselves an evil person. If you had asked Al Capone or Joseph Stalin, they would have probably said that they were, for the most part, good people. This is the wide-gate mentality. We need to remove these thoughts from our hearts, tie a millstone around them and cast it into the sea.

Allow me to make clear another salient point the modern church has failed to illuminate to their constituents; we will not be judged by our faith, but rather we will be judged by our works. I know I have just set off serious alarm bells in my readers' heads, because everyone knows salvation is by faith and not of works. (Eph 2:8-9), and likewise, I am in agreement with this truth. However, I did not say this is how we are saved, I said this is how we will be judged; by our works! For the Apostle Paul has told us that salvation is "*by grace ...through faith ...not of works.*" (Eph 2:8-9) Nevertheless, the manifest evidence of salvation, to ourselves and to others, is our works, which is commonly referred to in scriptures as fruit.

This is so opposite to what the church has expressed that I will have to take a moment to demonstrate this from a multitude of scriptures.

> *And the dead were **judged** ...**according to their works**. (Rev 20:12) And each one of them was **judged according to their works**. (Rev 20:13)*

*...then He shall reward each one **according to his works**. (Mat 16:27)*
*...who will render to each **according to his works** (Rom 2:6)*
*Reward her as she has rewarded you, and double to her double, **according to her works**. (Rev 18:6)*

Notice below that three times God repeats what He is going to do with non-fruit bearing trees.

...every tree which does not bring forth good fruit is cut down and cast into the fire. (Mat 3:10, Mat 7:19, Luk 3:9)

I know many members of the church, who have been raised in the age of easy grace, will take issue with my exegesis, stating things like; "*I am mixing up the two judgments*," or "*I am comparing salvation to rewards*," or "*that I am comparing salvation to earthly punishment*." However, I will ask you to bear with me a little longer while I prove my case.

The Apostle Paul, the celebrated teacher of grace, emphatically warned us "*to be not deceived; **God is not mocked**: for whatsoever **a man sows, that shall he also reap**.*" Furthermore, this teacher of grace states quite clearly, that it is, "*not the hearers of the law are just before God, but **the doers of the law shall be justified**.*" (Rom 2:13) This verse is in agreement with the Apostle James' admonition to "*be doers of the word, and not hearers only, deceiving yourselves*." (Jas 1:22) Notice also in both cases the apostles warn self-proclaiming Christians to "*be not deceived*" by their hearts. For Jeremiah cautions, "*The heart is deceitful above all things, and desperately wicked: who can know it?*" (Jer 17:9)

Moreover, notice that each time King Messiah addressed the seven churches in Revelations He began with the phrase, "*I know your works*." The Messiah did not say to these Christian churches, "*I know your faith*," but rather, He said, "*I know your works*." To one of these churches He even stated, "*I will give to every one of you according to your works*." (Rev 2:23) Finally, consider His emphatic warning later in the same book:

*Blessed are they that **do his commandments**, that they may have right to the tree of life, and may enter in through the gates into the city. (Rev 22:14 ESV)*

This leaves us in quite a quandary. We are justified by grace and not of works. It is Jesus' finished work. It is His perfect sacrifice that allows us to enter the kingdom of heaven. However, when I arrive at the pearly gates, I will be judged by my works, which are never righteous before God! This is the same perplexity Paul spent seven chapters building up to when he finally cries out in despair, "*O wretched man that I am! Who shall deliver me from the body of this death?*" (Rom 7:24) However, thankfully, a few verses later the apostle gives us the answer to this quandary:

> *There is therefore now no condemnation to them which are in Christ Jesus, who walk not after the flesh, but after the Spirit. **For the <u>law of the Spirit of life in Christ Jesus</u> hath made me <u>free from the law of sin and death</u>.** For what the law could not do, in that it was weak through the flesh, God sending his own Son in the likeness of sinful flesh, and for sin, <u>**condemned sin in the flesh**</u>: That the righteousness of the law might be fulfilled in us, **who walk not after the flesh, but <u>after the Spirit</u>.** (Rom 8:1-4 KJV)*

Within a few days after He cursed the fig tree, Jesus reinforced His lesson with the parable of the vine. It is not difficult to imagine Him teaching in a vineyard setting, walking over to an exceptionally large vine, proclaiming, "*I am the True Vine.*" Saying afterwards, as He points to a man tending the grapes, "*My Father is the Vinedresser.*" Then adding, as He holds up a branch not bearing fruit, "*Every branch in Me that does not bear fruit, He takes away.*" Subsequently, with the other hand, He takes hold of a branch bearing some fruit and says, "*And every one that bears fruit, He prunes it so that it may bring forth more fruit.*" Imagine the impact this message would have had on the agrarian-minded disciples. It is obvious to them that it is necessary to cut off the unfruitful branches. All the branches in the vine, including this unfruitful one, share its nourishment. The fact that it is not producing fruit makes it obvious that pruning is necessary. For that reason, while Jesus is teaching on this specific point, it is easy to envision the vinedresser cutting off the unfruitful branches, and throwing them on the ground.

After this, our Faithful and True Witness, holding a dead, cut off branch in His hand, takes this opportunity to explain how this imagery is analogous to our relationship with Him and our ability to bear fruit, saying, "*Now you are clean through the Word which I have spoken to you. **Abide in Me**, and I in you. **As the branch cannot bear fruit of**" *itself **unless it remains in the vine**, so neither can you unless you abide in Me. I am the Vine, you are the branches."* (Joh 15:3-5) Imagine how distasteful the non-fruit bearing branches appeared to the disciples. He then walks over to a branch, brimming with fruit, an exceedingly delightful sight in their agrarian-eyes, and He says, *"He who abides in Me, and I in him, the same brings forth much fruit; for without Me you can do nothing."* (Joh 15:5)

All of this is so obvious to the disciples. If they owned that vineyard, they would do precisely the same thing. Now it becomes clear that God did not save us just for our sake, but also for the world's sake. Not only did He save us, but He also placed us in the vine, giving us the ability to bear exceedingly good fruit.

I recall when I was first saved, like all immature children; I thought it was only about me. I remember inquiring of God, *"Since I am now saved, why do not You immediately take me to heaven?"* I did not comprehend the fullness of His magnificent plan of salvation. What else is there to do if you have already given your life and your heart to Jesus? However, there is much for the Christian to do, for we must be about our Father's business (Luk 2:49) while it is day, that is to say, while we are alive, for the night comes when we will pass away, and no man can work. (Joh 9:4)

Returning to the vineyard, at the climax of this analogy, Jesus points to the vinedresser, now gathering the dead branches and says, *"If anyone does not abide in Me, he is cast out as a branch and is withered."* Then He says *"And they gather and cast them into the fire, and they are burned,"* as the vinedresser throws the dead, cut off, unfruitful branches into a nearby fire. This imagery is so intense. The fire is already burning unfruitful branches. In the meantime, the vinedresser continues to cast in more kindling that causes the crackling flames to surge and the air to become thick with the smell of burning timbers. Then, in what seems like only a moment in time, the blaze violently engulfs the last of these unfruitful branches, turning this once proud, heaping pile into nothing more than a few charred remains and an ash heap that the wind easily overcomes and disperses into the air.

Can you imagine how intently the disciples must have been watching Jesus as He expounded upon this imagery? Jesus may now have just watched the vinedresser continue to gather additional dead branches and throw them into the fire, allowing His message, *"If anyone **does**"* *__not abide in Me__, __HE IS__ ... cast ...into the fire, and ...burned"*, to permeate the disciples' thoughts. At that moment, I would have been dumbstruck; thinking to myself, *"I do not want any part of that fire! I am staying in the vine!"*

Thankfully, He did not conclude His discourse at this point.

> *If you abide in Me, and My Words abide in you, you shall ask what you will, and it shall be done to you. In this My Father is glorified, that you bear much fruit, so you shall be My disciples. (Joh 15:7-8 MKJV)*

Notice that Jesus ends His lesson with another message on faith. In like manner, in cursing the fig tree, which also stunned the disciples, He concludes the teaching with a message on faith, saying, *"Have faith in God."* (Mar 11:22) Therefore, both stories accentuate the astounding promise that if you have faith in God then **you WILL bear** much fruit and your prayers **WILL be** answered! This is not a command, but rather a tremendous promise from the Word of Life! Nevertheless, let us not become so enamored with the promise that we forget our ominous warnings that judgment looms over the unfruitful, clearly marked by the sentence of the withered fig tree and burning branches in the background.

> *Behold then __the kindness__, and __the severity__ of God; on those having fallen, severity; but on you, kindness, if you continue in the kindness. Otherwise you also will be cut off. (Rom 11:22 MKJV)*

This balance appears to be severely missing in most modern churches. The greatest teacher who ever lived was Jesus. The words He spoke in His three and a half year ministry have endured over two millennia and have become the most expounded upon teachings in human history. It has not only had an enormous impact on Christianity, but the entire world, so that all religions magnify Him as a good and wise teacher. Why then does TV on Sunday mornings speak so much of the promises that accompanies faith but so little, if at all, of the detrimental choice of living an unfaithful and unfruitful *Christian* life?

Satan, it seems, loves to cause us to err by swinging the pendulum of truth from one extreme to the other. Let us remember that living waters flow directly from the Word of Truth, and this is the river that nourishes the Tree of Life, which bears its fruit in due season. (Rev 22:1-2) It is our desire to remain as close to the center of this river as possible and not to become too extreme in either direction so we do not find ourselves on the bank of falsity. When Calvin began to elucidate his doctrines on the depravity of man, our utter inability to come to God in our own strength and the glory and sovereignty of God, he was battling against the prevailing church teaching that was a mixture of man's works and God's works. His precepts were an enormous necessity because Christianity is not a work's religion. His primary desire when he wrote *"The Institutes of the Christian Religion"* was to sanctify the believer with correct doctrines and to bring Christians into a close, personal relationship with their Savior. However, if Calvin was alive today, I believe he would be utterly dismayed at how the misapplication of his doctrine has produced the opposite effect and become a license for lasciviousness. I am speaking of what I call ultra-Calvinism, which is the *Once-Saved, Always-Saved* ideology run amok that has become so prevalent in the modern church. In Calvin's time, he was warring against self-righteousness, that we can justify ourselves before a Holy God. In our time, we have swung to the opposite extreme, finding ourselves shipwreck on the other bank of falsity, that a person can be saved, and yet never have a changed life. Even though the concept *Once-Saved, Always-Saved* is true, the phrase has been distorted to imply all that is needed is a casual alter call to receive Christ's salvation gift without repentance, and thus without the fruit of a changed life. With this in mind, there is no need for self to die. There is no need to crucify the sins of the flesh. You have your insurance policy of salvation so live as your flesh desires. Is it not apparent that this teaching is as equally false in our time as the self-justification dogmas Calvin was battling in his time? The principle itself is correct and I wholeheartedly agree with it, in principle. We cannot save ourselves. We are not justified by our works. No one can pluck us out of the Savior's hand. Nevertheless, we are also earnestly warned in the Bible not to deceive ourselves, believing we can be saved, non-fruit bearing Christians.

You have been set free from the law of sin and death (Rom 8:2) and pulled out of the pit. For this cause, you should no longer wallow in the mire of your former lifestyle. (2Pe 2:22) You have been made a new creation, (2Co 5:17), renewed into the image of Jesus Christ; (Col 3:10), who purposed in you that you bear much fruit, of righteousness, and true holiness. (Eph 4:24) We are emphatically warned, *"not [to] be deceived, God is not mocked. For whatever a man sows, that he also will reap. For he sowing to his flesh will reap corruption from the flesh. But he sowing to the Spirit will reap life everlasting from the*

Spirit." (Gal 6:7-8) Therefore, my beloved, "*work out your own salvation with fear and trembling*" (Php 2:12) and "*let him who ...thinks he stands take heed lest he falls*" (1Co 10:12)

It is interesting, many rabbis around Christ's time were teaching the same *Once-Saved, Always-Saved* doctrine, saying, Abraham stands at the gate of hell to be sure no circumcised person would enter in. The thought was, they are God's covenant people, and God cannot break His covenants. How similar this is to our current interpretation of salvation. That old deluder, Satan, keeps rehashing the same deceptions upon the people of God throughout the ages. Consider John the Baptist's admonishment:

> ...***bring forth <u>fruits</u> worthy of repentance***, *and do not begin to say within yourselves, we have Abraham for our father. For I say to you that God is able to raise up children to Abraham from these stones. (Luk 3:8 MKJV)*

My beloved child of God, you should know there are many proof texts in scriptures stating you can lose your salvation, and there are just as many proof texts stating you can never lose your salvation. I could easily substantiate either doctrine by emphasizing the proof texts of one over the other. David Guzik suggests, "*Systems of theology are important, because the Bible does not contradict itself; but the way to right systems begins with a right understanding of the text, **not one that bends the text to fit into a system**.*" The eminent theologian Charles Spurgeon has also suggested that when we come to passages that contradict our own system of theology we should be "*prepared to cast away every doctrine of our own, rather than one passage of Scripture.*" Moreover, he has stated specifically on this subject, "*We had better far be inconsistent with ourselves than with the inspired Word. I have been called an Arminian[7] Calvinist or a Calvinistic Arminian, and I am quite content so long as I can keep close to my Bible.*"

It is human nature to attempt to reconcile apparently inconsistent passages in the Bible. I have struggled also, being tossed to and fro with the sovereignty of God's election and the free will of the believer. I have reconciled verses like, "***no one is able to snatch them out of the Father's hand***" (Joh 10:29) with seemingly contradictory verses like,

---

[7] Armenians held to the position that a person could lose their salvation.

*"those who were once enlightened ... and were made partakers of the Holy Spirit ... and **then fell away**"* (Heb 6:4-6) with various constructs. First, it is possible these believers were never truly regenerated believers, but rather they were self-professing, unsaved people. Calvin would likely agree with this view. On the other hand, how do you fall away except that you have first believed? Another approach is to consider the element of time. It may be the many promises that we cannot lose our salvation are spoken from the eternal perspective of an omniscient God. Alternatively, it may be the many passages that warn against falling away from the faith are spoken from our temporal perspective. Finally, when the subject has exacerbated me enough, I just throw up my hands and say,

> *O the depth of the riches both of the wisdom and knowledge of God! How unsearchable are His judgments, and His ways past finding out! For who has known the mind of the Lord, or who became His counselor? (Rom 11:33-34 MKJV)*

How then do faith and works work together? Do works produce faith? Does faith produce works? Do you recall that God's purpose for saving you was to produce good works? *"For we are His workmanship, **created in Christ Jesus <u>to good works</u>**, which God has before ordained that we should walk in them."* (Eph 2:10) The Apostle James explicates,

> *But someone will say, "You have faith and I have works." Show me your faith apart from your works, and **I will show you my faith <u>by my works</u>**. You believe that God is one; you do well. Even the demons believe--and shudder! Do you want to be shown, you foolish person, that faith apart from works is useless? Was not **Abraham our father justified <u>by works</u>** when he offered up his son Isaac on the altar? You see that **faith was active along <u>with his works</u>**, and **faith was completed <u>by his works</u>**; and the Scripture was fulfilled that says, "**Abraham believed God**, and it was counted to him as righteousness"--and he was called a friend of God. You see that **a person is justified by works** and not by faith alone. And in the same way was not also Rahab the prostitute justified by works when she received the messengers and sent them out by another way? For as the body apart from the spirit is dead, so also **<u>faith apart from works is dead</u>**. (Jas 2:18-26 ESV)*

When James said, "*a person is justified by works*", he meant that within the context of an active faith in God and God's works through us. James is never insinuating that we are saved by our works. Notice that he points out two different types of faith. There is the active faith that will affect what we do or what we call our works. Then there is the dead faith that mentally ascents to God's existence, but has no effect on a person's behavior. Demons have this same faith! They know God exists. Likewise, they know that He will judge the righteous and the unrighteous. However, they continue in their own will and follow their lusts. They do not have an obedient faith that is submissive to God's will. Instead, they have chosen their own way. This is why people who follow their example are called, "*the sons of disobedience.*" Paul explicitly warns us, "*Let no one deceive you with empty words, for because of these things the wrath of God comes upon the sons of disobedience.*" (Eph 5:6) Are you a child of God or a son of disobedience? Has your faith caused you to walk in the newness of a life-giving spirit; or is your religion vanity of vanities? Are you submissive to the Will of God; or have you acknowledge the truth of God and yet have chosen your own way? Are you a fruit-bearing fig tree; or are you a pretentious fig tree, going church every Sunday to sit in God's vineyard, and yet not abiding in the vine, and not bringing forth much fruit? Did the Seed of God fall on a stony heart that immediately sprung to life and yet was soon withered by the scorching heat of the sun because it never penetrated your stone-hard will (Mat 13:5-6); or did that Seed fall on the good ground of a compliant heart and yield much fruit? (Mat 13:8)

Jesus has made it clear that "*every tree is known by its own fruit.*" (Luk 6:44) He then elucidates more fully, "*A good man out of the good treasure of his heart brings forth the good. And an evil man out of the evil treasure of his heart brings forth the evil. **For out of the abundance of the heart his mouth speaks.***" (Luk 6:45) This is why I said earlier that if you spend time with Messiah you will not have a problem with profanity. This advice has never failed. This reiterates how significant our words are, and that we should exercise extreme care in their use. Paul also affirms this point when he advised the church at Ephesus, "*Let no corrupt communication proceed out of your mouth, but that which is good to the use of edifying, that it may minister grace unto the hearers.*" (Eph 4:29) Elsewhere Jesus says "*But I say to you that every idle word, whatever men may speak, they shall give account of it in the Day of Judgment. For by your words you* *shall be justified, and by your words you shall be condemned."* (Mat 12:36-37)

Do your words *"minister grace unto the hearers"* or are they *"the poison of asps ... full of cursing and bitterness"*? (Rom 3:13-14) The Fountain of Life beseeches, *"Either make the tree good and its fruit good, or else make the tree corrupt and its fruit corrupt; for the tree is known by its fruit."* (Mat 12:33) He who is Faithful and True gave this advice to Pharisees, who had an appearance of authentic religion, and yet did not bear the good fruit of faith. They were extremely pious and devoted in the eyes of the community, but Jesus appears to advise them to make the tree corrupt rather than continue in their present state; or specifically, that it would be better to live a life of open sin than to mask it with the pretense of a religious faith in God. In addition, this study has convinced me that the lowest depths of hell are reserved for those people who outwardly proclaimed The Righteous Judge as their savior but never submitted their stone-hard will to His kingly authority. For this reason, the Word of Testimony calls them, *"Offspring of vipers!"* and asks them *"How can you, being evil, speak good things?"* (Mat 12:34)

Therefore, do we say, *"Thank the Lord that I am not like those hypocrites. I go to church twice a week, and I pay tithes?"* However, The Parable of the Cross is teaching us that WE are the Pharisees. This is our old nature. This is that self-life that attempts to draw us out of the Light and the Glory of the Son of God and bring us back into the dark cave of sin and death. This is the flesh nature that raises its ugly head when we are tried by the fire of false accusations, tiredness, hunger and other tribulations, which God uses to bring this old man to his death. When the trials by fire arise, do we fall at the feet of Jesus and give Him our complete heart of worship or do we return to the cave, shackle our spirit to the flesh and rise in rebellion to God's good work? Christianity is not a *"been there, done that religion."* We are in the battle of our lives. The Enemy has built strongholds in the land of the flesh and he no desire to relinquish them to God. He attempts to speak into our spirit through the strongholds of the flesh, and even though he constantly accuses us night and day before the Lord, we have been promised that those *"gates of hell shall not prevail."* (Mat 16:18) Nevertheless, it is necessary for us to know who we are in ourselves and who we are in the Lord and choose the better part.

*"How can **you, being evil**, speak good things?"* (Mat 12:34)
Therefore, why even attempt to bring forth the filthy rags of our good
works since The Word of the Testimony informs us, *"No one is good
except God alone"* (Mar 10:18), and a corrupt tree cannot bring forth
good fruit (Mat 7:18), meaning we are absolutely incompetent to bear
the good fruit that is requited of us! O Lord of my Lord what an
enormous, insurmountable dilemma you have placed upon us. You
DEMAND good fruit and yet the wellspring within us is bitter waters
that poisons the ground of our own hearts and infects the tree that
brings forth the corrupt fruit of our lives and our testimony. When we
lay the profane sacrifice of OUR good works before your Holiness,
they are utterly despised and rejected! For this reason, You have said,
"There is none righteous, no not one." (Rom 3:10) Thankfully,
however, *"the things which are impossible with men are possible with
God."* (Luk 18:27)

It is on this account that Jesus, standing next to the withered fig tree,
says, *"Have faith in God."* (Mar 11:22) It is impossible for us to
crucify ourselves. Besides, why even contemplate it, considering we
have been so easily deluded, believing the pretense that we are living
righteously before God? Dying to ourselves is the insurmountable
mountain. We will never accomplish the monumental task of defeating
the Goliath within unless we come *"in the name of the LORD of hosts,
the God of the armies of Israel."* (1Sa 17:45)

When we accepted the Holy One of Israel into our heart, the first thing
He did was drive out the moneychangers. After that time, the temple of
God was clean and full of the Holy Spirit. For a while, our lamp
burned brightly, but like all people, our affection begins to fade as we
became more familiar with our loved ones. For this reason, it is a true
saying that *"familiarity breeds contempt."* This also, is why the
Bridegroom has said to us:

> *But I have against you that you left your first love. Therefore,
> remember from where you have fallen, and repent, and do the first
> works, or else I will come to you quickly and will remove your
> lampstand out of its place unless you repent. (Rev 2:4-5 MKJV)*

Therefore, do not be like that generation whose house was cleaned, and
yet not filled with the Word of God, so the unclean spirit returned to
find it empty and brought with him *"seven other spirits more evil than
himself"*, as a result of which, the last state of that man was worse than

the first. (Mat 12:43-45) Thus, *"seek first His kingdom and His righteousness."* (Mat 6:33) Seek Him first in all things. Give Him preeminence. Seek Him first thing in the morning. Seek Him last thing in the evening; for He is the Alpha and Omega, the First and the Last.

When you do this then you are having *"faith in God."* Then you are abiding in the vine. Jesus does not say go out and create much fruit or bring fruit with you into the vineyard. Notice how we will bring forth the fruits of righteousness.

> *I am the Vine, you are the branches.* ___He who abides in Me, and I in him, the same___ ___brings forth much fruit___; *for without Me you can do nothing. (Joh 15:5 MKJV)*

Do you see how degenerate our reasoning is? We always seem to get things backwards. When we read this parable, we think it is our responsibility to bear fruit or to be thrown into the fire. When I say we are judged by our works and not our faith, people automatically assume this is not biblical because we all know that we have been saved by grace and not of works. Now, however, notice the simplicity of the Lord. He does not ask us to become fruit-bearing vines, but rather that we abide in the vine. This is the key to everything. The sequence of these things is as follows: We have been grafted into the vine. There are other branches in the vineyard that are not of the vine and those branches are not producing any fruit. Since they cannot bear fruit by themselves, unless they abide in the vine, they are deemed worthless, removed, and thrown into the fire. (Joh 15:4) However, if you are abiding in the vine then you will bring forth much fruit, and God will judge your fruit. Therefore, the fruit is not the cause of your justification but the result of your justification. It is the end to your means. You are to focus on abiding in Jesus; the Father and the Son have placed you as a branch in the vine. Your only focus is to remain in Him. With this understanding, we can now begin to clear up any other misconceptions. Jesus informs us that will know them by their fruits, which also means that we will know ourselves by our fruits.

To crystallize the point, let us begin from the end of the sequence. If you have righteous fruit in your life, then you have given your heart and mind to the Lord of Glory and you have continued to abide in His Holiness, because this is the only way to bring forth the fruit of righteousness that will not be rejected by the Father. If you are not bearing fruit in your life then you are probably not receiving the life-giving, fruit-bearing sustenance of the vine. Therefore, have you continued to abide; *"remain, continue, dwell, endure, be present, stand and tarry"*[8], in the vine?

Again, the fruit is not the means by which we will be able to go to heaven, but the result of the means. The means is Jesus. He is and always should be our All in All. The fruit is what we see in our lives. It has been rightly said that the Father is a fruit inspector and this is exactly what Messiah is teaching us in this parable. He is the farmer, looking over his vineyard and removing the non-fruit-bearing branches that are taking up space.

We also know the scriptures have warned us that *"the heart is deceitful above all things, and desperately wicked."* (Jer 17:9) Amazingly, we cannot even know our own heart. The fall of man and the resulting sin in our lives has so degenerated our thinking that we are always justifying our works and ourselves. It has become the natural, spontaneous reaction to everything in our lives. Consider this for a moment. When a person accuses us, our immediate reaction is to recast the blame, even if we are completely responsible. This is the sin reaction we inherited from our forefather, Adam. Notice Adam's reaction when Jehovah God asked him if he had eaten of the tree. He answered yes, but then immediately shifted the blame to his poor wife and then ultimately to God.

> *The man said, "The woman whom **you gave to be with me**, **she gave me fruit** of the tree, and I ate."* *(Gen 3:12 ESV)*

We are so blind and disillusioned that we cannot even know our own heart. This is an astounding statement with enormous implications! If we accept this premise, then how are we going to be able to know that we are not deceiving ourselves? Fortunately, God made it extremely simple; fruit, the observable, outworking of the heart. Everyone can see the fruit of our lives, including us. Furthermore, this makes it very simple for God to judge the rest of the world. He will not have to contend with people about where their heart was because the video of their lives will bear either the righteous fruit of repentance or the unrighteous fruit of deception.

---

[8] Strong's Hebrew and Greek Dictionaries, G3306 - μένω (menō)

> **For sin**, *seizing an opportunity through the commandment,*
> ***deceived me*** *and through it killed me. (Rom 7:11 ESV)*

Consider how are continually warned in the Holy Writ to not be
deceived.

> *Do not be deceived: "Bad company ruins good morals." (1Co*
> *15:33)*
> *Do not be deceived: God is not mocked... (Gal 6:7)*
> *...the woman was deceived and became a transgressor. (1Ti 2:14)*
> *...impostors will go on from bad to worse, deceiving and being*
> *deceived. (2Ti 3:13)*
> *...by your sorceries all nations were deceived. (Rev 18:23)*

Strong's defines the word deceived, *"roam (from safety, truth, or*
virtue): - go astray, deceive, err, seduce, wander, be out of the way."
Have you gone astray in your thinking? The many times Paul uses this
word, he follows it with a laundry list of external works that we can
measure our internal heart by, which I call *"works of the flesh"*(Gal
5:19), so we may have a clearer picture if something is amiss in our
spiritual lives.

However, if we continue to abide in His light then we will see clearly,
and will not be susceptible to this deception.

> *For we ourselves also* ***were once foolish, disobedient, deceived,***
> *slaving for various lusts and pleasures, living in malice and envy,*
> *hateful, hating one another. (Tit 3:3 MKJV)*

This really brings to light how blind we are by our sin. John Calvin
used said we cannot see clearly without the Bible. He called the Bible
his spectacles. This seems to be a good analogy, yet possibly not
radical enough. The Bible is gives us an opportunity to see. We are so
lost that we are completely blind. We are like blind Bartimaeus crying
out, *"Son of David, have mercy on me!"* (Mar 10:48) Yet, notice that
blind Bartimaeus *"recovered his sight and* ***followed Him*** *on the way."*
(Mar 10:52)

Where does all this start? Jesus made it very simple for our hard hearts
to comprehend and our blind eyes to see. Abide. Abide in the vine. If
you are in Him and He is in you then you will produce much fruit.
Therefore, the True Vine, the Only Begotten tells us,

Bearing the Fruit of Faith

By this my Father is glorified, that you bear much fruit and so prove to be my disciples. (Joh 15:8 ESV)

Alternatively, to make it ever simpler for our simple minds:

HAVE FAITH IN GOD! (Mar 11:22 ESV)

chapter seven

MOUNTAIN MOVING FAITH

*And Jesus answered them, "**Have faith in God**. Truly, I say to you, whoever says to this mountain, 'Be taken up and thrown into the sea,' and does not doubt in his heart, but believes that what he says will come to pass, it will be done for him. Therefore, I tell you, whatever you ask in prayer, believe that you have received it, and it will be yours." (Mar 11:22-24 ESV)*

One could easily write volumes on either the Fruit of the Spirit or mountain-moving faith. Nevertheless, let us touch upon God's faithfulness and His absolute assurance of victory in the battles against the Goliath of our fears and conquering of the mountains of doubts that continue to inhabit strongholds within our hearts. If you will recall, we did touch upon the fruitfulness of possessing a prayer life that stems from a correct heart. Keeping this in mind, let us now plant the seed of true and authentic prayer in good soil and allow the Holy Spirit to bring forth the increase in due season.

"Have faith in God" cannot be repeated enough. That we must repeat this so often only further proves how clouded our reasoning has become since the fall. The teaching is so simple. Why then, is it one of the most difficult seeds to cultivate in our heart? Additionally, our intellect has become so degenerated that we cannot even begin to comprehend the vast divide between our holiness and God's Holiness. Somewhere in the dullness of our natural minds, lurks the belief that we are good, decent people that will satisfy God's righteousness. We have no trouble acknowledging the fall of our bodies, because it is easily observable that it is corruptible and temporary. The syllogism is very simple. Every living creature since the beginning of time has died. I am a living creature; therefore, I must die. Living creatures get sick. I am a living creature; therefore, I get sick. Thus, it is very easy for us to accept God's warning to Adam "he *shall surely die*" (Gen 2:17) if he eats from the tree of the knowledge of good and evil. We have a

perfect alignment between the concept and our material observations. However, when Jesus makes monumental statements like "*ask, and it shall be given*" (Mat 7:7) or "*ask whatever you wish, and it will be done for you*" (Joh 15:7), do we accept these statements at face value or do we attempt to reason away these simple, yet earth-shattering promises?

Consider the following simple dialectic using the metaphorical characters Faith and Doubt.

Faith begins with, "The New Testament is full of these types of promises, and they are also supported by the apostles' testimony that walked in them."

Doubt retorts from his theological studies, "Yes, but that was the dispensation of the apostles. Those promises were meant for them and not for us."

Faith then responds, "But many miracles have been performed by believers since the age of the apostles."

Doubt, "Maybe so, but not the ones like the apostles performed. I have not seen anyone walking on water or people raised from the dead lately. Have you?"

Faith, "No, but if Peter and the apostles were human beings, just as I am, and all the admonitions of the New Testament pertain to me, then does not it follow that the promises of the New Testament should pertain to me also?"

Doubt, "The promises do pertain to you, but you have to do a correct exegesis to interpret the promises properly within their context."

Faith, "But I think I am doing a proper exegesis. The book of Acts says that these promises were given to them, their children, and to all of us who are afar off."

Doubt, "Well there is your problem; you are not rightly dividing the word of truth. You cannot obtain doctrines from historical books like the Book of Acts."

Faith, "But the Bible says that ALL scripture is profitable for doctrine."

Doubt, "Then do you believe that you can raise someone from the dead?"

Faith, "If it is God's Will to raise someone from the dead then I believe He would give me the faith to accomplish it."

Doubt, "The Bible also says that Paul had a thorn in the flesh which he could not remove. Do you have more faith than Paul?"

Faith, "I would never compare myself to Paul. What was this thorn? We do not know, do we? However, we do know why God gave it to Paul. To keep him humble because of the exceeding revelations God was pouring into him."

Doubt, "Then why not go into the hospitals and lay hands on all the sick and heal the world."

Faith, "If God leads me to do this, then I will follow"

Doubt, "Who do you think you are? Are you greater than the celebrated dispensational teachers of our time? They have dedicated their lives to rightly dividing the word of truth. They hold doctors degrees and have written many books on the subject. Are you wiser than they are?"

Faith, "I am blessed by many of their teachings, but Jesus and the apostles are even greater than they are; therefore, I will have to follow what I believe they teach if there is a contradiction."

Doubt, "Do not you realize that your theology does not match reality?"

Faith, "I enjoy theology, but I prefer to read the scriptures on faith with the simplicity of a babe."

Doubt, "The Lord also said come and let us reason together. He gave you the ability to reason and the intellect so you could create systematic theology and doctrines to understand His admonitions and promises."

Faith, "But the Lord also said to receive the Kingdom of God with childlike faith."

Doubt, "Do you think you are some great apostle or profit?"

Faith, "No, I am just a simple vessel willing to be used by a Great God."

Doubt, "Is it not arrogant of you to think that you can do these kinds of things?"

Faith, "Yes, if I believed that I deserved these magnificent promises because of my good works, but God is no respecter of persons. It is not me but He who lives in me who performs the promise."

Doubt, "Well you seem to have great faith in your abilities."

Faith, "No, I have NO faith in MY abilities at all. I **have faith in God**."

Let us examine, for a moment, the minor conclusion discussed earlier; that our natural intellect has become so darkened that we cannot even begin to comprehend how absolutely helpless we are in our lost condition. Then, we can concentrate on the weightier matters of this discussion. This is a very significant point to ingrain into our minds. Consider, for example, that after God created Adam, He brought all the animals of the world before him, and Adam named every creature. Can you imagine the computer-like brain he must have had in order to accomplish this feat? However, because we have descended from Adam's fallen state, to learn it is necessary to repeat, repeat and repeat the lesson. "*Repetitio est mater studiorum,*" repetition is the mother of studies.

Why is this true? I contend that not only have we become slaves to sin because of our posterity in the fallen race of Adam, but also our ability to reason has become dull. Consider for a moment the metaphor God uses over 200 times in scriptures for His people, sheep. Sheep are one of the dumbest creatures in the entire animal kingdom. Have you ever noticed any sheep in the circus? The reason the sheep is not among the chimps, elephants, bears, lions and other animals is that they are too dumb to train. To underscore their ineptness, contemplate that they even have problems recognizing basic instinctual circumstances like danger. I read a story about a cute little lamb that kept wandering from the herd, which the shepherd would find walking in the midst of predators, ready to fall over cliffs, chasing butterflies! Of all the animals on earth, they are the only domesticated animal that has no ability to live in the wild. They either would starve to death because of their inability to find good pasture, or devoured as prey because of their inability to protect themselves, or die of thirst because they are afraid of fast moving waters. Furthermore, they are slow animals. If wolves attack the heard and begin devouring sheep, they do not even have enough sense to run; they will just watch and bleat while the pack of wolves devours them, one after another! Additionally, the shepherd has to watch what the sheep eat because they will eat poisonous plants, and if they stay in one area too long they will graze until they make themselves sick. Finally, they are filthy animals that cannot even perform the simple task of cleaning themselves.

On the positive side, they are gentle, quiet, innocent, affectionate, docile and passive animals. They love to follow their shepherd, who walks in front of them instead of pushing them the way cowboys do with cattle. In addition, it is these positive qualities, along with their utter dependence upon the shepherd for their sheer survival that creates this unique shepherd-sheep relationship, whereby shepherds have been known to fight to the death against the many predators that have been aroused by the smell and sound of the herd walking through the wilderness.

Nevertheless, our focus at this time is the level of our lost condition that God is attempting to communicate to us by using this sheep metaphor. There are two levels of being lost. First, I am lost and I know that I am lost. Second, I am lost and I do not know that I am lost. In the first condition, I will attempt to rectify the situation and find my way back. This makes the second condition far worse, because I will make no effort to solve the problem, because I do not even know that I have a problem. Sheep lose their way all the time without ever realizing they are totally lost. They are defenseless, depending on the shepherd for every aspect of their survival. Without the shepherd, they would be lucky to last even one day in the wild.

Therefore, let us accept that our immense intellectual abilities are equivalent to the reasoning of a sheep. We may have wandered in our reasoning and have chased butterflies in the midst of lions. Nevertheless, I have a remarkably simple solution to this problem.

HAVE FAITH IN GOD.

Stop trusting yourself and accept what God has to say at face value. Accept what He is telling you as if you are a little child. Trust the Good Shepherd. He will not leave you or forsake you and without His protecting hand, you are defenseless, dirty and completely lost!

HAVE FAITH IN GOD.

In addition, if you have been prone to wander from the simplicity of His promises or His admonitions then you may be in danger and not even know it. However, be comforted because the Good Shepherd will leave the other ninety-nine, go out, find you, and bring you back to the fold. (Luk 15:4) Therefore, allow the Good Shepherd to bring your reasoning back into the fold of His finished work and His promises for your life.

You say you believe in God, but what does that mean? We had already spoken of the mental assent type of belief that James was alluding to when he said that faith without works is dead. However, now let us focus on the object of the sentence, God. What does that word mean? What are the attributes that we comprehend about God?

Here are a few basic facts we know about God as revealed to us from scriptures. He created the entire universe simply by speaking it into existence and every moment, He sustains it. He knows our every thought, even before we have thought it. He cares when a sparrow falls from the nest, and yet, He cares even more for you; so much so, in fact, that He was willing to sacrifice His only Begotten and Beloved Son in order to have a relationship with you. This was required because God by His very nature is holy and we by our very nature are unholy. Therefore, the great expanse between God's holiness and our unholiness, needed to be reconciled by a person who could live according to God's perfect standard of holiness, and then pay the retribution for the rebellion of the unholy. At what cost? Death, "*For the wages of sin is death*", but thankfully, God gave us the gift of "*eternal life through Jesus Christ our Lord.*" (Rom 6:23) The incarnation of God, Jesus, is the greatest love story ever told in the history of humanity. God left His Holy throne to come into the filth of this world, allowed sinful man to disgrace His glory, and paid the enormous penalty for our sins, purely out of His love for us! For "*Jesus came into the world to save sinners*" (1Tim 1:15) and "*God commends His love toward us in that while we were yet sinners Christ died for us.*" (Rom 5:8) He is a supernatural God. He is above the universe, in power and glory, able to control it simply with the power of His word. He came to earth and healed the sick, cured the lame, cleansed the lepers, restored vision to the blind, opened the ears of the deaf, loosed the lips of the dumb and freed the demon-oppressed. He fed the four-thousand; the five-thousand, walked on water and stilled the storm. He raised people from the dead. At every encounter, He crushed the powers of darkness. However, at the climax of the war, the crucifixion of the Son of David, when it looked as though all was lost in defeat, He raised Himself from the dead to conquer the power of sin and death, walking in His resurrected body for almost two months proclaiming His victory over death! Finally, God glorified Him, taking Him into heaven in the sight of all the disciples. These are the revealed facts of God.

It is extremely exciting to consider the miracles the incarnate God performed while He walked in this world. However, these are extraordinarily small matters when compared to creating the entire universe simply by saying, *"Let there be...."* Our understanding of God's glory is only the smallest fraction of His true radiance. In fact, I would posit that it is impossible even to begin to comprehend His greatness! Even if we could contemplate His glory through that which He has made, it would be entirely from our human perspective. We cannot begin to reach the depth of His understanding or even begin to fathom the riches of His Glory and grace. We actually can only understand this extraordinary, supernatural God through our natural, human experiences. It is like comparing a hot day to the actual heat of the sun. Has anyone you know been to eternity? Have you ever witnessed something without a beginning or an end in this temporal universe? Has anyone ever seen the Spirit of God? The scriptures declare Moses saw His back. What does that mean? Does a spirit have a back? Can you see our dilemma? God fills the entire universe, and yet, He also exists outside of our time, space continuum in which we live. The natural world is all we know. For that reason, we must realize that even our language is inadequate when attempting to convey the concept of God, since humanity has framed these words from our natural experiences. Serious reflection upon this dilemma will cause us to appreciate that the Almighty is so far above our understanding that we are only able to comprehend the smallest sliver of His Glory.

Consider the following analogy. You have an ant farm contained within a glass that is a two-way mirror. You can see the ants, but they cannot see you. These ants are super intelligent. However, they are completely constrained by their environment within the two-way glass. Occasionally, they see you add food, so a few of them describe your hand in ant terminology. Sometimes you use a utensil to add the food. Therefore, to some ants, you are a hand and to other ants, you are a utensil. However, since these ants do not have hands, and they do not have utensils, they will not only err by attributing this small part to the whole, but they also will err in that they cannot even properly describe the small part they have seen! How close would you expect those ants to come to in their understanding to the reality of your life? They would not even begin to be able to contemplate your existence. In fact, you may smile and think you poor, ignorant beautiful ants. You have built cities, formed civilizations, created governments and established kingdoms. You have considered how large and beautiful these things are, and then you have attempted to describe me from within the experiential knowledge of these things.

Nevertheless, other ants within this ant farm would become so vain in their imagination that they would say, "*Nothing exists outside of this universe.*" Intuitively these ants understand that something else exists beyond the glass and beyond their understanding, yet the most intelligent of the intelligent have determined that this is foolishness. Would not you think that their wisdom is an astonishing ignorance and arrogance for a society that only has the smallest fraction of an ability to comprehend the riches and the glory of your existence?

This analogy is very fitting, as it does touch upon our own dilemma. Although, the irony is, the massive chasm between God and us is so vast that the analogy itself is just as inept as that which the moral of the story portrays. Hence, our Glorious God must find tremendously funny as He watches this ant pound out the words on his ant keyboard!

For this reason, many renowned intellectuals smugly ask utterly inane questions like, "*If God created the world than who created God?*" Ironically, while the academic basks in their brilliance, feeling they have demonstrated the foolishness of the argument, they have shown themselves to be foolish, not realizing that the question they just asked is a meaningless contradiction of terms. It is as if someone would ask, "*Why cannot black be white? And, why cannot white be black?*" You would not answer the question, but instead you would say to the person that the question itself does not make any sense, because by definition black cannot be white and white cannot be black. God by definition is uncreated. Therefore, the intellectual is asking the silly, nonsensical question, "*Who created the uncreated?*" Does that actually make any sense? Nevertheless, some of the most brilliant ants I have ever met have asked this feebleminded question. Anyone can see that the intellectual, ant, is attempting to experientially understand God, and since everything we have ever witnessed has a beginning and an end, then God also must have a beginning and an end.

How then, are we to know God, if we cannot comprehend Him through the world in which we live? The scriptures describe His revealed nature. Therefore, maybe God is a pair of eyes, since the Holy Writ says, *"the eyes of the LORD run to and fro throughout the whole earth."* (2Ch 16:9) Better yet, maybe He is a bird with eyes, since it is written, *"under his wings you will find refuge."* (Psa 91:4) Alternatively, maybe He is a big bird with eyes and hands, since *"The hand of the LORD was heavy against the people of Ashdod."* (1Sa 5:6) However, since no one has ever seen the Lord then He must be invisible. Although, if He is invisible then how did Moses speak with God face-to-face; and how then did God show him His glory by walking past him, allowing Moses to see His back? Do you see how foolish and limited we are in our capacity even to begin to fathom the depth of His inconceivable glory? The Bible says that we will spend eternity learning about God. Truthfully, that may not be long enough.

You would think that since emotions do not have the same limitations we could at least begin to understand God's emotions from our perspective, but even in this area, we fall far short. When we love someone and that person chooses not to return our love, we feel hurt. This is because we have lost something in our lives. God, in turn, loves His creation. When His creation rejects Him, as most people in history have done, then He also feels hurt. However, He is perfectly complete within Himself. He never needed creation to complete Himself. Therefore, He cannot suffer loss. It is also written that the Lord is jealous for His people, so what can this mean? He is jealous, not because of what He will lose, but because of what we will lose. His other centered focus is beyond even our emotions. We reason from our own inner perspectives. So even making statements like God is love falls far short in our comprehension, considering that we understand love from our human perspectives.

For this reason, I once again defer to Spurgeon's counsel to be *"prepared to cast away every doctrine of our own, rather than one passage of Scripture"* and to read the scriptures *"with the simplicity of a child."*

HAVE FAITH IN GOD.

If we have the faith of a young child, then we will truly begin to see the kingdom of His majesty. Consider how the ants in our analogy would discern your existence. If they continued to reason exclusively from their environment, even though you had told them otherwise, would they not look foolish? Now consider that you have chosen to reveal yourself to a young child ant, so that ant actually has greater revelations of you than the oldest, wisest, most learned ant in the colony. Even if the wise ant is pious and respectful, and has established many complex doctrines, the young child ant would still have greater insights, since he accepted your words with the simplicity of a babe.

It is for this reason, and because the pride of our heart is so rock-hard stubborn that, we have to repeat…

HAVE FAITH IN GOD.

Do you honestly believe that God created this entire universe with the Word of His mouth? Have you ever seriously contemplated this statement? We have never seen anything created out of nothing. If I were to make a napkin appear out of thin air, would you be amazed? Would it astonish you, if I could create an entire mountain from nothing, or add another moon simply by saying, "*Let there be a second light in the night sky?*" Would it amaze you if I created another sun? Have you ever considered how minuscule our solar system is in comparison to the enormity of the universe? That it is only a tiny part of the Milky Way, which itself is just a small fraction this vast universe. Some of the other non-believing, intellectual ants have asked, "*Do you truly believe God created the world in six days?*" To which I have said, "*I do, and I am surprised it took Him that long.*" However, it is possible God created everything in one glorious, instantaneous moment in time, since the Bible says, "*In the beginning, God created the heavens and the earth*" (Gen 1:1); and then, afterwards, began to order the universe from that created substance.

Consider all the stars that fill up the night sky. They are many light years away. Even with all of our technological expertise, we have only been able to traverse the short distance to our own moon in this galaxy. The Milky Way itself is enormous, yet infinitesimal when compared to the vast universe. Did you know there are an estimated 50 billion galaxies visible with modern telescopes? It is very conservative to estimate that another 50 billion galaxies exist that are not visible. Amazingly, some of those galaxies have hundreds of billions of stars!

Taking a low estimate of 100 billion stars in the 100 billion galaxies means that there are 10 thousand, billion, billion, properly known as 10 sextillion stars in the universe. This number is so large that it is virtually incomprehensible. Consider that one trillion seconds equals approximately 32,000 years. Since a sextillion is 1,000 trillion then a sextillion of seconds is 320,000,000, or 320 million years. However, we state that a conservative estimate for the number of stars in the universe is ten sextillion. Therefore, ten sextillion seconds are roughly 3.2 billion years, which is nearly the age of the earth, according to most scientific estimates. So when you say that God spoke all of this into existence, have you honestly comprehended the magnitude of what you are saying?

This is where the non-believing, intellectual ants will defiantly rise up and say, "*Yes this is ludicrous!*" Nevertheless, their explanation is even more foolish, believing that somehow random chance and an impersonal cosmos collaborated with each other in a spontaneous explosion that created all the order and design we witness in creation.

Nevertheless, our present subject is not an apologetic for the existence of our Great Creator but rather an appeal to trust in His Word. The same Word, by the way, that you say you believe created the grand universe that you see and live in every day. You say you believe all of these things, but God Incarnate says, "*Ask, and it will be given to you*" (Mat 7:7); do you genuinely believe Him? When, He follows that statement with, "*For everyone who asks receives, and the one who seeks finds, and to the one who knocks it will be opened*" (Mat 7:8), do you then trust and follow the Good Shepherd; or do you become a wandering lamb, chasing butterflies, attempting to confine the infinite, omnipotent power of His Word into that small box you call doctrine? When you stand before Him who overcame the world will He reprove you saying, "*O you of little faith, why did you doubt?*" (Mat 14:31); or will the Faithful Witness say to you, "*Well done, good and faithful servant*"? (Mat 25:23)

It is all right if you have difficulties with all of this, since God has told us that you will have problems comprehending His power and grace in our lives. This is because we attempt to understand a supernatural God with a natural mind.

> *But the **natural man** **receiveth not** the things of the Spirit of God: for **they are foolishness unto him**: neither can he know them,*

*because **they are spiritually discerned**. But he that is spiritual judgeth all things, yet he himself is judged of no man. **For who hath known the mind of the Lord, that he may instruct him?** But we have the mind of Christ. (1Co 2:14-16 KJV)*

Beginning in doubt is not sin, but ending in doubt is. Have you so clearly seen the mind of the Almighty that you will now instruct Him in your doctrine? Jesus set the example of how we are to follow God's promises.

*Jesus said to them, "Truly, truly, I say to you, the Son can do nothing of his own accord, **but only what he sees the Father doing**. For whatever the Father does, that the Son does likewise." (Joh 5:19 ESV)*

In one of His last appearances, our Raboni gave to us our marching orders, saying, "*As the Father has sent me, even so I am sending you.*" (Joh 20:21) Nevertheless, you say to me, "*I just do not have that kind of faith. I cannot let go of this thing I am I call reality.*" Remember that the natural mind cannot receive these things, and it is that same natural mind that desires to keep you shackled to the bottom of the cave where you are comfortable believing in the shadows of your illusions. I also have difficulties believing these grand promises. The Goliath of my fleshly mind rails against them, and the Philistine army of the Father of Lies shouts against me, "*Who do you think you are? Do you think you are so important or grand that you can walk in the Creator's steps? You are so arrogant; you are nothing but a mouse!*" At first, I shrink from this high calling, but then I realize that most of the things these liars have spoken are true. I do believe I am important. I am arrogant and yet, I really am a mouse. However, I also know what I am, dead. I also know who I am, for it is no longer I who live, but Christ in me. It is not I who have been commissioned to do these works, but He who has overcome the world. Therefore, if Christ is for me than who can be against me!

You see these grand promises have another hidden dilemma, which we have not discussed. For God has said,

*...**without faith it is impossible to please him**, for whoever would draw near to God must believe that he exists **AND that he rewards those who seek him**. (Heb 11:6 ESV)*

Do you see how important it is to believe that God will answer your prayers?

When we do not believe His promises, we do not please Him, who has called us to be His son, and to whom we call *"Abba Father."* Do you not believe your earthly father or mother when they make promises? In addition, parents, will you not give good things to your children when they ask?

> *Or which one of you, if his son asks him for bread, will give him a stone? Or if he asks for a fish, will give him a serpent? If you then, who are evil, know how to give good gifts to your children, how much more will your Father who is in heaven give good things to those who ask him! (Mat 7:9-11 ESV)*

"But I am a sinner, and I do not feel that God will listen to my prayers," you say. You are correct! You and I are sinners. We have a natural inclination towards sin. However, we have died to sin and death, and it is no longer I who live but Christ in me. We are free from being stoned to death as adulterers and admonished to go and sin no more. How does a sinner stop sinning? This is like telling a fish to breathe the air or a person to fly or a snake to run. We cannot do it! It is part of our nature to sin because we ARE sinners. The only choice is to die and let Jesus live! God will hear His Son, Jesus' prayers. On this, we have the historical testimony that God answered all of Jesus' prayers. Moreover, this is what He meant when He said pray in my name, which in the Greek means in His *"nature, character and authority."*

God will not answer your prayers because of your own righteousness, but He will answer Jesus' prayers because of His righteousness.

Here is our dilemma, how do we have so great a faith that we believe the answers to our prayers is yes and amen and therefore, be pleasing to Almighty God? The answer is, we cannot! This is the great test of faith. We are brought to a place where there is no escape. Pharaoh's armies are quickly descending upon us. We have no ability to part the Nile, because we do not have the faith to do it. At that moment, cry out to God, *"Help my unbelief!"*(Mar 9:24) Then He will say, *"Lift up your staff, and stretch out your hand over the sea and divide it, that the people of Israel [you] may go through the sea on dry ground."* (Exo 14:16)

Allow me to illuminate our predicament. We cannot please God without faith. Then we discover that, in ourselves, we do not actually possess faith. Therefore, we have to ask God by faith, for faith, in order to receive the faith, which we do not possess, in order to please Him. Like a dog chasing his tail, this is an impossible situation. It is very much like when Moses and the children of Israel were brought into the trap at the Nile, only to realize that they could do nothing to save themselves. Even the mustard seed of faith that we need to have in order to believe in God has to be given to us by God! So if you do not have faith that is all right. In fact, it is a good starting point to acknowledge. Apprehend this concept. Within us, no one has faith. Faith is a gift from God.

A man brought his possessed son to the disciples to cast out the demon, but they were not able to do this, even though they had cast out many demons from many others. Jesus firmly reprimanded His disciples saying, *"O faithless generation, how long am I to be with you? How long am I to bear with you?"* (Mar 9:19) It is unfortunate when the Lord has become so annoyed with our faithlessness that He has to ask Himself how long He will to have to tolerate us. The disciples brought the child to Jesus, and immediately the youth fell on the ground and began rolling on the ground and foaming at the mouth. His father, feeling helpless and heartbroken, agonized over his beloved son watching the scene play itself out again as it had done so many times before in his young son's tumultuous childhood. At that time, Jesus told the father, *"If you can believe, all things are possible to him who believes."* (Mar 9:23) To which, the father, knowing that his belief was not strong enough to win the battle, straight away cried out with tears flowing down his face, *"Lord, I believe. Help my unbelief!"* (Mar 9:24)

Do you feel this father's heart? Imagine this is you and your four or five year old child. Your young son violently convulses on the ground. This has been going on for so many years; in the middle of the night, at the babysitter's house, in church, at the supermarket, in school and all the other places in society. Not only has your son become a prisoner to this torment but also your entire family has become the prisoner of this torment. Not only have you and your family become ostracize from society, but you also fear for his life because this wicked spirit is constantly trying to kill this innocent child by causing him to be thrust into the fire or by leaping into the water. Now, however, Jesus looks at you and says this is no problem if you believe because all things are possible to him who believes. You have done all the right things; you brought the boy to the Mediator of our Faith, you asked the Healer to make him whole, but now the Light shines back on you, the father of this child, and says you *"I will heal him as long as __YOU believe__."* What! Do you mean your son's entire life now depends on your faith?

In the meantime, your child continues to convulse violently on the ground. You have seen this so many times. You brought him to the best doctors. You brought him to the finest rabbis. You brought him to the finest therapists. You changed his diet; his sleeping habits, his clothes, moved from the location where it first occurred, cried out to God in the synagogue and nothing has worked! All the experts who examined your child were professional specialists in their field, and they all confidently promised you they had seen this before, and they would be able to help. Therefore, you put your faith and trust into those professionals with the doctor's degrees and other certifications of higher learning. Nevertheless, nobody ever was able to help you with your child. Physically, you are completely beaten, mentally you are at your wits-end, and you have nothing left spiritually; your knees are bruised and your heart has become weak because you have spent so many years, day and night, calling upon a deaf God that appears to have no concern over the trivialities of your heavy burden.

Nevertheless, one small ray hope has shone forth in the dark night of this despair. You have heard about this man named Jesus, a healer being used mightily by God,. He has made the blind to see and the deaf to hear. His touch has cleansed lepers. He fed thousands with only a few loaves of bread and fish. He is beyond doubt a man of God. Now, where there was no hope, hope has sprung to life once again. You have one last, and final hope, and it is Jesus. Then after all of this, He says I will do this as long as YOU believe. You are aghast, thinking, *"What! Not me Lord. My faith has been shaken to the core. There is nothing left in me. Years and daily cries to God have not worked. I have become nothing but an unformed lump of clay."*

All these thoughts rush through your mind as your little child is vomiting and violently floundering on the ground. Nevertheless, Jesus is not even looking at the child; He is looking at you. He is looking you straight in the eye and He is saying do you have enough faith to believe because if you do then it will happen, but if you do not then your child is lost! There is no time to hide behind the platitudes of your doctrine or any other pretense of your systematized theology, you are now standing in front of the Light of the World and His Radiance and Glory are shinning upon you. There is only time for the naked truth. Then, the man prays one of the most marvelous prayers in the New Testament.

"Lord, I believe. Help my unbelief!"

What an impossibly astounding contradiction! I do have faith, but I do not have faith. I do trust, but I do not trust. I do believe but I just do not know if I truly believe enough. The Lord of Glory has brought us to this place, so He can reveal to us just how helpless we are. His eyes pierce the windows of our soul; intuitively we know He can see directly into our hearts. Standing in front of the Judge and the Creator of the entire universe, the inner thoughts of our hearts are laid bare naked before Him. We cannot lie to Him who searches the heart. We do believe. We just do not know if you believe enough. We do trust in Him, but we do not know if we trust in ourselves. Nevertheless, the Lord of Glory places the matter directly upon your faith, saying. "It is possible as long as YOU believe." He has reversed the responsibility of your son's life unto you, making the promise contingent upon YOUR faith after so many years of defeat. It is up to you. Do you have enough faith to overcome this spirit finally? Be honest, do you? If you were strapped to a lie detector at this time, would you be able to answer this question, yes? I know I would not. Neither was this man. He said I do believe, but I just do not know if I believe enough. Tears rolling down his face, his heart breaking, he realizes, if his son's life depends on him then all is lost. However, his prayer is so wise. He says to Jesus, *"I do trust in You, which is why I brought the child to you, but I have no trust in myself."* What an enigma this presents?

God requires faith, but then we learn we must go to Him to get the faith. We do not even have the smallest morsel we can offer as a burnt sacrifice to the Lord of Glory. We may only offer ourselves upon the altar of uncut stones rather than the finely manufactured altar of human wisdom. (Deu 27:6)

Therefore, we come to our Lord with the smallest mustard seed of faith, saying to Him, *"Lord I believe but not enough. Please help my unbelief."* Then the Lord of Glory does the work. It is not you, I, or any other superman of Christianity that has special powers that will cause God to answer the prayer. To believe such a thing, would be a sacrilege, reducing the immense glory of a God to the pawn of man.

There is no such thing as a superman in Christianity. The Lord said that the greatest would be the least. History confirms this axiom, because the Christians that have risen the highest have always had very low opinion of themselves in light of His glory and grace. Jon Bunyan became a spiritual prisoner for years believing that he had lost his salvation, by committing the unpardonable sin. Martin Luther, understanding the level of his depravity, spent six to eight hours a day in confession, wearing down the priests, who began to say to him things like, *"Come back when you have committed something worth confessing."* Later he attempted to find justification by taking a pilgrimage to Rome. After he arrived, he went to the Scala Santa, steps that led up to Pontius Pilate's praetorium, according to Christian tradition, got down on his hands and knees and crawled up the staircase, kissing and reciting the Lord's Prayer with each individual stair with tears streaming down his face. However, after he finished this ritual, he still did not find any peace, but rather was even more troubled than before he had begun the exercise. Then, consider Augustine of Hippo, who wasted many years in paganism, because he knew that he was not worthy of this God's glorious favor and grace. Thus, history confirms this truth repeatedly; *"he who is least among you all, he shall be great."* (Luk 9:48) Again, The Faithful and True Witness says,

> *The kingdom of Heaven is like a **grain of mustard seed**, which a man took and sowed in his field; which indeed is **the least** of all seeds, but **when it is grown** it is **the greatest** among herbs and becomes a tree, so that the birds of the air come and lodge in its branches. (Mat 13:31-32 MKJV)*

Notice that the mustard seed does not remain small. That is its beginnings but its ultimate state is to become so large that the birds of the air can reside in its branches. Has not Christendom lodged itself within the branches of great Christian teachers who at one time esteemed themselves as not worthy of God's glory?

Likewise, consider the prayer of faith, moving the mountain of doubt, in the story of Augustine's conversion. He states his mother went to church twice a day for years, pleading in tears for God to save her son. Her countless petitions finally caused the exacerbated bishop to tell her to go her way, concluding, that she had spent so much time weeping and praying that there is no way God could refuse her. Then Augustine correctly expresses in his book *"Confessions"*:

108

*My mother, your faithful servant, wept more for me than mothers weep over their children's dead bodies. **By that spirit of faith which she had from you**, she saw my death, and you graciously heard her…*

Although, the bishop's response was an irritated reaction to her never-ending pleading of her prayer of importunity, his mother received it as a message from God that He answered her prayer. Jesus alludes to this same type of prayer in the following parable:

In a certain city there was a judge who neither feared God nor respected man. And there was a widow in that city who kept coming to him and saying, "Give me justice against my adversary." For a while he refused, but afterward he said to himself, "Though I neither fear God nor respect man, yet because this widow keeps bothering me, I will give her justice, so that she will not beat me down by her continual coming." And the Lord said, Hear what the unrighteous judge says. And will not God give justice to his elect, who cry to him day and night? Will he delay long over them? (Luk 18:2-7 ESV)

However, elsewhere scriptures exhort us not to pray in *"vain repetitions, as the heathen do: for they think that they shall be heard for their much speaking."* (Mat 6:7) So which is it? Are we heard for our prayers of importunity, which involves much speaking and weeping? Alternatively, are we heard for our prayers of faith, which usually involves very little speaking? First, let us clarify the difference between a prayer of importunity and a prayer of vain repetitions. The prayer of importunity is a pleading prayer with the coherent logic of a normal conversation. You may be repetitious in the subject matter, which may also cause some repetition of the words, but you are not just repeating the same words over and over again. A prayer of vain repetitions is one in which the person repeats the same words. It is like Luther crawling up the Scala Santa on his hands and knees, hoping to bend the will of God, repeating the same words, repeating the same prayers, on every step, and then repeating the entire process over again. What is the magic number of prayers that will cause God to accept our request? Will God be required to obey us once we have reached that requirement? Have we become God's puppet master?

Imagine for a moment that you are a young child and your mother is cooking your dinner. You ask her, *"Mom when will dinner be done?"*

She says, "*In an hour.*"

Then a second later you ask her, "*Mom when will dinner be done?*"

She then says, "*I told you, in an hour.*"

To which you state, "*Mom when will dinner be done?*"

"*Are you hard-of-hearing? I said an hour.*"

Would you not become frustrated with a person who kept echoing the same thought over and over? How long would you tolerate this nonsense before sending your son out of the kitchen? Obviously, either he does not believe you, or he is not listening to your response, considering he is constantly inquiring, "Mom, *when will dinner be done?*" The key to good relationships is good communication. I could just as easily talk to a robot as a person who continues to steadfastly, like a broken record, replaying same words over and over again. Thankfully, God is not wearied so easily with our folly; however, we are not heard for our vain repetitions, hence if you pray in this manner I will suggest that your prayer life will yield more abundant fruit if you follow the exhortations of the Mediator of our Faith.

Now having clarified the difference between a prayer of importunity and a prayer of vain repetitions, we must return to our original question. Are we heard for our much speaking, which is the prayer of importunity? Alternatively, are we heard for our not much speaking, which is the prayer of faith? The answer is both. So then, which is the appropriate prayer?

First, let us consider Messiah's prayers of faith. When Satan stirred up the seas against Him and the disciples, He rebuked the storm saying, "*Peace, be still.*" (Mar 4:39) When Jesus saw the man in the synagogue with the unclean spirit, He rebuked the spirit saying, "*Be quiet, and come out of him.*" (Mar 1:25) When He raised the ruler of the synagogue's daughter from the dead, He simply said, "*Little girl, I say to you, Arise!*" (Mar 5:41) When He raised Lazarus from the dead, He said, "*Lazarus, come forth.*" (Joh 11:43)

Prayers of faith are usually remarkably short. They speak directly to, and take authority over the mountain. They speak the unthinkable, commanding the mountain to be cast into the sea. They are powerful. In all cases, they glorify God. If you find someone who prays with this kind of authority and yet glorifies himself, run as fast as you can in the other direction. However, in all of these cases Jesus acted as God's representative on earth. He had authority because He was under the Father's authority. Jesus, now sitting at the right hand of God, has appointed you as His representative on earth, having given the Helper of the Holy Spirit in order to accomplish this monumental task.

Now let us consider those evenings when Jesus retired from the crowd, to spend time with the Father in prayer. Moreover, let us not forget all the mornings when He rose early to be with the Father. Were those prayers of importunity? What do you imagine Jesus was praying for at those times? My supposition is this was a time to praise God, to embrace His fellowship, to receive His strength to endure and to seek guidance to abide in His Will. These morning and evening sacrifices were the Son's personal time with His Father. This time with the Father was a much-needed respite after spending an entire day healing and teaching the people. This was a time for God to revive His Servant's spirit, so the Son could be about His Father's business, and sustain the frantic pace of His three-and-a-half-year ministry. This was a time for Jesus to bless the Father for the wonder of the previous day's works, wrought through Him. It was a time to seek the Father's Will, so He would be prepared to take authority over the forthcoming day's obstacles. In short, it was a time to strengthen His relationship with the Father, and a time to build Himself up in the power of the Holy Spirit.

That is the key. The prayer of importunity is not a legal argument wrought by a lawyer. It is a time to build your relationship with the God of Creation, your Father in Heaven. Therefore, the question, *"Which is more important?"* is like asking which hand is more important, your right or your left. If you had to choose you would probably choose the stronger, but the best choice is both. This is also the case between the prayer of importunity and the prayer of faith, the best choice is both. The prayer of importunity is the seed that grows your faith by strengthening your relationship with the source of that power, Almighty God. The prayer of faith is the fruit of that seed.

Now it should be apparent, that God does not require rituals in order to hear your prayer. Your God is not like the idols the prophets of Baal prayed to on Mount Carmel that may only hear prayers after the people had aroused them into hearing with their many repetitive word-chants and elaborate displays.

And they cried aloud and cut themselves after their custom with swords and lances, until the blood gushed out upon them. (1Ki 18:28 ESV)

They spent the entire day chanting and dancing around like a bunch of fools. However, the Almighty did not allow their idols to answer the supplications, because this was a contest between God's prophet and the prophets of Baal. Meanwhile, Elijah began mocking them saying, *"Cry aloud, for he is a god. Either he is musing, or he is relieving himself, or he is on a journey, or perhaps he is asleep and must be awakened."* (1Ki 18:27)

The contest was to prepare a bull for sacrifice, lay it on the wood, and not create the fire; but rather, they would call upon their deity to bring down fire from heaven. After the prophets of Baal spent the entire day calling on their gods, it was now Elijah's turn. He had the people take four jars of water and drench the sacrifice three times. He did not do this as some sort of ritual, but rather, to prove to the people that it was a real miracle, no tricks or mirrors. Then he prayed,

O LORD, God of Abraham, Isaac, and Israel, let it be known this day that you are God in Israel, and that I am your servant, and that I have done all these things at your word. Answer me, O LORD, answer me, that this people may know that you, O LORD, are God, and that you have turned their hearts back. (1Ki 18:36-37 ESV)

How long do you suppose it took Elijah to say this prayer? Notice his purpose. It is not to make him a great prophet. It is not to elevate Elijah's prestige in the sight of men. It is to bring people back to God. It is for God's glory.

That is a charismatic prayer I can support! However, it is important also to comprehend that many charismatic prayers are answered, but they do not come from God. The Enemy, who has been sent *"with all power and signs and lying wonders"* (2Th 2:9), answers those prayers. Moreover, it is because the people making the request do not love truth; therefore,

*God sends them a strong delusion, so that they may believe what is false, in order that all may be condemned **who did not believe the truth but had pleasure in unrighteousness**. (2Th 2:11-12 ESV)*

As you can see, the motivation of your heart is the defining factor. Are you seeking prosperity and wealth so that you may live in luxury? This sounds like feeding the flesh, not that God does not want to bless you in this world, but we cannot serve both God and mammon.

Christian TV is constantly televising this type of preaching. My friends do not believe the charlatans that say, "*Send in $ 100.00 and God will bless you with $ 1,000.00.*" Do not do this! This dishonors God's immense glory. Will you now turn the radiant glory of God into a mere stockbroker, performing your bidding, in the financial markets?

If you have needs, do not worry, He will supply them. In fact, you do not even have to pray for those needs. Instead, you can just thank God for taking care of them; for if you "*seek first the kingdom of God and His righteousness; and all **these things shall be added to you**.*" (Mat 6:33) You can stand on this promise. If you do not have enough faith to hold onto this promise, then ask God to increase your faith. If you still have problems believing, then pray the prayer of importunity to build yourself up in the Lord and the power of the Holy Spirit, and then,

HAVE FAITH IN GOD.

To summarize what we have discussed thus far. Trust in God's promises, in His written word, even if it means putting aside your doctrine for a moment. Since, His ways are so much higher than our ways; we place absolute confidence in His precious assurances. We discussed the power of prayer and its two principal divisions. We also addressed that it is essential to have the heart of God, and not the heart of the flesh, as the wellspring from which these prayers may flow. Finally, we deliberated that we are Christ's representatives in this world, standing by faith in the promise that He abides in us, and by this, He is represented properly on earth; whereby, the Father is glorified in the Son through us.

Glorifying God in the earth is an unequivocal command of the Captain of our Salvation. It is clear, concise and unwavering, affording you no ability to feign misunderstanding your obligation due to ambiguity. Not to follow this express order, is direct disobedience, known in the military as insubordination. When we bring our troubles to Jesus, He looks **US** in the eye, and says, "*All things are possible **to him THAT BELIEVES**.*" (Mar 9:23) Therefore, the Son of Man calls our faith to the center of the stage, so it becomes the pivotal focus upon which the promise depends. You no longer can hide behind the curtain of pretentious religion. You are standing before God Himself. Do you honestly believe the astounding promises of His Word? Do you have that much faith? Do you have faith in your faith, or do you have greater faith in your doubts and failures? At that moment, do you stand shaking and trembling, having recalled all the past failures, which has destroyed your hope in the future? At that moment, with your present fears laid bare before you, convulsing on the ground, you must make a decision; will you believe in the Word of God or will you trust in your fears? Will you spend your time looking at your obstacle violently shaking on the ground, attempting to pull down the walls of your salvation and the promises in the Lord? Alternatively, will you look up at Jesus and trust in Him? God is looking you in the eye. You cannot lie to Him Who Searches the Heart; so, what is the answer? This is our great paradox, and the extraordinary power of this prayer; therefore, cry out to Jesus, *"I believe, help my unbelief!"*

The Lord admonishes us to take courageous stand.

> *Have I not commanded you? Be strong and courageous. Do not be frightened, and do not be dismayed, for the LORD your God is with you wherever you go. (Jos 1:9 ESV)*

Jesus, likewise, made it His promise just before He ascended to the heavens.

> *All authority in heaven and on earth has been given to me. Go therefore and make disciples of all nations, baptizing them in the name of the Father and of the Son and of the Holy Spirit, teaching them to observe all that I have commanded you. And behold, **I am with you always, to the end of the age**. (Mat 28:18-20 ESV)*

Now, having reviewed our marching orders, let us consider some of God's tremendous promises. When Jesus says *"ask, and it shall be given"*, do you believe Him? (Mat 7:7) When He says, *"whatever you ask in prayer, believe that you have received it, and it will be yours"*, do you then trust in His promise, or do you hide your unbelief behind a tower of your doctrine? When He makes the breathtaking promise *"ask whatever you wish, and it will be done for you"* (Joh 15:7), do you receive it as a child would accept the truth from a father, or do you mask your unbelief behind the pretense of false modesty and humility? Whereby, you say things like *"God could never use a sinner like me in this way."* Therefore, your tradition has made the powerful Word of the

Lord of none effect, because you have chosen to remain in the shackles of your natural mind, bound by Satan in the cave of sin and death. However, God has said to you, *"Awake, sleeping ones! And arise from the dead, and Christ shall give you light."* (Eph 5:14)

Praying in His nature, character and authority is the key:

> *For all the promises of God in Him are yes, and in Him Amen, to the glory of God by us. (2Co 1:20 MKJV)*

Therefore, stop looking at your soul agonizing on the ground and look up to God in heaven and believe His promises. He is, after all, the King of Glory, Creator of the Universe, Infinite in Power and Authority, and the Captain of our Salvation. He says to one come and he comes. He says to another go and he goes. He sets up rulers and kings. He knows the end from the beginning and nothing has occurred that He has not allowed. He is all power, all knowledge and all authority. The earth is the Lord's and all that dwell within it belongs to Him; even your mountain of obstacles. How much greater is God than your mountain? When He looks down on your mountains from above the stars in the universe does not this thing you call a mountain look like a speck of dust, no rather, less than a speck of dust to our awesome, amazing God of All Power and Authority. How little is our faith that we cannot believe in God?[9]

When Christ says, *"As the Father has sent me, even so I am sending you"* (Joh 20:21), and *"greater works than these he shall do"* (Joh 14:12), it is time to stop doubting, Thomas, and *"not be unbelieving, but believing"* (Joh 20:27), so that we may shout out to our loving Father in Heaven for the world to hear,

> *Abba, Father! My Lord and my God! Blessing and honor and glory and power be to Him sitting on the throne, and to the Lamb forever and ever. (Joh 20:27, Rom 8:15, Rev 5:13)*

How is this teaching applied in The Parable of the Cross? The answer is simply that this is the reward-promise of the obedient life. This is something that even the carnal mind can appreciate and wish to attain.

---

[9] The power of prayer and faith is a huge subject that is much larger than the amount of space that I am able to give to it in this book. I would recommend books by E. M. Bounds and a book by Dutch Sheets called, *"Intercessory Prayer."*

Nevertheless, the carnal mind cannot attain it. In fact, these promises are only for those who choose to live their lives after the manner of their Lord and Savior. This is one of the magnificent gifts of the spirit, which the Lord promised. Therefore, do not squander or forfeit these riches on small carnal pleasures.

The Lord gave me a dream that is so vivid and precise to the topic that I have to include it in our discussion. I was walking along a beach at sunset, so captivated by its beauty that I was upset that I did not have a camera to capture the moment. The light was glistening off the waves out on the vast horizon. The sun had serenely drawn a cloud of curtains over its face in the lower part of the sky, painting the horizon with a splendor of vivid colors. The breeze gently caressed my skin with her soft fingers, and the fresh, clean smell of the ocean breeze filled my senses and refreshed my soul. While I was admiring the Creator's glorious creation, a scantily clad woman, who walked into my sight, abruptly diverted by my attention. Immediately, I forgot God's glory. He was still there, His glory, His promises, and His beauty, but my mind was taken prisoner so quickly by this besetting sin that I completely lost focus on Him, choosing rather, to feed on the lusts of the flesh. O' how quickly, and easily we are drawn away.

This is the dilemma is it not? We can choose the dainties offered by the Father of Lies and fulfill the indulgences of the flesh, or we can choose not to feed those lusts and continue to look upon His Glory. Ultimately, we can only do one or the other. The beauty of that horizon is eternal; scratching that itch in the flesh is momentary and ultimately unsatisfactory. Choosing to remain in Him at all times is the most difficult and yet rewarding choice of our lives. It is, in fact, the battle of our lives. Will you let your flesh live and the spirit die? Alternatively, will you allow Jesus to live in you? This is The Parable of the Cross. The by-product of this walk is the benefit of a mountain-moving faith. However, the greatest mountain we need to move out of the way and cast into the sea is, ourselves! Nevertheless, this requirement is impossible for us to achieve. However, thankfully, what is *"impossible with men is possible with God."* (Luk 18:27) Therefore, I will leave one last thought to ponder. When you are in doubt, it is because you are trusting in yourself. Rather than trusting in our deservedness or ourselves; why not put your trust and reliance in Jesus Christ and His finished work? In other words, why not,

HAVE FAITH IN GOD!

chapter eight

WHO DO YOU THINK YOU ARE!

Now let us recap a few of the controversial incidents that occurred over the last week. Within a week of the Passover, Jesus raised Lazarus from the dead at Bethany. After hearing this, the Pharisees began to plot how they might surreptitiously arrest and execute Him. Next on Palm Sunday, the Ruler of Heaven and Earth openly proclaimed that He is Jerusalem's long awaited Messiah, riding into the city on a colt, and accepting praise and worship of the multitude. When the multitude lavished Him with adulation that seemed worthy of Deity, the Pharisees objected and ask Him to rebuke His disciples. Instead, the King of Glory dismissed their petition, telling them *"if these were silent, the very stones would cry out."* (Luk 19:40) Then He went to His throne room, the temple in Jerusalem, inspected it and found it wanting. Afterwards, He left for the day since it was late. However, the next morning, He drove out the moneychangers causing a huge commotion. This infuriated Jerusalem's spiritual and business leaders. The religious leadership, outraged by what they considered an audacious display of effrontery, most likely felt greater indignation since this action almost certainly cost them large sums of money. Now that the temple was no longer defiled, the Deliverer began healing *"the blind and the lame [who] came to him in the temple."* (Mat 21:14) While this was occurring, the children, caught up in all the excitement, began to repeat the words they heard their parents shouting the day before, *"Hosanna to the Son of David!"* (Mat 21:15) The children's relentless echo of praise drumming in the Pharisees ears was almost more than they could stand, until the cup of their indignation became so full, they insisted that God Incarnate put an end to these blasphemous acclamations. Once again, Immanuel ignored their criticism, to which He instead responded, *"Have you never read, 'Out of the mouth of infants and nursing babies you have prepared praise?'"* (Mat 21:16)

Can you imagine Pharisees faces flush with anger as the root of bitterness began to grow, and then blossom into insidious schemes, within their seething hearts of stone? Within a few days, the Resurrection and the Life raised Lazarus from the dead in the sight of an entire town. At the procession, he became walking proof of Messiah's power and the authority. Then The King arrived, riding on a donkey, publicly proclaiming Himself as the long awaited messiah. The next day, the Holy One of Israel drove the moneychangers out of the temple. All the while, people heap lavish praise upon Him worthy of God only, and He did not rebuke them, but instead, defended their actions, which by implication, also rebuked the Pharisee's disputation. In addition, the large sum of money the Pharisees must have lost and their concern that the Romans will take away would take away their power. (Joh 11:48)

Because of all of this, the chief priests and the scribes challenged, *"Tell us by what authority you do these things, or who it is that gave you this authority."* (Luk 20:2) The implication being, *"We have lost a lot of money because of you. Furthermore, you allow people to give you praise that is only worthy of God. And now you have the audacity to sit in God's temple healing people and accepting His praise, in the very spot you drove out good, honest business owners. Who do you think you are? You do not own this place. You do not sit on the council. You have no authority here, so who do you think you are?"*

Undoubtedly, this is a ridiculous question from the Christian perspective, considering they built the temple for God. Now God Incarnate is sitting in the temple, and yet, the individuals who claim to be His most devout followers, spitefully ask who gave Him the authority over His own temple.

Jesus responded, *"The baptism of John, from where did it come? From heaven or from man?"* (Mat 21:25) Then the Pharisees took council with each other and said, *"If we say, 'From heaven,' he will say to us, 'Why then did you not believe him?' But if we say, 'From man,' we are afraid of the crowd, for they all hold that John was a prophet."* (Mat 21:25-26) Therefore, instead of being truthful, they responded, *"We do not know."* To which the Word of Truth then answered, *"Neither will I tell you by what authority I do these things."* (Mat 21:27)

In order to make them realize the magnitude of their decision, Jesus told them the Parable of The Tenant Farmers, which is about a man who planted a vineyard and rented it out for a small portion of the profit of the harvest. When it came time to receive the return on his investment, three times he sent his servants who were treated shamefully and sent away empty handed. So at his wits end the owner said to himself:

> *'What shall I do? I will send my beloved son; perhaps they will respect him.' But when the tenants saw him, they said to themselves, 'This is the heir. Let us kill him, so that the inheritance may be ours.' And they threw him out of the vineyard and killed him. (Luk 20:13-15 ESV)*

If we simply glaze over the above text without much contemplation, it almost appears as if Jesus responded with a disjunctive rhetorical question in order to gain the advantage by catching His opponents off guard. However, we must remember that we are speaking of the mind of God; hence, we must consider that He may have both answered the question and asked a question at the same time. Taking this approach to the text, reveals a very small thread that weaves these seemingly disjointed teachings into a most beautifully ornate fabric. Jesus confronts the inquisition head-on by asking, who gave John the authority to baptize. If they do not believe the Baptist's testimony, and if they do not believe God's testimony (Mat 3:17) and if they do not believe the Holy Spirit is testimony of the miracles wrought in the Son of Man, then what will they believe? Their acrimonious question was merely a pretense, designed to capture Jesus in the moment. However, there was a very small mustard seed of truth hidden within the leaven of the Pharisee's purpose for asking the question, although, most assuredly, they did not realize it. The truth of the matter is that this was actually a very good question, especially if asked from the correct heart. However, the Son of God will not be tossed to and fro by their craftiness. Therefore, a superficial reading of the text will cause the reader to believe that Messiah's only goal was to win the argument by throwing the Pharisees off guard and humiliate them in front of the common people. That would not be very a loving response from our God of true love, yet a loving response is exactly what it is. When Adam and Eve sinned, they hid from God. God then asked Adam *"Where are you?"* (Gen 3:9) To which Adam responded that he hid because of his nakedness. This caused the Omnipotent God to ask, *"Who told you that you were naked? Have you eaten of the tree of which I commanded you not to eat?"* (Gen 3:11) This appears to be a very typical dance between the Almighty and man, throughout the scriptures. Why do you suppose the Omnipotent God always seems to ask questions when He already knows the answer? The answer is simple. He is prodding the person to see their true heart. He asks us to approach Him in truth, so we may be healed. For example, consider the question the Son of God asked a man at the pool of Bethesda, who had been an invalid for thirty-eight years, "*Do you want to be healed?*" (Joh 5:1-8) The answer appears so apparent that the question seems rather inane, yet it is one of the most profound questions in the entire Bible. Therefore, when Jesus answers their question with a question about John the Baptist, He is actually asking them, "*Do you really want to be healed?*" If they answer truthfully, then the Healer will heal them and make them whole. However, if they continue in a surreptitiously vain attempt to hide the truth of their naked sin from the God with Seven Eyes, then their sin remains.

Subsequently Jesus asked the Pharisees, "*What then will the owner of the vineyard do to them? He will come and destroy those tenants and give the vineyard to others.*" (Luk 20:15-16) To which they exclaimed, "*He will put those wretches to a miserable death and let out the vineyard to other tenants who will give him the fruits in their seasons.*" (Mat 21:41) In other words, they agreed that such an egregious crime deserved the most severe form of judgment. Then, Jesus, like Nathan the prophet moment, when he proclaimed, "*You are the man!*" (2 Sam 12:7) responded,

> *What then is this that is written: "The stone that the builders rejected has become the cornerstone'? Everyone who falls on that stone will be broken to pieces, and when it falls on anyone, it will crush him." (Luk 20:17-18 ESV)*

Of course, this caused the Pharisees, to fall on their faces, confess their sin and beg for mercy. Wrong! That was King David's proper response; instead, they seethed with bitterness.

> *The scribes and the chief priests sought to lay hands on him at that very hour, for they perceived that he had told this parable against them, but they feared the people. So they watched him and sent spies, **who pretended to be sincere**, that they might catch him in something he said, so as to deliver him up to the authority and jurisdiction of the governor.(Luk 20:19-20 ESV)*

Prior to this exchange, Meshiach told the Pharisees a short story of faithful and faithless obedience, commonly known as the Parable of the Two Sons. The son, who initially appeared to obey his father, actually demonstrated faithless obedience by ultimately not doing the will of the father, and the son who at first was disobedient, later changed his mind, ultimately demonstrating repentance and faithful obedience. Concluding the parable, Jesus asked, *"Which of the two did the will of his father?"* To which the Pharisees correctly responded the one who was disobedient initially, but in the end did the will of the father. Then Jesus said to these extremely pious-looking priests,

> *Truly, I say to you, the tax collectors and the prostitutes go into the kingdom of God before you. (Mat 21:31 ESV)*

Imagine how great the fire of indignation burned in the hearts of these pretentious, high-minded priests. Who did this man think he was coming into their temple, driving out the moneychangers and teaching the Word of God without the proper authority or formal training? He then had the gall to tell priests, who were officially trained in all aspects of the Law and the Prophets, that the most hated people in all of Israel, the cheating tax collectors and the most despised sinners, the shamefully wicked prostitutes, would have their place in heaven ahead of them; the piously devout, formally-acknowledge priest of God!

I cannot help but think of John Bunyan, thrown into prison for preaching the Word of God directly from the scriptures. Ironically, the church betrayed him, through an unholy church-government alliance that conspired to jail this virtuous man of God for twelve long, hard years. Nevertheless, neither the Enemy nor the prison walls could restrain the Word of His Testimony.

Either God would allow His servant a way out, or He would allow the Word to be written from that prison; as He did with Paul, writing over one third of the New Testament from various prisons. Therefore, John Bunyan, from prison, wrote the second greatest work in the history of the English language, *"A Pilgrims Progress"*, whose printing is surpassed only by the Holy Scriptures.

Nevertheless, before Bunyan this untrained upstart Jesus completely embarrassed the learned Pharisees. Who did this man think he was? They diligently began to study the Tenack at the age of five; learned so well most of them could recite the Torah, the entire first five books, solely from memory. In their minds, they were the caretakers of traditions, keepers of the law, guides to the blind, and lights to those who were in darkness. (Rom 2:19) Nevertheless, this unlearned rabbi threw down the gauntlet, and the contest had been enjoined.

Therefore, these pretentious priests conspired with the state to bring charges against the Truth, a tactic repeatedly used in the chronicle of fallen churches, whereby the false believers persecute the true believers. The pattern of this conflict is indelibly written in church history. The church, infused by the Enemy with pride and man's tradition becomes apostate. God then raises up a leader to oppose the false doctrines of this apostatized church. Although, scripturally astute, they become so blind by spiritual pride, they cannot see what the commoner can see, their righteousness is as filthy rags. (Isa 64:6) After challenging the doctrines of this fallen church, it then looks to the government to do its dirty work. Nevertheless, this is the way it has been from the beginning, for God's ways are the same yesterday, today and always. (Heb 13:8) Likewise, it appears throughout history that the heart of man has also been the same yesterday, today and always. As proof, compare the book of Judges, where "Every man did the right in his own eyes" (Jud 21:25), to church history. However, if that is too time consuming, then consider how these supposed pious priests of God reacted to Messiah's stern rebuke.

> ***Then the Pharisees went and <u>plotted</u>*** *how to entangle him in his words. And they sent their disciples to him, **<u>along with the Herodians</u>**, saying, "Teacher, we know that you are true and teach the way of God truthfully, and you do not care about anyone's opinion, for you are not swayed by appearances. Tell us, then, what you think. Is it lawful to pay taxes to Caesar, or not?" (Mat 22:15-17 ESV)*

The Pharisees, then created an unholy alliance with the Herodians in order entrap our Lord and Savior. Therefore, we have three groups who desired to destroy the Lamb of God.

At this time, it would be beneficial to discuss the differences between these groups; the Pharisees, the Sadducees and the Herodians. The name Pharisee means, *"pure or separated or divided."* Groups of rabbis believed Israel's subjugation was God's judgment against the nation's sin; therefore, these Pharisees began to add a multitude of rules in order to earn God's favor, so He would send a deliverer to free them from their Roman overlords. They followed these rules so precisely that they became inflamed with anger when Yeshua, the Lord of the Sabbath, healed the afflicted on the day of the Sabbath rest; having greater concern over breaking the letter of the law than rejoicing in miraculous healing and salvation. The Pharisees had two primary schools of thought within their own sect, the school of Shammai and the school of Hillel. The school of Hillel most likely had disciples like Nicodemus, Joseph of Arimathea and Gamaliel. Although they also were extremely devout, they had greater leniency and were fewer in number than their Shammai counterparts. For instance, their foundational doctrine was that men shall love the Lord their God with all their heart and love their neighbor as themselves. However, they were also just as fanatical in their creeds. Taking their liberality to the extreme, for example, they allowed a man to divorce over the minor infraction of a burnt dinner. The disciples from the house of Shammai, on the other hand, believed that fornication was the only justifiable grounds for divorce. Most of Jesus' teachings tended to validate Hillel's principles, associated with love, tolerance and mercy; but there were also times when He denounced Hillel's teachings as overly liberal in their freedoms and justified the house of Shammai. Of these two groups, the house of Shammai was the larger and more popular. The Zealots were probably the most extreme of the extreme adapts of the house of Shammai. The Zealots were violent revolutionaries against the yoke of Rome. They also actively looked for Yahweh's Meshiach-Deliverer to overthrow the oppressor and establish Israel's millennial kingdom, as foretold by the prophets.

Jewish scholars of both schools despised Roman rule, yet the house of Hillel was more open to Jesus' teachings about love, tolerance and mercy than their Shammai counterparts. For example, Jesus' teachings to *"not resist the one who is evil"* (Mat 5:39), to *"Love your enemies and pray for those who persecute you"* (Mat 5:44) and to *"love your neighbor as yourself"* (Mar 12:31); were easily accepted by the disciples of Hillel but vehemently rejected by the house of Shammai. The house of Shammai taught that resistance to the occupation good, but even more so, it sin to be pacifistic in the face of this evil.

Consider within the cultural and historical context how these two groups may have reacted to a few of Yeshua's teachings. We will begin with the Meshiach's teaching *"if anyone forces you to go one mile, go with him two miles."* (Mat 5:41) A Roman soldier could force any Jewish citizen to carry his shield for up to one mile according to the law. The Israelite could be plowing the field or bringing in the harvest and a soldier walking by could order him to drop everything and carry his shield. The citizenry and the Pharisees both despised this rule. Therefore, when Jesus made this staggering statement, it is easy to comprehend that the house of Hillel may have accepted this teaching, but the house of Shammai would have utterly rejected this doctrine. Another example is the story of the Good Samaritan. In this story, the responses of the priest and the Levite are shown to be inappropriate for having nothing to do with the beaten, half-dead man; whereas, the Good Samaritan is shown to exceed their righteousness by caring for the stranger. (Luk 10:30) This was in direct opposition to the house of Shammai, which taught to have nothing to do with the Gentiles, teaching that a person would defile himself simply by entering into one of their houses. Furthermore, the Samaritans were greatly despised, because they were a mixed race of Jews and Gentiles, so for Jesus to use these people to emphasize his story would have exacerbated the house of Shammai. On the other hand, although this teaching would have challenged the disciples from the house of Hillel, they may have been able to receive it since their emphasis was on love and mercy. However, the Shammites, who also taught that adultery was the only justifiable reason to divorce your wife, gladly received Messiah's teaching on divorce. (Mat 5:32)

Overall, the Pharisees were formal legalists, so concerned with following all the precise, minute, details of the law, that many times they lost the basic spiritual concept or contextual principle of the text.(Mat 23:24) They became so ritualistic that most of their ceremonies were devoid of any meaningful sacred significance. (Mat 23:27) They said long prayers (Mt. 23:14) publicly on the street corners. (Mat. 6:5) They had a trumpet blown before them when they gave alms. (Mat 6:2) They chose the best upper rooms at feasts (Mat 23:6) and sat in the chief seats in the synagogue. (Luk 11:42) They fasted at least twice a week (Mat 9:14), being sure to show disfigured faces, so to receive praise from men. (Mat 6:16) They believed overt rituals justified themselves before God, so they had no need for repentance. (Luk 18:11) They believed it was unlawful to eat or drink with sinners (Mt. 9:10-11), or even to be in the same house with them. (Luk 19:7) Nevertheless, they were highly esteemed by the unlearned masses. They were somewhat democratic, since they allowed anyone to join and advance through their strict set of teachings. However, their greatest error, and one that some sects of Christianity err in today also, was that they believed their oral laws held as much weight as Yahweh's Holy Scriptures.

The Sadducees, on the other hand, were the rich, ruling elite. In today's society, they are similar to the liberal, moral ethicists, primarily concerned with social justice rather than the spiritual significance of the scriptures. They were the aristocrats, separated from the masses by social class and wealth. They believed only the first five books of Moses, the Torah, were authoritative, and denied the Pharisees' oral traditions. They believed in the Creator, and yet, denied almost every spiritual aspect of His kingdom. For instance, they did not believe in a future state of punishments and rewards, or angels and spirits (Acts 23:8), or in the resurrection of the dead. (Mar 12:23) They openly supported Rome's rule over the people. Because of this, and their high-minded snobbery, the masses despised them immensely. The Herodians were a small division of this sect, called such because of their support for the loathsome King Herod, who most people correctly considered a despicable usurper.

Despite their vast disagreements, these two groups had two issues very much in common. First, they fervently disliked each other. However, since both groups were extremely powerful within the Jewish theocratic society, there was an uneasy tolerance of each other and an avoidance of certain provocative topics. We see a glimpse of just how volatile this relationship could be at Paul's inquiry before a commission of these two groups. With only two remarkably short sentences, he almost incites a violent riot, stating, *"Brothers, I am a Pharisee, a son of Pharisees. It is with respect to the hope and the resurrection of the dead that I am on trial."* (Act 23:6) Now consider the practically immediate explosion of violence, so easily ignited by setting such a small spark upon this controversial issue.

*And when he had said this, a dissension arose between the Pharisees and the Sadducees, and the assembly was divided. For the Sadducees say that there is no resurrection, nor angel, nor spirit, but the Pharisees acknowledge them all. Then a great clamor arose, and some of the scribes of the Pharisees' party stood up and contended sharply, "We find nothing wrong in this man. What if a spirit or an angel spoke to him?" And when **the dissension became violent**, the tribune, afraid that Paul would be torn to pieces by them, **commanded the soldiers to go down** and take him away from among them by force and bring him into the barracks. (Act 23:7-10 ESV)*

To appreciate this impassioned reaction more fully; picture our Senate debating taxes that leads to such a rage that the Democrats and the Republicans become so violent that the police have to separate them.

Nevertheless, *"politics makes very strange bedfellows"* and *"the enemy of my enemy is my friend."* Therefore, the second issue the Sadducees and Pharisees had in common was that their deep fear and bitter hatred for Jesus easily surpassed their fervent animosity for each other.

With this understanding, let us return to the scene where the Herodians collaborated with the Pharisees in order to confound the Omniscient Incarnate God. It is laughable how they believe they can craftily bait this thinly veiled trap with false flattery to catch Messiah off guard, saying, *"Teacher, we know that you are true and teach the way of God truthfully, and you do not care about anyone's opinion, for you are not swayed by appearances."* (Mat 22:16) It is also quite possible they know Jesus will see through their deception and yet the people will not. Either way their behavior is utterly duplicitous. However, is not this what one would expect from people influenced by the Father of Lies, who was the most crafty, subtle beast of the field? (Gen 3:1)

These deceitful, arrogant, elitist aristocrats, feign a humble spirit, then ask King Messiah, *"Is it lawful to pay taxes to Caesar, or not?"* (Mat 22:17) Imagine their glee believing they have completely ensnared Wisdom within their entangled deceits and placed the King of Glory into an impossible situation. The only Jews who enjoyed Roman rule were the Herodians and the Sadducees. The masses despised the Romans and the Zealots were fanatical in their hatred and resistance to this usurping power. Therefore, the masses yearned for the long awaited Meshiach Deliverer according to their prophetic interpretations of the scriptures. Thus, publicly accepting Messiah's praise created other problems for the Son of David. They believed the He would depose the Romans and setup Israel's Millennial Kingdom, according to God's promise to King David.

> *And I will appoint a place for my people Israel and will plant them, so that they may dwell **in their own place** and **be disturbed no more**. And violent men shall afflict them no more… And I will give you rest from all your enemies. … I will raise up your offspring after you, who shall come from your body, and **I will establish his kingdom**. He shall build a house for my name, and **I will establish the throne of his kingdom forever**. I will be to him a*

*father, and he shall be to me a son. ... And your house and your kingdom shall be made sure forever before me. **Your throne shall be established forever**. (2Sa 7:10-16 ESV)*

A thousand years later Rabbi Moshe ben Maimon (1135 – 1204), one of the greatest rabbinic sages in history and renowned scholar on Jewish eschatology wrote:

*The Messianic age is when the **Jews will regain their independence** and **all return to the land of Israel**. The Messiah will be a very **great king**, he will achieve great fame, and his reputation among the gentile nations will be even greater than that of King Solomon. His great righteousness and the wonders that he will bring about will cause **all peoples to make peace with him** and **all lands to serve him**.*

It is apparent from the above passages, the Jewish people expected an earthly king to set up his kingdom in Israel. However, Jesus never came to fulfill these earthly prophecies; but rather, came to set up a spiritual kingdom. Consider, for example, that Messiah informs Pilate, *"My kingdom is not of this world."* (Joh 18:36) Nevertheless, when Pilate asked if He is a king, the King of Glory affirmatively responded, *"You say that I am a king. For this purpose I was born and for this purpose I have come into the world."* (Joh 18:37) This interpretation of Messianic prophecies was so ingrained in Jewish eschatological understanding that even John the Baptist, who boldly proclaimed Jesus as the Meshiach earlier, sent his disciples to inquire, *"Are you the one who is to come, or shall we look for another?"* (Luk 7:19) To which Jesus then responded,

*Go and tell John what you have seen and heard: **the blind receive their sight**, **the lame walk**, **lepers are cleansed**, and **the deaf hear**, **the dead are raised up**, **the poor have good news preached to them**. And blessed is the one who is not offended by me. (Luk 7:22-23 ESV)*

These verses were also very well known Messianic prophecies; although with a much smaller degree of emphasis than the millennial kingdom teachings. Jesus points to these fulfillments to reassure John the Baptist and encourage him during his trial of faith by fire; for the Baptizer was now in prison and would soon give his life as the last martyred prophet of the dispensation of the law. These specific prophetic fulfillments found the book of Isaiah are as follows:

127

> *Then **the eyes of the blind shall be opened**, and **the ears of the deaf unstopped**; then shall **the lame man leap like a deer**, and **the tongue of the mute sing for joy**. For waters break forth in the wilderness, and streams in the desert; (Isa 35:5-6)*

> *The Spirit of the Lord GOD is upon me, because **the LORD has anointed me to bring good news to the poor**; he has sent me to bind up the brokenhearted, to proclaim liberty to the captives, and the opening of the prison to those who are bound; (Isa 61:1)*

Notice I have not cited any Old Testament passages about Messiah raising people from the dead, yet Jesus uses this as one of His proof texts for John the Baptist. That is because, the Jewish rabbis correctly taught this commonly understood prophetic fulfillment. They anticipated that the kingdom of God would be set up in Israel and that their ancestors would have a part in that kingdom. Do you recall what Martha said when Jesus told her that her brother would rise again? *"I know that he will rise again **in the resurrection** on the last day."* (Joh 11:24) This was why Jesus refocused her attention from the last day to Himself and His day:

> *Jesus said to her, "I am the resurrection and the life. Whoever believes in me, **though he die, yet shall he live**, and everyone who lives and believes in me shall never die. Do you believe this?" She said to him, "Yes, Lord; **I believe that you are the Christ, the Son of God**, who is coming into the world." (Joh 11:25-27 ESV)*

Should we then interpret all the Messianic Kingdom references in scriptures spiritually rather than expecting literal or physical manifestations? Absolutely not! Many times the spiritual realization occurs long before we witness the physical appearance of that fulfillment. For example, God told Adam *"of the tree of the knowledge of good and evil you shall not eat, for **in the day** that you eat of it you shall surely die."* (Gen 2:17) Adam ate of that tree, and we know he did not die in that day. In fact, he did not physically die until many years later. Was God's Word then unfulfilled? Absolutely not! Adam died spiritually, and then he imparted the chronic cancer of sin and **death** to his posterity.

The promised Davidic Messianic Kingdom of 2 Samuel 7:10-16 was being fulfilled, although, not in the observable, physical dimension. This is why Jesus strengthened John the Baptizer's faith by pointing him to current material manifestations. Yeshua also pointed to these same prophetic passages when He taught in the synagogue at Nazareth.

> *And the scroll of the prophet Isaiah was given to him. He unrolled the scroll and found the place where it was written, "The Spirit of the Lord is upon me, because he has anointed me to proclaim good news to the poor. He has sent me to proclaim liberty to the captives and recovering of sight to the blind, to set at liberty those who are oppressed, to proclaim the year of the Lord's favor." (Luk 4:17-19 ESV)*

Afterwards Messiah states, *"Today this Scripture has been fulfilled in your hearing."* (Luk 4:21) Thus, making it perfectly clear He is the fulfillment of these prophecies. What most casual readers miss is that He stopped the quotation of Isaiah in mid verse. The complete quotation of this verse is as follows:

> *...to proclaim the year of the LORD's favor, **and the day of vengeance of our God; to comfort all who mourn** (Isa 61:2 ESV)*

Christ's crucifixion fulfilled the day of God's vengeance when He recompensed our sin. However, Jesus pointed to prophecies manifested in the physical world during His life as evidence that He was Messiah. Hence, it was fitting that He would end the discourse in the middle of this verse. Although, *"the day of vengeance of our God"* was fulfilled in the spiritual plane, it will also be manifested in the physical dimension at the King's second coming. This comma, therefore, is a two thousand year pause in God's final judgment against this sinful world, which is quite fortunate for our generation. The Lord has demonstrated extraordinary patience with mankind, *"not wishing that any should perish, but that all should reach repentance."* (2Pe 3:9)

Against this backdrop, consider the Herodian's question. *"Is it lawful to pay taxes to Caesar, or not?"* (Mat 22:17) Jesus was in an impossible situation, since most people despised their Roman overlords, but even more so, because of their misconceptions about Messiah's true calling at His first coming. Ponder the magnitude of this confrontation. Consider how easily one wrong word could have derailed His entire mission by sending Him to the cross too soon; thereby, resulting in unfulfilled messianic prophecies and leaving so many of His most important discourses unspoken. Therefore, it is easy to appreciate our Wise King's response to the dogs that have encompassed Him roundabout within the snares of this cunning dilemma.

> *But he perceived their craftiness, and said to them, "Show me a denarius. Whose likeness and inscription does it have?" They said, "Caesar's." He said to them, "Then render to Caesar the things that are Caesar's, and to God the things that are God's." (Luk 20:23-25 ESV)*

Extraordinarily, His response appears entirely extemporaneous. When I face quandaries of much lower magnitudes, I am usually unable to find the immediate, correct answers. Of course, after contemplating the subject, I can think of many marvelous responses. However, the question, the people, and the opportunity for my testimony all have passed. This never seems to be the case for The Wisdom of God. Instead, He calmly engaged the question, and then offered a most remarkably wise reply, even though He knew He was walking directly into their attempted trap. Moreover, He appears to rely explicitly on the Holy Spirit in this case, considering the text seems to indicate that He has never seen a denarius, since He says, *"Show me a denarius. Whose likeness and inscription does it have?"*

The wisdom of the wisest of men attempting to confound the Wisdom of God is certainly a ludicrous proposition, although, this is exactly what we witness in this dialogue. Do we honestly believe that the knowledge of the most renowned, wisest intellectual could even amount to a grain of sand when compared to the vast universe of the secret knowledge that remains hidden within the Mind of God? In this scene, the intellectual elite of His time had the audacity to question the Lord of All Creation as He taught in His temple, *"Who gave You the authority to do these things?"* When that fails, are they actually so impudent they believe they can confound the Son of God? It is not our wisdom that reaches the heights of the universe; but rather, it is our vanity, our pride, and our self-righteousness. Considering this, we can truly appreciate the long-suffering, loving-kindness the Lord of Glory has with our astounding blind pride.

His response amazed these entrappers. *"And they were not able in the presence of the people to catch him in what he said, but marveling at his answer they became silent."* (Luk 20:26) Nevertheless, the submissive silence of vain imaginations never endures. Now comes the

Sadducees, whom you will recall denied the resurrection, with another great quandary, searching out the Lamb of God for blemish, inquiring:

> *Teacher, Moses wrote for us that if a man's brother dies, having a wife but no children, the man must take the widow and raise up offspring for his brother. Now there were seven brothers. The first took a wife, and died without children. And the second and the third took her, and likewise all seven left no children and died. Afterward the woman also died. In the resurrection, therefore, whose wife will the woman be? For the seven had her as wife. (Luk 20:28-33 ESV)*

The King of Heaven underscored their misinterpreted the scriptures that created a false doctrine and caused them to misunderstand heaven. Notice how our Gracious King answered their question, and also corrected their incorrect dogma at the end of His reply.

> *The sons of this age marry and are given in marriage, but those who are considered worthy to attain to that age and to the resurrection from the dead neither marry nor are given in marriage, for they cannot die anymore, because they are equal to angels and are sons of God, being sons of the resurrection. But that the dead are raised, even Moses showed, in the passage about the bush, where he calls the Lord the God of Abraham and the God of Isaac and the God of Jacob.* ***Now he is not God of the dead, <u>but of the living</u>, for all live to him.*** *(Luk 20:34-38 ESV)*

Considering the various schools of thought in that age, take note that the listening scribes remarked, "*Teacher, you have spoken well*", and not the Sadducees, who originally posed the question. By the way, much to the delight of the scribes and the Pharisees, Mark informs us Messiah concluded His discourse with "***You are quite wrong***." (Mar 12:27) O how we love to have our propositions validated! Even our most despised enemy, whose voice may usually cause us to wince, as if fingernails are screeching across a chalkboard in the back of our mind, can become beautiful music if only they can find some place of agreement with us, and validate our ego. This truism only serves to demonstrate the enormity of our lost condition and our spiritual blindness. Is there any cavern as deep and dark as the abyss of spiritual pride? Child of God beware of being led astray by the subtle thoughts and the vain imaginations of the intellectual elite.

Jesus, loathed by the Pharisees, the Sadducees, the Herodians and the scribes, ingratiated Himself to two of the groups because the truth He proclaimed happened to validate their doctrine. Subsequently, a scribe comes to Him with a semi-sincere heart and asks Him, *"Which commandment is the most important of all?"* (Mar 12:28) To which Jesus answers:

> *The most important is, "Hear, O Israel: The Lord our God, the Lord is one. And you shall love the Lord your God with all your heart and with all your soul and with all your mind and with all your strength." The second is this: "You shall love your neighbor as yourself." There is no other commandment greater than these. (Mar 12:29-31 ESV)*

Jesus then perfectly summed up His answer, stating, *"On these two commandments depend all the Law and the Prophets."* (Mat 22:40) Afterwards, the scribe once more responds with a positive affirmation, to which Jesus then concludes the subject with *"You are not far from the kingdom of God."* (Mar 12:34)

This scribe, probably a follower of the house of Hillel, is very close to salvation, since he clearly understands that it is not the works of the law by which salvation is received, having said,

> *...to love him with all the heart and with all the understanding and with all the strength, and to love one's neighbor as oneself, **is much more than all whole burnt offerings and sacrifices**. (Mar 12:33 ESV)*

Having approached the Mercy Seat of God with a semi-pure heart, the scribe's animosity appears to have dissipated; therefore, the Author of Salvation then attempted to move him and others into the next revelation of His redeeming grace. While they were all gathered, He asked them, *"What do you think about the Christ? Whose son is he?"* They replied, *"The son of David."* (Mat 22:42) To this correct response, Yeshua then offered these intellectual elites a quandary of their own, asking,

> *How is it then that David, in the Spirit, calls him Lord, saying, "The Lord said to my Lord, Sit at my right hand, until I put your enemies under your feet"? If then David calls him Lord, how is he his son? (Mat 22:43-45 ESV)*

In the Hebrew, this verse is saying *"Yahweh said to Adonai"*; Yahweh being the actual name of God and Adonai referring to His Kingship. This passage was widely accepted by the rabbis as a messianic promise. The Treasury of Scriptural Knowledge quotes Rabbi Joden stating that, *"In the world to come, the Holy Blessed God shall cause the king Messiah to sit at his right hand."* Likewise, Rabbi Moses Hadarson and Saadias Gaon state, *"This is Messiah our righteousness, as it is written, The Lord said to my Lord."*

Now these intellectuals have a serious problem. How does this make any sense? If David is the promised forefather of the Meshiach, then how can He be seen in a vision as a preexistent offspring and be Adonai? Furthermore, this had been an area of contention with Jesus and the intellectual elite several times in the past few years. When Jesus said, *"My Father is working until now"* they sought to kill Him, because He was *"calling God his own Father, making himself equal with God."* (Joh 5:18) When He said, *"Before Abraham was, I am"*, they sought to stone Him. (Jon 8:58-59) Likewise, when He said, *"I and the Father are one."* they *"picked up stones again to stone him"*, because they claimed He committed blasphemy, stating, *"You, being a man, make yourself God."* (Jch 10:30-33)

Considering past confrontations with Immanuel, and now presented with this riddle, the religious leaders become as speechless as Job when he demanded answers from God. Also intriguing, which most readers miss, is the common thread between this subject and the last subject, since most people read Messiah's discourses presented in the Gospels as disjunctive lessons. However, if you search for a common thread between these lessons, many times you will uncover a much deeper and glorious undercurrent supporting the clear meaning shown on the face of the water of the Word. When we juxtapose the question Messiah asked the Pharisees against the His response to which is the greatest of all the laws, we discover something very wonderful.

We begin our search with Yeshua's *"Shema Yisrael"* response to, *"Which commandment is the most important of all?"* (Mar 12:28) *"Shema Yisrael, Yehovah Eloheinu, Yehovah ached Yehovah"*, or *"Hear, O Israel: the Lord our God is one Lord."* This verse is so fundamental to the Jewish people that many scholars call this the creed of the Jews. Countless morning and evening services begin with this article of faith. To the Jewish mindset, they are affirming that there is only one God against the polytheism that most of the rest of the world asserts, of which, they believe Christians are among, because of their adherence to the Trinitarian concept. As Christians, we believe the three in one concept of the trinity affirms only one God. However, many others consider this nothing more than a game of antics with semantics, believing Christians have fallen into a trap of worshiping three gods, and are attempting to justify their pagan polytheism with some high-minded, abstract, theological theory. It is quite simple to them; three does not equal one and one does not equal three. No matter how you try to do the math this is an extremely easy equation. Three always equals three and never equals one. Hence, they believe these deceived Christians' worship three gods. However, this turns out to be a truly great and mysterious paradox, because the very Shema used to refute the Trinity, contains, hidden within it, the very concept of the Trinitarian doctrine!

Consider the meaning of the Hebrew words in the Shema. We will begin our word study with the word "*Eloheinu.*" This word is actually a combination of the words "*Elohim*" and "*nu,*" which is the same as "*God*" and "*our*". This word refers to God 2366 times in the Hebrew Bible, what the Christians call the Old Testament. However, another 216 times it refers to angels or false gods, when refuting the pagan worship of the surrounding nations, or condemning Israel's fall into those same idolatrous practices. Even some of the rabbis have written on this unique understanding. For example, the Treasury of Scriptural Knowledge quotes Simeon ben Joachi, "*Come and see the mystery of the word Elohim. There are three degrees, and each degree is by itself alone, and yet they are all one, and joined together in one, and are not divided from each other.*"

How can the same word, used so many times in the plural, also be the word of choice to refer to the singular, one true God? There is no getting around the fact that the word "*Elohim*" is the plural of "*Eloah.*" How then do we reconcile that our monotheistic faith, exemplified in the creed of the Shema, has within it the concept of a plurality? That is not the only hidden characteristic of this creed that should cause one to wonder. Consider the second to last word in this affirmation of Yahweh's revealed nature, "*achad*". This word describes the concept of a plural unity in the Hebrew language. For example, Numbers 13:23 uses this term to describe "***one cluster*** *of grapes*". Genesis 1:5 is the very first use of "*echad*" in the Word of God. "*So the evening and the morning were the **first [echad]** day.*" Again, note the singularity of "*the first day*", combined with the plurality of "*the evening and the*

134

morning." This is also used in Genesis 2:24 when the Lord says, "*Therefore, shall a man leave his father and his mother, and shall cleave to his wife and they shall be **one** flesh.*" This word is distinct from the Hebrew word "*yachad*", which is used to refer to a singular unity. Why does not the Shema use the word "*yachad*" instead of "*echad*" when describing Yahweh? The answer is remarkably easy, because it would be inaccurate. So now, consider what the Shema is literally stating. "Shema Yisrael [Hear Israel] Yehovah Eloheinu [our God(s)], Yehovah achad [a plural unity] Yehovah"; or "*Hear, O Israel, Jehovah God(s), Jehovah is one clustered, complex union Jehovah.*" Is it not also fascinating the Shema uses the word Jehovah **three times**?

Consider now the faint common thread connecting these seemingly disjointed passages. First, Messiah began with the Shema to establish the greatest commandment, which also contains within it the concept of the Trinity. Next, He quoted the messianic verse from Psalm 110, and asked the perplexing question, "*If then David calls him Lord, how is he his son?*" which points to a pre-existent Son of David, and implies His deity. As you can see, the common thread between these passages is the Meshiach is God. Taking precept upon precept and line upon line (Isa 28:10), let us contemplate other passages within the Tenack that also point to Messiah's deity. Consider, for example, Isaiah's testimony of the promised Deliverer of Israel.

> *Behold, God **is my salvation**; I will trust and not be afraid for the LORD JEHOVAH is my strength and my song; He also has become **my salvation**. And with joy you shall draw water out of the wells of **salvation**. And in that day you shall say, Praise Jehovah! **Call on HIS NAME**; declare His doings among the people, **make mention that HIS NAME is exalted**. (Isa 12:2-4 MKJV)*

In the above verse, the Lord promises salvation if we will call upon His Name. Hidden from our view, as English readers, is the Hebrew word for salvation, "*Yeshua.*" Is not it remarkable that Jesus' literal name, "*Yeshua*" in the Hebrew, is in the exact same verses the Almighty promises to be their savior? Now take the underlined words in the above verse, and replace them with "*Yeshua*", and you will have a particularly clear picture of the mysterious Incarnation of God. "*Behold, **God Yeshua**; I will trust and not be afraid for **the LORD JEHOVAH** is my strength and my song; **He also has become Yeshua**. And with joy you shall draw water out of the wells of **Yeshua**. And in that day you shall say, **Praise Jehovah! CALL ON HIS NAME**.*"

Behold, our Immanuel, our Savior, call upon His name, Yeshua is His Name!

However, Matthew also makes this very clear when he quotes Isaiah 7:14 stating,

> *"Behold, the virgin shall conceive and bear a son, and they shall call his name Immanuel" (which means, **God with us**). (Mat 1:23 ESV)*

Moreover, Isaiah also boldly affirms later in his writings,

> *For to us **a child is born**, to us **a son is given**; and the government shall be upon his shoulder, and his name shall be called Wonderful Counselor, **<u>Mighty God</u>**, **<u>Everlasting Father</u>**, Prince of Peace. (Isa 9:6 ESV)*

However, this is where the scribe, who began to receive the words of salvation, must withdraw, because these words do not line up with his taught, preconceived notions of Meshiach, although the scriptures consistently affirm these concepts. This is what happens to well meaning people of the book when they hold the scholars of the Holy Writ in higher esteem than the book itself. These teachings gone astray are precisely what Jesus battled in His day, and it is still somewhat of a problem for many believers in our own time.

> *And no one was able to answer him a word, nor from that day did anyone dare to ask him any more questions. (Mat 22:46 ESV)*

Notice there was no response. Many may not have been able to explain why *"David calls him Lord"*; however, for so many others, their prophetic dogmas blinded them to any possible interpretations of Messiah as God in the Flesh. Consequently, silent dissent was preferable over an open concession that the scriptures affirm Meshiach's preexistence and His divinity; therefore, if Yeshua were Meshiach, then His proclamation, *"Before Abraham was, I AM"* (Joh 8:58), was quite correct.

This chapter began when the Pharisees asked the King of Kings *"Who gave You the authority to do these things?"* (Luk 20:2) Amazingly, at the end of the day, after wrestling with God, they received their answer, although they did not know it. The authority is God. Not only the Father, who is in Heaven, not only the Holy Spirit, who was producing the miracles, but the King of Kings, and the Lord of Lords, who has now come into His temple. Yeshua is His Name! What an absurd question. It would be as if I asked the President, *"Who gave you the authority to be in the White House and run the country."* People would wonder how I became this insane; yet we do this all the time. Most believers, especially members of the luxurious Laodicean church of the West, continue defiantly to ask their Creator, *"Who gave you the authority?"* When the Spirit of Christ compels our conscience to let go of a sin we love, we ask Him who died for our sins, *"Who gave you the authority?"* When we do not spend time in the Word in the early morning or evening hours, and the Holy Spirit convicts us, we respond to Him who first loved us, *"Who gave you the authority?"* When we allow the lust of the eyes to fill our soul with all sorts of materialistic desires, we ask Him who made us Sons of the Most High God, *"Who gave you the authority?"* When we become sick and go directly to the doctor without uttering a single word of prayer, we confirm our belief that He no longer has the power to heal us, and we say to Him who has healed us from all of our diseases, *"Who gave you the authority?"* When we satisfy the flesh by indulging our thirst for revenge, and lie to our conscience calling it merely a defense of unrighteous persecution; we say to Him who taught us to turn the other cheek, *"Who gave you the authority?"* When we gaze too long at another person's beauty and allow desire to fill our hearts, we say to the Him who has made us a Holy nation, *"Who gave you the authority?"* When the Lord of the Sabbath says, put down the phone, or computer, or brief case, spend time with your spouse and children in the Lord, and we brush Him aside, we say to Him who never turned anyone away, *"Who gave you the authority?"* When we place loved ones, who were a gift from the Creator of All Things, above and beyond Him that is Eternal, and make them idols in our hearts, we tell Him who loved us more than His own life and freely gave us all things, including those loved ones, *"Who gave you the authority?"*

The list goes on and on and on, throughout our days, throughout our lives. Consistently, we affirm to all who will listen, Jesus is the King of Kings and the Lord of Lords, firmly seated on the throne in the temple of our hearts; yet witnessing against this testimony are convicting contradictions of our daily walk. We say one thing and allow another. We are able to leave a sermon, taught to turn the other cheek, and immediately lambaste another commuter on the way home. We can be taught to have faith in God and yet in the time of need not go to Him in prayer. Sadly, we do not even see that we are walking contradictions, consistently affirming one thing and living another. We say what we believe, and we believe what we say is good and true, yet we live our true convictions.

Allow me to share an example the Lord provided to reveal my own hypocrisy. A few days ago, my beautiful eight-year-old son had a runny nose. At bedtime, he asked me if I could give him some medicine to relieve his constant dripping, so I gave him an antihistamine. Lying in bed, he began to whimper that his nose was still dripping. I was very tired. In addition, I had to wake up extremely early in the morning to fly to Chicago, so I told him to calm down, be quiet and go to sleep. He continued to sob, so my wife decided to sit with him while they watched TV, so he may calm down and go to sleep. Immediately, the Spirit of Christ began to convict me of several things. First, I am more concerned about my sleep than my son's welfare. Second, why did I give him the medicine without a word of prayer? Do I genuinely believe what I am teaching in The Parable of the Cross? Do I honestly have faith in God? By the Spirit is conviction, I brought my poor despondent eight-year-old son upstairs, and laid him down in bed with me. I told him that he was going to be fine, and that I was going to pray for him. I rubbed his hair gently and softly prayed the Word of God over him. Within a few minutes, his nose stopped running; his breath became calm and he drifted into a deep sleep. The peace that surpasses all understanding quickly overshadowed his hour-long torment.

He is a child, but a mountain of faith, specifically because he is a child. If I could only become as childlike in my faith as my children, then I also would have that same mountain of faith. It is a remarkably simple equation for them. I am a good father. At least my family believes I am. I would never withhold any good thing from them. For the most part, I do what I promise. God is a good father. God will not withhold any good thing from us. God will do what He has promised. Why do we, adults, always attempt to hide our unbelief behind complex doctrines of faith? Can we just be honest with the Lord and say, "*I believe, help my unbelief!*" Without this simple statement of faith, we become through our own vain intellect like the Pharisees and the Sadducees, who denied their Meshiach, all while holding firmly to their doctrines of the Meshiach, and intently looking for the Meshiach. However, it was precisely the doctrines developed from scriptures, which blinded them from seeing the illustrious light of the King of Glory, standing right before their eyes!

I listened as my child began to breathe a bit easier after he had fallen asleep, although he remained somewhat congested throughout the night. This was his little cross to bear. I showed my son you should go to the Lord in prayer always. Our God may allow some discomfort, but He promised to take us through the valley of the shadow of death. He promised to take our burden if we would only take the light load of His yoke. He also promised all things are possible to him who believes. These assurances are not just some high-minded, lofty ideals, but rather, they are life-changing words from the Word of Truth.

At the beginning of this chapter, He Who Heals All of our Diseases, healed *"the blind and the lame [who] came to him in the temple."* (Mat 21:14) Meshiach validated His identity and thereby His authority by fulfilling all of these ancient prophesies. (Luk 7:22-23) All of this carries significant meaning in The Parable of the Cross. We also were blind when the Resurrection and the Life first called us out of the dark cave of our sin and death, seduced by the false reality of the images projected on the wall. We have now walked into the Light of the World, yet we still do not see things as they truly are, for who can walk into the light after living in extreme darkness and not be blinded by the light. We are like the blind man whom Jesus healed who said, *"I see men, but they look like trees, walking."* (Mar 8:24) To which the Captain of our Salvation, who has entered the temple of our heart and driven out the moneychangers, now continues to open our eyes to the truth of His Word. We were the lame who were not able to walk in the paths of righteousness without the healing touch of our Lord and Savior. We were the lepers whose souls were so defiled with sin that we were nothing more than an unclean thing, whose righteousness was as filthy rags. We were the deaf whose consciences were so seared that we were not able to hear the still, small voice of the Word of God over the deafening shouts of our flesh.

Nevertheless, He continues to sit in our temple and teach us His ways. Since His ways are higher than our ways, we acknowledge that we do not always understand His ways. At first, we must live uncomfortably with circumstances that appear to be extreme contradictions. For example, Yeshua was fully man, and yet He was fully God. In addition, God exists as the Father, the Holy Spirit and the Son for all of eternity, and yet this compound union of three is somehow one. As well, we must have faith in God's astonishing promises that at times completely contradict our intellectual understandings of this cause and effect world. We were the deaf, dumb, blind, lame, leprous, dead

Pharisees whose terrible condition required that God come to this earth and die as a righteous man for our sin. How wonderful it is that we have put our confidence, not in a man, but in God Almighty Himself!

In the stories discussed in this chapter, almost every person at some juncture was wrong. Obviously, the Sadducees, the Herodians, the different sects of the Pharisees and the scribes were wrong, but, in addition, even the greatest man ever born of a woman, John the Baptist, began to get it wrong. Only one group was entirely correct in this whole tale, the children.

> *Yes, have you never read, "Out of the mouth of babes and sucklings You have perfected praise?"(Mat 21:16 MKJV)*

O' that we would pick up the cross the Lord presents to us today. O' that we would allow the intellectual, elitist pride of our mind to die and allow the Lord to raise us as babes in Christ, whose praise is becoming perfected; so *"that He who has begun a good work in you will perform it until the day of Jesus Christ."* (Php 1:6)

chapter nine

JUDGMENT IN THE TEMPLE

Who does not love meek, mild-mannered Clark Kent? We all love him. Even the villainous Lex Luthor loves Clark Kent's gentle, docile nature. However, he despises Superman and seeks his ultimate destruction. Since we are the spectators of the story, we know the inside secret, that the two natures are really one in the same person. We know Superman's power and strength, is often veiled behind the character of an extremely shy, reserved, humble, daily-reporter. We know the real Clark Kent, whom Lois Lane believes is a dreadfully weak and timid soul, is actually the strongest, bravest man on the entire planet; able to leap tall buildings in a single bound. Nevertheless, she has great admiration for his alter ego, Superman. Her eyes light up and her heart melts every time he saves her from the calamity of a burning building at the precise moment it is about to collapse. She loves Superman as her protector but cares for Clark Kent as his protector. Lex Luthor, on the other hand, despises Superman precisely because of his strength and his courage, which our super hero uses to foil his plans of world domination. Alternatively, Lex Luthor has no issues what so ever with Clark Kent. He probably wishes all men were as he is; mild-mannered, avoiding controversies at all cost. Both have partially accurate pictures of the whole, and yet they are entirely inaccurate, because they are only one correct part made into the whole. We, the audience, on the other hand, have the full picture. How we wish Clark would tell Lois his true identity, so they could live happily ever after.

Such are the paradoxes in storytelling, and such are the complexities of life. There seems to be something in our human nature that desires to simplify and compartmentalize people into various categories or types. This is not necessarily a bad thing, in fact, if used correctly it can be quite good. It allows us to communicate information quickly to each other, and in ourselves, to develop complex ideas and opinions without having to rebuild the basic foundations of the argument. Alan Bloom, the author of "*Closing of the American Mind,*" speaks to this subject and argues that the belief that discrimination is immoral is incorrect. He posits that discrimination is actually a quite natural, indispensable function of the human mind, when used within its proper context and outside of the connotative meanings that now shade the use of this word. To be discriminate simply means to note or observe a difference, to distinguish accurately. In spite of that, in our modern vernacular, it has come to mean the exact opposite, which is to distinguish inaccurately. However, to distinguish inaccurately is not to be discriminate, but indiscriminate and prejudice, which is wrong. Therefore, to be discriminate is to take a neutral observation of the world and note the differences. We take people, places, situations and things, and we categorize this data into chunks of information, so we can better comprehend our environment. Sometimes after getting to know someone that we have quite naturally placed into one of these compartments, we discover the person is nothing like what we imagined; as a result, we then should change our preformed opinion. If we continue to hold to that incorrect initial assessment, despite having evidence to the contrary, and especially if that assessment was negative, then we are now acting upon our prejudgment of that person, which is prejudice and is wrong.

The Hindu religion asserts that no religion can perfectly know God, but rather, all religions see some form of God. They tell a parable that equates all religions to blindfolded people who are holding one part of an elephant. The believers then take the one portion as the whole. For example, to the person holding the tail, God is a snake; to the one holding the leg, God is a tree and to those touching the body, God is a wall. Christians agree with the Hindus that people and religions are blind and usually form very inaccurate pictures of God. However, we disagree that we cannot know God. In the Christian worldview, the saints in the Old Testament were like the blind men who had the opportunity to touch many different parts of the elephant. Because of this, they were the leading authorities in their time of God's revealed nature. Now, the people of the New Testament have had their blindfolds removed and have an opportunity to view most of the elephant. As I expressed earlier, it is utterly impossible for finite, temporal, physical humans living within the dimensions of our universe ever to understand the infinite, eternal, boundless spirit of an Omniscient, Omnipotent God fully. Nevertheless, just because we cannot completely and thoroughly comprehend our Maker does not mean that we should not attempt to understand what we are able to. Since God has chosen to reveal Himself through His creation (Romans

chapter 1) and through His Word, then we can infer that it is important
to Him that we learn of Him. If the basis of getting to know a person
was determined by having to know that person completely, then we
would never get to know anyone, would we? For, do we ever actually
thoroughly know anyone? So why then would we hold getting to know
the eternal spirit of God to the impossible standard that we do not hold
to physical beings? Which is easier to know? Is not the physical human
being easier to know? Do we not choose to learn about loved ones and
friends, despite knowing we can never know them perfectly? Finally, I
would submit to you that getting to know your Creator is the most
valuable thing that you can do and spending time doing this will lead
you to your greatest fulfillment and happiness. Our lives are much like
Pinocchio's, who went off into the world in order to find himself and
to become a real boy; but after many mishaps in his arduous
adventures he comes to himself and realizes that his true happiness was
with his maker and his father, Geppetto, so he decides to return home.
What a tender reunion when Pinocchio and Geppetto are reunited!
Then, Pinocchio's joy is full, and likewise, Geppetto is overjoyed,
since he has found the lost son he has been diligently searching for. At
that time, Pinocchio realizes his true purpose in life and becomes a real
boy!

As any Christian can see, this story has been completely stolen from
the pages of the Bible; for this is our story. In the story of Pinocchio,
we have the creation, the fall, the wandering condition of man, the
redemption and the reincarnation all wrapped up into one beautiful
story. Thus, Jesus tells us in the parable of the Prodigal Son; who took
the inheritance, wasted it in riotous living, and then became extremely
poor, that he came to himself

> *And he arose and came to his father. But when he was still a great
> way off, his father saw him **and had compassion, and ran and fell
> on his neck and kissed him**. And the son said to him, Father, I
> have sinned against Heaven and before you, and am no more
> worthy to be called your son. But the father said to his servants,
> Bring the best robe and put it on him. And put a ring on his hand
> and shoes on his feet. And bring the fattened calf here and kill it.
> And let us eat and be merry, **for this my son was dead and is alive
> again, he was lost and is found.** And they began to be merry. (Luk
> 15:20-24 MKJV)*

Nevertheless, how can we return to a father whom we cannot truly know? Besides, what is the way? Thankfully, Jesus has answered both of those questions for us. First, He affirms, *"He who has seen Me has seen the Father"* (Joh 14:9) Moreover, He also declares, He is *"the Way, the Truth, and the Life"* and that *"no one comes to the Father but by Me."* (Joh 14:6)

According to the bible, to *know* a spouse is the most intimate expression of love. (Gen 4:1, Mat 1:25). This is rightfully so, since whom do you truly know better than your spouse? Additionally, is it not painful when a small part of your character, or an isolated act, is equated to the whole of your personality? For example, consider a man whose nature is usually extremely patient and quiet. On an exceptionally challenging day, after completely reaching the limits of his patience, he explodes in a fit of rage in a public place. Most people, who do not know this placid soul, would conclude he is easily excited. It unlikely this man would know about their opinion or give it much thought. His wife, on the other hand, would surmise that he must have had an extraordinarily dreadful day, since she knows he never behaves in this manner. However, if his wife began to treat him as a hotheaded, insolent person, her husband would become extremely hurt, reflecting, *"That is not who I am. Apparently, she does not actually know me."*

Most Christians also do not actually know Jesus. They have seen one part of His dynamic, passionate personality and applied it to the whole. He is the image of the invisible God. Most of us have taken what we have learned and oversimplified His complex nature. It is no wonder that the lost cannot see God's loving-kindness in the Old Testament and His judgment in the New Testament. Most of them have never read the Bible. Moreover, for many the only knowledge of God they have acquired has been learned from people who are antagonistic to the faith. However, since most Christians today have never read the Bible, they also have fallen into this trap; the main difference being, they believe in the revelation of God as presented to them by their denomination. So many Catholics believe Jesus is a God of judgment, who needs to be approached with care and reverence. Because of this, they ask for intercession from the dead saints and His mother Mary to go before the Intercessor of God. They have overemphasized the angry Jesus, who throws the wicked city *"into the great winepress of the wrath of God"* (Rev 14:19), saying, *"I trod them in my anger and trampled them in my wrath; their lifeblood spattered on my garments, and stained all my apparel"* (Isa 63:3), whose *"blood flowed from the winepress, as high as a horse's bridle."* (Rev 14:20) These Catholics have touched the fury of the elephant's tusks. Although, I agree we should approach God with reverence and respect, for *"It is a fearful thing to fall into the hands of the living God"* (Heb 10:31), I also agree that we can draw near to the throne of God, as a son, saying, "Abba, Father!" (Rom 8:15) On the other hand, some Protestants have become so comfortable with the loving-kindness of God and the grace of salvation, that *"There is no fear of God before their eyes"* (Rom 3:18), which Paul uses to describe people who are lost. They have ridden in the carriage of the tame, domesticated elephant and have not appreciated his power and strength.

To the Catholics who have built layer upon layer of ceremonies, relics, intercessions, liturgical law and such, in order to have their prayers heard by the dreadful and sovereign God, I say, *"Cast all your cares upon **HIM** for he cares for you."* (1Pe 5:7) To the Protestants who say Jesus is their homeboy and treat sin so lightly, I say,

> *Do not be deceived: God is not mocked, for whatever one sows, that will he also reap. For the one who sows to his own flesh will from the flesh reap corruption, but the one who sows to the Spirit will from the Spirit reap eternal life. (Gal 6:7-8)*

Then the real revelation of God is not somewhere between these two extremes, but rather at both extremes. This is not so much a paradox, or a contradiction, but rather a comprehension of the complex nature of God. Should not this be the case? After all, how much more complex is God than our human loved ones, whom we agree are especially complex personalities?

G. K. Chesterton, in his book *"Orthodoxy"*, paints an extraordinary portrait of the complex, seemingly contradictory, nature of our Sovereign King and Loving Savior, in all His contrasting, beautiful colors of glory and grace, as revealed in the Gospels.

> *There I found an account, not in the least of a person with his hair parted in the middle or his hands clasped in appeal, but of an extraordinary being with lips of thunder and acts of lurid decision, flinging down tables, casting out devils, passing with the wild secrecy of the wind from mountain isolation to a sort of dreadful demagogy; a being who often acted like an angry god - and always like a god. Christ had even a literary style of his own, not to be found, I think, elsewhere; it consists of an almost furious use of the*

a fortiori. His "how much more" is piled one upon another like castle upon castle in the clouds. The diction used about Christ has been, and perhaps wisely, sweet and submissive. But the diction used by Christ is quite curiously gigantesque; it is full of camels leaping through needles and mountains hurled into the sea. Morally it is equally terrific; he called himself a sword of slaughter, and told men to buy swords if they sold their coats for them. That he used other even wilder words on the side of non-resistance greatly increases the mystery; but it also, if anything, rather increases the violence. We cannot even explain it by calling such a being insane; for insanity is usually along one consistent channel. The maniac is generally a monomaniac. Here we must remember the difficult definition of Christianity already given; Christianity is a superhuman paradox whereby two opposite passions may blaze beside each other. The one explanation of the Gospel language that does explain it, is that it is the survey of one who from some supernatural height beholds some more startling synthesis.

The Catholic, who understands and appreciates the fury of God's wrath against sin, will recognize the anger of Jesus we are about to discuss. However, the Protestant, who has allowed the world or his sect to define Messiah's character as one who overlooks sin, may find our Loving Savior's vehement response to the legalistic, self-righteous Pharisees a little stunning. Nevertheless, it is as essential to see the red fury of our Sovereign's character, as it is to see His peaceful nature and apply both to the portrait. Let us appreciate the complex and vast color array of our God's nature, and draw near to our Redeemer. For He is not only a God with *"lips of thunder and acts of lurid decision, flinging down tables, casting out devils,"* but He is also the God who speaks to us in a *"still, small voice"* (1Ki 19:12), entreating,

> *Come to Me all you who labor and are heavy laden, and I will give you rest. **Take My yoke on you and <u>learn of Me</u>**, for **I am meek and lowly in heart**, and you shall find rest to your souls. For **My yoke is easy, and My burden is light**. (Mat 11:28-30 MKJV)*

Therefore, the Catholic, who sees only the judgment of God in Christ, and the Protestant, who sees only the grace of God in Christ, are both incorrect when they have over emphasized one aspect of His complex nature, taking the singularity and applying it only to the whole. Despite this, both are correct in their singular assessments, so that this is not a contradiction at all but a complexity; and yet, t is as normal as any person's intricate personality whom you may know. Moreover, we should expect nothing less; after all, God did create us in His image. (Gen 1:27) Thus, in Christ Jesus, the King, the Righteous Judge, and the Peace of our Salvation, we acknowledge, "*Mercy and truth have met together; righteousness and peace have kissed each other.*" (Psa 85:10)

Recall when Jesus arrived at His temple, He immediately cleared out the moneychangers, threw down their tables, and did not permit them to take anything with them. In this act, He demonstrated the cleansing, sanctifying power of the "*water of the Word*" (Eph 5:26), so that out of our "*heart will flow rivers of living water.*" (Joh 7:38) This in turn was the fulfillment of another parable God hid in the Old Testament when "*Moses lifted up his hand and struck the rock with his staff twice, and water came out abundantly, and the congregation [the church in the wilderness] drank.*" (Num 20:11) For the Lord has promised in the Day of Christ, at our new birth:

> *And I will give you **a new heart**, and I will put a new spirit within you. And I will **take away the <u>stony</u> heart** out of your flesh, and I will give you a heart of flesh. And I will put My Spirit within you and cause you to walk in My statutes, and you shall keep My judgments and do them. (Eze 36:26-27 MKJV)*

Subsequently, the One Who Teaches Us All Things (Joh 4:25), began to fulfill His office as our instructor with the same spiritual authority of Moses, whose books became the first five books of the Bible, and are called by the Jewish people the Books of the Law. Then the intellectual elite of His day, the Sadducees, the Herodians, both sects of the Pharisees, and the scribes (the lawyers) all began to examine the Lamb of God. Despite their exceptional intellectual prowess, they were left dumbfounded by His answers and His final question. Thus, He fulfilled two prophetic types. The first of which was when God asked Job unanswerable questions, causing Job to respond, "*Behold, I am vile! What shall I answer You? I will lay my hand on my mouth.*" (Job 40:4) Secondly, He was the Passover Lamb of God found "*without blemish and without spot*" (1Pe 1:19) who had begun to be led "*as a lamb to the slaughter.*" (Isa 53:7)

After demonstrating His Kingship, His Sanctifying Power, and His Spiritual Authority, He was found to be an acceptable, blameless sacrifice for the sins of the world, fully examined, and worthy to be the unblemished Lamb of God. He now moved into His office as Judge of the World and openly proclaimed eight woes against the scribes and the Pharisees.

He begins by publicly exposing their sins for all people to see, fulfilling His earlier forewarning while speaking to His disciples:

> *Beware of the leaven of the Pharisees, which is hypocrisy.* **Nothing is covered up that will not be revealed, or hidden that will not be known.** *Therefore, whatever you have said in the dark shall be heard in the light, and what you have whispered in private rooms shall be proclaimed on the housetops. (Luk 12:1-3 ESV)*

Who are the Pharisees today? Are they Catholics that observe ritualistic rites of worship without a changed heart? Are they Protestants that legalistically hold various holiness doctrines? Maybe both groups are Pharisees, maybe they are not, but for our purposes, we need to recognize that you and I were Pharisees when Christ called us to come forth from the grave of sin and death, and we are still somewhat Pharisaical even after His Holiness has cleansed the temple. Our sanctification walk precisely parallels Jesus' walk after His triumphal entry and just before His crucifixion. He has pronounced these woes against us! Nevertheless, I hope that He is pronouncing these woes against the fleshly Pharisee, whom we no longer acknowledge as our kingly and priestly authority. The Pharisees greatest error was that they focused so intently on the outward, letter-of-the-law observance that they completely forgot what these rites were intended to accomplish, namely, the inward change of the heart, brought about by the spirit of the law. It is for this reason, that the Lord of Glory instructs, "*God is spirit, and those who worship him* **must worship in spirit and truth**." (Joh 4:24) In addition, Paul informs us "*circumcision is of the heart; in spirit and not in letter.*" (Rom 2:29) Despite these admonitions, old habits die-hard, and these subtle, legalistic, ritualistic traps consistently ensnare us; which means that even after Jesus comes to our temple there remains some Pharisaical imprint in our hearts and minds. It is the Spirit of Christ, which then begins to convict us of these transgressions. Fortunately, our gracious God does not choose to reveal all of our wrongdoings to the world, but be forewarned, abiding in those sins, while being convicted by the Holy Spirit, will eventually lead to openly exposing your nakedness to the world, as Adam was exposed in the Garden of Eden. We observe this so often today when the Lord publicly exposes one of His servant's sin in some breaking newscast. To which, the world's natural reaction is that religion is full of hypocrites While this is actually true due to our human condition, the inferred from the inverse of this logic is the presumption that the nonreligious are not hypocrites, which is just as false. Let us be candid, we are all hypocrites at some level. Thankfully, the Lord loves us, so He covers over a multitude of our sins (1Pe 4:8); however, *"The Lord is not slow to fulfill his promise as some count slowness, but is patient toward you, not wishing that any should perish, but that all should reach repentance."* (2Pe 3:9) Therefore, be forewarned; stop sinning, or the One Who Sees through the Darkness as the Light of Day, admonishes, *"be sure your sin will find you out."* (Num 32:23)

Our humble King was extremely patient with the scribes and Pharisees throughout His ministry, but it is now judgment day; hence, the hour has come for the Light of the World to reveal the transgressions covered deep within their hearts, just as He promised. He begins the fiercely pernicious discourse by defining the concept of a hypocrite, although he does not express it directly. However, also take notice, in the following passages, that Messiah does not associate the true doctrines of God with the false face of the pretenders, which is the misconception of many who ascribe the duplicity of the individual to the whole of that ideological school. Although a natural reaction, it is actually an extremely irrational response, also known in logic as a *"Hasty Generalization"* fallacy. If a person does not adhere to the doctrines of a belief system, it is nonsensical to identify this pretentious, non-follower with the belief system and call it wrong, or to paint the true follows with the same broad brush of hypocrisy. In short, the counterfeiters may be false, but the ideology can still be true and worthwhile. To this assessment, Jesus also agrees, asserting,

> *The scribes and the Pharisees sit on Moses' seat,* **so practice and observe <u>whatever they tell you</u>--<u>but not what they do</u>**. *For they preach, but do not practice. (Mat 23:2-3 ESV)*

This same duplicitous state of many self-proclaiming believers today has provoked many would-be-followers to forgo the Christian life. Although, every religion since the beginning of time has exhibited comparable levels of hypocrisy, which we should expect, since the Lord's horrific sacrifice would not have been necessary if we were all perfectly loyal and trustworthy subjects. Therefore, putting on a self-righteous, religious false-face is not the exclusive property of the casual, modern-day Christian, but it is actually a human dilemma that stretches across all times and all religions, as noted, for example, in the scriptures when Paul admonishes even Jewish believers of his generation.

> *You who boast in the law dishonor God by breaking the law. For, as it is written, "The name of God is blasphemed among the Gentiles because of you." (Rom 2:23-24 ESV)*

Nevertheless, the magnitude of this hypocrisy is not solely the badge of honor of all religions of all centuries, but rather, all people, including secular people, throughout all ages, may also stake a claim to the prize. How many nonbelievers would be willing to expose openly their hidden secrets to the world? For example, consider a dynamic, freethinking politician whose nakedness was recently quite literally exposed. In front of the cameras, this politician became the leading voice of the Democratic Party's liberal wing, fighting for social justice for the downtrodden against the cruel, oppressive right wing ideology, owned and financed by greedy capitalists. He was a rude, obnoxious, disagreeable sort; and yet, even if you objected to his approach, and even his political philosophy, you did have to admire his candid courage, which, in turn, led you to believe that at least he was genuine. As the Lord promised, his sin found him out. For after he walked out of the spotlight of his public image in front of the cameras, he quite literally exposed the nakedness of his secret life behind the cameras, betraying his wife, the integrity of his office and his honor by sexting women all over the country, sending grotesque images of his private parts. Hypocrisy, therefore, is not a religious problem, but rather, inherent proof of the degenerative human condition. It is a faithful saying that the only thing that does not change is that everything changes; however, this is not entirely correct, since the one thing that has not changed throughout history is man's heart; it is still prideful, stubborn and full of duplicitous pretense. How ironic, and hypocritical that we are all so willing to call each other hypocrites, when we all are hypocrites. The only thing to debate is; what is the magnitude of our hypocrisy?

How great was this burden? The lawyers of the law, known as the scribes, and the Pharisees created so many laws that it was virtually impossible to know your right from your left without their help to guide you through the maze of their directives. For example, these religious rulers extracted 613 commandments out of the Tanakh, crafted over 1,500 restrictions about the Sabbath, and imposed over 6,000 oral traditions. Most of these laws fell upon the average citizen; however, many laws also pertained only to the Pharisees' converts. Therefore, Messiah, referring to heavy burdens, spoke directly to the multitude and to the religious converts. Imagine what a welcomed relief it was for the people to hear Yeshua reduce those twisted, tangled labyrinths of edicts down to two basic commandments, saying, *"You shall love the Lord your God with all your heart, and with all your soul, and with all your mind. This is the first and great commandment. And the second is like it, You shall love your neighbor as yourself. On these two commandments hang all the Law and the Prophets."* (Mat 22:37-40)

Meshiach came to His people at a time when Pharisaism and their oral traditions were at its peak. The historian Josephus asserts there were about 6,000 Pharisees in Israel at this time. The group's size may appear rather large, although when compared to the estimated population of 3 million, the Pharisees become an extremely small fraction of that population. Nevertheless, despite their minute number, they held enormous influence over the people.

The demands placed upon disciples of the various Pharisaical sects utterly eclipsed every aspect of their life. Learning and memorizing the Torah's laws and restrictions, and the whole Torah, became their sole job. This heavy burden took years to complete, preoccupying their entire day. To demonstrate how extreme this had become by the time God Incarnate proceeded to the earth to set the captives free, consider the six main sects outlined in the Talmud. First, there was the **Shoulder Pharisee**, who literally wore his good deeds upon his shoulder. He stopped after completing every meritorious achievement to write it down and pin it to his shoulder. He was a true observer of the law, but he was not doing it for the law's sake, but rather, to receive praises from men for his many badges' honor. The **Wait-a-little Pharisee** had the unique ability, at any moment, to produce an entirely reasonable excuse for putting off a good deed. The **Bleeding Pharisee's** primary focus was the sin of lust. In order to overcome this sin, he shut his eyes every time a woman came within his vision, many times injuring himself by bumping into walls, buildings and other obstructions. The **Humpbacked Pharisee** displayed his humility by walking hunched over, dragging his feet on the ground, and tripping over even the smallest obstacles. The **Ever-reckoning Pharisee** kept a sort of balance sheet of his righteous deeds, so he could hold God accountable for his exemplary works. The **Timid Pharisee** was so afraid of God's judgment that he barely spoke loud enough to hear. Finally, the **God-fearing Pharisee** loved the law of God and sought to follow His Word, yet he also wore the heavy yoke of 6,000 oral traditions, 1,500 Sabbatical laws and the enormous weight of the Pharisaical life as a whole.

Imagine the following scene of these various Pharisaical sects on their way to the synagogue. As a woman passes by the Bleeding Pharisee, he immediately closes his eyes and walks head first into a building, knocking him down to the ground. Lying on the ground, bleeding, half-dazed with his eyes still completely shut, fearing that the woman is still in view, he asks for help. Unfortunately, the Wait-a-little Pharisee just happens to be walking by, who tells the Bleeding Pharisee that he will return in a little while to help him after he takes care of some extremely urgent business. However, in the distance the Shoulder Pharisee sees a tremendous opportunity to do a good deed and add to his paper medals he wears so proudly upon his vesture. Straight away, he comes to the rescue of the Bleeding Pharisee and helps him off the ground, but then the Shoulder Pharisee realizes he does not have any paper to write down his meritorious feat. Fortunately, the Ever-reckoning Pharisee is coming to the synagogue, and so the Shoulder Pharisee borrows a piece of paper. Now as the Shoulder Pharisee is pinning this righteous act to his shoulder, and the Ever-reckoning Pharisee is adding his good deed to his ledger, the Bleeding Pharisee, still afraid to open his eyes, walks right back into the same building and falls to the ground again. The Shoulder Pharisee, recognizing the opportunity to gain another medal shouts, *"I will help him!"* However, the Ever-reckoning Pharisee, who also sees a favorable occasion to add to his accounting of good works, moves quickly to help the poor Bleeding Pharisee. Nevertheless, he was not quick enough because the Humpbacked Pharisee just happens to be walking by, and he then trips over the Bleeding Pharisee. So now, both the Ever-reckoning Pharisee and the Shoulder Pharisee are happy because they can both add to their good deeds. In fact, the Shoulder Pharisee now realizes that if he just follows the Bleeding Pharisee and the Humpbacked Pharisee to the synagogue, he will have pinned many more meritorious honors to his shoulder than the other Shoulder Pharisees at the synagogue that day. Meanwhile the God-fearing Pharisee, who has watched the entire episode, asks the Timid Pharisee if it is permissible to allow the Shoulder Pharisee to enter the temple, since he has gotten some of the Bleeding Pharisees blood on him, thus making himself unclean. To which the Timid Pharisee, sore afraid of being wrong, replies that he is not sure. However, his answer is of none affect, since the God-fearing Pharisee cannot hear him anyhow, considering the Timid Pharisee's soft, trembling voice is nothing more than a faint whisper.

To the 21st century Christian, this appears to be like an episode of the Keystone Cops on their way to the synagogue; however, we should be careful not to cast stones from glass houses, considering that we believers have plenty of examples of extremist fleshly attempts to control our own fleshly appetites. For instance, within a few hundred years after Messiah's resurrection, men began separating themselves from society and retreating into North Africa with the idea of mortifying the flesh through fasting, self-flagellation, sleep-deprivation and refusing to wash. Gordon Rattray Taylor's book, *"From Shame to Guilt: Sex in History"*, points out several cases of adherents of the Christian religion who were just as radically zealous for their religious rites as the Pharisees were for their traditions.

> *Ammonius tortured his body with hot irons until he was entirely covered with burns; Macarius went naked in a mosquito ridden swamp and let himself be stung until unrecognizable; St. Simeon ulcerated his flesh with an iron belt; Evagrius Ponticus spent a winter's night in a fountain so that his flesh froze.*

Nevertheless, Pharisees from all ages did correctly assess the importance of conquering our deeply embedded sin-nature, the essentiality of this arduous battle of self-conflict, and the extremity of the solution. Even so, they have only partially diagnosed the cause of the disease, and therefore, they have incorrectly prescribed the remedy. They have correctly comprehended the sinful nature of their passions as fleshly. However, their remedy was to use their own power of the flesh, a determinant will, in order to throw off the shackles of fleshly desires. This is like attempting to put out a fire by adding another flaming log to the fire.

How did they come to this resolution that these passions were sinful? In most cases, people came to these conclusions through the revelation of the spirit by the Holy Word of God. However, there have also been Stoics and other philosophers, through self-examination and meditations on the subject of morality, who have come to this revelation by the spirit of the conscience that God has placed in them. (Romans 1) Both groups had this spirit in common. In other words, they surmised from the spirit that the fleshly nature wars with the spirit nature. To be a decisive general in this war of the flesh, we need to assess the battlefield definitively. Therefore, what is the fleshly nature that continues to torment us? Christians use the word *"the flesh"* to refer to both the temporary tabernacle of our bodies and the lower nature of our mind or soul. Nevertheless, we would do well to comprehend the conflict in light of C. S. Lewis' suggestion that, *"You do not have a soul. You ARE a Soul. You have a body."* In other words, when I say that the flesh is at war with the spirit, I am actually saying that the fleshly mind, the soul, uses this fleshly body to war against the spirit. Now that we have clearly diagnosed the disease, we can see that the remedy of using the body and the power of the fleshly mind to win this war is ludicrous. For if this is a spiritual battle, which it is; how in the world can you ever expect to win this battle with the power of the flesh? Can YOU raise yourself from the dead Lazarus? Did YOU break the bonds of sin and death in order to stand in the glorious Light of Messiah? *"Are you so foolish? Having begun in the Spirit, do you now perfect yourself in the flesh?"* (Gal 3:3)

Nevertheless, in today's society we consider the sin nature of man to be a very light thing and this same attitude has crept into the church, having *"take[en] captive silly women [church sects and members] laden with sins, led away by divers lusts."* (2Ti 3:6) The Pharisees were correct in understanding the enormity of the problem, but in the remedy of the solution, they were incorrect and ineffectual. Consider Jerome's (347 - 420) vigorous attempts to attack the problem, and yet, despite his dedicated resolve, he was unable to conquer the enemy.

> *How often when I was living in the desert which affords to hermits a savage dwelling place, parched by a burning sun, did I fancy myself amid the pleasures of Rome. I sought solitude because I was filled with bitterness.... I, who from the fear of hell had consigned myself to that prison where scorpions and wild beasts were my companions, fancied myself among bevies of young girls. My face was pale and my frame chilled from fasting, yet my mind was burning with the cravings of desire, and the fires of lust flared up from my flesh that was as that of a corpse. I do not blush to avow my abject misery. (Taylor)*

Are you more dedicated than this pious man of God? If he cannot win this battle, what makes you think you can? When you finally acknowledge this conclusion, you have just received the first key to the door of victory. Then, and only then, do you come to a place where the Captain of your Salvation can win it for you. At that time, you finally come to the place where you are willing to set aside your pride, throw yourself at His feet and remain in His Light, so Lord of Armies can win the victory for you.

How ironic that Yeshua compares the Pharisees' hypocrisy people who load heavy burdens on a man. These Pharisees are not willing to even to lift their powerless finger to wag it, and tell the man where to put the load down, considering Messiah's stern rebuke after they accused Him of casting out demons *"by Beelzebul, the prince of demons."* (Luk 11:15)

> But if it is by the **finger of God** that I cast out demons, then the kingdom of God has come upon you. (Luk 11:20 ESV)

In the first instance, the Pharisees use their wagging finger to bind up *"heavy burdens ...grievous to be borne, and lay them on men's shoulders."* In the second instance, the Lord of Liberty uses the finger of God to loose a man from his heavy burden. In the first, the Pharisees, sitting in the seat of Moses, assert their power over men with their wagging finger. In the second, Messiah stands in His temple taking authority over the powers of darkness. The first is the useless, ineffectual wagging finger of the man of the flesh. The second is the All-Powerful finger of God.

This contrast is so typical of the religious traditions of men who bind up heavy burdens upon their followers compared to the liberty the Lord of Glory has won for men. It was Satan that held us in bondage before we were set free from our chains of sin and death. For *"where the Spirit of the Lord is, there is liberty."* (2Co 3:17) Although we are not to use that *"liberty for an occasion to the flesh"* (Gal 5:13), but rather, we are *"delivered from the bondage of corruption into the glorious liberty of the children of God."* (Rom 8:21) Therefore, our liberty is not liberty to choose what is wrong, but rather power to choose what is right, by the indwelled authority of the Holy Spirit.

This issue of law versus God's liberty was at the heart of almost every confrontation between Messiah and the Pharisees. For example, consider when Jesus and the disciples began to pick some grain to eat on the Sabbath. (Mar 2:23-8) The disparity also comes into view when Jesus healed the man with the withered hand on the Sabbath. (Mar 3:1-6) The difference is magnified when He healed the paralytic at the Pool of Bethesda on the Sabbath, as well (Joh 5:1-15), and again, when Jesus did not participate in the ritual washings of the hands before and during the meal. (Luk 11:37-54) I could go on and on about the traditions of men being at the heart of the battle with our Immanuel, who attempted to free men from the heavy yoke of those burdens to adhere to the light yoke of the Laws of God. It was not that Jesus was dishonoring the Sabbath but that scribes and Pharisees had added to the Sabbath a labyrinth of laws. It also was not that Jesus was eating His food with filthy hands but that they had exaggerated this requirement to the ridiculous level that they would wash their hands even between the different courses of the meal.

Despite all of those interactions with the Pharisees they never clearly understood what was at the heart of the battle, so one day Messiah decided to spell it out for them plainly.

> *And he said to them, "Well did Isaiah prophesy of you hypocrites, as it is written, 'This people honors me with their lips, but their heart is far from me; in vain do they worship me, **teaching as doctrines the commandments of men.' You leave the commandment of God and <u>hold to the tradition of men</u>.**" And he said to them, "You have a fine way of rejecting the commandment of God in order to establish your tradition! (Mar 7:6-9 ESV)*

In like manner, the Lord of Glory also says, *"No one can serve two masters, for either he will hate the one and love the other, or he will be devoted to the one and despise the other."* (Mat 6:24) This is at the heart of the battle between the pure religion of God, and the religious sects of men, adulterating our chaste religion. Many churches have done precisely this, having led their followers astray by many false traditions of men, taught as the doctrines of God. We should be particularly careful to examine these things within our churches and our lives since this was at the heart of most of the confrontations between the Pharisees and Jesus Messiah in the gospels.

Let us return to the vast irony between the wagging finger of the Pharisee and the finger of God. Remember Jesus told the Pharisees that if He was casting out demons *"by the finger of God"* then the kingdom of God had come upon them. (Luk 11:20) To our ears, it appears as if Messiah was only stating an obvious fact, if God is involved in this miracle then the Kingdom of God is also among us. While this was true, this statement also carried with it an ominous, dire warning, completely understood by the scripturally astute Pharisees. The Tanakh uses the phrase *"the finger of God"* several times, carrying with it the understanding of God's active involvement with mankind, exercising His authority. The first mention of this phrase in the Holy Writ is when the Pharaoh's magicians could not reproduce the judgment of turning dust into lice, thereby declaring that this miracle was unquestionably the *"finger of God"*. (Exo 8:19) Messiah's use of this term rebuking the Pharisees underscores a perfect paradox between the true powers of God and the false powers of religious traditions, and the false accusations of the Pharisees and the true accusations of Messiah. Moreover, the imagery is so clear that Moses stood as God's true representative in Pharaoh's court amid powerless, religious charlatans, just as Jesus stood in His temple wagging the powerful finger of God at the powerless, religious charlatans of His time. It is also ironic that they made false accusations that Messiah derived His power from the prince of the devils, considering that the prince of the devils is the author of all false religions and the controverter of God's true worship. A second and third instance of this expression in scriptures occurs when God writes the law on the tablets of stone. (Exo 31:18, Deu 9:10) The narrative in Deuteronomy chapter 9 is a perfect parallel use of the expression in our investigation of this subject, considering that Moses was sternly admonishing Israel for their idolatry, for having raised the rituals of men above the commandments of God.

What a remarkably precise, paradoxical rebuke we have in this scene painted by the scriptures! It is incredible that the judging, powerless, ineffectual, wagging fingers of the Pharisees were judging the Judge of the World, God Incarnate, teaching in His temple with all power and authority, who, in reality, was judging their words and deeds with the genuine finger of God. They considered themselves so pure and intelligent in their understandings of the scriptures. However, God Almighty chose to blind the proud and reveal the Kingdom of Heaven only to the babes and the poor in spirit, who recognize their utter inability to save themselves.

Now it is time for the Lord of All Power and Glory to push aside the wagging finger of the Pharisee and to brazening write His judgments on the stone tablets of their hearts with the authentic finger of God. Therefore, He commented on their pious pretenses, stating,

They do all their deeds to be seen by others. For they make their phylacteries broad and their fringes long, (Mat 23:5 ESV)

It is intriguing, and ironic, that the Judge of All the Earth begins His tirade of accusations against Pharisaical laws, traditions and hypocrisies by pointing to the large phylacteries they wore on their foreheads or arms. A phylactery was a cube-shaped leather box, divided into four compartments with separate scriptural passages written in each, and bound to the individual by a leather band. In the first section was Exodus 12:2-10, which gives instructions about the Passover Lamb of God. The second held Exodus 13:11-21, which tells of the death of the first born of the Egyptians and the redemption of Israel. Deuteronomy 6:4-9 was in the third, which is the Shema Yisrael, discussed earlier, and the fourth compartment contained Deuteronomy 11:18-21, which was the Almighty's admonition to remember the Words of Scripture and to teach them to their children. These phylacteries became popular Pharisaical traditions from extremely literal interpretations of passages like:

You shall bind them as a sign on your hand, and they shall be as frontlets between your eyes. (Deu 6:8 ESV)

Therefore, they literally bound the four passages from Torah to their left arm or forehead within this leather box called a phylactery. These phylacteries served at least four distinct purposes, of which, the first three the Pharisees would have clearly acknowledged. The first was to help in memorizing these particular passages. The second was to assist with their prayers. The third was to gain respect from the laity, and lastly, they believed these things could serve as amulets to drive away evil spirits.

All of this would have been more than enough to topple the pretentious house of cards the legalists built over the years. However, God Almighty's judgments are so exact that He is like a demolitionist who precisely placed all the charges in a proud, tall building. At once, with the thunder of his speech, and the All-Powerful Finger of God, the building implodes, piling steel and concrete one upon another into a tightly compact, ruinous heap. These perspectives, between God on High and man below, are so entirely different. To the Pharisees, their building was a sturdy, robust, concrete and steel structure, built upon the firm foundation of the Torah. To God Almighty, it was nothing more than a house of straw built upon the shifting foundation of man's traditions. Therefore, consider the ironic implications of the scriptures contained within the various compartments of these phylacteries. In the first compartment were the passages that spoke of the sacrificial offering of the Passover Lamb of God. It is fascinating that the fulfillment of this prophecy, the actual Lamb of God, was now standing before them only days away from becoming God's ultimate and final propitiatory sacrifice for the sins of the world; and yet their blind pride would not permit them to see it. It is fascinating that in the second compartment of their phylacteries were passages pertaining to God's judgment on the Egyptians' first-born and the redemption of Israel; considering that the Firstborn of Creation, the Only Begotten of the Father, He who Became Sin for Us, and judged of the Father, was standing right before their eyes. It is intriguing that the verses in the fourth compartment directed them to keep these words in their hearts and minds, or else, as the passages that both precede and follow these admonitions forewarn, they would follow other gods and fall into idolatry. How ironic that by using these phylacteries as amulets, they fell into the forbidden idolatrous practices the verses within the phylacteries forewarned. Finally, consider the third compartment, which contained the Shema Yisrael. It is striking that these were the precise verses the Lord of Glory and the scribe in Matthew chapter 22 found a place of agreement. It was when our Raboni stated that this was the greatest commandment that the scribe gave his seal of approval to the Lord of All, pronouncing, *"You are right, Teacher."* (Mar 12:32) From this place of agreement, the Lord then responded, *"You are not far from the kingdom of God."* (Mar 12:34) However, the Teacher did not desire to leave him in this almost-saved condition; therefore, He attempted to take the scribe to the next level. I would suggest that it is quite possible the scribe was wearing one of these exceedingly large phylacteries on his forehead at the particular time that the Lord began to quote the Shema. In fact, I am quite sure this scribe, and many of the other religious leaders, felt as if the Lord of Glory had honored THEM by selecting that passage tied to their foreheads. Imagine the religious leaders' sheer joy as they pointed to their own phylacteries, and said, *"The Teacher has said very well, I have that same passage written in the talisman I wear."*

How easily man's heart stumbles into the folly of idolatry. If there is any consistent testimony throughout the history of humanity, it is this; man has an idolatrous heart. Several years ago, I decided to make idol worship a topic for my small group Bible study. When I began to organize the material, I quickly realized that to examine the subject thoroughly I would have to include almost the entire Bible, because the idolatry in man's heart is the dilemma in virtually every chapter. This is our lost condition and our spiritual blindness, which I have spent this entire book attempting to magnify. When Adam chose to eat the fruit of the forbidden tree, it was because he had a greater love for himself, becoming like god, then for his relationship with God. Within a few chapters after the creation of the world, people fell into every inclination of evil. (Gen 6) Thus, God began again with only eight souls after the flood. In few more chapters, man once again fell deeply into rebellion and depravity, building the Tower of Babel. (Gen 11) Again, God called Abram out of a city of idols, which appears to have been the family business. (Gen 12) What begins badly gets worse and worse, so this becomes the recurring theme of all of the scriptures.

What exactly is idolatry? Consider the International Standard Bible Encyclopedia's (ISBE) definition:

> *Idolatry originally meant the **worship of idols**, or the **worship of false gods by means of idols**, but came to mean among the Old Testament Hebrews **any worship of false gods**, whether by images or otherwise, and finally the **worship of Yahweh through visible symbols** (Hos 8:5, Hos 8:6; Hos 10:5); and ultimately in the New Testament idolatry came to mean, not only the giving to any creature or human creation the honor or devotion which belonged to God alone, but the **giving to any human desire a precedence over God's will** (1Co 10:14; Gal 5:20; Col 3:5; 1Pe 4:3).*

Notice from the ISBE's definition that the Holy Writ provides an ever-escalating revelation of idolatry. Originally, it was worshipping physical idols or false gods by those material idols. Afterwards, it came to mean any false worship. Subsequently, it included worshipping the true God by means of physical images. Finally, as we became the people of the spirit and not of the letter, it has come to mean anything that takes precedence over God's Will. In some respects, this is like Maslow's Pyramid, progressing from the most based forms of idolatry to true spiritual worship; beginning with false physical worship, then to false worship as a whole, then to false physical worship of the one true God, and finally, descending into the deep caverns of the heart that oppose God's Will. This also parallels a person's development from nonbeliever, to believer, and ultimately to disciple. Notice also that as God descends deeper into the dark recesses of our heart, we ascend higher into the light of His Will. In this respect, the Lord is like a heart surgeon who must begin with the exterior and work His way into the core of our heart. The deeper He goes, replacing our depraved heart with His heart, the more our will becomes His Will.

In short, a definition of idolatry is anything that comes between you and God. Idols are like eclipses of the sun. They just get in the way of seeing and enjoying the beauty and glory of God. They cause darkness, even though you may appreciate them, and in some manner believe they help. They are like my young son who believes that a candy bar would make a wonderful breakfast. I try to explain to him that this is not excellent for his nutrition, but he does not understand. Therefore, I must give him a precept that candy bars are not good for breakfast, and he must accept by faith that I have his best interest at heart.

Anything can become an idol, even things prescribed with holy purposes by God Himself. Consider that godly king, Hezekiah, who was on a quest to destroy all the idols in his kingdom.

> *He removed the high places, and broke the pillars, and cut down the Asherah.* ***And he broke in pieces the bronze serpent which Moses had made****; for until those days the sons of Israel burned incense to it. And he called it Nehushtan. (2Ki 18:4 MKJV)*

What a marvelous relic this would have been to display in the church? That is, if you believe churches should display such relics. Who told Moses to make the bronze serpent in the first place? Was it not God? What did that bronze serpent represent? Did it not represent Jesus' substitutionary sacrifice becoming sin for us, and our redemption? However, what was godly at one time, and entirely holy within the Will of God and by His command, became a debased relic, a desecrated idol in the house of worship. Hezekiah calls it Nehushtan, which means *"a thing of brass."* In effect, he was saying, *"This is only a thing made of brass. It does not have any more spiritual significance than that!"*

A personal example of something that became an idol to me that most would not believe, considering its holiness, the Bible. That is correct, the Holy Word of God, enthusiastically endorsed as necessary sustenance for the soul for this entire book. Before I became a believer, I never believed the Holy Bible was actually the Word of God. Nevertheless, after much investigation, I soon discovered that the preponderance of evidence that the Bible was the Word of God was more compelling than the evidence against it. How then could something so pure, holy and blessed become an idol to me? I could not get enough of it. I read it day and night, many times sixteen to eighteen hours a day for almost a year. If this were the genuine Word of God, then I wanted to know every minute portion of it. I wanted the words engraved on my heart and in my mind. I even put it under my pillow and slept with it. After about nine months of incredible growth in the Lord, I felt as if God said, *"Enough, put down your Bible and just spend time with me in prayer and worship."* I did not want to do it. I wanted to continue to attain to knowledge of the Almighty. However, *"Knowledge puffs up, but love edifies."* (1Cor 8:1) Therefore, seeking knowledge had become my idol, so now the God of Love requested that I put the Bible down. The result was an extraordinarily blessed period of praise, worship and prayer.

We are all idol worshippers; even the most devout Christian of all the Christians is still an idol worshiper. My immense desire is to give a greater awareness of our own deeply depraved hearts and these exceedingly enormous beams in our own eyes that cause our spiritual blindness. Then, after having removed these beams, and looking clearly into the mirror, we should begin to see that the sanctifying work of Jesus has destroyed the works of the devil in this world and is able to break and shatter the idols in our hearts, no matter how powerful these hideous strongholds have become. Nevertheless, this does not happen overnight, but rather, it is a process.

I have a friend who once told me that having images to look at while in his devotions helps him to feel closer to God. He is at the level in the hierarchy of a man that worships Yahweh with physical symbols and images. He is like the child that wants a snickers bar for breakfast. It tastes good and provides immediate gratification and energy, but in the end, it is not good for his soul. When he began to legitimize this practice, you could hear the sorrowful tone in his voice betraying his testimony. The man has a true love for God. He is a seriously committed Christian, who knows very well that using images in his devotion, he is breaking God's second commandment. Nevertheless, as I said, I also am an idolater, as are you also. God is working on each of us in His timing. Consider, for example, the following conversation that took place after the man of God, Elisha, miraculously cleansed the leprosy of the Gentile idol-worshipper, Naaman.

Judgment in the Temple

Then Naaman said, "...please let there be given to your servant two mules' **load of earth**, *for from now on your servant will not offer burnt offering or sacrifice to any god but the LORD. In this matter may the LORD pardon your servant: when my master goes into the house of Rimmon to worship there, leaning on my arm, and I bow myself in the house of Rimmon, when I bow myself in the house of Rimmon, the LORD pardon your servant in this matter." He said to him, "**Go in peace**." (2Ki 5:17-19 ESV)*

This passage is full of idolatry. Moreover, it is shocking that the prophet of God affirms, "*Go in peace*" after Naaman expresses his plans for to bring the dirt of Israel to his home country for use in his worship Nevertheless, should we expect spiritual babies to rise and run marathons? No, therefore, let us allow God to have His perfect work. I am confident the Lord continued to work with Naaman in order to free him from the bondage of his idolatry. The missionary, Smith Wigglesworth, recounts an example of such a response in one his books. While on a ship, he brought a woman to salvation in Christ. The woman was a habitual drinker and gambler. Later that evening, she asked if it was all right for her still to gamble, to which he said, "*Gamble all you like*." After that, she asked if it was permissible for her to drink, to which he responded, "*Drink all you like*." Lastly, she asked if it was acceptable to smoke and to which he said, "*Smoke all you like*." The next day, after the Holy Spirit's conviction, she returned and told him that she did not feel right about continuing in these habits. She freely gave up all of these vices. Glory to God, that the Love of God is stronger than any vice or hideous idol!

Even the smallest item can become an idol. Smith Wigglesworth also recounts receiving a coffee mug as a gift while on a mission trip. The mug was one of the few things that offered him any solace during his considerable hardships in the jungle. Because of this, he came to have a genuine appreciation for the mug. However, he gave it away around the time he was about to return to civilization. When asked why he gave away the mug, he said that he began to love this mug, and he would never allow anything to come between him and his love for God.

Now consider the Pharisees, wearing phylacteries, while Jesus was teaching in the temple. Were not these people devoted to God? Did they not give up all sorts of worldly comforts to pursue God? Could they not have quoted the second commandment word for word? Did they not know, at least at some level in their hearts, they were breaking that commandment? Moreover, like my godly friend who feels close to God when using idols in his devotion, they felt close to God by having the words of scriptures strapped to their foreheads or their arms. However, instead of commending them for their pious appearance, God Incarnate pointed directly to their sin with the actual finger of God, plainly exposing their idolatry.

Once a person begins to diverge into these areas, he becomes Satan's prey for all kinds of other superstitious beliefs. As amazing as this may sound, these pious believers and most devoted men to their religion actually began to believe that God Himself wore huge phylacteries and studied His own scriptures for three hours a day. Talk about creating God in our own image! What blasphemy!

Additionally, Messiah reveals they made *"their fringes long,"* which they did because God instructed Moses to tell the people, *"make tassels on the corners of their garments throughout their generations, and to put a cord of blue on the tassel of each corner."* (Num 15:38) They tied the tassels into 613 knots to remind them of the 613 laws of Moses, of which 365 were the *"you shall not"* prohibitions and 248 were the *"you shall"* exhortations. It was God's intention that these tassels would hang in full view of the public to remind the believer to walk according to His Laws, which in the Hebrew literally means, *"walk."* Therefore, their careful observance of this requirement was not the heart of the issue. After all, it appears Jesus also wore tassels in keeping with this commandment (Mat 9:20), but as usual, the Pharisees took this to the extreme and enlarged their tassels much more than others, so they would be esteemed higher than others and honored for their holiness. As a result, they became inflamed with spiritual pride, self-affirmed in righteousness, acknowledging their own superiority, and because of this, they in turn twisted God's noble ordinances into another one of their shameful idolatrous acts.

Now imagine this mindset. You are a Pharisee. You always arrive at the temple wearing your phylactery, and because it is the Passover, you choose the robe with your longest tassels. At the temple, you find a young rabbi calling the religious leaders hypocrites, because of their large phylacteries and their long tassels. You are outraged! However, even more outrageous, is that you are sitting in the temple with the Only Begotten of the Father and despising Him because He was not wearing a phylactery and your tassels were so much larger than His.

These phylacteries had become so large they obstructed their view from seeing the Son of Glory, standing right before them. Moreover, their tassels had become so large that when they attempted to walk in righteousness, they tripped over their own sanctimonious pride. We are these Pharisees. How desperate is our fatal condition. How blinded we become by our own self-righteous efforts.

The love of things is not a learned behavior, but rather, it is quite natural. This conduct is apparent, even at a very early age. Consider children, who have a favorite blanket, or a favorite seat, or a favorite bottle. Does this not confirm the desire to have idols is at the very core of our human nature? When I was a child, I had a lucky penny. I loved that penny. I believed it brought me good luck. When I lost that penny, I became terribly disappointed. I remember spending time admiring that shiny penny, while the world went by without notice. Now contemplate for a moment, no matter how small the idol is that you adore, it can blind you from the largest object, even from God Himself. After all, the size of the idol itself does not determine a person's blindness, but rather, how close you carry it in your heart determines your blindness. For example, the moon, which is much smaller than the sun, can eclipse the sun because it is closer to the earth. Likewise, a tiny penny when held close to the eye could also blot out the vastness of the sun, or even the world; therefore, the closer the item is to the heart the more it can blot out, even the glory of God. Moreover, this is exactly what idols do, since all the good that occurs in our lives, we stupidly attribute to the idol, rather than giving the praise and glory to God. Do not believe that the coveted idol of your desire, the Holy Spirit is convicting you of is so small that it does not matter to God. If He is revealing that you need to remove this beam from your eye, so you can see clearly, then listen to Him who sits in your temple, and do not hold so tightly to your large phylactery and long tassels.

Originally, these were the commandments of God, but that perverter of all that is good and righteous, Satan, caused men to err by turning these ordinances into idols. How many of our churches, where the human sanctuaries of the Holy Ghost commune, are full of these same idols of worship, in order to satisfy the desire of man's fleshly heart at the expense of God's commandment, written by His finger in stone.

*You shall not make for yourself a carved image, **or any likeness of anything that is in heaven above**, or that is in the earth beneath, or that is in the water under the earth. **You shall not bow down to*** *__them__ or serve them, for I the LORD your God am a jealous God, visiting the iniquity of the fathers on the children to the third and the fourth generation of those who hate me. (Exo 20:4-5 ESV)*

God promises to visit this iniquity. Do you honestly believe in God? He is not just a God of blessing, but also a God of curses. I realize that most people do not want to consider this aspect of the Righteous Judge of Heaven, but it is certainly the case. *"If you do well, will you not be accepted?"* (Gen 4:7) If you do wrong, will He not chasten you? (Heb 12:6) The verse above is God's promise to carry out a curse against those who blatantly violate this law, even if performed in the church, just as the Pharisees practiced in their day, in God's temple, as the Son of Glory pointed out their sin. Therefore, the Supreme Judge says to us,

Behold, I set before you today a blessing and a curse: A blessing if you obey the commandments of Jehovah your God which I command you today, and a curse if you will not obey the commandments of Jehovah your God, but will turn aside out of the way which I command you today. (Deu 11:26-28 MKJV)

Considering this, I will do as Smith Wigglesworth, and say, *"Keep your worthless relics and religious images. Keep as many as you like."* Then allow the Holy Spirit to convict you of your idols. In the meantime, the Spirit of Truth is contending with me, to remove beams in my own eye. Although, it is like taking candy from a baby, is it not? We fight, scream, cry and hold tightly to the candy that we know is not good for us, and yet the Lord, having our best interest at heart, continues to plead with our stubborn, immature rationalizations. Nevertheless, we clasp so tightly you would think that our very lives actually depended upon them. Even so, in this, there is some truth; our lives do depend upon these idols, not on the idols themselves, but our reaction to them; not to grasp them tighter but to let them go.

Then Meshiach expounds upon the motivation behind so many of these outwardly pious-appearing acts, stating,

...they love the place of honor at feasts and the best seats in the synagogues and greetings in the marketplaces and being called rabbi by others. (Mat 23:6-7 ESV)

Notice, they were not doing this out of their love for God, which may have been their motivation at one time, but out of their love for themselves. However, the Lord says, *"I am Jehovah; that is My name; and My glory I will not give to another, nor My praise to graven images."* (Isa 42:8) Again, He says, *"It is better to trust in Jehovah than to trust in man."* (Psa 118:8) Nevertheless, this was precisely the error that the Pharisees had fallen into, and because they had become the unfaithful shepherds of the people, the sheep, likewise, had fallen into this idolatry. Sadly, in their desire to become obedient they had, in effect, become the sons of disobedience. The Lord had provided them with the good seed of the Word, and yet they had taken the pure doctrine of God, and corrupted it with the traditions of men, so the pleasingly abundant field of wheat became teeming with the tares of traditions. Moreover, because of the countless catechisms of the faith they had heaped upon the pure word of God, it was difficult for anyone even to see if they were walking in these entanglements. Since this was the case, the lawyers', the scribes' and the Pharisees' word became even more significant than the Word of God; for who could navigate through this maze of manmade doctrines without tripping over it? Therefore, this was at the heart of their corruption, for the enemy had sown the tares of traditions into the hearts of these religious leaders (Mat 13:25), so they had become idols of the people, stealing God's praise, and so they followed the error of their father and became their own gods. Thus, the Latin idiom holds true, *"Corruptissima re publica plurimae leges"*, *"The republic is most corrupt, when the laws are most numerous."*

Then Messiah addresses the people's misplaced adoration, and superseding God's authority with the traditions of men.

> *But you are not to be called rabbi, for you have one teacher, and you are all brothers. And call no man your father on earth, for you have one Father, who is in heaven. Neither be called instructors, for you have one instructor, the Christ. (Mat 23:8-10 ESV)*

Now let us not become pharisaical in our interpretation of these passages. Is Jesus actually saying that I cannot call my father *"father"*? No. Is He saying that I cannot address a rabbi as *"rabbi"*? No. Is He saying that I cannot refer to a person in God's house as father? Once again, the answer is no. For if, this was the case then Paul would have been wrong to address the Sanhedrin as *"fathers"* in his defense of the Gospel in Acts 22:1. Likewise, Stephen would also have been guilty of this transgression in Acts 7:2 when he addressed the Sanhedrin in an equivalent manner. However, take note, in both cases that while, these godly men had given the respect of titles to these blind guides, they in no way conceded the supremacy God's Word by honoring their magistrates. For it is evident in this same discourse, that Stephen became so pointed in his diatribe against the Sanhedrin, that after *"hearing these things, they were cut to their hearts. And they gnashed at him with their teeth"* in anger. (Act 7:54) Therefore, the distinct understanding of this teaching is not that a title is anything other than a show of respect, but that the title should never supersede the authority of scripture and the supremacy of God's Word.

By applying this discourse to the historical perspective of Meshiach's timeframe, we are able to glean the appropriate understanding out of the very subtle nuances in this teaching. As noted earlier, He said this because the Pharisees had so greatly entangled the Word of God with the tares of men's religious traditions. In addition, because His Words are now in the plain language of the people, we may act as the Bereans and examine these doctrines to corroborate their testimony against the scriptures. (Act 17:11) If our interpretations are faithful to the Good Shepherd's Words, then these words ought not to contradict each other. Hence, do you call a teacher of Bible study teacher? Alternatively, do you call church instructors, fathers or rabbis? My exegesis of this passage says go ahead and call them by their titles, as long as you are not superseding the respect for their positions above the Words of God by allowing doctrines that contradict the Holy Writ to rein supreme in your heart.

How do we know this? Jesus promised He would never leave us or forsake us. (Heb 13:5) He also promised He would not leave us as orphans, but that He would send the Holy Spirit, who would guide us in all truth. (Joh 16:13) My advice, then, is to pray, and search the scriptures, when the Spirit of Truth is warning that the enemy is attempting to plant tares in the heart. *"But I need the pastor to explain the Bible to me because I cannot understand it,"* you say. To that I say, that if you do not understand the Word of God it is because you are not searching diligently enough. Jesus promised to send the Holy Spirit, who would guide us in all truth. Thus, He beseeches, *"Seek and ye shall find."* (Mat 7:7) Immediately, He then reinforces this supplication with, *"he that seeketh findeth"* (Mat 7:8) Notice that the King James Version adds the suffix *"eth"* to the text. The translators of this text did this to indicate to the reader that this Greek verb is in the present perfect tense, which denotes a present and a continuous future action. Therefore, we can interpret this verse as, *"He that seeks and continues to seek will find and continue to find.*" What a wondrous guarantee of God! In addition, this testimony is in perfect agreement with many other scriptures, where God promises, "*if you shall seek Jehovah your God... you shall find Him, if you seek Him with all your heart and with all your soul.*" (Deu 4:29) I believe it was for this reason that God chose to write the whole New Testament in Koine Greek, the common language of the people of that time. Additionally, 72 rabbis translated the entire Old Testament into this same common language around 250 B.C. in what we now call the Septuagint. Moreover, we know the truth of our spiritual houses ought to be "*built upon the foundation of the apostles and prophets, Jesus Christ Himself being the chief cornerstone.*" (Eph 2:20) Therefore, have not built our spiritual houses upon the shifting sands that desire to supplant truth through the traditions of men, or the supremacy of titles, but rather is a holy and sanctified dwelling place for the Spirit of Truth. (Eph 2:21)

Messiah then instructed that our assessment of people and what is actually important are completely backwards. In America, we are always hearing that we need to boost our self-esteem; however, a recent survey of the world's industrial nations found that America's youth ranks number one in self-esteem. Thus, you would think that we are entirely satisfied in fulfilling our own self-regard, and yet, this actually is not the case; for another survey has discovered that college students desire self-esteem encouragement from others over such things as eating favorite foods, drinking alcohol, going out with friends or sex. Is this not the sin of pride, and self-love, which has haunted the history of man through the centuries? Is not this desire the root cause of all our miserable sorrows? In spite of this, we cannot get enough of it. O' how we love to be loved by others, but even more so, how we love to have others help us to love ourselves all the more! Thus, our natural inclination is to seek the praise of men and to acquire a greater abundance of our own self-adulation, but to the radiant splendor of our magnificent God, we are an unclean thing in His sight when we are high and lifted up. As a result, our Glorious Immanuel implores us to see clearly the opposite of our dyslexic natural eyes.

> *But he who is greatest among you shall be your servant. And whoever shall exalt himself shall be abased, and he who shall humble himself shall be exalted. (Mat 23:11-12 MKJV)*

Notice that this verse corroborates our exegesis of the prior verses, because the issue at hand was the prominence of these leaders.

Therefore, if the position requires respect then give "*honor to whom honor is due*" (Rom 13:7), but if asked to transgress the Word of God, then our answer should be, "*We ought to obey God rather than men.*" (Act 5:29)

Now we come to an area of the scriptures commonly referred to as the Eight Woes of Matthew, and it is particularly intriguing that these verses also are perfectly antithetical parallels to the Beatitudes. The Beatitudes expressed the ultimate unattainable ideal. In those passages, the Immaculate Man set before us the Holy mountain of God's Kingdom and then gave us the impossible task of scaling its heights. Although, we fully acknowledge the impossibility of this task, we set these ideals before ourselves daily to walk in them. Paul as our example in Christ repeatedly exhorts us to "*press toward the mark for the prize of the high calling of God in Christ Jesus.*" (Php 3:14) Day after day, we strive to attain the unattainable, to grasp that which cannot be grasped, and to achieve the unachievable, because He, who has attained, grasped and achieved, has scaled the heights of the Holy Mountain of God and beckons us to come. Although we know, we can never reach its summit, until this corruptible mortal flesh has put on incorruptible immortality. Nevertheless, we press toward the mark, because in this mountain, out of the midst of His purifying fire, the terrible and awesome Omnipotent Creator, who speaks to the camp in lightning and thunders, will meet with us face to face, wiping away all our tears, and speaking softly in a still small voice. In that place, He shall be our God and we shall be His people, whereby we joyfully shout, "*Abba, Father!*" (1Co 15:54, Deu 5:4, Exo 19:16, Rev 21:4, 1Ki 19:12, Jer 30:22, Rom 8:15)

Even so, I have wrongly suggested the Beatitudes presents *works* we should strive to achieve, for if that were the case, it would be just another vain attempt of mankind toiling to build a tower to ascend into the heavens through their own labors. (Gen 11:4) After carefully examining these passages, it becomes apparent that these verses are not compelling us to strive to attain at all; instead, they are a list of character traits that should define the content of our hearts. This is the beauty of the Beatitudes, in that, fallen man is shown by the God-man how the perfect man should look. Therefore, in the Beatitudes, we do not have the "*thou shalt __do's__ and be blessed*" but rather we have the "*thou shalt __be__ and be blessed.*"

Judgment in the Temple

In the commandments given by God, we have the *"thou shalt **not do's** and be blessed."* In the Woes of the Pharisees, we have the *"thou art and thou art cursed!"* In the law, God gave us firm boundaries of acceptable behaviors, and although we do not care for restrictions, because of our naturally rebellious hearts, we can accept that the law is good and should be obeyed. However, in the Woes, the mirror of our current condition is held up, and we are repulsed by the image Immanuel has revealed; and unfortunately, most of us refuse to believe that this is who we truly are without God. However, in seemingly a complete contrast, in the Beatitudes we are not repulsed by the image but inspired. Do you see the implication smuggled in? Before I answer that question, allow me to ask a few more probing questions. Have you ever known anyone that has lived as perfectly as the ideals of the Beatitudes? Do you know of anyone who has not been angry with another person for a wrong reason? Do you know of anyone who has not retaliated, at some time, after they have been mistreated? Is there a man alive that at some time in his life did not look upon a woman with desire? Have you always loved your enemies as yourself? The clear, unambiguous answer to all of these questions is no. Now do you see the implication smuggled in? The Beatitudes are God's perfect and impossible standard that we can never achieve, which demonstrate to us just how far we have fallen from grace. They are so far above anything we can achieve within ourselves that these ideals might as well reside on the other side of the universe. The Beatitudes present the most inspiring, highest mountain of supreme blessedness; and yet, they also reveal the deep pit of our hopeless present state under the curse. Originally, Adam had perfect fellowship with God, walking with Him daily in the garden. In the Beatitudes, we strive as well to become what we once were. To enjoy that same fellowship, through God's indwelling spirit, and return to the highest ideals of a sublime character. Therefore, we are rebellious against the restrictions of the law, yet our conscience acknowledges that it is good. We are completely repulsed and in denial of the Woes of our current condition. Thus, we accept the Beatitudes with exceptional fondness, because they inspire us, despite the implications of our desperate existing circumstances.

To accentuate these points, imagine reading all three passages to the most notorious criminal in history. Which passage do you think he would prefer - the Law, the Beatitudes or the Woes? I think almost anyone would prefer the Beatitudes, even our imaginary infamous criminal. However, they appear so lovely in large part because they were delivered in a lovely manner. Now envision what the response would have been if Messiah had presented the opposite characteristic with its contingent outcome; so that instead of saying, *"Blessed are the poor in Spirit"*, He would have said, *"Cursed are the prideful."* Would history's most monstrous reprobate have received these words? Would we receive them? Our most base, fallen nature is not far from the most notorious criminal in history; for, *"But by the grace of God, there goes I."* What if He had taken it one-step further and said something like, *"Woe to you, you spiritually prideful ones, you have fallen into a pit and are cursed!"* Would we still find the Beatitudes inspiring, or repulsive?

Notice Messiah chose to deliver the Beatitudes in such a lovely manner at the beginning of His ministry and then chose the harsh delivery of the Woes at the end of His ministry, after His attempts to reach the religious leaders through reasoning had failed, and now their response had begun to reach critical mass. Thankfully, the Lord of Glory *"is long-suffering toward us, not purposing that any should perish, but that all should come to repentance."* (2Pe 3:9) Nevertheless, after three-and-a-half years attempting to bring their hard hearts to repentance, it was now time for the judgment of God Almighty, in which His last public discourse appears to be a final attempt to save them from the Last Judgment that takes all unbelieving souls as a thief in the night.

After speaking about how the Pharisees and the scribes had exalted themselves above the scriptures of God and His Messiah; Faithful and True then began to pronounce the dire outcomes of their choices by stating,

> *But woe to you, scribes and Pharisees, hypocrites! For you shut up the kingdom of Heaven against men. For you neither go in, nor do you allow those entering to go in. (Mat 23:13 MKJV)*

When we compare the substance of Messiah's first public address, the Beatitudes, with His last public address, the Woes, we find that they express the exact same message, yet delivered from different perspectives. In His first public address, He stands on the mountain of God and bids us come. In His last public address, He stands in the defiled temple of the earth and points out our failures. In His first public address, He implies what we are and inspires us to become. In His last public address, He explicitly states what we are and the resultant effect of remaining in that state. In His first public address, He pronounces states of blessedness that carry with it the implications of a supreme state of peace and inner joy. In His last public address, He pronounces woes, which carry with it impending doom and supreme judgment. Even more fascinating is that the substances of these statements mirror each other perfectly. In the first Woe, the Kingdom of Heaven is shut to the prideful, and in like manner, although delivered inversely; we see in the first Beatitude, that the Kingdom of Heaven is open to the poor in spirit, that is, those who recognize their spiritual ineptness.

Now the Father of the Fatherless and the Protector of Widows (Psa 68:5) says,

> *Woe to you, scribes and Pharisees, hypocrites! For you devour widows' houses, and pray at length as a pretense. Therefore, you shall receive* **the greater condemnation**. *(Mat 23:14 MKJV)*

Once more, the second Beatitude mirrors the same thought, stating, *"Blessed are they that mourn for they shall be comforted."* In this case, the Light of the World illuminates an area of extreme darkness, for these pious hypocrites used spiritual coercion to seize widows' property by exploiting their emotions, using, as a pretense, scriptural empathy for the victim. To which they would say things like, *"You will be so blessed if you give a large portion of your estate,"* or "Your husband would have wanted you to contribute to the Synagogue," or "In *this package we can pray for three hours and bless your children.*" Therefore, we understand that the actions of these false comforters was nothing more than the facade of compassion wrought out of a heart motivated by the desire for filthy lucre. This religious hypocrisy is a one of the supreme causes for many of the *lost* to view the church with such enormous contempt. It is also the oldest form of prostitution on the planet, stealing from the downtrodden, believing the garb of spiritual concern conceals their deeds, although these pretenders' conduct stands naked before the eyes of the secular masses. Nevertheless, in their own eyes, and likewise to those followers, ensnared in the bondage of this religious system of works, they are clothed in righteousness. As a result, we also should not be surprised that this is the first of two places in the Woes that the Supreme Judge discusses the extreme *"condemnation"* for such a pious masquerade of works. However, the King James Version translation of *"condemnation"* as *"damnation"* appears to give a much greater emphasis and significance to their outcome of their actions. Thus, take note that when the Father to the Fatherless looked upon these unscrupulous ecclesiastical charlatans with His eyes of flaming fire and stated, "*Therefore, you shall receive **the greater damnation***", He was clearly expressing that He Who Looks upon the Heart has reserved the most severe fires of Hell for the schemers of the destitute.

Then Messiah addressed the state of those pharisaical disciples held in the dark bondage of religious works, stating,

> *Woe to you, scribes and Pharisees, hypocrites! For you compass sea and the dry land to make one proselyte, and when he is made, you make him twofold more the child of hell than yourselves. (Mat 23:15 MKJV)*

Is it not remarkable that religious people entangled in their good works can be more difficult to bring to the light of God than overtly, unabashed sinners? Nevertheless, the need for good works is further testimony we recognize deep within our hearts something is amiss. We need something to bridge the vast chasm between our lowly degenerative estate and God's supreme Holiness, although we cannot attain it solely within ourselves. Therefore, we acknowledge something must stand between Him and us on the Day of Judgment, which for some people is their religious works, but for penitent Christians is the Lamb of God. Thus, those entangled in the bondage of a religious system of works are like people who are standing above a sinkhole, believing it is firm ground. They grasp for a sliver of light, permeating through the dark rocks of their good works, as the ground begins to collapse in their day of trial; for we are forewarned that "*the Day shall declare it*" and "*fire shall try each one's work as to what kind it is.*" (1Co 3:13)

Once again, we see the perfect paradoxal parallel in the Beatitudes when the Author and Perfecter of our Faith proclaimed, "*Blessed are the meek! For they shall inherit the earth*" (Mat 5:5), in contrast to, cursed are the prideful fanatics who compass the earth to make people two-fold more children of Hell. (Mat 23:15)

At this time, the True Light will begin to expound on how ridiculous these intellectual elites could be in there tangled twine of rules and laws.

Woe to you, blind guides, saying, Whoever shall swear by the temple, it is nothing; but whoever shall swear by the gold of the temple, he is a debtor. Fools and blind! For which is greater, the gold, or the temple that sanctifies the gold? And, Whoever shall swear by the altar, it is nothing; but whoever swears by the gift that is on it, he is a debtor! Fools and blind! For which is greater, the gift, or the altar that sanctifies the gift? (Mat 23:16-19 MKJV)

Money, money, money! It is amazing how many issues our Lord and Savior had to deal with the Pharisees that concerned religious pretense for monetary gain. Buried within the passages above is another of these issues. When a layperson made a contract with another layperson, they went to the temple to have the agreement bound by the scribes. Now if one of these lawyers was corrupt, as many apparently were around this time, he may have set up a deal with one of the parties to have the contract bound by an oath to the temple or to the altar. When it came time for the receiving party to pay for these goods or services already received, they would renege on their promise to pay, sighting the fine print in the law that stated that an oath was only valid when sworn by the gold on the temple or a gift on the altar. This is like one child saying to another *"If you give me your blue marble now then I will give you the red marble that is back at my house."* However, when it becomes time to give up the red marble this child says, *"Oh no, I cannot give you that marble, because I had my fingers crossed behind my back."*

This is why the Righteous Judge of All the Earth said, *"Let what you say be simply 'Yes' or 'No'; anything more than this comes from evil."* (Mat 5:37) This also may be interpreted as, you do not need all of this fine print in the law and these precise rituals of oath-swearing, but rather be a person of upstanding character and honor your word. This is splendid advice to our generation as well, which has become so litigious, that we have buried our courts under vast mountains of civil cases, due in large part, to people dishonoring the spirit of their promises for the purpose of monetary gain, and yet, feeling entirely vindicated by the fine print of their well-written contracts.

Notice the adjectives the Lord used as He gazed deep into the soul of these respected priests, lawyers, doctors and other well thought of intellectual elites of society, drawing out a two-edged sword, His words begin piercing their hearts, even to the dividing asunder of soul and spirit, vehemently reproaching, *"Hypocrites! Fools! Blind guides!"*

Can you imagine being in His presence when He spoke these thunderous words? My jaw would have dropped completely to the ground. This is equivalent in our day to someone exposing the corruption of a reputable Senator, a brilliant lawyer, an astute author, a shrewd executive, or a highly regarded priest who sold his integrity for filthy lucre, who is renown at a national level. Moreover, Messiah was not only exposing just one of these powerful, well-respected, wealthy, elites, but rather, He was exposing all of them at the same time, standing in the midst of His enemies (Psa 23:5) and bringing to light that which was done in the dark. (1Co 4:5)

Once again, we witness another perfect parallel to the Beatitudes where the righteous shall be filled and the unrighteous are cursed.

In addition, He continues to slay them with His diatribe, stating,

> *Woe to you, scribes and Pharisees, hypocrites! For you pay tithes of mint and dill and cummin, and you have **left undone the weightier matters of the Law**, judgment, mercy, and faith. You ought to have done these and not to leave the other undone. Blind guides who **strain out a gnat and swallow a camel**! (Mat 23:23-24 MKJV)*

What these leaders called weighty, Messiah called light, and what they proclaimed light, He proclaimed as heavy; namely, the Law, or what we refer to in our time as the Bible. They superseded the Word of God with the traditions of men, and justified it by the fact that they were the keepers of the Law for so many centuries, which naturally made them the finest interpreters of God's Word. In their mindset, the Oral Torah, held nearly as much weight as the written Torah, but in reality, it had actually dethroned God's Holy Word. For who could interpret the Word of God, except rabbis who spent their entire lives learning the Torah. Only the greatest sages added to the Oral Torah; therefore, most teachers commented on the scriptures solely by quoting past rabbis. This is why Messiah's teachings astonished the people, causing them to say, "*No one ever spoke like this man!*" (Joh 7:46) For example, He never said, "*The scriptures say this, and Rabbi so and so interprets it as thus...*" but rather, He said with commanding authority, "*You have heard it said... but **I say to you**...*" Moreover, when Yeshua proclaimed, "*You have heard it said...*" He was not only taking authority over the interpretation of scripture, but He was taking authority over the accepted teachings of rabbis and sage's in the past.

The interpretations of religious scholars had exceeded the teachings of the Law, but now the Word of God in the Flesh took His rightful place, liberating the people from those heavy, binding pronouncements of past rabbis. We should also be quite aware of this subtle tactical wile of the devil when reading our own commentaries and catechisms.

John Gill's *"Exposition of the Entire Bible"* elucidates that the phrase *"straining out a gnat"* was more than just a colorful expression in Messiah's time, but rather it was a literal process alluded to by the Lord in His transcendent teaching. Gill, for example, quotes various Jewish sources who stated things like, *"One that eats a flea, or a gnat; they say is an apostate."* In addition, *"whoever eats a whole fly, or a whole gnat, whether alive or dead, was to be beaten on account of a creeping flying thing."* As well as, *"a man might not pour his strong liquors through a strainer, by the light [of a candle or lamp], lest he should separate and leave in the top of the strainer [some creeping thing], and it should fall again into the cup, and he should transgress the law."*

This rule was followed to the utmost degree because of their fanatical interpretation of God's restriction, *"And every creeping thing that creepeth upon the earth shall be an abomination; it shall not be eaten."* (Lev 11:41) Imagine the scene, as the Lord of Glory enters Jerusalem, while devout men piously strain their bowls just after spiritually coercing money from the widow and reviling blind beggars, whom they believe were born that way because of their parents' sin. (Joh 9:34) So the Lover of Our Soul says to these it is fine for them to be careful to count out all the little pieces of mint, dill and cummin; *"One for the Lord nine for me, one for the Lord nine for me,"* but not to withhold the more important matters of fair *"judgment, mercy [love] and faith."* (1Cor 13:13) O' how the Wicked One loves to bury the truth under the rigid details of man's self-righteous religious traditions.

Thus, at the beginning of His ministry He proclaimed, *"Blessed are the merciful: for they shall obtain mercy"* (Mat 5:7); and now, at the close of His ministry He proclaims cursed are the merciless for they shall not obtain mercy, but rather they are under judgment.

Messiah then continues the lambasting the Pharisees giving explicit examples of their duplicity.

> *Woe to you, scribes and Pharisees, hypocrites! For you cleanse the outside of the cup and of the dish, but inside they are full of*

extortion and excess. Blind Pharisee! First cleanse the inside of the cup and of the dish, so that the outside of them may be clean also. (Mat 23:25-26 MKJV)

Notice that in the prior verse, Yeshua pointed to a tradition of straining gnats out of their cups. Now He smoothly transitions to a metaphor that they are the cup. It would have been unthinkable for them to leave the gnat in the cup and clean the outside of the container; therefore, they should not conclude that all of their external traditions clean an unclean heart. The process of cleaning cups was also an allusion to the Pharisaical Oral Torah traditions, as exemplified by entire pages in their Talmud, that gave explicit instructions as to how, when, where and every other exacting detail that must be precisely followed or the violator would be considered an apostate. Once again, we witness the perfect paradoxical parallel of the woe that accompanies the corrupt heart of the Pharisaical, self-justifier, to the blessing of the chaste heart of a truth seeker in the Beatitudes, when Our Righteousness states, *"Blessed are the pure in heart! For they shall see God."* (Mat 5:8)

Then the Lamb without Blemish intensifies His diatribe against the self-justifier's heart, which at first He compared to a vulgar dead thing in their cup, now comparing it to a dead person in the grave.

Woe to you, scribes and Pharisees, hypocrites! For you are like whitewashed tombs, which indeed appear beautiful outside, but inside they are full of dead men's bones, and of all uncleanness. Even so you also appear righteous to men outwardly, but inside you are full of hypocrisy and iniquity. (Mat 23:27-28)

We can appreciate the dramatic imagery of this comparison; however, to the Pharisees this would have been the height of uncleanness. Once again, take note that this verse is a perfect paradoxical parallel to the Beatitudes, which subsequently declares, *"Blessed are the pure in heart! For they shall see God."* (Mat 5:8) Again, notice also that we could rephrase the opposite implication of the above verse, by saying, *"Cursed are the impure in heart for they are dead, and corrupt and will not see the Kingdom of Heaven."*

This is also a perfect picture of what we once were, if you will recall from the chapter *"Lazarus Come Forth"*, before the Resurrection and the Life called us to come forth out of our corruption. Notice also that these noblemen could not see their own corruption, just as most people cannot see theirs. Moreover, they were extremely well regarded by most as exceedingly pious, devout souls, for Faithful and True admits, *"indeed [they] appear beautiful outside."* Was this not our former state and is this not the current condition of almost all the lost? The supreme machination of the Schemer is to make people believe they can live a good enough life to please God. However, corruption does not belong in heaven, and neither do dead souls. Therefore, the dead will live with the dead in a Kingdom of Corruption under a deceitful, ruthlessly tyrannical king.

Consider Messiah's masterful transitions from straining the dead gnat out of the cup, to the Pharisee being the cup and cleaning its outside. Then, to the Pharisee being worse than the dead gnat in the cup, and more like an unclean, dead man in an exquisite whitewashed sepulcher; and finally, to the sepulchers built to the prophets their fathers have slain.

> *Woe to you, scribes and Pharisees, hypocrites! Because you build the tombs of the prophets, and decorate the tombs of the righteous, and say, If we had been in the days of our fathers, we would not have been partakers with them in the blood of the prophets. Therefore, you are witnesses to yourselves, that you are the sons of those who killed the prophets. (Mat 23:29-31 MKJV)*

As one would expect, this is another opposite parallel to His first public address. In these Woes, the Pharisees are righteous pretenders persecuting genuine righteousness. However, in the Beatitudes, the faithful are akin to the persecuted prophets of old, afflicted by the unrighteous. To which Yeshua says, *"Blessed are those who are persecuted for righteousness' sake, for theirs is the kingdom of heaven."* (Mat 5:10) In the Beatitudes, His first public discourse, the result of this walk is *"the kingdom of heaven."* Therefore, it is only fitting that Logos should end his last public discourse with its mirror-opposite and the consequence of this Pharisaical walk.

> *Serpents! Offspring of vipers! How can you escape the condemnation of hell? (Mat 23:33 MKJV)*

He uses not only a perfect paradox in precise relation to his first public address, but also uses the climax of this fiery diatribe as an ideal segue into the consequences of these choices. Hence, the Author of Life punctuates His entire discourse by giving these corrupt souls a glimpse into their actual miserable condition. He does this first by stating that they have testified against the actions of their fathers who killed the prophets, yet He that Knows All Things can see the subtlety of their feigned reverence and false hand of fellowship, attempting to hide their true passion for blood. Therefore, the True Witness makes ti known that a man cannot separate his walk from his character, and, in fact, the man who does is nothing more than a blind fool and a hypocrite. Thus, the Lord of Glory makes it abundantly clear that the actions of a snake define a snake.

Is not it compelling that the very first time the word "*serpent*" is used in the scriptures was in reference to Satan, and his primary characteristic is that he was "***more subtil*** *than any beast of the field*"? (Gen 3:1) Yeshua, Our Righteousness, essentially places people into one of two camps; the quick and the dead, walking in darkness or living in the light, you are either a son of the Most High and Holy God or a son of Satan, the Prince of Darkness. There is no in between. There is no other way, for He has said, "*I am the door of the sheep*" (Joh 10:7) and "*he who does not enter the sheepfold by the door but climbs in by another way, that man is a thief and a robber.*" (Joh 10:1) In addition, Paul later affirms this testimony, by the inspiration of the Holy Spirit, stating,

> *And you were dead in the trespasses and sins in which you once walked, following the course of this world, **following the prince of the power of the air,** the spirit that is now at work in the **sons of disobedience**… (Eph 2:1-2 ESV)*

In an earlier confrontation with the Pharisees, the Son of God made it quite clear that their actions defined their inner character, stating,

> *If you were Abraham's children, **you would be doing the works Abraham did,** but now you seek to kill me, a man who has told you the truth that I heard from God. This is not what Abraham did. (Joh 8:39-40 ESV)*

Later, in this dialogue He once again divides people into one of two camps, the Kingdom of God and the Kingdom of Satan.

> ***If God were your Father,** you would love me, for I came from God and I am here. I came not of my own accord, but he sent me. Why do you not understand what I say? It is because you cannot bear to hear my word. **You are of your father the devil, and your will is to do your father's desires**. He was a murderer from the beginning, and has nothing to do with the truth, because there is*

180

no truth in him. **When he lies, <u>he speaks out of his own character</u>,** *for he is a liar and the father of lies. But because I tell the truth, you do not believe me. (Joh 8:42-45 ESV)*

Messiah tells them to *"fill up the measure of your fathers"* (Mat 23:32), which is used as an ominous metaphor understood by those religious leaders to drink from the cup of the wrath and the judgment of God. Subsequently, Everlasting to Everlasting retorts, *"How can you escape the condemnation of hell?"*

Finally, His Omniscience concludes His diatribe with a prophecy about how these same religious leaders will treat the leaders of His true church.

> *Therefore, behold, I send prophets and wise men and scribes to you. And you will kill and crucify some of them. And some of them you will scourge in your synagogues and persecute from city to city; so that on you may come all the righteous blood shed on the earth, from the blood of righteous Abel to the blood of Zechariah the son of Berachiah, whom you killed between the temple and the altar. (Mat 23:34-35 MKJV)*

Note our Alpha and Omega's remarkable accuracy in this prophecy. For the God of the Bible declared, *"I am God, and there is no other; I am God, and there is none like me, declaring the end from the beginning and from ancient times."* (Isa 46:9-10) Likewise, God With Us also says, *"I have told you before it takes place, so that when it does take place **you may believe**."* (Joh 14:29) However, what is it we should believe? That Jesus and the Father are one and that whosoever has seen Jesus has seen the Father. (Joh 14:9-10) Secondly, and similarly, not only do these prescient words prove Yeshua is Elohim, but the fact that He will send His *"prophets and wise men and scribes"* after His death proves He is the Everlasting Father and the Prince of Peace. (Isa 9:6)

Also, consider that the interaction between the Light of the World and those in bondage of the chains of darkness is precisely what we discussed earlier in the chapter *"Lazarus Come Forth."* He who has descended from heaven is now telling the earthly of heavenly things (Joh 3:13), and they would not receive Him (Joh 1:11), because they *"loved the darkness rather than the light because their works were evil."* (Joh 3:19) Surprisingly, this is in complete agreement with the revelations of Socrates, whom, although a pagan, was a brilliant philosopher, and who asked the rhetorical question about a man attempting to free people from their bondage, *"[would not] they kill him?"* Nevertheless, the scriptures speak many times that people who seek truth, like the pagan philosopher Socrates, are able to discover very profound truths. For example, John tells us that Jesus was *"the true light that gives light to every man"*, yet many in the world do not know the Light by which they have been enlightened. (Jon 1:9-10). This is one of the great mysteries of spiritual blindness. It is also the greatest weapon of the Perverter of the Truth. Nevertheless, receiving a truthful revelation of the light of God, and then placing that epiphany upon a false foundation, only gives a partial restoration in this life and no restoration whatsoever in the life to come. Truth, twisted, is no truth at all, but delusion, completely devoid of saving grace. Socrates, for example, received an exceptionally true revelation of how men prefer the bondage of darkness to the light, and yet his foundation was not the one and only Savior bringing people to the Light of God, but rather, his foundation was himself, and others, who had attained his level of knowledge, whom he called the philosopher kings.

Once again, this final woe about the persecutors is in perfect alignment with the eighth and the ninth Beatitude, which speak about the persecuted, in which Jesus Messiah says,

> *Blessed are those who are persecuted for righteousness' sake, for theirs is the kingdom of heaven. Blessed are you when others revile you and persecute you and utter all kinds of evil against you falsely on my account.* ***Rejoice and be glad****, for your reward is great in heaven, for so they persecuted the prophets who were before you. (Mat 5:10-12 ESV)*

If only Christians in our time could do as the Suffering Servant and our Example in the Faith exhorts us while being pressed under the heavy weight of persecution, *"Rejoice and be glad!"* This one directive, if followed, would set the world on its head, especially in our culture, where most live in the lap of luxury and do not know how to endure suffering. Consider the testimonies of the early martyrs of the faith. For example, when King Herod Agrippa sentenced the apostle James, Son of Zebedee, to die, his accuser asked James to forgive him, after witnessing the apostle's joy, and then asked the king to sentence him to death as well. The king beheaded both and James became the first martyred apostle. Likewise, Polycarp converted many pagans in the Roman Coliseum just before he was burnt alive, joyfully praying,

"Lord God, Father of our blessed Savior, I thank Thee that I have been deemed worthy to receive the crown of martyrdom, and that I may die for Thee and Thy cause." Again, contemplate the many souls that were saved witnessing Cyprian of Carthage shouting out in victory, *"Thanks be to God!"* just before he was beheaded. Additionally, consider Perpetua's enormous impact on the Roman Empire; after she emphatically told the emperor, she would not worship him and boldly proclaimed her love for Christ. She then led a group of martyrs into the Coliseum singing psalms just before the wild beasts tore them apart. Witnesses in the stands later described her as a *"young and beautiful," "pure and modest Christian lady" "with shining countenance and calm step, as the beloved of God, as a bride of Christ, putting down everyone's stare by her own intense gaze."* Her bold testimony that *"I am a Christian and cannot deny Christ"* became a mantra throughout the Roman Empire.[10] These martyrs and others like them set the world ablaze, transforming a pagan world into a Christian world by keeping the word of their testimony while under the fire of affliction, and holding firmly to the tenants of a strange, small Jewish cult called Christianity.

We have spent many pages examining the Lord of Glory's final public discourse, which begs the question, *"How then does all this fit into The Parable of the Cross?"* The answer to this question is fourfold; this is what we were, this is what the world is, this is what we should not become, and yet, this is what we still are.

We have devoted much discussion to the foolish arrogance of these aristocrats, their trivial behaviors, and their spiritual pride that blinded them from the Light of the World, standing right before their eyes. In many ways, they have become like the men of Sodom and Gomorrah, who continued throughout the night to seek out the angels in Lot's house in order to fulfill their vile passions, despite God's judgment having struck them blind. This is the irrational state of following sin to its absolute fulfillment, which is actually a lie, because it never completely fulfills, but rather, promising the delusion of ultimate satisfaction, it falls far short, into the momentary pleasure of scratching

---

[10] 1. Peter Hammond. Remember the Persecuted. Available at: http://www.frontline.org.za/articles/Remember%20the%20Persecuted.htm [Accessed November 14, 2010].

a passionate itch, only to return later with greater intensity. The Supreme Judge struck the men of Sodom and Gomorrah blind, and yet, instead of concern over the condition of their eyes. They were captivated by their feverish, passionate impulses driving their sole desire to feed these fleshly appetites. This is an extraordinarily accurate picture of the bondage of sin. These Jewish aristocrats were in the same state, although it was not their sexual perversion driving their hunger, but rather, their blood lust to kill the Only Begotten Son. How could these pious men sit in God's temple, the church of their day, attempting to entrap and kill the long-awaited Messiah, and have been so blind not to see the hypocrisy of their own murderous desires?

Now in our own Nathan the Prophet experience, we come to realize, *"You are the man!"* (2Sa 12:7) We are the blind Pharisees standing before Christ, who called us out of the bondage of sin and darkness. He Who Loves Us and Died for Us raised us from our formerly dead consciences. We were lame, not able to walk in righteousness, blind, not able to see the truth, diseased, completely infected with the leprosy of sin, and all the while, we enjoyed feeding upon the death and decay of our own souls. Moreover, we sat on the throne of this kingdom of debauchery and spit upon, humiliated, beaten, scourged and crucified the Lord of Glory! Amazingly, He, whom we spent our entire life despising, loved us so much *"in that while we were yet sinners [He] Christ died for us."* (Rom 5:8)

However, some will respond, *"I never despised Christ, nor have I ever ruled over a kingdom of debauchery. In fact, my life was decent and moral before I became a Christian."* To which, I must counter, we usurped the King of All Creation by taking His rightful place on the throne of our heart. We chose to do the things that brought our happiness. It was always about our desires. We usurped the Righteous King. We followed the desires of our own heart, rather than the desires of God and make no mistake it was sin. It was the payment for this terrible sin, which caused God's wrath to requite the high cost of the cross from the Lamb of God. Make no mistake about it; at one time, we also sat on the Judgment seat and declared, *"Behold the man!"* (Joh 19:5) We did not say behold *"My Lord and my God!"* (Joh 20:28), or fall to our knees and say, *"Blessed is He who comes in the name of the Lord"* (Mat 23:39), or *"Hosanna in the highest!"* (Mat 21:9) Instead, we said, *"Behold the man!"* He was a good man, although some of His dogmas are now too strict for our open, tolerant society. He was a man who spoke the truth; although it seems many of His ideas were superstitious. He was a brilliant teacher of God's laws; although the God I serve, would never be so cruel as to send people to the Lake of Fire for eternity. He was a man who did many marvelous things for the sick and the poor; although He thoroughly deceived them with His hocus-pocus-psychosomatic trickery and false hope in a kingdom to come. He was the most renown teacher of philosophical morals the world has ever known; although He was quite delusional, making insane, monstrous assertions like being the "*only begotten Son*" of God (Joh 3:16) and "*Whoever has seen me has seen the Father.*" (Joh 14:9) Nevertheless, it was because of this sin that God "*made Him to be sin who knew no sin*" (2Co 5:21), so that the full fury of God's righteous, indignation against our unrighteousness may be recompensed.

Therefore, instead of saying, "*Behold, My Lord and my God!*" we said, "*Behold the man!*" By the time we finished recreating the Creator, He was so thoroughly marred that He no longer even resembled the Son of Man. (Isa 52:14) Is there anything more reprehensible than to disfigure perfection, the King of Creation Who Loves You? What greater crime is there than to utterly contort the actual Image of God, making Him into our own image? Are we not the ones who need to conform to the image of Christ? This is the most supreme debauchery, to recreate the Creator!

Many times, in the past, God brought Jesus before the judgment seat of your heart, and you asked, "*So you are a king?*" To which He replied, "*You say that I am a king.*" (Joh 18:37) His response to you seems like some sort of game of words. "*I did not say you were a king, I asked if you were a king.*" However, the King of Glory already knows what is in your heart; by the grace of God, you had some light within you. This light recognized the Lover of Your Soul, King Above All Kings, the Light of the World, when He called you to come out of darkness. You sat as judge in the judgment seat of the Judge of All Creation. When Messiah asked to take his rightful place on the throne of your heart, to Lord over your passions and desires, and it was those same passions and desires that screamed, "*Crucify Him! Crucify Him!*" (Joh 19:6)

This was the sorry state of our former existence, and so, this is what we were.

Now let us discuss what we should not become. Occasionally, we stumble in our walk with Messiah. This is the state of our current existence. We choose our passions over the Lord's passions and over our passion for the Lord. How happy we are to barter carelessly away the eternal riches and the glory we have in Christ Jesus (Col 1:27) for a meager moment of satisfaction. We are so effortlessly led astray, like lambs led to the slaughter by a hireling, deceitful Sheppard. The wolf, who seeks to steal, kill and destroy, has once again enticed us as a friend in sheep's clothing. He desires the exact opposite of what God desires for us. He deceives us with false riches of pleasures that are here today and gone tomorrow. He is the moneychanger in our temple, selling immediate gratification for a portion of the tried and true gold of our eternal inheritance. He is the nagging voice in our belly, whispering to our mind, "*Sell your birthright for this tasty morsel of bread.*" He makes tremendous promises of fulfillment, and yet, after the height of momentary bliss, we are empty, unfulfilled, and guilty. At that time, we realize our enormous blunder. We have not dealt wisely with our inheritance. Therefore, we return guilt-ridden from our riotous living in disgrace, and to Him Who Bore All Our Sins, "*Father, I have sinned against heaven and before you. I am no longer worthy to be called your son.*" (Luk 15:18-19) Then the Father runs to us and embraces us and kisses us and says to His servants,

> *Bring quickly the best robe, and put it on him, and put a ring on his hand, and shoes on his feet. And bring the fattened calf and kill it, and let us eat and celebrate. For this my son was dead, and is alive again; he was lost, and is found. (Luk 15:22-24 ESV)*

Thankfully, we serve a gracious God who is long-suffering for us. We are consistently falling to our besetting sins, and yet, He remains faithful to us, even in our unfaithfulness. We should desire Him with the desire that He desires us. We should desire to serve Him with the desire that He has to serve us, for He rules over our hearts in order to serve our hearts. He is a great, compassionate, and loving God. Do not sell your inheritance for such a cheap price to the enemy of your soul. This is what we should not become, and yet, it so often is what we become.

It is not difficult to see what we were before we were regenerated in Christ. It is also clear that this is what the world is without Christ. In addition, it is quite apparent that this is what we should not become, since this is precisely what Yeshua saved us from; namely, our legalistic, self-justifying, self-righteous systems of works. However, if this is what we **were,** then how can I say "*yet this is what we still are?*" This seems to be a contradiction, since, if we **were** saved from this state then how is it I can say this is the state in which we still remain? It is the fundamental question that crystallizes the true battle between what Paul calls the old man and the new man. It is here that we comprehend our real **need** for the cross. It is this revelation that gives clarity to what Jesus meant when He said, *"And he who does not take up his cross and follow Me is not worthy of Me."* (Mat 10:38) We pick up the cross because the old man cannot enter the Promised Land, flowing with milk and honey. We pick up the cross because we can now see the blurred image of what we were, and what we still are, and because of grace it is becoming clearer that this is what we no longer desire to be. (1Co 13:12)

The world does not see this degenerate deficiency when it looks into the mirror. Instead, they see them**selves** as justified and righteous. Take note, at the center of their systems of works is self. In this courtroom, self is the judge, jury, and defendant. Since self is the judge, then the defendant, self, is self-justified. It is also self who deems itself as righteous. In the kingdom of the world, self serves itself, and therefore, self is both king and servant. In the church of the world, it is self who is loved, worshiped, and adored. As you can see, it was self who usurped the King of Glory in every aspect that is rightfully His! Thus, the world is self-justified, self-righteous, self-serving, self-centered, and selfish, because they are under no other authority but their own in order to make these declarations. The Apostle Paul intimates to these worldly systems of self-deception, imploring,

> *...you should not walk from now on as other nations walk, in the* **vanity of their mind**, *having the* **understanding darkened**, *being alienated from the life of God through the ignorance that is in them,* **because of the blindness of their heart**. *(Eph 4:17-18 MKJV)*

Nevertheless, we are no longer like a blind man attempting to look into a mirror. Rather, Messiah partially restored our vision at the time of salvation. Therefore, our current condition is very much like the blind beggar that met the Savior at Bethsaida.

> *And He took the blind man by the hand and led him out of the town. And when He had spat on his eyes and had put His hands on him, He asked Him if he saw anything. And he looked up and said, I see men as trees, walking. And after that He put His hands again*

on his eyes and made him look up. And he was restored and saw all clearly. (Mar 8:23-25 MKJV)

Have you ever wondered why the Omnipotent God in the Flesh did not completely heal Him the first time? Was it because He was tired? Was it because He did not rub his eyes correctly the first time? Is this not the same Jesus, who walked on water? Did He not fed the five-thousand simply by giving thanks, calm the storm by saying, *"Peace, be still"* (Mar 4:39), cleanse the leper by saying, *"Be clean"* (Mat 8:3), raise Jairus's daughter by saying, *"Little girl ... arise."* (Mar 5:41) Did He not perform these miracles and many more with all power and authority, speaking so few words? Did He not speak with all power and authority? Did He not execute all of those astounding feats correctly the first time? Something is surely amiss. This same Jesus was so precise in word and deed, He confidently stated, *"Not one jot or one tittle shall in any way pass from the Law until all is fulfilled."* (Mat 5:18) Moreover, this same Jesus said, *"The heaven and the earth shall pass away, but **My Words shall not pass away"*** (Mat 24:35); meaning, everything He said during His life would transpire before the end of the age. Therefore, if Messiah spoke with all power and authority, then why did Jesus not heal the beggar completely the first time? After our walk with the Sacrificial Lamb of God in The Parable of the Cross, we can begin to discern the answer; namely, that this incident appears to suggest that our vision, in this life, has only been partially restored. That the disease of our mind, our wrong thinking, is not healed completely. This partial healing is the down payment on our salvation. Nevertheless, we will receive the entire payment, our complete restoration, and our full sight, and see things as they really are, when *"this corruptible shall have put on incorruption"* (1Co 15:54), in the resurrection life.

Again, this lines up perfectly with Paul's letter to the Corinthians.

For we know in part, and we prophesy in part. But when the perfect thing comes, then that which is in part will be caused to cease. For now we see in a mirror dimly, but then face to face. Now I know in part, but then I shall fully know even as I also am fully known. (1Co 13:9-10,12 MKJV)

The blind beggar saw men walking as trees. Paul saw himself dimly, as a blurred vision in the mirror. Thus, the first considers the revelation of men, and the second considers the revelation of self. In the blind beggar's initial healing, he sees humanity as it truly exists upon the earth. In his complete and final restoration of his vision, he sees humanity as it will be in its full and final restoration, after we have received payment in full of the great hope that is within us. Therefore, even though the blind beggar is looking at the world, and Paul is looking at self, both allude to the same problem, the current state of our vision.

Now consider the implications between the blind beggar's partial restoration of his vision and the vision itself. The blind beggar sees men walking as trees, which is actually a clearer spiritual vision of mankind, although his physical sight was only partially restored; for this is how God sees men walking upon the earth. Therefore, at the time of our salvation, we begin to see things as God sees them, as they really are, although, they do not have that physical appearance in the world. For this reason, the Lord of Glory says to us, "*For I know the plans I have for you, declares the LORD, plans for welfare and not for evil, to give you a future and a hope.*" (Jer 29:11) We need to realize that there is so much more that the Lord of Glory has in store for us, both in this lifetime, and even more so, in the life to come.

Would you desire to be born as a walking tree? Would you be satisfied with that condition if you knew you could be so much more? This is the Pinocchio analogy. He was born of wood. He saw the other boys created complete in the flesh; and how he desired to be like them. In like manner, we have the seal of hope, which is the Holy Spirit that speaks to our spirit and confirms our adoption. Nevertheless, we acknowledge a partial restoration only, living by faith, and the assurance of the reasonable expectation of the hope of our full restoration. This is the true faith walk of a Christian. Again, in like manner, Pinocchio did not receive his complete restoration until transformed by something much greater than his works, his father's love. Similarly, we are fully transformed in the spirit of this life by the love of Christ, receiving our final restoration when greeted by the Grace of our Sovereign Lord in the life to come.

Considering our adoption into the family of God, how should we live? What if you had been adopted into the house of a king? Would you not live as a prince? Nevertheless, until we come to an age to comprehend our princely calling, we are nothing more than a slave. (Gal 4:2) Likewise, we were all slaves prior to being set free from the bondage of sin and death. However, we then became new creations, although, we still find ourselves struggling with some of the same burdens of sin, like a princely child who has not yet come into the full realization of his freedom, and the glory of his high calling in Christ Jesus. Therefore, consider that the King of All Creation has adopted you! Will you now wallow in the mud like a common sow?

In the world, there are a great number of trees. Most are alive. A few are dead or infected with the disease. However, the opposite is true for the spirit of man in this world; most of them are dead. Most of the healthy trees bear abundantly good fruit, but some produce little or no fruit. This is similar to the spiritual condition of the born-again believer in this world. In the garden of God, the Husbandman is patiently eradicating many formally chronically infected trees. After treating the disease, these trees can begin to provide some healthy fruit. The more the disease has been successfully eradicated, the more abundantly wholesome the tree's fruit.

Considering these things, the blind beggar correctly saw people as trees, which alluded to the true spiritual condition of man. Then our Healer-Redeemer touched the man again, and he received the complete, final restoration. Thus, Messiah healed his physical eyes after having given him spiritual insights from God's perspective. How wonderful it is to receive the spiritual gifts upon His first touch. Nevertheless, how important it is to be properly equipped in order to witness to a physical world. It would have been highly impractical of God to give this man the wrong equipment to walk in this material world.

Years ago, I spoke with a well-respected pastor in the Detroit area who told me of another pastor that prayed fervently for the ability to see things as they actually exist spiritually. One day the Lord granted this holy man his request. The dreadfully fallen condition of the world horrified him. He literally saw the degenerate state of man, demons and evil everywhere. Soon he no longer wanted this capability, but he could not turn it off. He began to lose his mind and was committed to an institution. The pastor said that he diligently sought the Lord on behalf of his friend through praying and fasting. Eventually, his sanity was restored after receiving his natural vision several weeks later.

This story demonstrates two important principles. The first is that God will give to us the tools we need in order to live in our physical existence. He does not give lungs to a fish or gills to a human.

Secondly, the tools we are given will affect our interpretation of this world. Therefore, it is important to recognize our limitations, and overcome them, by seeing spiritual things with our spiritual eyes and physical things with our physical eyes, but far too often we view the world through our old material eyes only, causing us to see very little of the spiritual landscape.

The Parable of the Cross demonstrates the problems with spiritual interpretations in our existence. For example, most believers despise the cross when it comes into their lives. Immediately, they examine themselves and ask God what they have done to deserve this trial. This we should do, but it is not the only reason trials come into our lives. If a believer is walking by the spirit and not by the flesh, then it is quite possible the Lord brought the cross into their lives, not as an instrument of punishment, but rather as a reward for their good, and a refining fire for their sanctification. For this reason, James implores us,

> *My brothers, **count it all joy** when you fall into different kinds of temptations, knowing that the trying of your faith works patience. **But let patience have its perfect work, so that you may be perfect and entire, lacking nothing.** (Jas 1:2-4 MKJV)*

The scriptures also translate the word *"temptations"* above as *"trials,"* and the word *"perfect"* implies a maturing in the faith. This is the desire of every true believer, yet when God is gracious enough to grant our desire, we wine, cry, and fall to our knees, pleading, *"God, how could you have allowed these things to come into our lives? Please take it away immediately."* However, we must allow *"patience [to] have its perfect work."* Therefore, the mature, spirit-filled Christian should not respond in this manner. Moreover, to this end, Messiah informs us that we are blessed, not cursed, when trials come into our lives.

> ***Blessed are you** when others revile you and persecute you and utter all kinds of evil against you falsely on my account. **Rejoice and be glad,** for your reward is great in heaven, for so they persecuted the prophets who were before you. (Mat 5:11-12 ESV)*

This was the attitude of the early church. Immediately, after Jesus' ascension, and the gift of the Holy Spirit, the apostles transformed from shrinking, trembling cowards in hiding, to resolute, courageous heroes of the faith boldly witnessing the truth of the gospel of God in the public arena. What was God's reward for these virtuous feats?

They suffered public disgrace and were thrown into prison like common criminals. (Act 5:18) Then, before they were released, the rulers *"beat them and charged them not to speak in the name of Jesus, and let them go."* (Act 5:40) Nevertheless, instead of shrinking from their high calling to be God's *"witnesses in Jerusalem and in all Judea and Samaria, and to the end of the earth"* (Act 1:8), they

> ...*left the presence of the council, **rejoicing that they were counted worthy to suffer dishonor for the name**. And every day, in the temple and from house to house, **they did not cease teaching and preaching Jesus as the Christ**. (Act 5:41-42 ESV)*

In Acts 1:8 quoted above, the Greek word for *"witnesses"* is *"márturos,"* from which we derive the English word martyrs. Notice also that the Apostles' reaction of was the opposite of what you would have expected. This was because they viewed this persecution through their spiritual eyes rather than their physical eyes. Instead of asking why bad things happen to good people, they rejoiced, as Faithful and True commanded in the Beatitudes. This is our upside-down thinking returning to correct thinking. This logic makes no sense to the world, but it frees every believer to be victorious over every circumstance in life! This is how we attain *"the peace of God which surpasses all understanding"*. (Phi 4:7)

John Calvin understood he could not interpret the world correctly with his physical eyes, and his human intellect, without using the Word of God. For this reason, he called the Bible his spectacles. In addition, one of the greatest, most renowned presidents in the history of the United States, Abraham Lincoln, affirmed this same thought when he said, *"But for it [the Bible] we could not know right from wrong."* Again, John Burton's Hymn *"Holy Bible, Book Divine"* also alludes to this sentiment, stating, *"Precious Treasure, Thou art mine; Mine to teach me whence I came, **Mine to teach me what I am**"*. Furthermore, this concept is also expressed by God, through the prophet Jeremiah, stating, *"The heart is deceitful above all things, and desperately wicked; who can know it?"* (Jer 17:9) Thus, the revelation of man's degenerate, desperate, fallen condition has been taught to the people of the book for many centuries.

Many of the great philosophers of the past came to realize the enormous divide that exists between man's current fallen condition and the Holiness of God on High. For example, the theme of Plato's

"Allegory of the Cave," is that we are deceived in this life when viewing the world through our natural eyes. In addition, Socrates declared, *"the unexamined life is not worth living."* Gautama Buddha, sensing something was amiss, began his search for happiness in hedonism, then turned to extreme asceticism, which he also later denounced, and eventually founded the Buddhist system we know today. In fact, every religion on the planet begins with one underlying assumption; man is a fallen creature, and God will not accept him in his present state. It is precisely this innate realization that is the catalyst for all systems of works built into every religion, except true Christianity. The Buddhists, for instance, follow the *"The Noble Eightfold Path."* The Hindus, likewise, attempt to overcome the cosmic gulf by seeking the awareness of God and the blessings of Devas, benevolent supernatural beings, by venerating icons in shrines at home or in temples. Muslims, as well, attempts to straddle this vast chasm with the *"Five Pillars of Islam,"* which involves things like a pilgrimage to Mecca and the Salat, a ritual prayer performed five times a day. In addition, the root of every Christian cult is a rigorous system of works that promises to justify you before a Holy God.

Sadly, the lost world has correctly diagnosed the disease but has incorrectly prescribed the remedy. However, as people of the book this should not surprise us, since God has revealed to us that the *"heart is deceitful above all things, and desperately wicked; who can know it?"* (Jer 17:9) Nevertheless, even the most renowned philosophers and sages of the great religions have deceived themselves and their followers into believing they could traverse this great chasm through their works. This remedy is as absurd as the Babylonians attempting to build a tower to reach into the heavens. Imagine a tower that spans from the earth to the outer reaches of the universe. Is this not an absurd notion? If I began to create such a tower brick by brick and spent my entire existence in this endeavor, would I not be the fool of all fools? Yet this is exactly what so many people choose to do with their lives when they endeavor to justify themselves before the awesome Holiness of God and to ascend into the heavens through their works. Humanity, looking up at their tower of works, may find them to be innocent, noble souls holding the highest standards of decency that even most Christians can truly appreciate. However, God, looking down on this tower of works, from the outer reaches of the universe must consider these endeavors to be the vanity of all vanities. For this reason, the Lord of All Creation has told us many times throughout His Word *"all our righteousnesses are as filthy rags."* (Isa 64:6) Moreover, no human being could ever traverse the immense expanse that exists between man and God; thus, the Almighty accomplish the feat through the incarnation and a substitutionary sacrifice on the cross. For this reason, we fall on our knees in praise of Great God and Savior Jesus Christ (Tit 2:13), sitting upon the throne of our hearts, saying,

> *Thou art worthy, O Lord, to receive glory and honour and power: for thou hast created all things, and for thy pleasure they are and were created. (Rev 4:11 KJV)*

The crown cast before our Savior is the crown of life, given to the believer after the Light of the World calls him to come from the darkness of sin and death. Nevertheless, did Lazarus perform any good deed while in his dead state to earn this crown of life, no, not one thing! He did not come out of the cave and say thank you Lord for bringing me back to life. It is fortunate I was living such a virtuous life in my utterly dead condition, so I could merit your favor to receive everlasting life. No! In fact, if you review the passages about Lazarus, you will find he never says or does anything, except follow and fellowship with Jesus; and yet, for these reasons, he is called the one whom Jesus loved. (Joh 11:3)

As you can see, there is a part of us, after the Holy Spirit's regenerative work, that remains fallen and corruptible, which the Bible calls the flesh. There is also a part of us that is been quickened and made alive to the Spirit of Christ, where God resides and communes with fallen man in a temple not made by hands. This corruptible man has been dethroned and taken prisoner by your love for God and His Righteousness. However, the fallen man continues to war with the spirit in this life, *"For the flesh lusts against the Spirit, and the Spirit against the flesh. And these are contrary to one another."* (Gal 5:17)

Like most wars, there are obvious areas where the general sets his armies in battlefield array and the front lines are drawn. For the Christian, scriptures make these quite apparent, calling them the lust of the flesh, the lust of the eyes and the pride of life. Additionally, many lost souls can appreciate these battlegrounds as they attest to them throughout history, unless they have fallen into vain philosophies; like materialism, hedonism or existentialism, which has scarred their conscience. Therefore, as Christians we battle diligently against these very apparent enemies of God; seeking His Righteousness, and trusting that His Holiness will lead us to victory, and our sanctification. This is our continual battle in this life. This is what we still are.

Like most wars, there are areas of the conflict that are less apparent, which include things like espionage, surveillance and reconnaissance. Many times these activities are not visible at all to the public. The newspapers or history books may give all the details of a general's victorious campaign, but may have no knowledge of the intelligence gathered that furnished the leader with the information to devise the triumphant stratagem. These subtleties determine the battles' key victories, and ultimately, the war's outcome. Consider General Benedict Arnold, who plotted to deliver West Point to the British, which Washington discovered when British Major John André was captured carrying papers that exposed his scheme. If not for this incident in the American Revolution, we very well could be speaking the King's English today. Likewise, as guardians of the temple of God, we have been fervently protecting ourselves against all the corruptions of the flesh entering the sanctuary of our temple and gaining strongholds. We are exceedingly careful to bar the door against the lust of the flesh. We most diligently watch for the pride of life, consistently turning him away at every attempt. We are careful to close the shades to the lust of the eyes. Nevertheless, while having been most diligent in these battles has humanism been smuggled into the sanctuary? Does materialism now sit in the congregation? Have other worldly thoughts come into the holy place and the pure doctrines of Jesus? As Christians, with partially restored vision, we know of the enemy's subtle schemes; therefore, we examine ourselves daily, guarding against particular concepts that may have crept in privily. (Jud 1:4)

Nevertheless, many times the greatest enemy is that which appears to be your most obvious friend, and therefore, becomes the least obvious, most harmful adversary. We have done well guarding the rear door against the subtleties who sought access to the temple of God but what about the woman who walks in the front door *"arrayed in purple and scarlet"* and *"gilded with gold and precious stones and pearls"* (Rev 17:4), who calls herself righteousness and holiness for your sanctification. She enters the sanctuary, greatly esteemed by human reason, because she is beautiful to our earthly eyes, but inside, she is full of corruption. She is trusted, because she looks righteous, as Benedict Arnold appeared when given the command at West Point, and as Judas Iscariot seemed when entrusted with the moneybag. She preaches in the temple of God, *"All you have to do is follow my rules, and my religious rites, and then you will be able to save yourself,"* but this is a lie! Remember Lazarus, you cannot save yourself; so once you have been saved, why did you allow this woman to carry you away with the most heinous of all sins - spiritual pride.

Remember the Beatitudes begin with *"Blessed are the poor in spirit"*, and likewise, the Eight Woes warn of falling into the spiritual pride of the scribes and Pharisees.

The Parable of the Cross is a picture of our sanctifying walk with Christ, throughout the course of our lives, and also through our daily experiences. In the course of Christian lives, we have already discussed; being raised from the dead, being born-again, the anointing of the Holy Spirit, water Baptism, cleansing of the temple, bearing the fruit of faith, moving the mountain of ego and acquiescing the throne of our hearts to the Lord of Glory. In addition, in the daily experience of this parable, we have discussed that Logos told us to pick up our cross daily and follow Him, and the Word of God, likewise, affirms we are to die daily. So that the central thought behind The Parable of the Cross is; to deny ourselves, pick up our cross and to follow Him. Therefore, we understand that:

> *I have been crucified with Christ.*
> *It is no longer I who live,*
> *but Christ who lives in me. (Gal 2:20a)*

This is the only rule that we need to know as Christians and yet is the forgotten message of our generation. You do not need to go to church to be saved; although you should do so, to build your faith. You do not need to take communion to be saved; although you should do so, to self-examine your walk, and remember the cost of your freedom, and partake of the body and the blood of Christ. You do not need to read the Bible to be saved; although you should do so, to nourish your soul in order to bring forth righteous fruits in this life. You do not need to pray to God to be saved; although you should do so, to maintain the strength of your fellowship. The Pharisees were doing all of these things, and yet, the Lord utterly lambasted them, although they are things that should have been done, as we have acknowledged. Nevertheless, the act does not create sanctification, but rather, the motivation for the act. The scribes and the Pharisees were able to be obedient through discipline and the desire to make themselves righteous before a Holy God. Christians, likewise, should not be doing these things out of an outward obligation to perform duties before God but out of the desire to perform these duties out of the passionate love for our Great God and Savior. That is the key. The pride of the spirit, entering the temple decked in kingly purple and sacrificial scarlet, seeks to allure you into her enticing deceits by calling herself holiness, righteousness and sanctification. However, in reality, she is asking you to perform specific outward ritualistic acts in order to justify yourself, and make yourself righteous, by which, you perform these rituals in order to save yourself. This is exactly why she is wearing the kingly purple and the blood sacrificial scarlet. This is precisely why she is decked in fine gold and jewels, because, like Judas Iscariot, she is beautiful to our earthly eyes. Moreover, in The Parable of the Cross, the very next stumbling block created by the enemy of believers is the woman, who pretends to be holiness, but her real name is LEGALISM!

> And on her forehead was written a name of mystery: "Babylon the great, mother of prostitutes and of earth's abominations." And I saw the woman, **drunk with the blood of the saints, the blood of the martyrs of Jesus.** And when I saw her, I marveled with a great marveling. (Rev 17:5-6 ESV)

We observe the same scenario in Messiah's day, when the church of God, the synagogue at that time, initiated severe persecution against the saints. Nevertheless, when Stephan was before the council, he correctly asked, *"Which of the prophets did your fathers not persecute?"* (Act 7:52) The inference is not that the Jewish people always persecuted the true believers, as some anti-Semites might suggest, but rather, that the false, legalistic church of man's traditions has always persecuted the true followers of the Word of God. In this church, the Enemy can find an enthusiastic stronghold of zealous followers searching for God to do his bidding. They are ripe for deception, having been deluded by tradition, bound by legalism, blinded by rituals and seduced by relics. In the past, and with a superficial view, this has primarily been the Christian church, acknowledged by the world. However, with a deeper view, it is evident that this is a false church when its actions do not match the doctrines of Messiah it claims to follow. A few basic questions can make this abundantly clear. Was Christ the persecutor or the persecuted? How then can a Christian church, espousing to follow Messiah, be a persecutor?

When the church has usurped the place of the King of Glory, believing that she is protecting the faith of God, she becomes a fearful thing, worthy of *"great marveling."* This pre-Christian church persecuted the prophets of old, this apostolic age church laid waste to the first disciples and this post-apostolic age church committed horrendous atrocities against humanity throughout many centuries. Moreover, it is this church that has stolen the majestic purple from the King of the Universe and seized the sacrificial scarlet from the Author of our Salvation, demanding all the affections of the saints, which is only permissible to be given to the One who is worthy of glory and honor and power. (Rev 4:11) However, the Almighty rejects this traditional legalism in all its pomp and splendor, stating, *"I am Jehovah; that is My name; and My glory I will not give to another, nor My praise to graven images."* (Isa 42:8)

Now, imagine that the blind beggar was standing between the Savior and the Pharisees after Messiah restored his sight to some extent. After hearing from these respected and learned men of the church for a while, the young believer turns away from Jesus and begins to look to the Pharisees. Although the blind beggar received his vision partially, is he currently looking at the pure truth of Christ, who called him to come forth into the light, or at similar corruptible traditions of men who held him in spiritual bondage before the Light of the World beckoned him? Take note that it was a form of legalism that previously held the blind man in the darkness of sin and death, and it is a comparable legalism to which he is now returning, the only difference being, which law to follow and who will be the judge of that law? In the beggar's former state, the judge was himself, but now after receiving some sight he has given that judgeship over to a church of tradition, which has corrupted the pure doctrines of the Lord of Glory. Either way he becomes a slave shackled to a legalistic framework; albeit, the second condition is worse than the first, having become *"twofold more the child of hell."* (Mat 23:15)

What is fascinating is that the world now has better eyesight than the partially restored vision of the beggar. Only they see the church in the blind beggar, following the legal traditions of men. When this church eventually begins to persecute and lay waste the true church of God, the lost look on and say things like, *"if that is religion, then I do not want any part of it."* Even though, Messiah spent most his entire ministry fighting against precisely these legalistic traditions in order to rescue us from its captivity. Thus, Mahatma Gandhi has correctly observed, "*If Christians would really live according to the teachings of Christ, __as found in the Bible__, all of India would be Christian today.*"

After being raised from the dead and given partial spiritual sight, will you now turn to the legal traditions of a Pharisaical system of works to find your sanctification? Our Lord warned the believers in His day, saying,

> *If you __continue__ in My Word, you are My disciples indeed. And you shall know the truth, and __the truth shall make you free__. They answered Him, We are Abraham's seed and were never in bondage to anyone. How do you say, You will be made free? Jesus answered them, Truly, truly, I say to you, Whoever practices sin is the slave of sin. And the slave does not abide in the house forever, but the Son abides forever. Therefore, if the Son shall make you free, you shall be free indeed. (Joh 8:31-36 MKJV)*
>
> *...they picked up stones to throw at him... (Joh 8:59 MKJV)*

This was the very first enemy of the early church. All of John's epistles deal with this error of adding to the Gospel. In addition, the book of Hebrews and letters of Paul to the churches at Corinth and Colossi address these types of errors. However, the most poignant letter on the subject is Paul's epistle to the Galatians, which begins addressing this heresy immediately following his salutation.

> *__I am astonished that you are __so quickly__ deserting him who called you in the grace of Christ and are turning to a different gospel-- not that there is another one, but there are some who trouble you and __want to __distort__ the gospel of Christ__. But even if we or an angel from heaven should preach to you a gospel contrary to the one we preached to you, let him be accursed. As we have said before, so now I say again: __If anyone is preaching to you a gospel __contrary to the one you received__, let him be accursed__. (Gal 1:6-9 ESV)*

Paul gets to the point immediately in this letter. In today's culture, this would be equivalent to writing "*Dear Jane, I am astonished...*" The salutation comprises the leading five verses of the letter, so that the very first verse after the greeting instantly begins to address the issue. This demonstrates not only how serious the issue is, but also how passionately disconcerted Paul was after he received the news. It almost appears that he hears the news and immediately begins to dictate this letter to the Galatians.

The entire theme of this letter is set against this backdrop and deals directly with the issue that we are currently attending to in The Parable of the Cross; therefore, let us now overview Paul's concerns, observations and arguments against returning to a legalistic framework in order to continue the sanctification process and to see the world clearer.

After setting the subject matter for the letter, Paul vindicates his apostleship by testifying of his unique calling by the Lord Jesus Himself. (Gal 1:11-17) This is something that he contends with in many of his other epistles; therefore, it appears these false teachers who arrived after Paul, who wished to spy out these new believer's freedom in Christ and bring them back under their yoke, always attempted to undermine his authority by attacking his apostleship. This was an easy mark for these teachers of the law, who wished to retain their ceremonial rites and traditions and combine them with the sacrifice of the Lamb of God, even though the scriptures made it quite clear that He "*had offered **one sacrifice for sins forever**, [and then] sat down on the right hand of God.*" (Heb 10:12) They were very much like those who attempt to put new wine into old wineskins, to which "*the skins burst and the wine is spilled and the skins are destroyed*". (Mat 9:17) For Adonai of Israel declares from ancient times "*I will make a new covenant*" (Jer 31:31), which will "*not [be] like the covenant that I made with their fathers*" (Jer 31:32), "*but this is the [new] covenant...I will put my law within them, and I will write it on their hearts. And I will be their God, and they shall be my people.*" (Jer 31:33)

From Galatians 1:18-2:10, Paul continues to confirm his apostleship, and yet, at the same time, he masterfully begins to interweave points that advance his argument against returning to legalism. In the first portion of this section, he explains that the leaders of the church accepted him into the body of Christ. Then he met with the church leaders' again in Jerusalem fourteen years later to deal with the very same issue troubling the Galatians presently. The council not only affirmed his apostleship, but the leaders, who were present, at what became known as the Jerusalem Council, affirmed his unique calling as the apostle to the Gentiles. However, the question that brought the group together was not Paul's apostleship, but rather, which rites should bind the Gentiles to the church; the primary of which was the issue of circumcision. Paul then adds as proof to his contention that these false teachers are so compelling in their arguments that Titus, a preacher in the church, who had accompanied Paul to discuss the matter, was himself once deceived and circumcised. (Gal 2:3) Finally, this section concludes with the confirmation that legalistic rituals were no longer part of the new covenant, when James, the brother of Jesus, and the apparent head of the first church, settled the matter, giving only four prohibitions.

> *Therefore, my judgment is that we should not trouble those of the Gentiles who turn to God, but should write to them to abstain from the things polluted by idols, and from sexual immorality, and from what has been strangled, and from blood. (Act 15:19-20 ESV)*

In the next section (Gal 2:11-14), Paul affirms the issue of rituals was also settled when Peter and Barnabas fell into hypocrisy after separating from the Gentiles when Jewish leaders came to eat with the church, so they would not be judged unclean by their brothers in the flesh. At that time, Paul then confronted their duplicity immediately in front of everyone. This example continues to prove his case that we are no longer under the ceremonial law.

In the next section (Gal 2:15-20), we come to the heart of the matter, "*that God is no respecter of persons*" (Act 10:34) and we are all "*one new man*" (Eph 2:15) in Christ Jesus, "*knowing that a man is not justified by works of the Law, but through faith in Jesus Christ.*" (Gal 2:16) However, how is it that we are no longer under the yoke of the law and the ceremonial observances? The answer may surprise you because many churches teach today that the law passed away, but it is not the law that passed away, but rather, we are no longer under the law because WE have passed away! "*For through the Law **I died to the law**, that I might **live to God**.*" (Gal 2:19) Now, in this verse we return to the central message of The Parable of the Cross.

> ***I have been crucified with Christ, and I live; yet no longer I, but Christ lives in me.*** *And that life I now live in the flesh, I live by faith toward the Son of God, who loved me and gave Himself on my behalf. (Gal 2:20 MKJV)*

If we are no longer under the law, does that give us the right to satisfy our sinful desires? To this Paul states emphatically, "*Let it not be said! For if I **build again the things which I destroyed**, I confirm myself as a transgressor.*" (Gal 2:18) That which was "*destroyed*" was the body of sin and death and the subjection of the will to the flesh. Therefore, as followers of Christ, we are now able to keep His commandments, not out of an external obligation to duty, but rather out of our love and desire for Messiah Jesus. It is for this reason that Yeshua, the Song of Solomon, says to us *"If you love me, you will keep my commandments."*(Joh 14:15) This is the primary motivation for following Christ and lusting for God. This is the central message of Christianity, love, not obligation. Notice God does not write the law in our mind, because we already have some conscience that God gives to every man, but rather, God says, *"I will write it on their hearts."* (Jer 31:33) This means that we do not follow God because some well thought out mandatory outward observances or obligatory rules, but rather, we follow God because we passionately desire Him. Thus, the real question is *"Do we desire to please Him more than we desire to please ourselves?"*

In the section that follows (Gal 2:21-3:5), Paul clearly demonstrates the ultimate conclusion implied by a justification by works soteriology, is *"if righteousness were through the law, **then Christ died for nothing**."* (Gal 2:21) We have no comprehension, as we validate our righteousness through works, that we are stealing glory from God. This is the contamination of our sin-infected mind. The result of which is our misguided perception and our disjointed logic. If there was any other way, would not God have given His Beloved Son a way out at the Garden of Gethsemane, when his soul became exceedingly sorrowful (Mat 26:38), and His agony became so acute that *"His sweat became like great drops of blood falling down to the ground"* (Luk 22:44). However, the Father never capitulated, despite having heard His Son's fervent request three times, *"My Father, if it be possible, let this cup pass from me; nevertheless, not as I will, but as you will."* (Mat 26:39) Paul then says to us Galatians, who have now begun to justify ourselves through a system of works:

> *O foolish Galatians, who bewitched you not to obey the truth, to whom before your eyes Jesus Christ was written among you crucified? ...**Did you receive the Spirit <u>by works of the law</u>, or <u>by hearing of faith?</u>** Are you so foolish? **Having begun in the Spirit, <u>do you now perfect yourself in the flesh?</u>** ...Then **He supplying the Spirit to you and working powerful works in you, <u>is it by works of the law</u>, or <u>by hearing of faith?</u>** (Gal 3:1-5 MKJV)*

After this, Paul makes it exceedingly clear, in the subsequent section (Gal 3:6 - 4:12), that heirs to the promise are those who become the *"sons of God **through faith**"* (Gal 3:26), not those who *"rely on doing* *the works of the law"*, for they *"are under a curse."* (Gal 3:10) He does this by expounding upon the faith of an Old Testament saint, Abraham, who lived during the dispensation of the law, and yet, he was justified by faith also and not by works This flies in the face of hyper-dispensationalism many adhere to today, which teaches that God had one plan for the Old Testament saints and a different plan for the New Testament saints; however, as noted from Paul's example above, the Changeless God, always had only one plan fulfilled in Messiah Jesus, the Lamb of God. The Old Testament saints knew *"it is not possible that the blood of bulls and of goats should take away sins."* (Heb 10:4) This is why the prophets said, *"In burnt offerings and sacrifices for sin You have had no pleasure."* (Heb 10:6) Additionally, that God *"desired mercy and not sacrifice, and the knowledge of God more than burnt offerings."* (Hos 6:6) Again, the God of the Old Testament also says, *"I hate, I despise your feast days, and I will not delight in your solemn assemblies"* (Amo 5:21), although these solemn assemblies took place because of His ordinances. Moreover, King David makes the matter particularly obvious, stating,

> *For You do not desire sacrifice; or else I would give it; You do not delight in burnt offering. The sacrifices of God are a broken spirit; a broken and a contrite heart. (Psa 51:16-17 MKJV)*

The Old Testament saints never completely saw the entire picture that we now enjoy from the vantage point of the New Testament, yet they always understood that these rituals were only symbolic of something much greater to come. They may have not had a full understanding of what that thing to come, but they knew that God would provide the lamb (Gen 22:8) and that Messiah would show them all things (Joh 4:25), which has now come to pass in our dispensation. For this reason, Paul states, *"Before faith came, we were held captive under the law, imprisoned **until the coming faith would be revealed**."* (Gal 3:23) In other words, as already stated, the believers prior to the coming of Messiah followed God's ordinances out of faith that there was coming a more permanent solution to the problem of sin. Therefore, Paul makes this point apparent, stating, *"Even as Abraham **believed God**, and it was counted to him for righteousness."* (Gal 3:6) Additionally, he affirms, *"The just shall live by faith."* (Gal 3:11) *"Therefore, know that those of faith, these are the sons of Abraham"* (Gal 3:7), and in him *"shall all nations be blessed"*. (Gal 3:8) Thus, *"those of faith are blessed with faithful Abraham."* (Gal 3:9)

The question, therefore, is: "*If the Old Testament saints, who were under the law were not justified by the works of the law, but rather by faith; how is it that the New Testament saints, upon whom the fullness of faith has been revealed, are now going to justify themselves by works?*" When we fall into the snare of this trap, and the Holy Spirit brings this error to our conscience, then consider Paul's emphatic plea, "*O foolish Galatians! Who bewitched you not to obey the truth?*" (Gal 3:1)

Next, Galatians chapter four tells us that we are heirs in Christ, and yet, no different from slaves, if we do not mature enough to know the freedom of the spirit. How, then, do we learn of our freedom? Again, the answer is, through the Word of God, and not through some outward observance of rituals.

Subsequently, in Galatians 4:13-20, Paul pleads that his desire is wrought from his tremendous love for them, because he has fathered them into the faith; to which he says, "*My children, for whom I again travail until* **Christ should be formed in you**." (Gal 4:19) Once more, we have returned to the central message of The Parable of the Cross; that the cross is both necessary and desirable, because its end purpose and its ultimate effect, is to form Christ in us. What a message! Not by works, lest anyone should boast (Eph 2:9), but through faith; faith that Christ died for us, so we could die to ourselves, for Him who has risen, and wishes to raise us in victory from the body of sin and death. Praise God! Selah!

Now, Paul demonstrates the truthfulness of his message by using the mothers of Abraham's two sons as a shadow prophecy of the two covenants of God. (Gal 4:24) "*For it is written: Abraham had two sons, the one out of the slave-woman, and one out of the free woman.*" (Gal 4:22)

> *But then even as he born according to flesh persecuted him born according to the Spirit, **so it is also now**. But what does the Scripture say? "Cast out the slave-woman and her son; for in no way shall the son of the slave-woman inherit with the son of the free woman." Then, brothers, we are not children of a slave-woman, but of the free woman. (Gal 4:29-31 MKJV)*

However, notice also that the fleshly son persecuted the spiritual son. The one born according to the flesh is the lost world, which includes those who imagine they have accepted Christ's gift of salvation, and yet, continue to follow their own path of salvation by works. This was precisely the Pharisees' error. This also is the same mistake of the infamous apostasies of the Christian church throughout the centuries. Moreover, the false church, born according to the flesh, has always persecuted the true church, born according to the spirit. Comprehending this principle will help clarify actual church history. In Messiah's day, Stephan brought this understanding to light to the Pharisees, saying, *"Which of the prophets did your fathers not persecute?"* (Act 7:52) Once again, we must affirm, they were walking according to the fleshly path of salvation by their own righteous works. Even so, it would be incongruous of us not to concede that the greatest persecutor of Christians, before the 20th century, was the false church, clothed in the veneer of Christian worship, rites and man-made traditions. Thus, it is obvious, even to the lost, that this harlot was *"drunk with the blood of the saints"* (Rev 17:6), and because of this hypocrisy, the name of God is blasphemed among the skeptics even today. (Rom 2:24) However, because the facade so closely resembles the Christian church, many have incorrectly attributed these atrocities to the Christian church and true believers, despite the fact that the authentic church has always fought the counterfeit church; as Jesus did, and the apostles then followed, and then the early church fathers, the reformers and as we do in our time.

Because of the affection to feed our passions and because of our corrupt logic, Galatians reminds us, even though we are justified by faith, we are not free to live lascivious lives. The New Testament stresses this subject matter so many times, that many of the non-legalistic, faith-following churches have become so afraid of creating legalistic, self-righteous children, that they throw good works right out the window. Thus, in Galatians chapter five, begins once again to affirm our freedom in Christ. However, the chapter then ends by comparing the lusts of the flesh, *"Those who practice such things will not inherit the kingdom of God"* (Gal 5:21), to the fruit of the spirit, *"Against such things there is no law."* (Gal 5:23) The former creates ungodly, irreverent false believers and the latter produces good works *"from a pure heart and a good conscience and a sincere faith"* (1Ti 1:5)

In addition, because of our deficient logic, we must be reminded time and time again, against the will of the flesh.

> *But those belonging to Christ **have crucified the flesh** with its passions and lusts. If we live in the Spirit, let us also walk in the Spirit. (Gal 5:24-25 MKJV)*

The letter concludes with some final instructions for the practical application of living a life of faith in this world. Then, the epistle brings to light the hypocrisy of these legalists, and their motivation for bringing the Galatians under their yoke, saying, *"For they themselves, having been circumcised, do not even keep the Law, but they desire you to be circumcised so that they may boast in your flesh."* (Gal 6:13) Subsequently he closes with his central theme, and the central theme of The Parable of the Cross:

> *But may it never be for me to boast, except in the cross of our Lord Jesus Christ, **by whom the world is crucified to me, and I to the world.** (Gal 6:14 MKJV)*

The Old Testament also shows us *"a shadow of the good things to come"* (Heb 10:1), when God spoke to His people at Mount Sinai and gave them the law. Moses pled with the people to draw near to God and hear His Words (Exo 20:20), but instead they responded, *"You speak with us, and we will hear. But let not God speak with us, **lest we die**."* (Exo 20:19) They were correct in this saying, because God Himself has said, *"You cannot see My face. For there [is] no man can see Me and live."* (Exo 33:20) This is true for you as well, for you cannot look upon the face of Immanuel and live as you did formerly, but rather, the flesh will be crucified with its passions and lusts (Gal 5:24) and you will be transformed in the renewing of your mind in Christ Jesus. (Rom 12:2)

Obviously, this legalism existed in us in our former lives. This is what we were. In addition, it is also acutely apparent that these same legalistic behaviors exist in the world today; hence, this is what the world is. However, since we are a *"new creation"* in Christ Jesus, and since all things have been made new (2Co 5:17), then we should not return to our former ways. Therefore, this is what we should not become. Even so, if this is what we were, and this is what we should not become, then how can I say this is what we still are? For how can we still be something that we were, or how can we be on guard not to become what we already are? It seems that we have entangled ourselves into a very great contradiction with this answer, and yet from deep within our hearts, we know that this is the truth, because it speaks to our spirits as truth. How then do we explain this?

Nevertheless, what appears to be a contradiction, which any legalistic rationalist would throw out, is rather a complexity that once it is unraveled will present the discoverer of these treasures deep, and meaningful spiritual insights. For most people, Christianity is a collection of supremely magnificent, and yet disjunctive teachings. They come to Sunday service once a week and discover that God has a uniquely personal message for their lives, even though the preacher may be preaching to hundreds of people with texts that are thousands of years old. This is truly a wonderful mystery, affirming that God still speaks to His children through His Word even today. Then, the next week comes, and the pastor speaks a new breathtaking message. Once again, the parishioner leaves with a revitalized spirit, and a heart fulfilled by the Word of the Lord. However, many times the message from one week to another does not have any inter-relation for the laity, even though both are true. In this way, the average Christian leaves the congregation from week to week with extremely powerful insights for their lives, and yet, their meanings seem somewhat disjunctive, like a jigsaw puzzle that has been left in the box. Nevertheless, when we disentangle this apparent contradiction against the backdrop of The Parable of the Cross, the artistry of God's purpose in our lives will be visible to us in new and exciting ways.

Every evening I stand in awe of the beauty of a new sunset. As the day draws to a close, the Great Artist of All Creation paints a novel, majestic portrait on the canvas of the horizon for the world to see that which has never before been seen. Our Christian life is very much like the canvas of that horizon. We should follow God's example, take all the individual lessons that God has prepared for us, and apply them to the canvas of this marvelous parable. After we have begun to do this, we will find that like the sunset, our tremendous contradiction is nothing more than a complex collogue, filled with the rich hues and the majestic colors of God's purpose and meaning for our life.

The canvas is The Parable of the Cross. The paint is the lesson God is speaking to you in your Christian life; a message from the pulpit, a daily devotion, a Bible study, and so on. As you begin to learn these lessons and apply them to the canvas of this parable, you will begin to see a beautiful picture of the new creation that is unlike any other creation God has ever created, which is your meaning and purpose in life. Then, the lessons will begin to have inter-related meanings, and the disjunctions will start to disappear as you apply more and more paint to the canvas. Before this understanding, you may have never applied the paint to the canvas, because you did not know about the canvas, or you did not realize that the paint was for the canvas. This is very much like a young toddler who is told not to touch a hot stove. The next day he is told not to touch a hot fireplace. To a very young child, these are two particularly important messages, but the stove is in the kitchen, and the fireplace is in the family room; therefore, they do not have anything to do with each other. Nevertheless, as a mature adult we can easily see that the common factor that inter-relates these teachings is the fire, so we apply this commonality to the canvas of their learning experience.

When I first gave my life to Christ I had no understanding of this purpose for my life; I only knew that I was saved. In fact, one of the very first questions I asked the Savior was, *"Now that I am saved, why not just take me to heaven right now?"* My reasoning was as follows:

> **I** have been saved,
> **My** sins have been forgiven,
> **I** am now in perfect relationship with God,
> **I** would prefer heaven to earth, and therefore,
> **I** could never fall away from the faith.

Did you notice who was at the center of my thoughts when I was a babe in Christ? My questions, therefore, gave the answer. It also answers the question *"Why do we need this sanctification walk in this world with the Lord?"* It provides a benefit both for the Christian and for the world. When Daniel was in the lions' den, his faith became stronger by acting upon his faith, but he also became a witness to the unsaved world. When Nebuchadnezzar threw Shadrach, Meshach, and Abednego into the fiery furnace, their faith became stronger, and they also became witnesses to the unsaved. In fact, you cannot find a single trial in the Bible, withstood by the faithful, without seeing these two principles working side by side. Likewise, you will see that behind your trials is the dual purpose of your sanctification and your faithful witness to a watching lost generation. For this reason, we have not been transliterated into the heavens at our new birth, but rather, we continue to endure to the end and grow in sanctification both for ourselves and for the lost.

Although this is an outstanding principle to aid in our understanding of spiritual matters, it, nonetheless, does not answer the apparent contradiction, *"If this is what we were, then how can I say, this is what we still are?"* The partial answer is we continue to grow in our sanctifying walk with the Lord of New Creations. Still, the answer to this question is so profound and meaningful that we need to probe deeper into the matter in order to extrapolate its full significance in our lives. Many Christ followers learn early on that we are to present our bodies as a living sacrifice, which is our reasonable service. (Rom 12:1) In addition, most of us have learned that a living sacrifice has the ability to get up and walk away from the altar. However, so many of us have failed to ask, *"Why do we have to do this?"* To which the answer is contained in the very next verse.

> *And do **not be conformed to this world**, but be transformed <u>by the renewing of your mind</u>, in order to prove by you what is that good and pleasing and **perfect will of God**. (Rom 12:2 MKJV)*

So many Christians have never grasped this profound truth, and because of this, they at no time have clearly understood God's sanctifying work in their lives. Saying things like, "I *do not know what God's Will is for my life*," although, the answer is set right before them in the black and white pages of the Word of God. So many Christians ask questions like, *"I do not understand why I am going through this trial,"* and yet, they will quote Romans 8:28, saying, but I *"know that all things work together for good to those who love God, and to those who are called according to His purpose."* (Rom 8:28) Can you see the common canvas of God's work in the Christ follower's life? These are both excellent examples of our disjunctive understanding of the scriptures and our non-cohesive comprehension of God's purpose in our lives. The mature Christian should never ask either of those questions, because the answer is in the very next verse, because they are not attempting to inter-relate a stove and a fireplace, but rather, they have comprehended that the common element is fire. Look at the second half of the verse *"to those who are called according to His purpose"* (Rom 8:28); what is His purpose? Answer this question and you have now removed the veil, and seen the canvas, upon which God is painting the portrait of His purpose for your life. Again, the answer is in the very next verse:

*For whom He foreknew, **He also predestinated to be conformed to the image of His Son**, for Him to be the First-born among many brothers. (Rom 8:29 MKJV)*

YOU ARE BEING CONFORMED INTO THE IMAGE OF CHRIST! Please set this book down right now and contemplate the magnitude of this unbelievable statement for the meaning and purpose of your life. Spend the entire day meditating upon, and walking in this amazing truth, and you will become a transformed, new creation walking upon the earth. At that time, you will have died to yourself and have allowed Christ, the King of Creation, to live in you. Then you will be walking a sanctifying walk, which is holy and acceptable (Rom 12:1), and you will become a witness to the nations.

Nevertheless, as much as I would like to conclude our discussion upon this grand note; as magnificent as it is, it is still not the most glorious understanding of this teaching; for if we dig just a little deeper, we will discover an even greater treasure. We have now confirmed that being conformed into the image of Christ is God's purpose for our life. In addition, we have already discussed that the cross is God's method to bring about this plan. However, the complexity that I brought to your attention earlier has still not been completely disentangled. We have discussed the duality that exists in the Christian between the "*old man*" (Eph 4:22), and the "*new man*" (Eph 4:24). We have also discussed that the "*old man*" is what we were, and what we should not become, and yet, in some capacity, what we still are. Thus, our objective is to become the new man. Nevertheless, the problem with this understanding is that we now find ourselves working to become something that is impossible, although, thankfully what is impossible for man is possible for God. However, how do we become, because it seems that the harder we strive to become transformed by the renewing of our mind the more we fail? Once again, the answer is contained in the question. Because, becoming involves your work, it will always fail, but rather, it is a matter of "*being*" rather than "*becoming.*" Becoming involves your work and is, therefore, forever trapped within our temporal time dimension. Being transcends time because it involves faith. Becoming looks to the future and says this is what I wish to be. Being looks to the past as says this is what I have already become.

Now against the canvas of The Parable of the Cross, we can affix this very wonderful understanding:

*If then you **WERE** raised with Christ, seek those things which are above, where Christ is sitting at the right hand of God. Be mindful of things above, not on things on the earth. **For you DIED**, and your life has been hidden with Christ in God. (Col 3:1-3 MKJV)*

Now, consider your life from God's eternal perspective. God already knew you would come to Christ *"before the foundation of the world, that we should be holy and without blame before Him in love."* (Eph 1:4) God is not constrained by the time dimension that He created. This may be the most profound and overlooked understanding of God that many Christ followers have not fully contemplated. The Father placed you in the Son at the time of Christ's crucifixion. It is not a matter of **becoming** in the future, which involves your works, but it is a matter of **being** in the present, which involves faith in Messiah's accomplished work for your life, already accomplished at the cross in the past.

We are living in this time dimension, but outside of this time dimension is eternity. For most people, eternity is confused with infinity and interpreted as time that just goes on and on and on, but it actually means a dimension in which time has never existed. It is because of this, that God can say to us, and mean it in a truly literal sense, that He

Has raised us up together and made us sit together in the heavenlies in Christ Jesus. (Eph 2:6 MKJV)

While we live in this time dimension, we can now comprehend that we died in Christ, and were raised with Him in the past, some 2,000 years ago at the cross, and that we are now, presently, sitting in the heavenlies in Christ Jesus. Moreover, because Messiah already accomplished this in the past, we can presently, walk according to this truth in our time-constrained-existence and **become** what we already **are,** in the heavenlies, which is outside of this time dimension.

*For **now** we see in a mirror dimly, but **then** face to face. **Now** I know in part, but **then** I shall fully know even as I also am fully known. (1Co 13:12 MKJV)*

*For if anyone is a hearer of the Word and not a doer, he is like a man studying his natural face in a mirror. For he studied himself and went his way, and immediately **he forgot what he was like.** But whoever looks into the perfect Law of liberty and continues in*

it, he is not a forgetful hearer, but a doer of the work. This one shall be blessed in his doing. (Jas 1:23-25 MKJV)

What do you see when you look in the mirror? Do you see a fallen, sinful creation? Do you see Jesus? Look harder, Christian; if you are a Christ follower, He is in there.

Ye are of God, little children, and have overcome them [the spirit of this world]: because greater is He [Christ] that is in you, than he that is in the world. (1Jn 4:4 KJV)

Now walk in this truth today, for

He who says he abides in Him ought himself also to walk even as He walked. (1Jn 2:6 MKJV)

If you are abiding in Christ in the heavenlies, seated at the right hand of the father, will you not walk according to your calling? Will you not *be* what your new nature *is*, or will you continue to see yourself in the mirror? This is our sanctification and the faith walk of this world. Selah.

chapter ten

WALKING IN THIS WORLD

I knew immediately after accepting Jesus as my savior, I would never be cleaner than I was right at that moment. The Supreme Judge pardoned all my sins. All debts paid. All accounts settled. I literally felt washed and refreshed. Others have told me, as well; that they genuinely felt as if an enormous weight was removed. When the burdensome weight of sin was loosed, they actually felt lighter and freer. I realized, no matter how closely I walked with the Lord in the future, I would never be in more perfect relationship than I was at the time I initially received His redeeming grace. I had accepted Him into my heart. I was entirely complete in Him at that moment. No matter how much I confessed my sins in the future, I could never be more absolved than I was at the instant I was born-again in the spirit. I would never feel more love for God and more of God's love than at this birth. I would never feel a greater gratitude. I would never have more of the Holy Spirit. As I began to ponder this, I understood that I was already standing on the apex of the mountain of God, and since I was at the summit, I faced only two possibilities. I could remain, or, I could slide down the mountain into the mire of my sin. For this reason, I asked God, "*Why not take me right now,*" for it seemed to me, after that moment, I had everything to lose and nothing to gain.

Although the Lord immediately gave all the same gifts I currently enjoy many years later, there was one thing I was missing; and it was rooted in the mind that would even ask that question. It was a me-mentality that the Lord now desired to grow into an other-centered spirit. He took me out of the Egyptian bondage of slavery to my sins, brought me into the wilderness for my training, and was ready now to take Egypt out of me.

This Christian growth is analogous to training princes in monarchial societies. When a king has a son, immediately the child is heir to the entire Kingdom. At the moment he is born, there is nothing more than he will be given that he has not already received. However, until he has knowledge, and has been equipped by training to rule the Kingdom, he will remain in the care and control of his teachers. As a babe, he has no knowledge of anything other than his bodily desires. In his mind, he is the center of the universe. The world revolves around him, and those physical needs. As he grows older, and his mind becomes more sophisticated, he then begins to play games and to appreciate the joys of the imagination, but he is still immature and very self-centered. Nevertheless, if the instructors and the king have trained him properly, then he will grow to serve the nation that serves him.

Now there is only one King of kings and that is King Jesus. Nevertheless, notice that we call Him the King of kings. This is because all of the saints have been born into the kingly family of God at the time of the new birth, for He has *"made us kings and priests to God."* (Rev 1:6) Once you begin to contemplate your high station in life, you will have to wonder how it is that we are so easily beset by our sins when the Deceiver wishes to pull us down from our high estate to wallow in the mud of sin.

When I say Jesus made you a king, you can immediately imagine all the splendor of glory and honor that accompanies royalty. This is not inaccurate, or wrong. However, you do not receive your crown in this life, or this dimension of time, but rather, you received the crown of life in the heavenlies, where your life is hid in Christ, so the experience is manifest *"when this corruptible shall put on incorruption."* (1Co 15:54)

Because we are enticed by this vision, we must admit that glory and honor are desirable. It does not matter what your station is in life, whether you are in the most prestigious position, or in what you may consider, the least significant spot on the planet. Even if, you are rich or poor, intelligent or foolish, powerful or frail, you desire appreciation. This is an aspect of glory and honor. It is an extremely basic human desire, stemming from both below and above. From below, we seek the praise of men. From above, we seek the praise of God, also as a result, for God. From below, many have desired glory and honor so strongly that they seem to be willing sell their very souls for the honor. From above, many have desired heavenly honors so passionately; they have been willing to suffer slander and persecutions as the scum of the earth in order to seek the glory of God.

Nietzsche was correct observing that this drive was even greater than the basic instinct to preserve one's life, because men throughout history have risked everything, including their lives, to gain glory and honor. Thus, he reasoned, the most compelling force within man was what he called the *"Will to Power."* To Nietzsche, this is the most supreme purpose for our existence, and therefore, the highest morality is to fulfill the *"will to power,"* which may require stepping outside of the cultural mores restraining us from attaining this lofty ideal. In many respects, this was a natural extension of the Darwinist model, postulating that the greatest driving force in creatures is survival, which propels the force of natural selection. As a result of the intellectual thought of that era, Nietzsche created his model within this framework, contending that Darwin almost had it right, but missed the enormous psychological drive in man for honor and glory. A drive is so powerful, that men have voluntarily risked their lives and the lives of others, including loved ones, for the opportunity to attain these things.

Most Christians do not accept Nietzsche's observations, because they reject his worldview, as I do also. However, if his observations are found to be truthful, profound and insightful, is it necessary to reject them because they came from a man whose philosophical framework I reject, or is it possible, to accept one and reject the other? The unsaved world has much to offer Christians, but we need to build our philosophical houses upon the foundation of the revealed reality of a biblical worldview, then we may correctly evaluate causes and effects. Beginning with a foundation that does not align scripture will always result in erroneous conclusions.

Nietzsche believed the most predominant driving force in a person's life is the will to power. I agree with this observation, except, I would contend that it is a fundamental desire rather than the foremost principal instinct. We also agree that this driving force is an innate characteristic, common to all human beings. However, we disagree upon the supposition of its origin. Nietzsche, reasoning within an evolutionary framework presupposes the truth of Darwinism as part of his philosophical house, and therefore, concludes that this drive came about because of evolution. On this assumption, I disagree because it is in contradiction to a biblical underpinning. Nevertheless, we both agree about his observation, that the will to power is an extremely powerful driving force in humanity, but disagree on the presumption of its origin.

It is fascinating that about 250 years earlier an extremely devout man, John Calvin, dealt with this same issue in Book II of the *"Institutes of the Christian Religion."* In this book, Calvin contends that everyone has an innate understanding of our fall from God's glory. His argument is as follows. Adam's fall, in the Garden of Eden, transformed Adam from a perfect man, made in the image of God's glory, into a corrupted man with the severe infection of sin. All of Adam's posterity, the entire human race, then inherited this sin-disease. Additionally, buried deeply within our subconscious, and yet so rarely comprehended by most people, is the knowledge of what we were in Adam before the fall. It is for this reason, *"the whole creation groans and travails in pain together"*. (Rom 8:22) What caused this immeasurable agony in all of creation, except the inherent understanding that we lost something we used to possess? All suffering is grief over a lost possession. Consider the following examples. If a loved one dies, you are sorrowful, because you feel a loss. However, people are dying all the time, and yet, you are not constantly in distress. If you lost an immense sum of money, you would be troubled. However, everyday people lose money, and you have no regrets. If you become sick, you feel miserable, because you lost your health. Returning to the travail of all creation, what is it that we are missing that has caused this extreme anguish, except some faint comprehension of our current lost condition and our desire to regain what we once possessed? How can we have any idea about our desired state, except that the concept already exists within us? Moreover, if this idea exists within us, then where did it come from? Is it possible that it is a faint memory from our distant ancestor, stored somewhere in the deep recesses of the mind? What a profound thought! This also seems to line up quite well with scriptures, *"For I reckon that the sufferings of this present time are not worthy to be compared with **the coming glory** to be **revealed** in us."* (Rom 8:18) It is this earnest expectation of this future glory that we so eagerly desire to reclaim, after much patience, fulfilling the promised manifestation to become the sons of God. (Rom 8:19) Notice also, the entire Bible deals with the same theme of creation; paradise created, paradise lost, God's plan to reacquire paradise and paradise regained.

Now in this life we groan and travail because we comprehend the lost glory and honor we once possessed in Adam. We are fallen creatures, and predisposed to sin, but O' how we desire to regain our former state of glory. In Adam was all the perfection of humanity. He was not prone to disease, sin, selfishness or any of the other imperfections that are so ingrained into our fallen nature. Now we know that in Christ

Jesus, all of these things have been taken away, and we have been made kings and priests, and are hid in Him in the heavenlies. We also know that we will receive the manifestation of these gifts when this corruptible body puts on incorruption after being translated into the Kingdom of God at the resurrection. Nevertheless, in present time and existence, we desire both the honor and glory, which we once had in Adam.

Then comes Satan, with perversions and deceits he uses to corrupt this faint memory of what we lost in Adam into a desire of honor and glory from and over men. It is the pride of life. It is a perversion of a natural desire. The Almighty leaves this sense of loss within us to draw us back to Himself. Satan, on the other hand, uses this innate drive to deceive sinners into the believing that the means to fulfill this hunger is to achieve superiority over others to gain glory and honor.

Since the Lord created this drive within every human being, it is not wrong to desire glory, as many have falsely concluded; however, the misdirected focus of the object of that desire is immoral. The world desires glory and honor of self, for self, which is what the Fallen Angel of Light (2Cor 11:14), Lucifer, desired when he fell from grace and became Satan. (Isa 14:12) As Christians, we should seek the honor and the glory we once had in Adam, as we were in paradise before the fall. This honor and glory can only be found in the Glory of God, which means we have to be in Him in order to regain this glory. Thus, this desire is not wrong, as most people would have you to believe, but the real question is; who is the object of this honor and glory, yourself or God? God, then, is the object of our desire, and we are the contingent receptacle of glory in Him. In like manner, the moon has no glory of its own, but rather, it is dependent upon, and merely a reflection of, the antecedent radiance of the sun.

We have been made kings. Not in the manner that the world commonly understands royalty; but rather, we have been made kings in the likeness of our Father in Heaven. Now we know that "*No one has seen God at any time*" (Joh 1:18), but we have seen Yeshua, the "*image of the invisible God, the firstborn of every creature.*" (Col 1:15) We also know that children bear the likeness of their parents. Thus, "*The Spirit Himself bears witness with our spirit that we are children of God*", whereby "*we cry, 'Abba! Father!'*" (Rom 8:16, 15) Moreover, I am thankful that the Holy Writ never describes Yeshua Messiah in physical terms, implying we should not focus upon His earthly appearances and fall into idolatrous worship. Instead, our Example in the Faith is described in character and spirit. He is, therefore, the first fruits, radiant image of the Son of God, whose likeness we should bear as His offspring, since *"all who are led by the Spirit of God are sons of God."* (Rom 8:14)

In what manner did the King of Kings and Lord of Lords come? In addition, what manner did He reign while manifest in the flesh? We know that the Creator of the Universe chose to come to earth as a vulnerable babe in a manager, wrapped in swaddling clothes, born into a poor family, in the small, obscure town of Bethlehem (Luk 2:11-12), in the powerless, conquered nation of Israel. This is not the manner, which I would have come to earth if I were God devising a plan of salvation. I think I would have chosen to appear as a full-grown adult, in strength, and power, and majesty, like Alexander the Great in his prime, entering the world in a triumphal, victorious procession. Instead, the Lord tells us to *"let this mind be in you which was also in Christ Jesus,"* (Php 2:5)

> *...who, **though he was in the form of God**, did not count equality with God a thing to be grasped, **but made himself nothing**, taking the form of a servant, being born in the likeness of men. And being found in human form, **he humbled himself** by **becoming obedient** to the point of death, even death on a cross.*
> ***THEREFORE** God has **highly exalted him** and bestowed on him the name that is above every name, so that at the name of Jesus every knee should bow, in heaven and on earth and under the earth, and every tongue confess that Jesus Christ is Lord, **to the glory of God the Father**. (Php 2:6-11 ESV)*

To recap, the King of All Creation came to earth, born in the likeness of men, taking on the form of a bondservant, humbling Himself in absolute obedience, even onto death; therefore, God has highly exalted Him. Now the practical application of this for our lives is *"**let this mind be in you** which was also in Christ Jesus"*. (Php 2:5)

This is the likeness of the glory of the Son, our lives should reflect for the world to see in the darkness of this age. How do we reflect this glory? We serve. First, by serving God, for *"You shall love the Lord your God with all your heart and with all your soul and with all your mind."* (Mat 22:37) Secondly, by serving man, for *"You shall love your neighbor as yourself."* (Mat 22:39) Therefore, the world should witness a reflected glory of a graceful, servant king because "*the Son of Man came not to be served but to serve, and to give his life as a ransom for many.*" (Mat 20:28)

The distinction between domineering leadership and servant leadership played itself out during the last supper, when the disciples began to contend with each other about who would be the greatest in the Kingdom of heaven (Luk 22:23-24), to which Messiah responded,

> *You know that the rulers of the nations exercise dominion over them, and they who are great exercise authority over them.* **However it shall not be so among you.** *But whoever desires to be great among you, let him be your servant. (Mat 20:25-26 MKJV)*

After the supper, Messiah rose from the table and "*laid aside his outer garments, and taking a towel, tied it around his waist. Then he poured water into a basin and began to wash the disciples' feet:*" (Joh 13:4-5) All the disciples looked on in astonishment, because, in their culture, it was the duty of the lowest servant to wash the feet of the guest. What a dramatic moment. The one that they called Master was now served them as the lowest of all the slaves, which caused the disciples to be dumbstruck; that is, until Jesus came to Peter. Thankfully, however, Peter's impulsive spirit drove him to speak; otherwise, it would be extremely difficult to interpret the spiritual significance of Messiah's gesture. Next, Peter, adamantly objected, saying to the Lord, "*You shall never wash my feet.*" (Joh 13:8) To which the King responded, "*If I do not wash you, you have no share with me.*" (Joh 13:8) This, in turn, caused the zealous disciple to reacted, "*Lord, not my feet only but also my hands and my head!*" (Joh 13:9) Then the King of Glory explains the parable saying, "*The one who has bathed does not need to wash, except for his feet, but is completely clean.*" (Joh 13:10) In another teaching, later, Messiah reaffirms this principle, saying,

> **Already you are clean** **because of the word that I have spoken to** **you.** *(Joh 15:3 ESV)*

If the disciples were already clean, then why did Jesus feel it was necessary to wash their feet, saying, "*If I do not wash you, **you have no share with me**"?* (Joh 13:8) The answer to this question is so simple and yet so profound. The scriptures make it clear we are sojourners in this life (1Pe 2:11), and that our Kingdom is not of this world. (Joh 18:36) Because of this, we are sent as ambassadors for King Jesus (2Co 5:20); therefore, we are in the world but not of the world. (Joh

17:16-18) That is the key. We must be part of this world, because the Captain of our Salvation has decreed the mission, having said, *"As You [the Father] have sent Me into the world, even so I have sent them into the world."* (Joh 17:18) Add to this the Holy Spirit's exhortation through Paul, *"How beautiful are **the feet** of those who preach the **gospel of peace** and bring glad tidings of good things!"* (Rom 10:15) and you have the answer. He has sent us into the world, to reach the lost in our daily walk, but those feet get dirty, because we must walk in a polluted world. (2Pe 2:20)

In all of this, Messiah was our example. If His only purpose were to die for our sins, then He could have done that immediately, coming into the world as a full-grown adult going directly to the cross. However, other items were also part of the incarnation agenda. To list a few of these, consider that God chose that His Son would receive knowledge in the same manner as any other man, *"And Jesus increased in wisdom and in stature and in favor with God and man."* (Luk 2:52) Secondly, the Father determined that His Son must be *"tempted as we are..."* (Heb 4:15) Lastly, the Father resolved that Christ would be the perfect sacrificial offering, the Mediator, and Captain of our Salvation through suffering. In this way, He could then relate to all of us, in our human frailty, in our pain and emotions brought about by our various trials.

> *For it was fitting that he [Christ], for whom and by whom all things exist, in bringing many sons to glory, should make the founder of their salvation **perfect through suffering**. (Heb 2:10 ESV)*

After Christ washed the disciples' feet, He said, *"I have given you **an example**, that you also should do just as I have done to you."* (Joh 13:15) So many times, I have heard from our shepherds in the pulpit the correct interpretation shared with you, but what I never heard is another equally correct interpretation from an alternative perspective. The most prominent teaching is from the disciples' vantage point, which elucidates we must wash our feet in the water of His Word. Nevertheless, we should not overlook that Jesus said, He gave us *"an example,"* as we ought also to serve one another. Now, many have taught that this is a model as well, which is equally correct. However, I have never heard any teach that Messiah wants us to wash the feet of OUR disciples. Now, unless you are a pastor or a church leader, my previous statement probably caused you to say, *"I do not have any* *disciples.*" To this, I answer you are quite incorrect. We all have disciples. They may not be formal students, but we all exert an influence on other people, many times without any realization. I have three sons, that I lead every morning in devotion; they are my disciples. I have a wife who looks to me as the spiritual leader in the house, which makes her a disciple. I have people at work who may ask my opinion on spiritual matters, at those times; I wash them in the water of the word, which makes them disciples. Coaches have players. Teachers have students. Bus drivers have passengers, and the list goes on and on, as we begin to comprehend how we affect each other in our social interactions.

The Parable of the Cross perspective, should cause use to appreciate the affect we have with other people. We should always be washing them with the water of the Word.

Additionally, we see from Heb 2:10 that Jesus, the Founder of our Salvation, was made "*perfect through suffering*". This is why the cross is so crucial to our sanctification. This is why we are at all times, even in times of suffering; we should be giving thanks to God.

> *Count it all joy, my brothers, when you meet trials of various kinds, for you know that the testing of your faith produces steadfastness. And let steadfastness have its full effect, that you may be perfect and complete, lacking in nothing. (Jas 1:2-4 ESV)*

In addition, this means that Jesus needed a Judas to bring Him to the cross, or at least, to help Him, who is fully deity, understand the pain of betrayal by a loved one, in His full humanity. Now, when people betray us, we can find comfort in Immanuel, who also suffered in like manner, but even greater treacheries in the flesh during His incarnation. Then, after being bitten by the false kiss of friendship, we can help others who have experienced this pain as well. As a result, our ministry becomes more perfected as we begin "*to heal the brokenhearted, [and] to proclaim deliverance to the captives*" (Luk 4:18)

All the events, disputing who would be the greatest, washing of the disciples' feet and Judas' betrayal, all occurred after our Messiah instituted one of the two biblical sacraments of the Christian faith.

> *That the Lord Jesus on the night when he was betrayed took bread, and when he had given thanks, he broke it, and said, "This is my*

body which is for you. Do this in remembrance of me." In the same way also he took the cup, after supper, saying, "This cup is the new covenant in my blood. Do this, as often as you drink it, in remembrance of me." (1Co 11:23-25 ESV)

The literal interpretation is, the bread is Jesus' body, and the wine is His blood. However, we also can look for other contingent, supportive biblical imports for these symbols that the Lord chose to represent His sacrifice. In other words, the Omniscient God, who diligently inspired every word of scriptures, so *"not one jot or one tittle shall in any way pass... until all is fulfilled"* (Mat 5:18), must have had some rationale for choosing bread and wine as symbols for the New Covenant.

After conducting a systematic study of the bread, and Jesus in the New Testament, we discover that Jesus is the Bread of Heaven (Joh 6:41) and He is the Word of God in the flesh. (Joh 1:1) Therefore, the bread is also symbolic of the Word of God, as seen when Messiah told Satan during His temptation in the wilderness that *"Man shall not live by **bread** alone, but by every **word** that comes from the mouth of God."* (Mat 4:4) In addition, we find a similar comparison between the wine and the spirit when the Apostle Paul says, *"be not drunk with **wine**, wherein is excess; but be filled with the **Spirit**."* (Eph 5:18) Therefore, literally, we comprehend that the Sacraments were to be done *"in remembrance"* (Luk 22:19) of Christ's body and blood, but from a figurative perspective, we also acknowledge that the bread is symbolic of the Word of God, or the scriptures, and that the wine is symbolic of the Spirit of God. Following this line of logic, we discover additional revelations. We need bread, which synonymous with food, daily to nourish the body, and in like manner, we need the Word of God daily to nourish our spirit. Nevertheless, be forewarned, that we need both the bread, which is the letters of the Word of God, and the wine, which is the Spirit of the Living God, daily for our spiritual sustenance. In this manner, *"we serve in newness of spirit and not in oldness of the letter"* (Rom 7:6), because God has now put a new spirit within us (Eze 11:19), having written His Word upon our hearts. (Jer 31:33) Therefore, we do not follow His ways because of some outward religious obligation, but rather, because our innermost desires have changed.

In Messiah's days, the Pharisees were good at living by the letter of the law, but had very little spiritual discernment. We also have seen this same error many times in church history. In contrast, we have also witnessed the drunkenness of Christianity, which made spiritual revelations so significant that they superseded the Letter of God. The sacraments symbolize Christ's death, and the remembrance thereof, but they also demonstrate our need for both the Word of God and the Spirit of God, together for salvation and proper scriptural discernment. Therefore, when we sit at the table to feed our disciples, we should be sure to fill them with the body and the blood of the Son of God, which are both His Word and His Spirit.

I began this chapter discussing the controversy that arose from the disciples after the meal of the Last Supper. I purposely started at the end of the evening, rather than taking the events sequentially, in order to finish at that same point. If you will recall, our discussion that the desire for glory and honor are God-given attributes, which Satan attempts to fulfill with deceits and perversions. Nevertheless, God leaves this drive within us, so we will seek the Glory of God, which is the only satisfying fulfillment of this need. Now, consider that this was the last meal the disciples would eat with their Beloved Savior. Furthermore, notice that they knew His time was coming, because Messiah said them, *"I have earnestly desired to eat this Passover with you before I suffer."* (Luk 22:15) The fact that He must suffer, only reinforced what He told them on at least three other occasions:

> *The Son of Man will be delivered over to the chief priests and scribes, and they will condemn him to death and deliver him over to the Gentiles to be mocked and flogged and crucified, and he will be raised on the third day. (Mat 20:18-19 ESV)*

There is no doubt in my mind that the disciples loved Jesus, after all, they left everything and followed Him faithfully for over three years. However, notice that instead of comforting Messiah, or praying, or any consideration of His turmoil, they chose to contend with each other over who would be the greatest. The pride of man, the heart of man, and the blindness of man is so dark that these loved-ones could not, for one moment, put aside their own selfish desires, even for this final evening, they knew would be their last supper with the Lord of Glory. Are you now beginning to comprehend our desperate need for the cross? This is why we praise the Sovereign God of the Universe, who has created us for a higher purpose, so that all things would work together for our good, especially the shame of the cross.

chapter eleven

WHERE THE BATTLE IS WON

"Jesus said to him, 'What you [Judas Iscariot] are going to do, do quickly.'" (Joh 13:27) *"When he had gone out, Jesus said, 'Now is the Son of Man glorified, and God is glorified in him.'"* (Joh 13:31) Notice that the Example of our Faith had no problem glorifying Himself, because it is the glory of God through Him as a vessel, which is its proper place, and where it also existed in the first Adam, before Adam sought his own glory. We have already clearly delineated this fundamental observation in the previous chapter, but now, in order to advance our discussion on The Parable of the Cross, notice that the Lord of Host declares the victory before the battle has even been manifest before our eyes.

This is how faith always works. Faith is something that has already occurred in the past. Hope is something that will assuredly appear in the future. Faith for the born-again Christian looks back at the center of time, which is the triumph of the cross, and claims the body and the blood of Jesus as victorious over all circumstances. For *"faith is the substance of things hoped for, the conviction of things not seen."* (Heb 11:1) Notice that faith is a *"substance"* or an *"assurance"* as the ESV translates, which implies it already exists; and yet it is something that is hoped for, which implies it does not exist. Moreover, this is made clear by the subsequent phrase, stating it is *"the conviction of things not seen."* Additionally take note, that the Resurrection and the Life claimed victory prior to the substantive manifestation of Lazarus rising from the dead, saying, *"Father, I thank you that you have heard me."* (Joh 11:41) He does not say, *"Father thank you that you will hear me"*, but instead, He says, *"you have heard me,"* speaking in the past tense. Now consider the verse at the Last Supper. Notice that the Captain of our Faith says, *"Now is the Son of Man glorified."* He does not wait for the cross, the resurrection, or any other future event in order to claim the victory, but claims the victory solely upon the initial incident that springs all the succeeding events into action. That is, Judas' betrayal,

224

because all the consequential actions flow from this preliminary catalyst. For example, I recall the first time I jumped out of an airplane. I was terrified. I thought to myself, *"How do I always get myself into these things?"* as I walked to the door to jump. Nevertheless, in my mind, I was thinking of the recruiter's office when he suggested I become a paratrooper. That momentary decision was the initial catalyst for all the successive actions that followed; boot camp, airborne training, deployments and such. The catalyst for the cross, the event that sprung all other events into action, was Judas leaving the Last Supper with a heart of stone, determined to betray Immanuel, the Son of God. Because this was the catalyst to all the other future events, the Captain of our Faith, could rightly say, in faith, *"**Now** is the Son of Man glorified."*

The Lamb of God then set His house in order because soon He would be leaving His disciples. This is only fitting since His disciples had come to depend upon Him for everything. First, He lets Peter know that he will fall but assures him, and the others, that He will see them again in heaven. Secondly, He teaches that they should trust in God through the ministry of the Holy Spirit, also known as, the Spirit of Truth (Joh 14:17), the Comforter (Joh 14:16), the Spirit of Promise (Eph 1:13), the Spirit of Holiness (Rom 1:4), the Spirit of Life (Rom 8:2), the Helper (Joh 14:26), and the Spirit of Christ (Rom 8:9), among others. Thirdly, He warned them that they should remain strong in the face of persecution and steadfast in their faith, because *"A servant is not greater than his master"* (Joh 15:20), and because you have been born-again in the Spirit of Christ; therefore, you have been made in the image of your Master. Thus, you have been chosen out of the world, and so, *"the world hates you"* also (Joh 15:19); nevertheless, he that endures to the end shall be saved. (Mar 13:13) Then Our Salvation said, *"I have said all these things to you to keep you from falling away."* (Joh 16:1) In other words, He has told us before hand, so when we suffer these things, we will know that Our Sovereign Creator has all things under His control, implying that even our suffering is God's Will. Fourthly, Messiah subsequently enjoins the disciples in prayer for Himself, His disciples and believers throughout time. Afterwards, He retreats in solitude to the Garden of Gethsemane for personal prayer with the Father.

Then Jesus asked three of His closest disciples to come with Him for prayer and support. It was the end of one of the longest days of an extremely long week. Jesus had many things to set in order prior to His suffering. Likewise, the disciples also had a unusually demanding day. Their day probably began, walking from the Mount of Olives to Jerusalem, since Luke informs us that it *"was his custom"* to go out *"to the Mount of Olives"* (Luk 22:39) for an evening of prayer after spending the time ministering in Jerusalem. More than likely, Jesus spent this entire day teaching in the temple. The disciples, on the other hand, spent much of their time preparing the Last Supper; acquiring the room, setting up the room, buying and sacrificing the lamb, and gathering, preparing and cooking the dinner. To accentuate the disciples' labors, let us contrast them to Thanksgiving dinner preparations in our own time. Preparing this feast is a lot of work for the host; however, we have contemporary conveniences that make it much easier, like, supermarkets, freezers, refrigerators, stoves, cars and other modern advantages. The disciples, conversely, had none of these amenities; so, these preparations were extremely laborious. Afterwards, they ate a large, leisurely dinner. When Jesus discussed future events, then they contended with each other about who would be the greatest in Messiah's Kingdom. On the way to the Mount of Olives, Gethsemane, Jesus continued to pray with, and for, and teach the disciples. These teachings included, preparing a place and the Holy Spirit (Joh 14), and the Parable of the Vine (Joh 15). Now consider how tired you are after hosting a Thanksgiving meal for your loved ones. Additionally, if you spent any time teaching you can also appreciate how draining this can be. Now let us return to the Messiah and the disciples' state of being. Then they finally reached Gethsemane, at the end of both a truly fulfilling day of fellowship, and yet, a day filled with controversies and contentions, but most of all, a time in which the death of their beloved Messiah continued to loom particularly heavy upon all of their psyches. They were exhausted. Jesus then chose three of His closest disciples; Peter, James and John, to join Him in prayer, because He who has ministered unto others was now hoped they would minister onto Him in His hour of need. Not only for His comfort, but also, He purposed, they would seek God's strength in order to fortify themselves for their own fiery trial. We see this, as well, in the church today, that the Holy Spirit will inspire the leadership to break away for a time of special prayer and guidance to lead the flock.

> *Then he said to them, "My soul is very sorrowful, even to death; remain here, and watch with me." And going a little farther he fell on his face and prayed, saying, "My Father, if it be possible, let*

this cup pass from me; nevertheless, not as I will, but as you will."
(Mat 26:38-39 ESV)

Notice that The Way asked the Supreme Judge if there was any other way, and if there was, then to let the cup of God's wrath to pass from Him. We know, however, the Father's answer to His Only Begotten Son. There is no other penalty that would pay for all of mankind's injustice, lawlessness and wickedness that has piled so high in the ledger books of God's perfect law. For He has said, *"on the day of judgment people will give account **for every careless word** they speak, for by your words you will be justified, and by your words you will be condemned."* (Mat 12:37-38) If that is the case, then how much greater is the penalty for all the murders, rapes, adulteries, wars and other atrocities man has committed throughout the centuries. All these actions can be summed up into one exceedingly great slight against God throughout human history, which is the mantra, *"We choose our way and not Yours, O God, King of the Universe!"* We are the lump of clay that has said to the Potter, *"I have made myself, and I will rule myself, who are You, O God, to tell me how to live!"* In wickedness, we threw off the restraining Hand of God, meant for our good and called it the evil shackles of oppression, in order to follow our lusts. All the misery on earth can be traced back to this one exceedingly great folly of man; *"I choose my own way and not your way, O God!"* How long would the list of these indictments read against humanity throughout the centuries? What punishment could be equal to the abomination of these crimes? IT IS UNFATHOMABLE! Even while pondering this, I have to admit, that my feeble, small mind, cannot come to a full understanding of a settlement that would have been a payment worthy enough to remit the terrible atrocities man has committed throughout the centuries. Nevertheless, the Son of God understood it perfectly, and it was for this reason that He was *"sorrowful, even to death"* (Mar 14:34), and for this reason, He said, *"My Father, if it be possible, let this cup pass from me."* (Mat 26:39)

Next, consider when the Lord of Glory said, *"My soul is very sorrowful, even to death"*. We tend to take it as figurative language, which is possible that is all that was meant; yet, it is also very possible the King of Glory meant this in a very literal sense. For notice the third time He goes to the Father in prayer, His soul was so troubled that *"his sweat became like great drops of blood falling down to the ground."* (Luk 22:44) In this case, the word *watch* may have a dual meaning when Messiah tells the disciples, *"Remain here and watch."* (Mar

14:34) He may have been saying something like *"keep an eye on me because my anxiety is so great I may pass out or die."* The verses *"My soul is sorrowful, even to death"* and His sweat becoming *"like great drops of blood"* give some credence to this possibility; and when we take into consideration, the incredible payment required for the sins of humanity throughout the ages, this possibility becomes even more plausible. Nevertheless, even if we believe that the Lord had meant this in a dual sense, we should not lose sight of the view that this word watch also means to be on guard and diligent in prayer. Reviewing other passages for the Greek word *"watch,"* or *"gregoreuo,"* offers greater insight into its meaning:

> **Watch**! *Stand fast in the faith! Be men! Be strong! (1Co 16:13)*
> *Continue in prayer and **watch** in it with thanksgiving (Col 4:2)*
> *...let us not sleep as the rest do, but let us **watch**... (1Th 5:6)*

The word appears to imply concepts of guarding your soul, standing fast in the faith, being diligent in your devotions, being strong in the Lord and the Power of His Might, and being thankful that He has won and is our victory. Consider that the Good Shepherd reminded his sheep, *"Remember then how you have received and heard, and hold fast, and repent."* (Rev 3:2) Furthermore, He, who is Faithful and True, warned the flock, *"if you will not **watch**, I will come upon you as a thief, and you will not know what hour I will come upon you."* (Rev 3:3) Again, the Wall of Our Salvation, admonished, *"Be sensible and **vigilant [watch]**, because your adversary the Devil walks about like a roaring lion, seeking whom he may devour."* (1Pe 5:8) Notice, as well, that this roaring lion is *"The thief [that] does not come except to steal and to kill and to destroy."* (Joh 10:10) Additionally, we also know *"that if the master of the house had known what hour the thief would come, he would have **watched** and would not have allowed his house to be dug through."* (Luk 12:39)

Returning to the disciples, Jesus tells them to watch, in two very real senses, watch me, and watch your soul. This is an incredibly important point that I will return to later in the chapter to expound upon when we begin to apply this to The Parable of the Cross.

Finally, although the Son of God prayed that His Eternal Father take away the cup filled with His wrath (Rev 16:19), He was extremely careful never to seek His own will, but rather, to seek the Will of His Father. That is our greatest problem. We are our own worst enemy. We have forsaken our God, and everyone has followed what is right in his own eyes (Jdg 17:6); but that was not the case for Faithful and True. Who at the time of His greatest anguish asked if there was any other way, but never shrank from God's purpose for His life, no matter how difficult the path. This should be the life verse of every Bible believing Christian, *"not as I will, but as you will"* (Mat 26:39) O God, King of the Universe and King of my heart!

The Son of God must set aside His deity, and go to the cross as the Son of Man. After one final display of power, performed to protect His disciples, and demonstrate to an unbelieving world that no one takes His life from Him. Rather, He lays it down willingly for the flock, so He may take it up again. (Joh 10:15-18) This final exhibition of His supreme authority occurred at the time of His arrest, when Judas arrived at the garden that dark evening with a small army of soldiers. He Who Knew All that was about to come upon Him, stepped forward to confront the cohort, and asked, for their benefit, *"Whom do you seek?"* (Joh 18:4) To which *"They answered him, 'Jesus of Nazareth.'"* Then, He who walked on Water and Calmed the Raging Storm, responded with the name of God, which the New Testament translates as *"I AM!"* Instantly, this entire army of physically powerful men was thrust backwards to the ground, simply by the power of His Word. Immanuel's next statement was, *"I say to you, I AM: so if you seek me, release these to go their way."* (Joh 18:8) After being thrown to the ground by the power of His Word and confronted twice with the name of God, shaking in their military boots, they do as Yeshua commanded, and allow His followers to go. This was the last display of His deity, for now, His face was set as a flint, as He walked towards His destiny and His Father's purpose for His life, the cross. He must go to the cross as A MAN, who knew no sin, to become sin, to pay the penalty of sin, for those who have been born into sin. For, it was A MAN, who rebelled against God. Moreover, and as Adam's descendants, we were people without hope, born from his seed, who acted according to our nature. Mankind committed all the terrible atrocities throughout history, so it must be a man, who is obliged to pay its enormous penalty.

What benefit would Jesus be to us, who have fallen so far from grace, if He did not appear as fully man? For this reason, the Son of Man said, *"I have given you an example, that you should do as I have done to you."* (Joh 13:15) Likewise, the Apostle Peter admonished, *"Christ also suffered on our behalf, leaving us an example, that you should follow His steps.*" (1Pe 2:21) How hollow would these words be if the Example of our Faith did not go through these trials as a man? Thus, He emptied His divinity, taking on "*the form of a servant, being born in the likeness of men*" (Php 2:7), in order to be tempted in all points (Heb 4:15), and "*became obedient unto death, even the death of the cross.*" (Php 2:8) Yet, who, or what can tempt God? (Jas 1:13) Furthermore, who can kill the Everlasting God? Jesus, the Son of Man was tempted in all points, as we are also tempted. He humbly submitted to the Father, being obedient even unto death. For this reason, He set the glory of His deity aside, to embrace the shame of the cross, and became our example in the faith.

Knowing these things, will we now diminish the work of the cross and the trials and temptations suffered by Jesus, by saying, "*He was God*"? We are so quick to point to the deity of Christ when we need to justify our sins, saying things like, "*He WAS God.*" Conversely, we are just as quick to dismiss His deity and His Lordship when we wish to follow our own ways and fulfill the desire of that same sin. We are such rational beings, although our reasoning many times lacks coherency. We justify not following Jesus' as an example because He was God, then we rationalize not submitting to the King of Creation because we want to lord over our own lives. We do this to justify ourselves in our own eyes and fulfill our earthly passions. This is nothing more than a self-deluded house of cards that the fiery trial will quickly turn to ashes.

Many consider Jesus' greatest accomplishment was the cross, but I believe that is not correct. What Jesus accomplished on the cross was the result of His greatest accomplishment, which was walking in perfect obedience to the Father. The work of the cross would have been meaningless without the Son of God's perfect submission to the Father. Thus, He could only have accomplished the work of the cross out of a perfectly obedient life. Consider, for example, when Satan used the Pharisees to tempt Him on the cross saying, "*If he is the King of Israel, let him now come down from the cross, and we will believe him.*" (Mat 27:42) How easy this would have been for Immanuel to do! Alternatively, consider the time people were brutally beating Him, ripping out His beard, crowning Him with thorns and spitting upon Him. How easy it would have been for Him to call upon "*more than twelve legions of angels.*" (Mat 26:53) Thankfully, for our salvation, He continued to remain fully submissive to the Father's Will. It was

God's judgment against humanity that brought Him to the cross, but it was Yeshua's love and obedience that kept Him on the cross.

If you choose to follow your sin, do not diminish the work of the Savior by saying, "*He was God*." It is true that He is God, but He went to the cross to bear the sins of all men throughout the course of history, past, present and future, as a man. Besides, how can we compare the small temptations we face with one so great, and then, justify them by saying, "*He was God*"? Our degenerate minds know no bounds when it comes to justifying and satisfying the lusts of those sinful desires. Furthermore, how quickly we are beset by small temptations and willing to sell our birthrights in Christ for a mere morsel of bread.

We have discussed Christ as the great I AM, which is to say, He is fully God. In addition, we have discussed that the work of the cross proves He was fully man, because God cannot be tempted and God cannot die. What benefit would we have received if God went to the cross AS GOD, and then called this our example, since we could never be God?

With this understanding, let us return to the low point of Jesus' physical existence on earth, a time when He quite literally had the weight of the world on His shoulders, and a time when He was so sorrowful that He literally could have died from grief. I have often wondered how He was able to have enough stamina to endure the coming trials, after reaching this low point. Physically, it was an extraordinarily difficult week, teaching the entire day, constantly tested by the scribes and the Pharisees. This final day was probably consistent with the other days, in that He taught in the temple, after rising early to spend time in prayer and before spending time with the disciples at the Last Supper. Later, they walked to Gethsemane, and there He was in prayer for several hours. At that time that He told His disciples, "*My soul is sorrowful, even to death*." Nevertheless, this was only the beginning of the physical nature of these trials. He will have to go through six tribunals, without food, without rest, while enduring beatings and lashings, and He must accomplish the mission of the cross or all humanity is lost! After spending eighteen hours working in His ministry, He will now have to endure another fourteen hours of physical trials. All of this was accomplished with the ultimate dread in mind, that, at the time the Supreme Judge transposes all the sins of humanity onto His sinless soul, the Father will turn His back on His Son, causing His Beloved Son will cry out in anguish, for the first and only time in eternity, "*Eli, Eli, lama sabachthani? That is, My God, My God, why have You forsaken me?*" (Mat 27:46)

How did the man Jesus find enough physical strength to endure these trials and overcome death, by dying on the cross and rising from the grave? Fortunately, Doctor Luke provided the answer, "*And there appeared to him an angel from heaven, strengthening him.*" (Luk 22:43) Well there it is you say, "*Jesus was able to go to the cross because an angel strengthened Him. When I am tried, I do not get that kind of support.*" However, you are wrong; God did not provide anything for Jesus, concerning this strengthening, that He had not also provided, at other times, for His prophets when they faced extreme circumstances. For example, at Elijah's low point,

> *...the angel of Jehovah came to him the second time and touched him, and said, Arise, eat, because the journey is too great for you. And he arose, and ate and drank, and **went in the strength** of that food forty days and forty nights to Horeb the mount of God. (1Ki 19:7-8 MKJV)*

Consider when Daniel told the angel of the Lord, "*no strength remains in me, and no breath is left in me*". (Dan 10:17) The angel touched him and strengthened him. (Dan 10:18) Additionally, the spirit of the Lord, at various times, strengthened Samson, Jeremiah, Ezekiel and Isaiah. In like manner, the Father strengthened Stephen, in the New Testament, at the time of his stoning when he saw "*heavens opened, and the Son of Man standing at the right hand of God*" (Act 7:56), allowing him to pray for his persecutors, "*Lord, do not hold this sin against them.*" (Act 7:60)

Jesus, our Example in the Faith, demonstrated how to overcome when faced with an extreme trial. He went to God in prayer, the source of our strength and God heard His prayer. Then, the Father and gave His Son the power to endure. This is consistent with scriptures, "*where sin abounded, grace did much more abound*" (Rom 5:20); or to put this into a simple precept, God will always provide enough grace to overcome the sin, or the trial, when you seek the Almighty.

History, as well, bears witness to this truth. When the church imprisoned Martin Luther, he spent the evening in prayer. The next day, at the time of his trial, he was able to find the strength to stand in his convictions. John Wycliffe, likewise, endured many trials in his time by standing in his faith and gaining strength through prayer. God also afforded John Hus this same strength during his fiery trial, in which the church court convicted him of heresy. What followed was one of the most despicable scenes ever recorded by *civilized* society. As his enemies brought him to the place of his execution, people bombarded him with clumps of dirt. In order to humiliate this man of God, the church officials placed on his head a hat painted with three devils. Afterwards, they repeatedly cried out anathemas against him, committing his soul to the devil and his disciples. In order to take away any last vestige of human dignity, his persecutors then undressed him, prior to tying him to the stake. Next, they bound his neck with a chain to the stake, piled straw up to his neck and began to burn him alive. Witnessing all the people spewing hatred, cursing his soul to hell, as the flames began to consume his flesh, God gave him the strength to love his enemies, and so he died, praying:

> *Father in Heaven, do not hold against them the sins which my enemies commit against me, and let mine eyes see them blissfully with thee, when their souls fly to thy throne after an easy death. O Holy Spirit, enlighten their deceived hearts, so that the truth of the holy Gospel may open their eyes and its praise be spread everywhere, forever and ever, Amen.*

What was this heretic's infamous crime? He taught the word of God directly from the bible.

The Parable of the Cross is meaningless if Christ does not go to the cross as a man. This is the underpinning of Christ as faith exemplar. This is also the foundational understanding of this wonderful parable, whereby we now can begin to comprehend God's purpose in our lives, and how the cross fits into this divine destiny. Nevertheless, take to heart that the battle is not won at the time the battle is fought, but rather, it *was* won in the prayer that preceded the battle; making its outcome a foregone conclusion. This is why we can say, "*If God is for us, who can be against us?*" (Rom 8:31), and "*we are more than conquerors through him [Jesus Christ] who loved us*" (Rom 8:37)

chapter twelve

BETRAYALS AND BETRAYERS

Jesus said to him, *"Judas, would you betray the Son of Man with a kiss?"* (Luk 22:48)

How long have we betrayed each other, and been betrayed by each other? You have to go back to the very beginning of the propagation of the human race. Adam and Eve were the active participants in contracting the hereditary disease we now call sin, but after *"Adam knew Eve his wife, and she conceived and bore Cain"* (Gen 4:1), sin from the father's seed was passed into Cain, as were many other genetically inherited traits. When they became adults, *"Cain rose up against his [younger] brother Abel and killed him."* (Gen 4:8)

Was this the very first betrayal in the human race? The answer is no. The very first betrayal occurred when the serpent, Satan, betrayed Eve's trust, and beguiled her into thinking that God desired to keep something good from her. She then betrayed the goodness of God, by believing the serpent rather than the Word of her King. Adam's sin, however, was even greater than Eve's because Adam was not deceived. (1Ti 2:14) Because of this,

> ... *sin came into the world through one man, and death through sin, and so death spread to all men because all sinned... (Rom 5:12 ESV)*

What was Adam's great sin? Did he lust for the fruit, seeing that it was good to eat? Did he desire forbidden knowledge? Did he become prideful and want the same glory as God, rather than to be content as a reflection of that glory? Did he want to be God? On the other hand, did unbelief cause him to trust more in the words of the created thing, Satan, rather than the Word of the Creator? All the seeds for human corruption are in the above list, from which all sin was born, but the greatest offence, seems to be disbelieving the goodness of God and His Word. Consider, in times past, if we had followed two remarkably simple and reasonable requests of God, "*Love the Lord your God …and your neighbor as yourself.*" (Luk 10:27) Then, we would not have been adulterers, killers, and betrayers, our history books witness against our supposed civilized nature. Instead, these books corroborate the truth of our fallen, irreparable condition. With great repetition, we have made the same error, whereby we chose, throughout the centuries, to believe and give credence to, human reason more than the Word of God.

The greatest liar the world has ever known, Satan, who perverts all truth, turning it upside down and inside out. He is so adept at this that Messiah even warns believers that the Serpents minions; "*false christs and false prophets will arise and perform great signs and wonders, so as to lead astray, if possible, even the elect.*" (Mat 24:24) Earthly ecclesiastical institutions have led many astray. For example, before Martin Luther found grace and became born-again in the faith, he despised John Hus, believing his judgment to be burned as a heretic was just. Moreover, the secular world has correctly judged the atrocities committed by the church, throughout the centuries, like indulgences, the Crusade massacres, anti-Semitism and the Inquisition, as crimes against humanity, but they have wrongly attributed these transgressions to the Word of God and His genuine followers. It has now become a common axiom that religion is the cause of all wars and human suffering through the ages. Since the Christian faith was the official state religion of the Western culture that committed these atrocities, it is stands to reason it is the worst of them all. However, the pilgrims, who were intensely religious people, suffered dreadfully severe persecution at the hands of the official state church. They also believed these heinous crimes were wrong, but they believed Satan framed the wrong party as the cause. Most people believe religion is the root of all the ills in society. Therefore, we need to either stamp out or, at least, diminish the effect of the Word of God. Alternatively, the pilgrims believed the exact opposite, and I also, think the historical facts confirm their case. The period most of these crimes occurred is known as the Dark Ages, so called because society appeared to digress rather than progress, and the culture did not seem to create many works of art, literature or philosophy. It was also a time when the church authorities hid Word of God from the people, reading it only in Latin, which the commoner did not understand. Because the church restricted the Holy Oracles of God, they could now hold the people in bondage to superstitions and the traditions of men. What ensued were some of the greatest atrocities ever committed. Because of this understanding, seventeen years after the pilgrims landed at Plymouth Rock, they started a school and passed a law called the "Ole' Deluder Satan Act," which required that the Bible be read in their public schools.

It being one chief project of the old deluder, Satan, to keep men from the knowledge of the Scriptures...

It is therefore ordered, that every township in this jurisdiction, after the Lord hath increased them to the number of fifty householders, shall then forthwith appoint one within their town to teach all such children as shall resort to him to write and read...

Is it not interesting that the very first school and the very first law about school, ever sanctioned by the government of America, mandated instructors to read and teach scriptures in the classroom? So much for the wall of separation between church and state, but that is a different topic.

Betrayal is always born from a web of deceit. Many secular historians also know the facts previously discussed, yet because they are averse to Christianity, they twist the truth into an elaborate hoax. Additionally, because we esteem these intellectuals and their academic prowess, we then swallow these poisoning deceptions. In like manner, many within the church have allowed these secular humanist ideas to permeate their beliefs, and as such, have given this web of lies some traction within the body of believers.

Therefore, we consistently, and with great repetition, see betrayal between the false church and the true church, and between false believers and true believers. Cain slew Abel. Ishmael persecuted Isaac. Jacob betrayed Essau for his birthright. Essau betrayed his birthright for a morsel of bread. Joseph's brothers sold him into slavery. Then, Potifer's wife framed him. Samson's people gave him to the Philistines. Later, Delilah betrayed him. Saul betrayed David. Then, Ahithophel, his friend and counselor, betrayed him, helping his son Absalom betray his father. Solomon's brothers betrayed him, attempting to seize his throne. Almost every story in the Old Testament and many of the teachings in the New Testament has some element of betrayal. Therefore, it would be correct to say that the Bible is full of betrayals, but it would be wrong to say that the Bible teaches betrayals. Instead, the Bible shows betrayal so clearly to us because it is a translucent mirror of the human heart.

Is religion the cause of this duplicity? Is religion the heart of the betrayal cancer that infects our thoughts? If we only witnessed this behavior in the church, then it would be a stronger argument, but we see betrayal throughout human history. The Athenian rulers betrayed Socrates and put him to death. Julius Caesar's friend and counselor, Brutus, whom Caesar considered a son, betrayed him. Genghis Khan's life was full of betrayals and conspiracies. Early on, his brother Jamuka betrayed him by starting a revolt. Then, some of the generals of this revolt betrayed Jamuka to Genghis Khan. Afterwards, Genghis Khan betrayed the generals by putting them to death who had betrayed Jamuka. Some believe that the Scourge of God, Attila the Hun, met with death when he was poisoned at the hand of his bride, on their wedding night. Finally, consider the treachery and betrayal of kingships throughout history, against their own blood, in order to secure the power of the throne.

No, betrayal and treachery are at the very heart of humanity, with or without religion. The truth of the matter is that as much as we despise it, somewhere in the deep recesses of our perverted minds, we receive a certain satisfaction by feeding upon these dark desires. Consider the fascination the ancients had with Greek Tragedies. Consider the modern people's delight with dramas full of intrigue and deception. Consider the famous Shakespearean tragedies that have enthralled audiences for over four hundred years. Desdemona betrays her father by marrying Othello. Iago betrays everyone and even stabs his wife after she betrays him to Othello. Othello betrays his wife, Desdemona, by smothering her. Consider King Lear, who betrays one of his daughters by giving her inheritance to the other two daughters. The two daughters then betray King Lear and drive him insane. Consider Hamlet's uncle, who betrays his brother by killing him with poison. Hamlet's mother betrays her husband, according to Hamlet, by marrying his brother far too soon. Hamlet plots to betray his uncle, his uncle plots to betray Hamlet. Every scene is filled with someone plotting to betray another person. In fact, the play begins with Hamlet's father coming back from the grave to conspire with Hamlet to seek his revenge! Over the last four hundred years, audiences have been glued to their seats, not because of the eloquence of Shakespeare, which is only a small portion of this lovely morsel, but rather, because it fulfills some deep, dark desire that we do not want to admit is a part of our nature. Therefore, as much as we hate Iago, we would not have the delightful story of Othello without him; and because of this, we also greatly appreciate Iago. We not only appreciate Iago, but we actually need him in order to satisfy these dark appetites of our corrupt human nature. Hence, we find ourselves in a self-contradictory, uneasy place; we love to hate these vile characteristics, and yet, we almost feel as if life would be less enjoyable without them.

Now let us return to the betrayer of all betrayers, the most notorious betrayer in all human history, Adam. He was immaculate, perfect in all his ways, and because of this, he had a completely personal relationship with God in His dimension. Daily, the King of the Universe walked and talked with Adam in the garden. God gave him dominion over the entire world except for ONE tree. However, the Father of Lies found a deception he could use to induce Adam to commit the greatest betrayal of all time; man betraying His God, creature betraying His Creator.

Consider everything Adam was willing to gamble on the risk that this loving, personal God, who generously gave him an entire planet, may have wanted to keep him from becoming a god, like Himself. Every spiritual person on earth seeks a stronger relationship with God. What we would give to be able to walk with God personally in His garden daily and to be physically in His presence? Christians today have this in the Holy Spirit, but in comparison, it is merely a down payment of the assurance that one day we will be in the actual physical presence of our God! Adam had this and threw it on the black jack table. How many times has man desired to rule the whole earth? It has never occurred, but the closest it ever came to happening was with Adam. He ruled everything except one tree! What if God gave you this offer, would you not be grateful and have no concern over this one tree? How often has humanity searched for the cure for diseases and prolonged life? Would you be happy if God gave you eternal life, without the possibility of growing old or getting sick? Adam took all of these gifts and threw them on the craps table, betting that God was a liar. For what reason did he do this? He was already an immortal being. He already had dominion over the earth. He already was perfect in health. He would never grow old. He was perfect in intellect, not forgetting one thing. He was an entirely perfect being. If Adam were to walk the earth today in that same state, many people would consider him a god! Nevertheless, he wanted more. He wanted to be on the same level as the God of All Creation. However, that will never be, because God will not, nor should He, share His glory with anyone! O' betrayals of all betrayals!

The second greatest betrayal in human history, ranking far above the next highest betrayal, was when Judas betrayed God With Us, Jesus Messiah. So why was this betrayal, without a doubt, the next greatest in history? It cannot be due to their relationship, since Judas only knew Jesus for a little over three years. There have been plenty of black widow betrayals in history, whereby women killed their life-long lovers. It cannot be because of their natural relationship. After all, is it not a greater perversion against nature when a woman kills her children? Consider Diana Lumbrera, who smothered six of her children, over a period of thirteen years, including a three-month-old daughter. Even so, in search for the greatest betrayals in human history, Diana Lumbrera does not even make the list. Why is this? Is it because Judas' betrayal is more famous than her betrayal, or is it because the magnitude was not as great?

Depending upon your worldview, you will arrive at two entirely different answers. If you come from a secular worldview, you will conclude that the story of Judas' betrayal is more widely known, so it is more infamous. If you are of the Christian worldview, which believes that "*all have sinned and fallen short of the Glory of God*" (Rom 3:23), then you should believe that the depth of Judas' betrayal can never be reached by another human. This is because Jesus was the only person to be born without, and never to, have sinned. The implication is staggering; we are then asserting that we all deserve to die because we have all sinned by betraying our God. Adam gave us a state of betrayal, which was our heritage at birth, but the act of betrayal began as soon as we were mature enough to act upon that inherited nature. This seems almost absurd when considering an innocent, newborn baby, but we are making a grave error of confusing innocence with vulnerability and dependence. What would happen if that young child were given a grown man's body suddenly? How fearful that would be! Among a baby's first words are "*mine*." We have to teach children not to bite, throw, hit and to share. It is intriguing that we do not have to teach children how to be bad, that seems to come quite naturally, but we do need to train them to behave well. Augustine does quite well in explaining this childhood condition of sin in his book "*Confessions*".

For my wants were inside me... And so I would fling my arms and legs about and cry, making the few and feeble gestures that I could, though indeed the signs were not much like what I inwardly desired and when I was not satisfied - either from not being understood or because what I got was not good for me - I grew indignant that my elders were not subject to me and that those on whom I actually had no claim did not wait on me as slaves - and I avenged myself on them by crying.

Am I saying that the betrayal of Jesus was a greater crime than the woman who betrayed her three-month-old daughter, because the daughter is born into sin? Yes. That statement, more than likely, will cause all our deficient human reasoning to begin railing within our imaginations. Remember, our thinking lacks precision because of our inherent fallen nature and the presence of sin in our intellect. Take a moment to contemplate the case from God's perspective, according to His Word. Who is more deserving of death, one who sins, or one who is without sin? The scriptures are abundantly clear that the only reason death even exists is because of sin. It is our just wages. *"For the wages of sin is death."* (Rom 6:23) If God sees it this way then who are we, O' Fallen Ones, to judge the Supreme Judge or His Righteousness?

Lumbrera's betrayal appears to be a greater offense because she violated a natural, God-given mother's instinct to protect her children. Betraying the mother-daughter relationship is a greater betrayal than Judas' betrayal of his friendship with Jesus. Nevertheless, once again, we have erred because we viewed this betrayal through our natural eyes and not from a biblical perspective. Calvin might say, *"It is time to put on our spectacles in order to see the world correctly."* The relationship Jesus had with Judas is even more binding than a woman's relationship with her natural-born child. Jesus is Creator God, by whom *"all things were created through him and for him"* (Col 1:16), *"and without him was not any thing made that was made."* (Joh 1:3) Judas would not have been pro-created by his parents if Jesus, his God, the Creator of All Things, had not formed his inward parts and knit him together within his mother's womb. (Psa 139:13) It is appalling to see a son betray his father, or a mother betray her daughter! This crime offends even the fallen natures of the lost, because, by the Grace of God, some moral conscience of right and wrong remained within us after the fall. However, how blind we are not to see that the betrayal of children against their pro-creators, their parents, is a small offense when compared with creation's betrayal against their Creator!

Mankind has never created one thing; not a single, solitary atom. We re-manipulate objects in our world and call it creation. We cut down trees, mill them into lumber and build houses. We have only taken one material and re-shaped it into another form. In all of our creative efforts, we are nothing more than pro-creators, or re-manipulators, working with the true Creator's wealth of original works.

Jesus created Judas. He loved Judas as much as his father and mother pro-creators loved their son. No, He loved Judas more. He loved Judas as his Creator and his God. He loved Judas with a perfect love that we can barely comprehend, for God not only loves His creation, but He is love. (1Jn 4:8) God not only acts out of perfect love toward us, but He is the true essence of love. What human being is so untainted by sin that they are able to love as fully and perfectly as God? Is it even possible to fathom such a thought? This is the perfect love that Jesus had for Judas when He said to him, "*Judas, would you betray the Son of Man with a kiss?*" (Luk 22:48) His love for Judas was beyond anything we are able to comprehend, because we can only know to a very small degree of what true love is in our fallen natures. The pain Jesus must have felt to see him bringing the soldiers to betray Him with a company of evildoers, Judas, His friend, His disciple, His brother in the Lord, His son, His creation. What an incredible betrayal!

Nevertheless, Yeshua knew this would occur, and so He prepared Himself for the spiritual battle through prayer. However, if you believe this was the only time Jesus Messiah was betrayed, then you have not surveyed the scriptures. Consider when the Pharisees accused Him of being born of fornication (Joh 8:41), with a Samaritan. (Joh 8:48) Was this the first-time people threw that insult at the Lord of Glory? I am quite sure, like today, there were many people in Nazareth who did not believe His mother was a virgin and conceived a child by the Holy Spirit. How many children betrayed His friendship with this slanderous insult? How many parents forbid their children from playing with that little boy Jesus, because they considered Him the bastard son of Mary? Consider the time when His brothers and His mother sought, at the beginning of His ministry, "*to seize him ...saying, 'He is out of his mind'*" (Mar 3:21), attempting to ensnare Messiah by calling Him out of the crowd. (Mar 3:31) Consider another time, when His brothers were so exasperated with Jesus; they suggested He go openly to the feast (Joh 7:2-4), knowing the Jewish leaders would probably kill Him. "*For not even his brothers believed in him.*" (Joh 7:5) Reflect upon the people in Jerusalem, who glorified Him as Savior and King, and then, only a few days later, had a change of heart and insisted that the authorities brutally crucify Him as a common criminal. For these reasons, we can say that the Savior truly died from a broken heart, for it is written, *"Reproaches have broken my heart."* (Psa 69:20) Moreover, consider when *"one of the soldiers pierced his side with a spear, and at once there came out blood and water"* (Joh 19:34), indicating that the Lord of Glory both literally and spiritually died from a broken heart; the blood coming from the heart and water from the pericardium sac.

When considering the betrayal of our Immanuel, a sinless man, who was perfect love in order to destroy the only being that has ever created anything; how heinous the crime! Is there any crime that compares? No wonder Yeshua sternly warned Judas, *"woe to that man by whom the Son of Man is betrayed! It would have been better for that man if he had not been born."* (Mat 26:24) Judas was probably shaking in his sandals, but he still resolutely rose from the Last Supper determined to betray the Son of God. Therefore, the greatest betrayal in the history of mankind was when Adam, the creation, betrayed his Creator. However, this betrayal was very similar to the first, because Judas also was Immanuel's creation. Moreover, the Son of Man loved him so much that He came to die for his sins, and yet, Judas' stony heart chose to conspire in the murder of this great love, his only Hope, his only Salvation.

It is intriguing, that recently some Secularist and neo-Gnostics, the modern-day members of the New Age movement, have run to Judas' defense, after National Geographic published a translation of the Gnostic *"Gospel of Judas"* in 2006. This account, like all lies from the Father of Lies, takes the known events just prior to the crucifixion and completely turns the story on its head. Judas is not the most infamous betrayer in all history, but instead, the most valuable insider to secret knowledge; and as such, instead of being history's greatest villain, he becomes one of history's greatest self-sacrificing heroes! It is remarkable that Secularists and New-Agers are so eager to throw out large portions of the validated, ancient manuscripts in the New Testament, which surpass all tests for historical credibility, and yet, so quick to adopt even the smallest fragments of ancient writings that discredit the Word of God, even though, they fail every test for historical trustworthiness. For example, their hypocrisy is evident in that, we know these writings are early second-century at best, written over two hundred years after Christ's death. These same groups discredit the Gospels as unreliable because of the timeliness of the transcriptions despite the fact most were written less than forty years after Yeshua's death. In addition, there are so few fragments of these Gnostic Gospels, which they accept as valid, and throw out New Testament texts, even though, we have over 5,000 Greek manuscripts corroborating the testimony to their authenticity. Furthermore, thousands of letters from the Anti-Nicene writers quote the text so frequently that ninety-five percent of this text could be recreated from these letters alone. They also receive the credibility of the writer of the Gospel of Judas, knowing he could not possibly have written the document; thereby, accepting testimony from a person they know is lying about his identity! These are the same pseudo historians who wish to throw out the Gospels, although, almost all historians agree to be written by; Matthew and John, Jesus' disciples, Mark, a follower of Jesus and Luke, a first-century proselyte and historian that personally went to Judea to investigate the claims of the apostles. On the other hand, they raise the bar so high for the Gospels; we would not be able to accept any manuscript as trustworthy, secular or religious, if we applied these same standards to other ancient writings, since the New Testament is the most credible and validated document in history. Conversely, these groups attempt to drop the bar so low that virtually any writing found in history should be considered valid by these standards. However, even more amazing, like the Pharisees and the Sadducees, these people do not even recognize their own duplicity.

The fundamental question is; why are Secularists and New Agers so fervent in their desire to transform history's most treacherous, self-serving villain into history's most misunderstood, self-sacrificing hero? The answer offers valuable insights in understanding the lost, but even more important, it offers powerful insights into understanding ourselves. To the lost, if the Gospels accurately depict the story of Judas' betrayal, then it means that Jesus actually is Messiah and the Savior of the World. Further, it means that anyone who rejects the Only Hope for Mankind is like Judas, who also rejected God's plan of salvation through Jesus Messiah. Judas did not want to follow Ben Joseph, the Lord's Suffering Servant, but rather, Judas wished to follow Ben David, God's conquering king, who would establish the one-thousand-year reign of Israel on earth. Judas rejected Jesus' plan. These groups, in like manner, also reject Jesus' plan; therefore, it is important to change the story in order to remove their condemnation, indictment and hopelessness in this world. Thus, if Judas is history most misunderstood hero, then they have also discredited the validity of all the other truths found in the Gospels, such as the Lamb of God avowal, *"I am THE way, and THE truth, and THE life. **NO ONE comes to the Father EXCEPT through me.**"* (Joh 14:6)

How is it by understanding why these groups have these reactions to Judas the betrayer, we can gain greater insights into our own Christian lives? The answer to this lies in the same reason that we both despised and loved Iago, and the Shakespearean tragedies, which are filled with betrayal and conspiracy, and have withstood the test of time as some of the most loved plays ever written. A part of us still relates to Judas! *"What!"* you say, *"Never!"* However, I beg to differ. Please put down your Pharisaical blinders for a moment, and put on your biblical spectacles, to look at yourself in the mirror to see an accurate reflection of who you truly are. Christians every day, including myself, betray Christ. We are all betrayers. When we rise to defend ourselves, we betray Christ's teaching about turning the other cheek. When we burst out in anger at a loved one, we defy Christ's teachings. When we gossip about a friend, we rebel against His authority. In fact, if we are totally honest with ourselves, and we take an accurate survey of the ideals expressed by our Example in the Faith, we will find that we are much more similar to Judas than to Jesus. That is sad to say, but it is also the first and most critical step in recovery, and the transformation process.

There have always only been two choices in the Bible. The words of Moses, inspired by the Holy Spirit, *"I have set before you life and death, blessing and curse"* (Deu 30:19), have been echoed repeatedly by God's prophets, by His Son and by the Apostles throughout the scriptures. Joshua, likewise, said, *"choose this day whom you will serve... But as for me and my house, we will serve the LORD."* (Jos 24:15) These choices are personified in choosing either Jesus, or Judas. If we choose our own way, apart from the pure teachings of Jesus, as presented in the Holy Writ, then we choose to betray our Messiah, as Judas also had done. If we choose to lay our lives down, as our Example in the Faith had done for us, then we choose obedience out of love, just as the Son of Man had done out of obedience to the Father for us. It is set before you today, and every day. Will you choose blessing or curse, life or death?

Understanding our Judas mentality makes Judas the most important disciple for our study. Either we identify with Messiah and God's Way, or we associate with Judas and our own way.

Nevertheless, The Parable of the Cross is a perspective of our sanctifying walk, which places us in the footsteps of Jesus, so we may be become conformed into His image. What, then, is the lesson from this perspective? The answer is extremely easy. We all have a Judas inside of us. We cannot live in this world without being betrayed or betraying one another daily. As clearly demonstrated, the Lamb of God suffered the most heinous, heart-breaking betrayal of all time. We, also, suffer betrayals, if we are walking in Christ, for scriptures declare we are "*fellow heirs with Christ, provided we suffer with him*". (Rom 8:17) Thankfully, we can take significant comfort that our God in the Flesh can relate to our pain, because He suffered more; therefore, "*as we share abundantly in Christ's sufferings, so through Christ we share abundantly in comfort too.* (2Co 1:5)

Consider that Judas was a disciple of Christ. He looked like all the other members of the church. Jesus knew Judas would betray him, and we may not know, but we will suffer loss at the hands of false brethren. Jesus did not shrink from this; instead, He allowed Judas to remain, even though He knew his intentions. This is turning the other cheek to your enemy. If He had chosen to remove Judas, the Lord of Glory may not have gone to the cross to save the world. This clearly demonstrates that we must allow certain individuals, at times, to remain in our lives to bring us to the cross. The common reaction is to turn away from these people, but these people are in our lives to accomplish two purposes. First, they need us as a witness, or a martyr. Secondly, we need them to bring us to the cross in order to be "*conformed to the image of his Son*", for which we have been "*predestined*". (Rom 8:29)

The disgust we feel for Judas is how much we ought to loath our sin nature, which the bible calls the *old* or *outer* man. Only after we have reached this level of conviction and hate for our sin, we will be willing to kill *self*, who keeps rising in us against the King's rule.

Consider Martin Luther revelations on the subject from his book "*Explanations*".

> *True sorrow must spring from the goodness and mercies of God, especially from the wounds of Christ, so that man comes first of all to a sense of his own ingratitude in view of divine goodness and thereupon to hatred of himself and love of the kindness of God. Then tears will flow and he will hate himself from the very depths of his heart, yet without despair. Then he will hate sin, not because*

245

of the punishment but because of his regard for the goodness of God; and when he has perceived this he will be preserved from despair and will despise himself most ardently, yet joyfully.[11]

This was the central, fundamental teaching of Christianity, but now, how few churches offer these insights into ourselves, and yet, how desperately needed they are for our church, and our times. For this reason, I called this book "The **Lost** Parable of the Cross."

---

[11] Martin Luther and Stephen J. Nichols. Martin Luther's Ninety-Five theses. Phillipsburg N.J.: P & R Pub., 2003. Print.

chapter thirteen

TRIALS

Modern man commonly misinterprets readings from earlier societies
due to two grave errors. First, because our society is more
technologically advanced, most people extrapolate we have progressed
in other areas as well, such as wisdom, jurisprudence and humanity.
Secondly, because those societies were more devoutly religious than
our modern societies, many also conclude by extension, the individuals
were more virtuous and pious. Either one of those propositions could
be correct, but in either case, the premise does not necessitate the
conclusion. These propositions, as well, are mutually exclusive,
meaning, one could be false, and one could be true, in different
comparisons to earlier societies. Setting both of these commonly held
errors in the forefront of our minds as we begin to examine, and
interpret, the events of Jesus' trial is of the utmost importance. Doing
this, we will be able to comprehend fully the travesty of justice against
the Son of Man with an acute awareness.

Speaking to the first point in a general sense, do you think, because our
society is more technologically advanced, we are also wiser, more
judicial and more human than earlier societies? Most moderns view the
ancients with disdain, thinking that they superstitiously attributed
every inexplicable event to the gods. In part, they may be correct. After
all, many cultures in antiquity did ascribe natural phenomenon to the
gods; however, if you believe in God, then you must acknowledge that
their assumption is not entirely without merit; not in the conclusion of
the earthquake's physical explanation, but in its cause. This is a
common and critical error in logic; that an explanation of the physical
manifestation of an event, excludes God as its true source. However,
this is not necessarily the case, many times God will, and does, work
from within His physical laws. At times, He chooses not to. It is His
choice. He made the material world. He is the ultimate, unlimited God
and He can do as He well pleases. This does not sit well with us, since

most of the time, we want to control God rather than submit to His authority over our world.

Are we wiser as a result of our technological advancements? Sadly, although I am an adamant proponent of using technology and work in the field, I must admit, technology has made our society less intelligent in many respects. Considering the effect of our society's technological progress with cultures from antiquity can be extremely difficult, because we lack standardized measures across those times, in order to make objective assessments. Nevertheless, if we can demonstrate that there is not a binding relationship between the technological advancements and more recent culture's overall level of wisdom, when consistent measures have existed, then we can conclude the premise is false. Thus, in an effort to either disqualify or validate the precept that modern people are wiser than ancient people were, we will review the last fifty years, in which scientific advancements have occurred at a breakneck speed. Furthermore, we will focus on the U.S. as one of the most advanced societies today.

Technological breakthroughs are increasing so rapidly that computers are considered obsolete in less than three years. It is remarkable to note that just over one hundred years ago most people did not drive cars, make phone calls, watch television or listen to the radio. Today, we all own cars with radios, have televisions in every room, and mobile phones that allow us to listen to the radio or watch videos from anywhere at any time. These tremendous technological advancements have contributed to the vast wealth of information mankind has been able to accumulate in recent times. Consider for a moment that accumulated knowledge doubled from the Year of our Lord to the year 1750. Then, it only took another 150 years for it to double. In 1950, fifty years later, it doubled once more. Again, in 1960, and once again in 1968 it doubled. Presently, the vast accumulation of knowledge is doubling every two and a half years. Furthermore, consider that a laptop now has more processing power in it then all the mainframes put together that NASA used in 1969 to send a man to the moon. The laptop I am currently using is more powerful than the most complex assemblies of mainframe computers, filling extremely large rooms, in the most technologically sophisticated nation of the world less than fifty years ago. If there is a direct correlation between technological progress and intelligence, we could easily conclude during this period the skulls of our succeeding generations would double in size, just to hold the vast amounts of knowledge.

Unfortunately, we have witnessed quite the opposite, as Americans have become more advanced, we have become dumber. The statistics are staggering. Consider, for example, that among the top 30 developed nations, we rank 25th in math and 21st in science. To our shame, this will be the first generation less literate than the preceding generation.

Who is to blame? Teachers blame the parents. Parents blame the teachers. Progressives blame lack of funding, and conservatives blame the system. Who is holding the child accountable? How do you hold them answerable? By building into them an objective sense of responsibility and ethics, but we have instead thrown these antiquated ideals out the window and to our surprise, education went with them. For example, charts show a substantial increase in immorality and a considerable decrease in academics right about the time three significant events occurred in our recent history. When the Supreme Court declared prayer in school unconstitutional in 1961, when abortion became legal in 1973 and when divorces became as easy to acquire as a candy bar at the nearest store beginning in 1969. I am not advocating for any of these positions, although I do in my personal life; however, the blame for our stupidity should not be attributed to bad teachers, detached parents, or broken systems. No, rather, the fault lies with only one person, Adam. As a result of his disobedience, we are fallen race, full of sin and full of pride. Instead of taking advantage of these tremendous technological advancements and becoming better people, we have squandered the opportunity. To underscore the truthfulness of this statement, I withheld the fact that our children do rank first in one category, self-confidence.

To highlight this further, I would like to tell you a story about an extremely poor child, raised as a farmer. By the time he turned fifteen, he could barely read or write, having about the equivalent of one year's worth of education. He lost his mother at the age of nine and worked exceptionally long days on the farm. Although his father considered education worthless, he instilled into this young man values of integrity and honesty. Since he did not have enough money to buy books, he had to borrow them, sometimes walking as far as twenty miles. He was so poor, he did not have enough money to buy paper, so when he read a book, he wrote notes on a log. According to this child's profile, by our standards today, he had no chance to be anything other than someone perpetually trapped on the lower rung of society, but instead, because of his work ethic and integrity, he became a distinguished lawyer, then a congressional representative, and ultimately, one of the greatest presidents in U.S. history. About one hundred and fifty years ago, Honest Abe Lincoln became one of the most learned and eloquent leaders the world has ever seen, prevailing over the difficult and challenging circumstances of his childhood.

In summation, wisdom is the result of hard work. This is a morality issue. Laziness is immoral. The laws I pointed out earlier all indicated, as a society, there was an unprecedented paradigm shift in our morals during that period. In direct relation to this, we see exponential increases in abortions, sexually transmitted diseases, unwed mothers, teenage pregnancies, and dramatic decreases in literacy, math and science skills and graduation rates. We should be ashamed of ourselves! Likewise, our children should be ashamed of their stupidity, but they are too dumb to realize it, after all, they are the most self-confident people on the planet.

I know this seems a little harsh, but consider people interviewed by Jay Leno, who did not take issue that the interviewer asked about America gaining its independence from Greece, Winston Churchill as a Revolutionary War general, the original thirty colonies and America formally becoming a nation in 1922! Do you think children reared from Christian homes would fare better? Consider when I asked a nine-year-old granddaughter of one of the best pastors I have ever known who was the first president of the U.S. she responded with "*Jesus Christ?*" Are you kidding me! This not only underscores her lack of American historical knowledge, but even worse, her lack of knowing Jesus Christ as a historical person!

To my own shame, if Abe Lincoln were in my family, he would use his laptop to watch movies and play games. He would spend most of his days watching TV, playing video games and failing his classes. The reading he longed to do by candle light, after twelve to fourteen hours of hard work, my children consider punishment. O' how far we have fallen!

Are we wiser than ancient generations? Are we able to memorize the first five books of the Bible, as Paul and the other Pharisees were required to do? No, technology has benefited people in many areas, but it has also given the immoral a greater ability to satisfy their desire for idle entertainment, crass amusement and slothfulness.

Maybe our culture is not wiser than previous societies, but at least we are more humane. Consider, after all, the cruel methods ancient man used to kill each other. The Ninevites skinned people alive. The Persians began nailing people to crosses around 400 B.C. Vlad Dracula impaled his enemies. Consider the horrifying tortures of the Inquisition. Yes, we have become more humane in how we kill each other. In our recent history, Hitler benevolently sent millions of Jews to the gas chambers. Mao Zadong was quite magnanimous in starving, beating or working 45 million Chinese to death. Stalin, of course, was exceedingly gracious spending his evenings scrutinizing death lists, killing 20 million souls. Yes, we are a much more benevolent and sophisticated culture. We can kill millions in a flash with our nuclear weapons technology. The methods of the past were appalling, but the magnitude of the present, completely outweighs our claim as a more humane society. Today, we are able to kill without looking at the person, face to face. We can kill people before they see the light of day from inside the womb of the mother. Furthermore, I would not be surprised that we will soon be mercifully killing the elderly, and the physically disadvantaged in order to free them from their reduced quality of life and our society from having to provide their care. Our desensitized decline in compassion should come as no surprise, because we despised and hated God's laws, and He has forewarned us *"all who hate me love death."* (Pro 8:36) Nevertheless, when the world chooses to throw out God, they also choose to follow Abaddon the Destroyer (Rev 9:11), and then, they become like him.

At least our laws are more civilized than these ancient cultures, correct? Here, again, we also make a false assumption. Our laws are directly derived from England, in which the common law and the Magna Carta were foundational to our Declaration of Independence and our Constitution. However, the origin of English law was Roman law and the Judeo-Christian ethics of the Bible. So that, in the trial of Jesus, we have both the Jewish and the Roman elements involved, which have also shaped our laws. A person would expect that as time goes on the laws would become superior, and this may be the case, but concerning civil liberties of the accused, the Jewish laws of antiquity actually afforded greater protections, which we will discuss in detail as we begin to unfold the text.

We shall also reserve the second fallacious common assumption, that, because ancient societies were more devoutly religious, they also have a greater degree of honesty and integrity, for later as well.

Let us review the trials of Jesus in light of the Jewish and Roman laws at that time. To begin with, we will overview the chronological events of the arrest, trials and crucifixion and ascribe time when none is given based on location of that event and the known location of the subsequent event. My point is that even though the actual hours may vary, since we are not given this information most of the time, the chronology is extremely detailed, and scholars are almost all agree about the basic time of the day.

Jesus and the disciples arrived at the Garden of Gethsemane an hour or two before 10:00 PM., Messiah prayed for about 3-4 hours. Judas, then, betrayed Him sometime after midnight. Once again, the following times are approximations:

1:00 AM.	– First trial before Annas, the former high priest
2:00 AM.	– Second trial before Caiaphas
3:00 AM.	– Imprisoned at Caiaphas' palace
5:00 AM.	– Third trial by most of the Jewish leaders
6:00 AM.	– Fourth trial before Roman governor Pilate
6:30 AM.	– Fifth trial before Herod Antipas
7:00 AM.	– Sixth trial before Pilate
8:00 AM.	– Jesus begins to carry the cross
9:00 AM.	– Jesus is crucified (Mar 15:25)
12:00 PM.	– Darkness covers the land (Mar 15:33)
3:00 PM.	– Jesus dies (Mar 15:34)

Two things should jump out at us as we begin to survey this timeline. First, that so many of Jesus' trials were conducted at night, and secondly, that there were so many trials. Immediately, our sense of right and wrong, developed out of our culture, sends out warning signals that something is amiss. If you cannot get the guilty verdict, you desire, and then keep trying the poor soul until you get the death sentence you sought. How outlandish, by the time most of us punch in at work, Messiah had already undergone, six trials, beatings, mocking, scourging and other tortures, and on His way to Calvary, carrying the cross He would soon be nailed to.

Since this culture is so far removed from our own, we fall into those two logical fallacies I spoke of earlier. First, the society was less sophisticated than our own; therefore, they offered fewer protections. Secondly, the people were intensely religious; therefore, these leaders conducted their affairs with a higher level of integrity than our culture, despite their strict legalities. However, something seems to ring untrue and irreconcilable with these premises. We discover what appears to be a sham of a trial, judging from our 21st century perspective, is even more of a charade in the first century, because their system of justice was actually more protective of the accused, and the leaders conducting the inquiry were far from virtuous.

It seems these leaders violated at least eighteen or more of their own laws in order to secure the verdict of guilty and the sentence of death. Now the abuse of power is even more egregious, because we cannot excuse it due to culturally relativistic ideals, since their own laws convict the court as corrupt and duplicitous.

Let us consider the many serious violations of their own law. **The first violation** is that it was illegal to conduct a trial at night. This stands to reason, since thirty or so of these leaders would constantly have to leave their homes in the middle of the night. It is also more difficult to conduct trials and have all the witnesses present at that time. Therefore, the alarm bell that began to ring in our conscience that something was amiss was correct. **The second violation** occurred when the King of the Jews was examined by Annas as the sole judge, for the Mishna states *"Be not a sole judge, for there is no sole judge but One."* **The third violation** was a lack of formal, specific charges brought against the accused, but rather, the trial began as an investigative inquiry, which tried several accusations, until they found a couple that would stick. At that time, there were no grand juries, the trials had to convene with an explicit charge, and if that accusation could not be proved then the case was dismissed. **The fourth violation** of their law occurred when one of the officers struck Jesus for answering Annas, saying, *"Why do you ask me? Ask those who have heard me what I said to them; they know what I said."* (Joh 18:21) **With the Fifth**, they violated their law by conducting the trial on a holy day, because this was the morning of the first day of the Feast of Unleavened Bread and the Eve of the Passover. Once again, their Mishna witnesses against their hypocrisy stating, *"They shall not judge on the eve of the Sabbath, nor on that of any festival."* **The sixth violation** is evident as the Mishna states, *"The morning sacrifice is offered at the dawn of the day. The Sanhedrin is not to assemble until the hour after that time."* This not only disqualified the trial, because this was the Passover sacrifice that would be offered that day, but it also disqualified and desecrated the sacrifice itself. This is especially compelling, considering that, God would no longer accept this form of sacrifice, but rather, He now would only accept the one-time sacrifice of the Lamb of God for the propitiation of sins. **The seventh violation** of their law was that the execution and the conviction occurred on the same day. The Jewish people, once again, affording the accused every opportunity not to be falsely convicted in a rush to judgment, made it their practice that judges go home for at least one evening to fast, pray and consider any alternative that would allow them to acquit the accused. **The eighth violation** seems a little strange, but it makes sense when considered more carefully; "*A simultaneous and unanimous verdict of guilt rendered on the day of the trial has the effect of an acquittal.*" In our courts, we require a unanimous verdict of twelve jurors, which many times is extremely difficult to achieve; however, in this court, there were over thirty jurors, so in the Jewish mind, every single juror in agreement meant something must be wrong with the trial. **The ninth violation** was that the condemnation of Jesus was pronounced in a place that was forbidden by the law. In a trial of capital offenses, the Sanhedrin was required to meet in a place known as the Hall of Hewn Stones. **The 10th violation** of their law was that many of the judges were not permitted to have bias in the case and no feelings of animosity towards the accused. **The 11th violation** of their law was that Messiah was not presented with a defense. Many people tend to justify the actions of these religious leaders by stating that they misunderstood Jesus' defense, which He was not required to prove at all by their standards, but rather Messiah was afforded no defense. If this case had been conducted during the daytime, then Lazarus, the blind, the lame, the deaf and many others that the Great Physician had healed could have been brought forward to confirm His Messianic claims. **The 12th violation** revealed that the judges could not get their false witnesses' stories to agree. Surprisingly, the testimony of witnesses, they apparently coached, contradicted each other enough that the false faces of piety and reverence to the truth these judges wore to the tribunal caused them to dismiss the charges they had so carefully conspired to produce. **The 13th violation** was that not all the Sanhedrin were present, but rather, only those leaders who despised Messiah were notified of the proceedings as we are told later in scriptures that "*Joseph ...of Arimathea ...a member of the council ...had not consented to their decision and action*" (Luk 23:50-51)

Astoundingly, that is not all, but rather I have extracted the following from scriptures, so I may expand upon all the rapid violations within just this small section of testimony.

*Now the chief priests and the whole Council were seeking false
testimony against Jesus that they might put him to death, but they
found none, though many false witnesses came forward. At last two
came forward and said, "This man said, 'I am able to destroy the
temple of God, and to rebuild it in three days.'" And the high
priest stood up and said, "Have you no answer to make? What is it
that these men testify against you?" But Jesus remained silent.
And the high priest said to him, "I adjure you by the living God,
tell us if you are the Christ, the Son of God." Jesus said to him,
"You have said so. But I tell you, from now on you will see the Son
of Man seated at the right hand of Power and coming on the
clouds of heaven." Then the high priest tore his robes and said,
"He has uttered blasphemy. What further witnesses do we need?
You have now heard his blasphemy. What is your judgment?"
They answered, "He deserves death." Then they spit in his face
and struck him. And some slapped him... (Mat 26:59-67 ESV)*

The public testimony was not strong enough to convict Him by their
standards, even after the chief priests illegally set up the trial and
conspired with witnesses to present false testimony. Again, their laws
appear to provide greater protections than our legal standards today.
Consider that the two false witnesses testimony was remarkably
similar. One testified that Messiah stated, "*I am able to destroy the
temple of God, and to rebuild it in three days.*" (Mat 26:61) Another
witnessed that Messiah said, "*I will destroy this temple that is made
with hands, and in three days I will build another, not made with
hands.*" (Mar 14:58) Yet, these statements were not considered a
strong enough consensus of facts to convict a man of a capital offense
worthy of death. Mark informs, "*Yet even about this their testimony
did not agree.*" (Mar 14:59) Then, out of extreme frustration and
desperation, because of various time constraints, like, when Pilate
holds court and the coming Passover, the high priest in a matter of
minutes broke so many of their laws that the other priestly conspirators
must have been ashamed and astonished at the same time. He
addressed the accused, "*Have you no answer to make? What is it that
these men testify against you?*" (Mat 26:62). "*But Jesus remained
silent.*" (Mat 26:63) He remained silent at that time, because, according
to their law, the defendant could not incriminate himself, and so the
Law and the Testimony, Jesus, held His accuser to his own imperfect
laws by not answering. Breaking the law, in **the 14th violation**,
Caiaphas hypocritically presses on by putting the accused under an
oath of God, saying, "*I adjure you by the living God, tell us if you are*

the Christ, the Son of God." (Mat 26:63) In short, Messiah said yes. However, the longer answer was, *"You will see the Son of Man seated at the right hand of Power and coming on the clouds of heaven."* (Mat 26:64) Well versed in the Tanakh, they understood perfectly that Jesus was affirming that He was the fulfillment of Daniel's messianic vision. *"I saw in the night visions, and behold, with the clouds of heaven there came one like a son of man, and he came to the Ancient of Days and was presented before him."* (Dan 7:13) However, not only did He affirm that He was Messiah, and the very essence of God, since His is the only begotten of the Father, but also that He was the Ancient of Days Himself; in other words, God! After this statement, court broke out in complete mayhem. The high priest ripped his priestly garment. People began shouting, and then, in **the 15ᵗʰ violation** of their law, the judges and jurors, in this farce of a trial, *"Then ...spat in His face and beat Him with the fist. And others struck Him with the palms of their hands."* (Mat 26:67)

Meanwhile in the background of these events was Peter and his cross. Before this time, Peter said, *"Lord, I am ready to go with You, both into prison, and into death."* (Luk 22:33) Now, however, when this cross was laid before Peter by the hand of God *"...he began to curse and to swear, I do not know the man. And immediately the cock crowed."* (Mat 26:74) This is a perfect picture of the battle that lies outside us, and the war within. Outside, we are brought to the cross by the Lord's hand, in order to bring about the destruction of the flesh. The world and this mortal realm rule over vast lands of the heart, even after we have been called out of the cave of sin and death. The Lord of Glory slowly and certainly brings these internal conditions to light by causing the idolatrous kings and lovers who reign over those regions of our heart against us. In Peter's case, he was in love with his own strength and abilities. He was a leader of men, who more than likely also ran a fishing business prior to being called into service by the Lord. In Peter, we see a extraordinarily capable, courageous, outspoken, self-made man of the world. Yet the gifts that God had given to him became his idol, because Peter claimed these for himself. He was now like, Nebuchadnezzar, the king of Babylon, who once said, *"Is this not great Babylon that I have built for the house of the kingdom by the might of my power and for the honor of my majesty?"* Where did Peter derive his strength and power when he made the statement *"I am ready to go with You, both into prison, and into death"*? The answer was, by his power and by his majesty, because he lost the battle in the Garden of Prayer, at which time Jesus *"came to the disciples and found them sleeping. And he said to Peter, 'So, could you not watch with me one hour?'"* (Mat 26:40) In Peter's denial of the cross, we see our own failures when we also choose to go into battle without the power of the spirit strengthened in prayer. In Peter, we see the born-again Christian, with all the courage and talent of the flesh, and yet powerless in the spiritual battles to which we have been called. To which the Captain of our Faith has said, *"...the gates of hell shall not prevail against it."* Nevertheless, some of those gates have been erected and continue to reign over vast regions within the Christian heart; *"For we do not wrestle against flesh and blood, but against principalities, against powers, against the world's rulers, of the darkness of this age, against spiritual wickedness in high places."* (Eph 6:12) So, how can Peter win this spiritual warfare exclusively through the strength of his flesh? The answer is, he cannot. That is precisely what we see. In contrast, while this is occurring in the background, the Champion of our Faith is walking in the victory He prepared for in the Garden when He prayed *"My Father, if it be possible, let this cup pass from me; nevertheless, not as I will, but as you will."* (Mat 26:39) To which the Father answered *"...yes, and in Him Amen, to the glory of God."* (2Co 1:20) *"Yes, it will be My Will, and no, there is no other way."* *"And for this I have made you stand, to make you see My power, to declare My name in all the land."* (Exo 9:16) *"And there appeared to him [Jesus] an angel from heaven, strengthening him."* (Luk 22:43) So that Jesus could draw His strength for the battle from God the Father, and because of this, He became steadfast in His course, setting his face as a flint, knowing that the Lord God would be His helper and that He would not be put to shame. (Isa 50:7) When we are presented with the cross by the Hand of God, the Lord of Glory says, *"My grace is sufficient for you, for My power is made perfect in weakness."* (2Co 12:9) To which we should respond in like manner as the Apostle Paul, *"Most gladly therefore I will rather glory in my weaknesses, that the power of Christ may overshadow me."* (2Co 12:9) What a beautiful portrait the Lord painted, by intertwining both scenes at the same time. In Peter, we see the impotent ability of the flesh to secure the victory over our spiritual battles. In perfect opposition, in Jesus, we see the power of the spirit as the complete victory over the flesh. It is these circumstances that our works are tried by fire, when the Hand of God uses the world to come against us so that *"each one's work shall be revealed. For the Day shall declare it, because it shall be revealed by fire; and the fire shall try each one's work as to what kind it is."* (1Co 3:13) In Peter, we see wood, hay and stubble that *"shall be burned up, [and] he shall suffer loss. But he shall be saved, yet so as by fire."* (1Co 3:15) In Jesus, we see gold, silver, precious stones, whose work remains when tried by fire. (1Co 3:14) In Peter, we see our utter inability to be victorious in the battles to which we are called, and in Jesus, we see our absolute victory to stand in what He has already accomplished. One is the old man. The other is the new man. They both are alive, and neither one will submit to the other. Both rule over various regions of the Christian heart, but Jesus reigns supreme as the King of Kings and the Lord of Lords and the King of Jerusalem. Nevertheless, there are still many regions within the Christian where the gates of Hell shall not prevail, but they are many times only exposed when the Hand of God lays the cross before us to be taken up in victory; for in of our weakness we are made strong in Him and become valiant for the fight. (Phi 4:13, Heb 11:34)

We already know quite clearly that our victory is in Christ. In this, I have not stated anything new or insightful, but that was not the point I was attempting to make. The point is that we need the cross in order to grow in our Christian lives. However, Jonah, although the cross is crucial to burn up the works of the flesh, when the Hand of God leads us to the next victory over our flesh, we shun the trial and go in the completely opposite direction. We do this repeatedly, even though, the Lord of Glory said, *"If anyone desires to come after Me, let him deny himself and take up his cross and follow Me."* (Mat 16:24) Thus, we say to the Lord by our actions *"I will affirm myself. I will choose the wide and easy gate of the flesh. I will not pick up this cross, and I will not follow you to Calvary."* Therefore, Jonah, you only postpone the inevitable, which is, you will do the Lord's Will and accomplish that to which you have been called. You can go directly to Nineveh and proclaim the Word of God, or you can sail to the opposite end of the earth, but either way, you will carry the cross, or you are none of His. For, He is the Lord of Armies. (1Sa 17:47) He will have victory over the flesh. The Captain of our Faith did not come to bring peace to these unconquered regions of our hearts, but rather, a sword. (Mat 10:34) Hence, you can continue to grow in the power of His might, or you can postpone the inevitable, even to the day of your death, but would you not rather grow in God's glorious plan and continue to *"press toward the mark for the prize of the high calling of God in Christ Jesus"*? (Php 3:14)

Now, let us return to this abomination and farce of a trial. **The 16th violation** of their law was that the leaders should have arrested and tried the many false witnesses, who gave conflicting testimony. For the Law of Moses says, "...*if the witness is a false witness and has testified falsely against his brother then you shall do to him as he had thought to have done to his brother.*" (Deu 19:18-19) Thus, the judges should have put them to death, but then, these lying witnesses may have turned on their co-conspirators and indicted the religious leaders. **The 17th violation** of their law was when the leaders changed the charge from blasphemy to treason, after Pilate confronted them to respond why Messiah deserved death. **The 18th violation** of the law was that the judge, Pilate, declared the Spotless Lamb of God innocent, saying, "*I find no guilt in him.*" (Joh 18:38), and yet, they scourged and crucified Him anyway.

Why was it necessary to go over all of these unbelievable violations of the law of their culture and time? The purpose was twofold. First, so you will know, after loved ones, friends or the state falsely accuses you that Christ suffered far greater atrocities. Secondly, so we could remove the mask from these diligent, letter-of-the-law followers.

We have already proven Jesus suffered the greatest betrayal in history. We determined this because He was the spotless Lamb of God without blemish, and therefore, because He never sinned He did not deserve betrayals. We cannot comprehend how deeply it must have hurt to have the ones He loved so perfectly consistently betraying Him throughout His life. Those same arguments hold true for His trial because it was a complete betrayal by His brothers in the flesh, whom Jesus continued to love throughout the ordeal. Therefore, our Blessed Example in the Faith showed us the way to walk in truth when life confronts us with these types of circumstances.

History witnesses when Christians have followed in the footsteps of The Way, enduring such travesties of justice, that God the Father has blessed land with the harvest of that reward. William Tyndale comes to mind as a powerful example of a man who followed in these footsteps of the Messiah. Henry Phillips betrayed him. Phillips, whom Tyndale befriended, pretended to be concerned with Tyndale's work of translating the scriptures, feigning his desire to become his apprentice. Phillips' pious pretense and false intensions completely fooled Tyndale. In reality, Phillips was a despicable human being. He betrayed his parents by gambling away a large sum of money his father had entrusted him to give to someone in London. He was an enemy of the state due to his enormous debts. By the time the ecclesiastical authorities and the government acquired his services to capture the elusive outlaw Tyndale, he was without a friend in the world. Tyndale actually was an outlaw, because he broke the law of the Constitutions of Oxford passed in 1408, forbidding anyone from translating or reading vernacular versions of scriptures. In this case, Tyndale, like our Lord, he was breaking from the traditions of men and following the higher law of God, to which, even the Apostle Peter once defiantly told the church of his day as they attempted to restrain the going forth of the gospel, that *"We must obey God rather than men."* (Act 5:29) Henry Phillips, feigned ardent love and admiration for Tyndale, and yet, secretly despised and hated everything he stood for, betraying him into the hands of his enemies after a dinner for a small sum of money. Tyndale's prosecutor was even more corrupt and cruel. He sat as the prosecutor, judge and jury in most cases, extracting confessions after long periods of imprisonment and under many diverse tortures. He received a considerable fee for hunting down heretics and a portion of the confiscated property, so he could hardly have been an unbiased judge. Tyndale spent five-hundred days imprisoned in deplorable conditions at Vilvoorde Castle near Brussels. The following letter, written in his last days, gives us both a glimpse into his suffering during his time in the foul smelling, rat-infested dungeon and into the heart of this holy man of God, as well.

I beg your lordship, and that of the Lord Jesus, that if I am to remain here through the winter, you will request the commissary to have the kindness to send me, from the goods of mine which he has, a warmer cap; for I suffer greatly from cold in the head, and am afflicted by a perpetual catarrh, which is much increased in this cell; a warmer coat also, for this which I have is very thin; a piece of cloth too to patch my leggings. My overcoat is worn out; my shirts are also worn out. He has a woolen shirt, if he will be good enough to send it. I have also with him leggings of thicker cloth to put on above; he has also warmer night-caps. And I ask to be allowed to have a lamp in the evening; it is indeed wearisome sitting alone in the dark. But most of all I beg and beseech your clemency to be urgent with the commissary, that he will kindly permit me to have the Hebrew Bible, Hebrew grammar, and Hebrew dictionary, that I may pass the time in that study. In return may you obtain what you most desire, so only that it be for the salvation of your soul. But if any other decision has been taken concerning me, to be carried out before winter, I will be patient, abiding the will of God, to the glory of the grace of my Lord Jesus Christ: whose spirit (I pray) may ever direct your heart. Amen.

On October 6, 1536, the executioner strangled William Tyndale at the stake and then burned his dead body. The strangling was an act of mercy by the state that acknowledged his holy and pious life and thereby desired to ease the suffering of the execution. His last words, he zealously cried out, praying, *"Lord! Open the King of England's eyes."* After his death, Miles Coverdale, a Tyndale disciple, accelerated the effort of translating the entire Bible into English and quickly completed the project. Then, in August 1536, King Henry VIII issued royal injunctions requiring that a Bible written in the common language of the people be placed in every parish of the country. Within three years of Tyndale's death, his dream of bringing the Word of God to the lay people was realized. He was such a gifted translator that scholars estimate approximately 85% of the King James Bible is directly derived from his work.

It is difficult to comprehend the tremendous impact this one man's committed effort to God's call has been to our history. He changed England forever. Because people were able to read the Bible, the government abolished the slave trade. Churches dispatched missionaries all over the globe, because being convicted by the words they read in the bible. Because the Pilgrims read the Bible, they left England to form a purer Christianity. It was the call from the Bible that caused the Puritans to make the New World, America, into a city upon a hill for the propagation of the pure religion. The English Bible directed and guided the American Judeo-Christian ethic; we now call traditional American values, and became our democratic form of government. One man totally disposed to God's Will, and the world once held in the shadow of superstitions and traditions of men was set free. He was only one man, a tiny mustard seed of faith that God caused to grow into a great tree of Christian freedom, upon which we now are able to nest within the strong branches of many translations of the Holy Writ, which inspire and guide our behavior.

William Tyndale never set his sights on man, and the cares of this world. He did not *"fear those who kill the body"*, but rather, he feared *"Him who can destroy both soul and body in hell."* (Mat 10:28) He did not care about the temporal. He cared only for God's Eternal Will to be carried out on earth as in heaven. He steadfastly pressed hard *"toward the mark for the prize of the high calling of God in Christ Jesus."* (Php

3:14) When Tyndale looked at Jesus, he saw the Author and the Finisher of his Salvation, but he also saw our Example in the Faith, in His sacrifice, our salvation, in his walk, the embodiment of our sanctification. The latter is the message of The Parable of the Cross. His final letter to his best friend, John Frith, made it quite apparent the high calling that drove Tyndale's burning desire to follow Christ's Way.

> *Your cause is Christ's gospel, a light that must be fed with the blood of faith... If when we be buffeted for well-doing, we suffer patiently and endure, that is thankful with God;* ***for to that end we are called.*** *For Christ also suffered for us,* ***leaving us an example*** *that we should follow his steps,* **_who did no sin_**. *Hereby have we perceived love that he laid down his life for us: therefore we ought to be able to lay down our lives for the brethren... Let not your body faint. If the pain be above your strength, remember: "Whatsoever ye shall ask in my name, I will give it you." And pray to our Father in that name, and he will ease your pain, or shorten it... Amen.*

The honorable Tyndale not only points to Jesus as our Example in the Faith, but also points out that He never did anything to justify the world's ill treatment, for He *"did no sin."* This small phrase speaks to my point earlier. Even if, someone had a case more unjust than our Savior's trial, it still is not equivalent to the injustice done to Him, because we are sinners by nature, and He never knew sin, until the Father placed the sins of the world upon Him at the time He paid its penalty at the cross. Furthermore, He was God in the Flesh, who came to earth with only one purpose in mind, to save humanity. What was the Kings of King's reward for so gracious a cause? That He would be despised and rejected of the very men He came to save. Even virtuous Tyndale, who lived so holy before the Lord, that prisoners in the dungeon with him said, *"If he was not a Christian, then than there is no such thing as a Christian."* Nevertheless, he was born with a sin nature, and therefore, deserving of death. This statement rails against our intellect, but remember, the corrupt reasoning of our sin nature has forever tainted our thought processes. Sin has only one punishment by God's decree, death. We now have the choice, because of Christ's victory over sin and death, either to die to ourselves, which is our sin nature, or to die in our sins.

262

Now let us return to Jesus and Peter at the time of His trial, in order to compare their actions. Jesus was fully prepared through prayer to manifest the victory He had already won in the Garden. Peter, on the other hand, was completely ill equipped due to spending his time asleep, which in this case is a metaphor to us, symbolizing not diligently watching over the heart and falling into sin. Jesus embraced the cross, because He was strong in the spirit. Peter denied the cross, because he was strong in the flesh. Jesus fulfilled the Will of God. Peter denied God Himself. Jesus was victorious in death, and, at this time, Peter was defeated in life.

Fortunately, for us, and for Peter, this is not the end of his story. He was completely despondent after denying the Lord three times, at which time "*the Lord turned and looked on Peter.*" (Luk 22:61) It is easy to consider that Peter's fate could have been the same as Judas' fate, since they both denied the Lord. However, the heart of Peter and the heart of Judas were altogether different. Nevertheless, if Jesus did not pray that Peter's faith would not become shipwrecked after Satan had sifted him like wheat (Luk 22:31-32), then it is relatively easy to imagine Peter taking his own life at this time. Instead, he "*went out and wept bitterly*" (Luk 22:62), and remained with the faithful. Later, an angel instructed Mary Magdalene and Mary, the mother of James, in the empty tomb of Jesus to "*go tell His disciples **and Peter** that He goes before you into Galilee.*" (Mar 16:7) Notice the restoring work of Faithful and True after Peter's fall! The angel specifically tells the women to inform Peter. Additionally, consider one of the final meetings in the book of John. We see the exchange between them, when Jesus asked three times if Peter loved Him. In this exchange, Jesus used the highest word for love, "*agape*," and Peter responded with the lower form of brotherly love, which is "*phileo.*" The old Peter would have proudly responded that he was wholly given over to the Lord, and therefore, full of agape love for the Lord. However, that Peter no longer exists, because that part of his flesh was burned up in the fiery trial. Thus, the new, more humble Peter says, yes, I do love you so much, but I am afraid of my pride, therefore, I will not presume "*agape*" but will attest "*phileo.*" Soon, this Peter will open the doorway to the Holy Spirit on Pentecost, bringing down fire from heaven, because this Peter is now a man whom the Lord will use, fulfilling our Lord's prophecy when He said,

> *You are blessed, Simon, son of Jonah, for flesh and blood did not reveal it to you, but My Father in Heaven. And I also say to you*

that you are Peter, and on this rock I will build My church, and the gates of hell shall not prevail against it. And I will give the keys of the kingdom of Heaven to you. (Mat 16:17-19 MKJV)

Peter was given the keys to the Kingdom of heaven, and those gates were opened to the Jews by his sermon at Pentecost (Act 2:14-36), at which time 3,000 souls were added to the Kingdom. Later, the Holy Spirit sent him to Cornelius' house to open the door to the Gentiles. (Act 10) Therefore, he who denied Christ three times, and refused the cross, was given the distinguished honor of opening the gates of heaven to Jews and Gentiles alike. This man, once he began to walk in the Spirit of God and not in the power of the flesh, did great and mighty things for God. Later, when he also had finished his course, he embraced the cross, being crucified in Rome upside down, at his request, saying, he was not worthy to die in the same manner as his Lord.

I am grateful the Lord chose Peter. I am also especially thankful the gospel writers spoke openly about their defects. In Jesus, I see the ultimate ideal of what it means to be a Christian. In Tyndale, I see a man that lived so well towards that principle that I almost cannot identify with him, although, I greatly appreciate and admire him. However, in Peter, I see a man that was strong in the flesh and weak in the spirit, who through God's grace, became a powerhouse in the spirit, having died to the flesh. In Peter, I see hope for myself, that God could use such a one as Peter. That He could so profoundly transform his strengths, and his pride, into a mountain of faith and submission to the Will of God. In Peter's transformation, is hope, that God will do the same in me.

We will all fall from grace at some time in our life-walk with the Lord. However, the Lord came for restoration. We see this work out particularly well in Peter's life. If we are not too prideful to weep bitterly over our failures, then the Lord is quite gracious to restore us again. Not that He needs to save us over and over again, but that there are times when our relationship needs to be repaired; for, God is our Father, and a father cannot disinherit a son, but a son can go off into a far-off country, and be without the relationship of his father.

Tyndale was an ideal example of a man who followed in the footsteps of the Messiah. Thomas Cranmer, on the other hand, is a perfect example of a weaker vessel that was restored after denying his faith.

He was imprisoned during the reign of Mary Tudor, who we know today as Bloody Mary. After three torturous years anguishing in prison, he recanted his faith on six separate occasions. His final recantation was in writing, which he agreed to read in public. Later, when he went to the podium to address the public, he withdrew his recantation. At the time of his execution by fire, he thrust his right hand into the fire asserting, "*As my hand offended, writing contrary to my heart, my hand shall first be punished.*" Thus, Thomas Cranmer, who wavered in his faith, as we do also, is a perfect model of a man who was restored to faith, and finally able to achieve victory, embracing the cross.

We spoke of embracing the cross and reviewed four examples of Christ followers who embraced the cross all the way to their martyrdom. However, if it were only a singular event in our lives, then God would bring us to that point immediately after receiving our salvation. Instead, embracing the cross means picking it up when it has been set before us in so many of our ordinary daily life circumstances.

At the time of this writing, I met with a long-time brother and sister in Christ to celebrate the exciting news that the Lord had blessed them with a child. They tried several times in the past to conceive and failed, but now, the Creator answered their prayers. They affectionately called the unborn child, Lilly. At the end of the dinner, they asked my advice on an issue causing them some trouble. Apparently, one of the grandparents lived out of town and the mother-to-be sent her an email asking for addresses, so they could send out invitations to a baby shower. She wanted to be sure to do this early enough to allow everyone an opportunity to share in the celebration of this wonderful news. However, Lilly's future grandmother responded somewhat curtly that it was highly inappropriate for a woman to plan her own baby shower. The future grandmother's response devastated the young woman. She went from extreme elation over the blessing of pregnancy to immediate distress over the reply from her mother-in-law. She sadly kept repeating, "*You know my heart.*" As she continued to recount the affair, I could see the emotional toll of her grieving heart and troubled spirit. At the same time, I was in complete wonderment that such a strong Christian woman could so easily have her peace taken away. Christian peace is not something that resides in the peripheral circumstances of our day-to-day experiences, but rather, it is something that exists deep within us and in our strong relationship with Jesus. For, the Prince of Peace has decreed, "*I have spoken these things* *to you so that **you might have peace in Me. In the world you shall have tribulation**, but be of good cheer. I have overcome the world."* (Joh 16:33) Now, I needed to console her troubled heart, and at the same time, make her realize that she serves a sovereign God, who allows these crosses to come into our lives for our growth and His Glory. He glories when we embrace the cross and respond with the peace, and the love that Jesus gave to us as an example. I knew the Lord had perfectly arranged the timing of the writing of this chapter, the dinner, my time in that town, their pregnancy and this trial, in order to grow their faith. Therefore, I had to find a way to get them to stop looking at the circumstance and to start looking at the Lord. I also knew the Lord placing a cross in front of me, to bring this delicate message to my long-time friends, whose company I so rarely have the opportunity to enjoy.

How can I tell them without damaging our relationship? Maybe I should just console them and leave it at that, but instead I felt the Holy Spirit prodding me to bring this teaching to their attention. The fact that I have to teach this lesson so often to mature Christians is why I have felt a prevailing need to write this book.

I told her, *"Yes, I do know your heart, but you need to apologize to your mother-in-law."* I said to her that they both have a correct heart and correct intentions. The mother-in-law may have been looking out for her, so she does not seem to have violated some traditional ethic. She was raised in a different generation when traditions were more rigidly formal. She needed to appreciate that frame of mind and let the mother-in-law know that she did not realize she overstepped these boundaries. It was not an apology for wrongdoing as much as it is an apology for not realizing she broke some tradition. Then I began to explain The Parable of the Cross, how the Lord allows these things to come into our lives, so we can grow as Christians and become witnesses of our faith to the world. I talked about Jesus, and the things that He said and endured, in order to provide us this example, so we can also overcome the world and not allow our peace to be stolen. Then, I gave them testimony of some of my own trials, when I took up the cross He laid before me, and how, in the end, the Lord rewarded my obedience by working all things towards my good. (Rom 8:28)

Now the moment had arrived. Would they accept the message or would they reject the message and me at the same time? Thankfully, they embraced the message. I left feeling very good that night. They said they did not seek the Lord in prayer about the matter, and their time with the King had wavered. They were encouraged that I had used the words of the Bible as a solution to their problem and decided that they needed to create a habit of spending time in devotions for themselves and for their future daughter.

Several days later, the young woman emailed me and said she found her peace, and that she forgave her mother-in-law. She also said her mother-in-law subsequently wrote an email apologizing for her remarks, and that they had begun to reconcile their relationship. How many times do we not allow the Lord to have His perfect work because we do not want to follow His example, embracing the cross, and turn the other cheek? If she had sent an email back expressing her hurt or decided to withdraw from her mother-in-law, altogether it could have damaged their relationship for a very long time. Instead, she embraced the cross and then the Lord worked all things for their good. Praise God!

Jesus endured one of the most corrupt, unjust trials in history and experienced betrayal at every turn. It may not have been the most unjust trial ever, but never was a man accused as innocent as He was. For, He knew no sin and not only did He love perfectly, but He was the actual manifestation of love in the flesh. He stood spotless and blameless before an evil and adulterous generation, and submitted gracefully to the cross. Now, we also are called to endure these betrayals, trials and tribulations. We know there is one who suffered for us, who will provide us with the strength to endure; one who never deserved this treatment, but rather, it was us that deserved this dreadful punishment. For this reason, we should stop asking, "*Why do bad things happen to good people?*" Instead, we should be asking, "*Why do good things happen to us at all, who deserve death for our sins? Why does a righteous God even give to us such ardent love, affection and grace? Why did He love us so much that He sent His only Begotten Son to die on our behalf?*" Let us stop looking at the bad that is the consequence of an evil world and blaming God because of Adam's disobedience. Instead, let us begin to look at the good, God still allows to fall upon our unworthy souls. Every day I breathe the air. Every day my heart beats, and every day I have the life He gave. Every day I eat food and enjoy the company of others, and yet, I am sad to say, every day I give so little praise for all I have received.

chapter fourteen

THE LAST WORDS OF THE CONVICTED

The Passover celebration was a particularly intense time for Roman soldiers stationed in Judea. During this time, Jerusalem's population swelled, tripling in size, with the arrival of many zealous Hebrew pilgrims, who desired to celebrate Yahweh's deliverance of the Jewish people from enslavement by the world's greatest superpower of that day. The parallels between the period of Egyptian oppression and the current Roman overlords were obvious. Not only was this a celebration of the past, but it was also a time when the Jewish people looked to the present and to the future for the hope of Messiah, who would come in the same manner as Moses and deliver them from their current repression to set up His Kingdom on earth. The rabbis clearly understood Moses as a Messiah-type. Many people, as well, believed the actual Deliverer of God was due to arrive around this time. Considering all of this, it is remarkable that they were not able to see Yeshua, the Lamb of God, standing among them, in their midst. Nevertheless, from the Roman perspective, these were Messianic superstitions; and yet, they were dangerous concepts that could ignite the fire of insurrection, so the entire government and the soldiers anxiously served on high alert during these days.

Normally, Pontius Pilate administered Judea from a palace in Caesarea, which was half-way between Jerusalem and the Sea of Galilee on the coast, but because of a higher probability of a revolt during this time; he chose to reside temporarily in Jerusalem.

According to Rome, Pilate already made three critical errors, which meant his political career hung by the thinnest of threads. After he had become the governor of Judea, he did something no other Roman leader dared; he rode into Jerusalem bearing standards with images of eagles and the emperor, causing a protest and a near rebellion in that zealous city that lasted five days. Shortly after this, he took money from the temple treasury, in order to fund an aqueduct from Bethlehem to Jerusalem, which instigated a riot and bloodshed. His third blunder occurred when he set up several golden shields at his headquarters in Jerusalem that also met stern opposition from the Jewish leadership. His archenemy, Herod Antipas, then was able to use this against him in an appeal to Rome.

Now with the backdrop of this information let us begin to review the last words of the convicted. However, I fear that you have assumed that I was speaking of Jesus, because He was the one convicted of the world, when in fact I am speaking of the world because we are the ones that convict ourselves by our the hypocrisy of our actions against our words. From our perspective it is Jesus who is on trial, but from God's perspective it is the world that is on trial; Jesus is innocent as proclaimed by all parties and yet He will die a death that was reserved for only the greatest of criminals. In fact the more Pilate attempts to satisfy the blood lust of the Jewish leadership and set Jesus free the more he will cause the Him to suffer even greater torment at the hands of an ungodly world.

The Jewish leaders arrived early in the morning at Pilate's headquarters with the *"malefactor"* Jesus. Besides arriving at the governor's office at daybreak, they refused to enter his chambers, so they would not defile themselves for the Passover, forcing the governor to come out to them. Imagine Pilate's contempt, considering the damage to his reputation due to incidents from serving in Judea, and now these leaders, the cause of so many of his problems, now not only demand to see him, but on their terms. If Pilate's power had not so utterly eroded due to his previous missteps, it would be easy to imagine an entirely different outcome to this demand by the Roman government's subjugated leaders, but due to his precarious situation the ruler submits himself to the demands of the ruled. *"So Pilate went outside to them and said, 'What accusation do you bring against this man?'"* (Joh 18:29) To which, the Jewish leaders gave a highly ambiguous answer, *"If this man were not doing evil, we would not have delivered him over to you."* (Joh 18:30) This is almost like saying, *"Do not ask us why we brought him to you. Just do as we say and put him to death."* Once again, the response clearly demonstrates Pilate's tenuous position as a leader ruled somewhat by those whom he should be ruling. From The Parable of the Cross perspective, we see this in our own lives on a daily basis, whereby the flesh attempts to rule over the spirit and choose its own way, despite our conscience giving clear objections.

Straight away, Pilate comprehended it was a violation of their religious laws, which Rome chose not to entangle themselves in these cultural matters; therefore, they allowed the conquered provinces to rule over their own religious issues and customs, and so he responded, *"Take him yourselves and judge him by your own law."* (Joh 18:31) Having forced their hand, the Jewish leaders made known their purpose for bringing Messiah to the Roman governor saying, *"It is not lawful for us to put anyone to death."* (Joh 18:31) The response also demonstrates that the charges were never as important to the leadership as its primary purpose, which was to put Jesus to death. As we had seen earlier, the charges kept changing until they could find one that would stand, in order to achieve its ultimate aim, which was the death of this man, who proclaimed they were snakes, vipers, thieves and hypocrites, all within the ears of the people.

Applying this scene of Christ's Passion to The Parable of the Cross, the Pharisees represent strongholds and passions of the flesh. Pilate symbolizes the battleground of the intellect, which must choose between the powerful pulsating demands of the flesh's strongholds or the gentle prodding of the Holy Spirit. The Lord represents the Holy Spirit, or the moral conscience God has given to every man, even to the lost to know the difference between right and wrong. In each case, it appears that the statements of the rulers carry with them extremely profound applications to this hidden parable. In this case, the strongholds of our passions, the Pharisees, state, *"It is not lawful for us to put anyone to death."* (Joh 18:31) This is precisely how Christians, including myself, continually attempt to win the war of enmity between the spirit and the flesh, using our passions to defeat our passions and our flesh to conquer the flesh. Occasionally, we win small victories through our own strength and the pride in the spirit, but in the end, we always lose the war, for who can nail himself to the cross. You can attach both feet and even a hand, if you have the will power to endure the pain, but who will put in the final nail at the cross to secure the victory for the particular battle you have been commissioned to fight. Fighting in this manner is like a person who has nailed himself to the cross, but now only has one remaining arm and is unable to complete the victory. Eventually, you will use the free hand to release your other hand and then your feet, and before you know it, those passions you thought the spirit had crucified now live and reign supreme once again in your mortal soul. Time after time, we go through this exercise in futility until we finally cry out in despair, "*O wretched man that I am! Who shall deliver me from this body of death?*" (Rom 7:24)

If it is not lawful for us to put ourselves to death, then why does the Bible tell us "*those belonging to Christ have crucified the flesh with its passions and lusts*"? (Gal 5:24) However, if we were able to crucify the flesh solely on our own, then would we not be able to glory in it before God? Would we not then be achieving the ongoing work of our salvation, which is our sanctification, by our works and not by faith, which is contrary to the scriptures? No, there is only one method to crucify the flesh. By the example, Christ has given to us, which is to allow the evil in the world to purge the evil in our hearts, and thereby submitting ourselves to the crosses the Sovereign Lord allows to come into our lives. If you wish to grow stronger in the faith, to grow closer to the Lord, and to walk in His spirit, this is the only way, because there is far too much of us in us, and not enough of Christ, without the cross. For this reason, we ought to praise God when He brings these crosses into our lives, instead of dropping them and running the other way. We should thank our Lord for the opportunity to become more like Him, and closer to Him, rather than praying fervently that He takes it from us.

This is why Jesus showed us the Way to the Cross. This is why Jesus told us through the prophet Isaiah:

> *The Lord Jehovah has opened My ear, and **I was not rebellious, nor turned away backwards. I gave My back to the strikers, and My cheeks to pluckers; I did not hide My face from shame and spitting**. For the Lord Jehovah will help Me; therefore I have not been ashamed. On account of this I have set My face like a flint, and I know that I shall not be ashamed. (Isa 50:5-7 MKJV)*

Moreover, Isaiah explicates:

> ***Yet it pleased Jehovah to crush Him; to grieve Him;*** *that He should put forth His soul as a guilt-offering. He shall see His seed, He shall prolong His days, and the will of Jehovah shall prosper in His hand. (Isa 53:10 MKJV)*

Now consider that the Way to our Salvation has said, "*I have given you an example, that you should do as I have done to you.*" (Joh 13:15) He

271

has also said, "*If anyone desires to come after Me*"; that is, to follow His Way in their lives, then "*let him deny himself and take up his cross and follow Me.*" (Mat 16:24) John the Evangelist, likewise, tells us, "*He who says he abides in Him ought himself also to walk even as He walked.*" (1Jn 2:6)

If this is Jehovah's doings, and it has pleased Him to crush us, then why are we always defiantly turning away from the cross that is our destiny, and the evil used to destroy the evil strongholds in our lives? The answer is, we do not think properly any more since the fall of Adam. Our sin nature has infected our minds so deeply; what we think is good for us is usually bad and what we think is bad is generally good. As we begin to get these concepts straightened out, the world then begins to look upon us as a peculiar people. The truth is that we despise the cross, yet we should be grateful for it! For our faith is called to be tried by fire. We are admonished to endure to the end, and to "*continue in the faith ...that through much tribulation we must enter into the Kingdom of God.*" (Act 14:22) "*For you yourselves know that we are destined for this.*" (1Th 3:3) This is God's plan. If it pleased Him to grieve His Only Begotten, Sinless Son in this manner, then it pleases Him to grieve our corrupts souls in the way, as well. For He has told us from long ago:

> **Awake, O sword, against My Shepherd**, *and against the Man who is My companion, says Jehovah of Hosts; strike the Shepherd, and the sheep shall be scattered.* **And I will turn My hand on the little ones.** *(Zec 13:7 MKJV)*

Therefore, it is now our turn, Little Ones, to be stricken. This may cause you to look at the Lord Almighty with fear, but that is your sin nature screaming out from within you, just as the loudest participants in this scene, the Pharisees, made their demands upon their ruler Pontius Pilate. This is our current upside-down state of reasoning, in which, the flesh constantly attempts to usurp the clear logic of the gospels, because without this logic setting our minds straight we cannot come to the truth. We need to die to ourselves, since we love ourselves more than anyone or any god!

Returning once more to the scene, the Pharisees came up with charges Rome considered worthy of death, so they "*began to accuse Him, saying, 'We have found this one perverting the nation and forbidding them to give tribute to Caesar, saying himself to be a king, Christ.'*"

(Luk 23:2) Next, Pilate began a private examination of Messiah and asked, "*Are you the king of the Jews?*" (Joh 18:33) To which Jesus responded, "*You say it*" (Luk 23:3), which is to say, "*You are correct.*" Subsequently, He added, "*My kingdom is not of this world. If My kingdom were of this world, then My servants would fight so that I might not be delivered to the Jews. But now My kingdom is not from here.*" (Joh 18:36)

Luke 23:3 may stand as the most astounding words Jesus ever spoke! Furthermore, the fact that he responds with the calm, cool, matter-of-fact statement, "*You say it*", makes it even more remarkable. It is as if someone was to ask me if my name was Don Lett, to which I would quite naturally respond in a matter-of-fact tone of voice, "*Yes.*" Yes! He is the King of the Jews. He is Immanuel, God With Us, born of a virgin. (Isa 7:14) He is the "*...Lord Jesus Christ, the only begotten Son of God, begotten of his Father before all worlds, God of God, Light of Light, very God of very God, begotten, not made, being of one substance with the Father...*"[12] He is the one who has fulfilled over 300 prophetic descriptions of Messiah in the Holy Writ. For this reason, the world stands convicted before the Supreme Judge, because He fulfilled all the promises to such a degree that anyone truly seeking God will find Him in history and in the scriptures. As a consequence, God the Father can rightly say on judgment day "*O man you are without excuse.*" (Rom 2:1)

Consider how precisely Jesus fulfilled just a few of these prophecies in the final hours of His life. Scriptures predicted Judas' betrayal stating, "*Even my close friend in whom I trusted, who ate my bread, has lifted his heel against me*" (Psa 41:9), even foreseeing the exact cost of his treachery, saying, "*So they paid me thirty pieces of silver.*" (Zec 11:12) In addition, the Holy Scriptures foretold Judas throwing money into the temple and the religious leaders choosing to buy a Potter's field with the blood money. "*So I took the thirty pieces of silver and threw them into the house of the LORD, to the potter.*"(Zec 11:13) Furthermore, the scriptures predicted false witnesses would testify against Him, saying, "*Malicious witnesses rise up.*" (Psa 35:11) They prophesied Messiah's response to His trial and His false accusations, saying, "*...he opened not his mouth.*" (Isa 53:7) They predicted His followers would desert Him, saying, "*Strike the shepherd, and the*

---

[12] Taken from the Nicene Creed.

sheep will be scattered." (Zec 13:7) The Holy Scriptures predicted; He would be flogged, His beard would be ripped out, He would be spit upon (Isa 50:6), and He would be beaten so badly that His form would be *"beyond human semblance."* (Isa 52:14) He would be mocked (Psa 22:7), and scorned (Psa 109:25) by His enemies. He would be crucified (Psa 22:16) with transgressors (Isa 53:12), even though, He was innocent of any crime (Isa 53:9), in order to pay the price for our transgressions (Isa 53:5). While He was on the cross He would thirst (Psa 22:15), and they would offer Him sour wine to drink. (Psa 69:21) Moreover, they would divide His garments among them and cast lots for His tunic. (Psa 22:18) While His detractors shook their heads at Him (Psa 22:7), and stared and gloated over Him (Psa 22:17), His friends and family would be standing afar off. (Psa 38:11) However, Messiah's reaction to all of this would be that He would pray for His persecutors. (Isa 53:12) He would be pierced in the side (Zec 12:10), and He would both literally and figuratively die of a broken heart. (Psa 22:14) Despite the prophecies of this man being despised, rejected and tried as a enemy of the state He would be buried with the rich. (Isa 53:9)

If that is not enough, consider this prophecy, which occurs in the future when Israel cries out to God for help, just as the armies of the world are about to annihilate her. *"Then the LORD my God will come, and all the holy ones with him"* (Zec 14:5), which is preceded by a massive earthquake, and *"the Mount of Olives shall be split in two from east to west".* (Zec 14:4) Notice also that this is the same mountain of Messiah's ascension, when the angels told the men of Galilee, *"This Jesus, who was taken up from you into heaven, **will come in the same way** as you saw him go into heaven."* (Act 1:11) Then, according to Zechariah's prophecy, written a little over 500 years before Christ was born, *"they shall look on Me **whom they have pierced**, and they shall mourn for Him, as one mourns for his only son, and shall be bitter over Him, as the bitterness over the first-born."* (Zec 12:10) Not only did Zechariah write this before Messiah was crucified, but it describes crucifixion even before the Persians invented the practice around 400 BC. Furthermore, notice that God foretells Israel that they will not recognize Jesus, until He returns in the Last Days with the marks in His hands and feet. Then, having realized their error, they will become as grief stricken *"as one [who] mourns for his only son."*

This scene in the Last Days is what Messiah referred to in His last public address to Israel when He said, *"You shall not see Me from now*

on until you say, 'Blessed is He who comes in the name of the Lord.'"
(Mat 23:39) Can you imagine that day? Israel will look at His pierced
hands, and they will realize that they did not know Him through all
these centuries. Instead of celebrating the most miraculous victory in
history, their hearts will be full of sorrow. Their bitterness is
accentuated by the fact that not only have they been delivered from
certain annihilation by their long-awaited Messiah, but also, their
Messiah is Yahweh Himself, standing amongst them, in their midst. In
proof of this, note that the context of Zechariah chapter 12 is God
speaking of Himself, in either the first or the third person. He says,

> *I will make Jerusalem a cup of trembling... (Zec 12:2)*
> *I will make Jerusalem a burdensome stone... (Zec 12:3)*
> *I will strike every horse with terror... (Zec 12:4)*
> *I will make the governors of Judah like a hearth of fire... (Zec 12:6)*
> *Jehovah also shall save the tents of Judah... (Zec 12:7)*
> *Jehovah shall defend around the people... (Zec 12:8)*
> *I will seek to destroy all the nations that come against Jerusalem... (Zec 12:9)*
> *I will pour on the house of David... (Zec 12:10)*

Finally, concluding these series of events in which God is actively
involved in Israel's salvation, He says *"And they shall look on __ME__
whom they have pierced."* In the small verse of Zechariah 12:10 is the
deliverance of Israel and the sorrow for having missed their Messiah
through all these centuries. Although the Deliverer is God Himself, He
must also be a man, because He is pierced. Therefore, it can only be
our Immanuel, God in the Flesh, *Yeshua Ha Meshiach*, which is Jesus
Messiah.

Is Jesus the King of the Jews? These twenty-eight prophecies are not
your average, every-day horoscope or fortune cookie types of
prophecies. They are extremely specific. It would have been virtually
impossible for any one person to fulfill these prophecies alone. Now
contemplate the practical impossibility of one person fulfilling the
other, over 270 explicit prophecies we have not discussed. These
verses make extraordinarily precise predictions about His life, birth,
ministry and death. In the Old Testament patriarch Joseph, the
scholarly rabbis saw a suffering messiah they called *ben Joseph*, which
means son of Joseph. In David, they saw a victorious messiah they

called *ben David*. If God Incarnate came to earth as ben David, Israel would have accepted Him with open arms, but in God's grace, He came first as ben Joseph, in order to bring *"many sons to glory"*. (Heb 2:10) In the scriptures, we read, *"And Joseph knew his brothers, but they did not know him."* (Gen 42:8) Later, after experiencing many trials, *"Joseph made himself known to his brothers"* (Gen 45:1) and they all wept with a mixture of emotions of sadness and joy. Superimposing Zechariah 12:10 with the stories of Joseph and Jesus, paints a detailed picture of the Messiah and demonstrates the coherency and the continuity of the Word of God. In all three are images of rejection, spiritual blindness, deliverance and bittersweet joy after discovering their deliverer's actual identity at their reunions.

Had the nation of Israel ever rejected the King of the Universe? When Israel demanded to have a king rule over them in the Tanakh, God told Samuel, *"For they have not rejected you, but they have rejected Me."* In like manner, all who reject Jesus as the King of the Jews not only rejects Him, but they reject God, for Jesus rightfully said, *"the one who rejects me rejects him who sent me."* (Luk 10:16)

Is Jesus the King of the Jews? As you can see from our earlier discussions on Zechariah 12, the answer to this question carries enormous implications. To be the King of the Jews means that Jesus Messiah has to be God Himself. Now understanding all the monumental ramifications when Yeshua answers, *"You say it"*, we find ourselves stuck squarely in the middle of C.S. Lewis' trilemma; that is He is either our Lord, or a liar or a lunatic. This statement utterly pulls the middle ground that He was only a revered teacher and a moral man out from under our feet. When Messiah point-blankly affirms, *"You say it"*, He is saying, *"Yes, I am the King of the Jews, the promised Messiah, Yahweh Himself in the Flesh, the God-Deliverer"*! Not to believe He is God, even though, Jesus clearly affirms that He is God, forces us to conclude that He was either the greatest charlatan, who has fooled billions of Christian believers through the centuries, or the most self-deluded lunatic in history. As remarkable as it may seem, it is actually more rational to believe that Jesus truly was born of a virgin, walked on water, healed the sick, calmed the storm, was crucified and rose from the grave and then ascended into heaven. As we progress forward in our reasoning, we now only have two choices, He is either God of very God, or we have to believe the greatest conspiracy ever perpetrated on mankind, which makes us conspiracy theorists of the highest magnitude. Not to believe that Jesus is God, suggests that

276

somehow He had to change over 300 prophecies in all the copies of the Tanakh and then fulfill them all in the historicity of His life. It is clearly easier to believe in a Supernatural God than to become the alternative, a conspiracy theorist who believes in the greatest hoax in history.

Is Jesus the King of the Jews? This is the most important question in every person's life. If He is the King of the Jews then should He not also be the king of our heart?

Next, in Christ's dialogue with Pilate, He says, "*Everyone who is of the truth listens to my voice*". (Joh 18:37) To which Pilate cynically responds with rhetoric, "*What is truth?*" (Joh 18:38) What irony! Here is Pilate, who knows the truth in this instance, but whose life is neither guided by it nor can recognize its principles when making monumental life decisions, and yet, he is now standing face to face with the embodiment of The Truth of God, looking Truth directly in the eye and asking, "*What is truth?*" To this, Jesus offers no response, because He has already answered it, saying, "*Everyone who is of the truth listens to my voice.*"

Then cold, calculating Pilate, whose truth vacillates according to the circumstances of the day, makes the determination that Jesus is not guilty. This is such a fascinating scene the Omnipotent God has painted for us. We have politically expedient Pilate, living by the principle that there is no one truth, now comes to the truth that Jesus is innocent. This is the terrible irony, as well, for all who bear the politically correct standard of relative truth as the moral banner for their lives; in every way they are walking, irrational contradictions. All actions and decisions testify against this cornerstone to the foundation of their philosophical houses. They ultimately make choices, which means they settle upon some truth in that situation. The dogma of relative truth itself is a contradiction, because it sets itself as the pinnacle of absolute truth while attempting to hold fast to its fundamental creed that circumstances defines the meaning of truth. What the right hand gives the left hand takes away. You may ask, "*Is all truth relative?*", and they would say, "*Yes.*" Then, you may ask, "*Then how about the truth that all truth is relative?*" To which they may say, attempting to gloss over the obvious contradiction, "*Yes this is the only truth that is absolute; that all truth is relative except for the truth 'all truth is relative.'*" As you can see, the more they struggle to free themselves from this tangled twine the more they find themselves entangled within it. This is very much like watching a dog chase his tail. The more frantically they attempt to resolve the impossible contradiction, the more frantically they chase their tails. Thus, on the issue of Christ's innocence, reciprocating Pilate appears to have drawn an absolute line in the sand and now leaves the presence of the Lord to walk out and address the Pharisees of his verdict.

However, when one's cornerstone is made of sand than the circumstances of the storm can easily wash away one's convictions. Jesus elucidates, *"Everyone then who hears these words of mine and does them will be like a wise man who built his house on the rock"* (Mat 7:24); whose life will stand firm in the face of the storm of adversity. The other option is to choose your own truth, which the storms of this life will soon reveal its faulty foundation.

Is your foundation on the solid ground of God's absolute Truth, or is it based upon the shifting ground that truth is relative to circumstances and opinions? The answer to the following questions will assist in that assessment. Do you waiver when you are tossed to and fro by life's storms, like a ship on the ocean or do you stand fast in His truth? Is your peace easily stolen, because you choose not to continue to abide in His rest?

Pilate never sincerely asked, *"What is truth?"* Instead, by asking this rhetorical question, he was stating emphatically there is no such thing as truth. Once again, I am struck by the irony that he looked Truth in the face as he made this statement. Pilate, the creature of God, stood before the Incarnate Creator and Supreme Judge of the earth, to judge whether He should live or die. If I was God, I think I would be offended at this time, but not His humble servant Jesus. No, instead Jesus, the manifest Love of God, always reaching out to the lost, looked upon cold calculating Pilate with the warm, gentle eyes of a Loving Creator. In His speech was the calm, reassuring voice of an affectionate parent who spoke to Pilate with the overtones of, *"Come to Me… you who labor and are heavy laden, and I will give you rest."* (Mat 11:28) Thus, when Pilate looked into His eyes, he saw the lover of his soul. He saw His tender compassion, and most inexplicably of all, He saw a man who was more concerned with Pilate's judgment than His own judgment. This did not make any sense to shrewd, politically expedient Pilate. When he looked into those eyes, he should have seen a pleading criminal or a conniving manipulator, but instead he saw a Loving Creator's concern for His creation. When he looked into these eyes, he recognized, at that moment, no other person knew him as well. His wife knew him, his best friend knew him, and he even knew himself better than any other man, and yet, at that time, he realized this man understood him more than his wife, best friend, or himself. For this short period in Pilate's life, he apprehended no one ever loved him more, because not only did God's eyes of mercy look upon him with care and concern, but also, He continued to love Pilate, even though He knew all his faults and failures. During this short exchange, Pilate found the peace and the love of God. What else should we expect? After all, he was standing in the presence of the Prince of Peace and the embodiment of His love.

While Pilate felt this serene peace in his soul, his mind was set ablaze with all sorts of questions. Who was this man? Why was He so different? What could He have done to these priests to cause them to desire His death? Why was this man not groveling at his feet pleading for mercy? Thus, in Pilate's heart, he knows there is something truly remarkable about the man who stands before him. Intuitively, he knows this man is so gentle He would not break a bruised reed or quench a smoking wick. (Isa 42:3) However, it has been unusually long indeed, since cold, calculating Pilate has allowed his heart a voice in his decision-making. All his decisions came entirely from his cool, calm intellect. It was weakness to allow his heart any voice in these political matters. So for the time being, he set aside all of these questions and premonitions and turned away from so great a salvation and cynically retorted, *"What is truth?"* Once more, he chose the relative truth of political expediency and condemned the objective truth to the cross.

How could this be? How could he stand face to face with the Truth, and yet, choose political expediency over God's truth? The nature of Pilate's question is indicative of why he is not able to see the answer standing right before his eyes. He appears to have already arrived at a conclusion before he asks the question, *"What is the truth?"* Furthermore, his conclusion driving the rhetorical question carries with it the implication that no one really knows the definition of truth. It implies that our definitions are based upon words, and words upon cultures, and so the truth is not in any person or place but just a something that is created by societies. However, if Pilate had sincerely asked, *"Where is the truth"* or *"Who has the truth,"* then he would have gotten an entirely different response from our Lord, rather than silence.

"For everyone who asks receives, and the one who seeks finds." (Mat 7:8)

Even one of the greatest pessimists of all time can elicit a response from the Lord of Glory when he asks the correct question from the correct heart; for *"Thomas said to him, 'Lord, we do not know where you are going. How can we know the way?'"* (Joh 14:5) To which the Lord was pleased to answer, *"I am the way, and the truth, and the life. No one comes to the Father except through me."* (Joh 14:6) In the Lord's answer, He uses the definite article *"the"*, which carries the extraordinary proclamation that there is no truth outside of Him. Additionally, He uses this same definite article calling Himself *"the way"* to God. He ends His response, as well with the definite article by saying He is *"the life."* As a result, we can now see that knowing the truth is not a matter of a personal definition or a conglomeration of aggregately agreed upon moral standards of a society, but rather, it is a place to be sought out; for the Lord has promised us *"the one who seeks finds."* (Mat 7:8) Therefore, Yeshua's response is more than fitting, because if the truth is a place, then how do we know how to get there and who will show us the way? To all of these, and many more questions, the Lord of Truth has given us a most concise and insightful answer. Jesus is *"the way"*, Jesus is *"the truth"* and Jesus is *"the life."* Notice the beautiful progression of these truths. Jesus will show us *"the way"* to *"the truth"* in order to find *"the life."* For this reason, He has told every believer to *"Follow Me"* (Mat 4:19), which is to say, walk in His footsteps during our pilgrim's progress in this world. Although the personal details are decidedly different for every Christian, the basic journey is the same for all. We must lay the heavy burden of sin aside on our journey to the Celestial City. We must avoid the wide and wicked gate of Mr. Wordly Wiseman, Mr. Legality and his son Civility, choosing rather, the far less traveled straight and narrow King's highway. On this journey, we will find a vast number of challenges and snares, like Giant Despair and the dungeon in Doubting Castle. Our reward for staying in the way and progressing on our pilgrimage is, to find, and become, filled with more and more of the truth. Ultimately, we discover what we have been searching for all of our lives, escape from the City of Destruction and entrance into the Celestial City. Thus, the story of every Christian life; we follow His way, He fills us with truth, and we eventually gain the manifest promise of the crown of eternal life.

NOT WORKS! Jesus gives us the promise of eternal life at the moment we welcome Him as our Lord and our Savior by faith alone. If He is our Lord, then we should follow Him as He has instructed. As we travel with Him in this life, we will find that the scales of our blind sin will fall from our eyes and we will begin to see His full manifestation within us. Then He fills us with greater and greater revelations of Him and His truth. This is our promise of eternal life; that the Son abides in us. (1Jn 2:24-5)

These are astoundingly distinct, definitive affirmations. Jesus declares that He is "*the way*", "*the truth*" and "*the life*." The definite article "*the*" completely forbids any possibility of any other way. If that was not clear enough, The Way of Truth to Eternal Life supports this fantastic affirmation with an even more astoundingly definitive universal negation saying, "***NO ONE*** *comes to the Father except through ME.*"

How do we find *the way* to the Celestial City? Where is *the truth*? How do we discover *the life* force of God? It is through Jesus and His guiding life force within us, called the Spirit of Christ. He is all things to the Christian. He is a way, or a journey. He is a place, or a destination. Yet, He is also a person with whom we can have a relationship, Jesus Messiah. Therefore, we rest in His finished work as we sojourn in our travels in this life. To which a large part of this journey is to accept the crosses that try our faith, which the Sovereign Lord has placed in the way, so the scales may fall from our sin-soaked eyes. As they fall, we begin to recognize that our voyage was only necessary in order for us to see what we already had become in the Lamb of God. This is the believer's profound understanding of time. We journey in this life, bearing our crosses, only to discover what we already became 2,000 years ago. For the Christian, our sanctification is a journey of the present, walking into the future, in order to realize our eternal victory He already attained for us in the past. We progress into the future by regressing into the past and proclaiming our victory at the Cross of Calvary. The Cross of Christ, therefore, stands as the centerpiece of time. The Old Testament saints looked forward to their deliverance in Messiah, but the New Testament saints look to the past for theirs. However, it stands not only as the centerpiece in time of human history, but also as a symbol, that should be the showpiece of our lives, as well. So, how do you find life? How do you find victory over sin? It is through death that we find life, and in His victory of the past we find the future. This is the great paradox of Christianity and the lost message of The Parable of the Cross.

As I have said, we should follow His way in the present, in view of the truth of our victory in Him in the past, ultimately, to receive the crown of eternal life in the future. However, is that all there is for this life? Is the only purpose for our present life to be offered as a sacrifice for our future? This is what many unbelievers believe about Christianity, and unfortunately, this is what many believers believe as well. In keeping with this thought, the Lord of Life told us *"he who hates his life in this world shall keep it to life eternal."* (Joh 12:25) He has also told us *"I have come so that they might have life, and that they might have it more abundantly."* (Joh 10:10) So where is this abundant life? Furthermore, how are we to achieve this if we are to hate our lives in this world, which gladly motivates us to pick up the cross and walk with the Lord of Glory to Calvary? In this case, the Greek behind the English translation offers us a much greater insight into this apparent contradiction. Notice the two different Greek words that the Resurrection and the Life uses when He says, *"he who hates his life [psuche] in this world shall keep it to life [zoe] eternal."* If this were the only verse that spoke of the sacrifice of our *psuche* life in this world to preserve our *zoe* life in eternity, then we would have to infer that we are called to ransom our current existence for a future existence. In contrast, notice which Greek word the Lord of Glory used when He said, *"I have come so that they might have life [zoe], and that they might have it more abundantly."* So is the Lord suggesting He will give us an abundant life in the future with this promise? That also does not seem to make much sense. That is like someone saying when you swim under the water you will become wetter by swimming deeper. How can we receive something in greater abundance of life than the full payment of the promise of eternal bliss with our Savior? No, all expositors have interpreted this verse to mean that the Lord of Life has come to give us life more abundantly in the present. Therefore, the Lord has *"come so that they might have [zoe] life, and that they might have it [zoe] more abundantly."*

Then, what is the difference between *zoe* life and *psuche* life? *Zoe* is the life force of God; it is the spirit life within man. *Psuche* life is the soulish life of man. It is the battleground of the intellect. This is where Freud, and so many other materialists have focused their attention. Freud defined these regions as the id and the ego, which is to say the lower regions of the mind, driven by bodily needs and the passions of the flesh and the upper regions of the mind, influenced by higher aspirations, which we also know as the spirit. This is an incredible trade that the Lord has offered the world. He will trade the temporal, soulish, *psuche* life for the eternal life force of God, the *zoe* life, if you are willing to offer this *psuche* life as a living sacrifice. In order to receive some clarity about this, consider the following:

> ...*whoever desires to save his [psuche] life shall lose it [zoe], and whoever desires to lose his [psuche] life for My sake shall find it [zoe]. (Mat 16:25)*
> ...*If anyone comes to Me and does not hate ... [even] his own [psuche] life also, he cannot be My disciple. (Luk 14:26)*
> ...*the Son of Man did not come to be served, but to serve, and to give His [psuche] life a ransom for many. (Mat 20:28)*

The Resurrection and the *Zoe* Life tells us that He is the way, the way of the cross and the truth. He shows us the truth of who we are in Him and the life, the life-giving force of God, the all-powerful, victorious, eternal *zoe* life in our present existence. We are asked to trade our *psuche* life, the lower regions of our mind, for the life-giving *zoe* life force of God's presence in our current being. What an astounding trade! This is like a car dealership freely offering to give you a brand-new car for your old, beat-up car! Why free? Because it was Jesus, who paid the price for so great a salvation, and for the abundant *zoe* life offered to you, now and into the future. This is why the Psalmist ecstatically proclaims with an abundant heart, filled with joy, "*O taste and see that the LORD is good!*" (Psa 34:8)

Now we can begin to understand the utter deceptions Satan uses against the world and carnal Christians. The world is doing all they can to preserve their *psuche* lives, and gratify the desires of this existence. Carnal Christians often look very much like the world. Most of them have never been taught the difference. It is also sad that many strong, dedicated believers have never learned the difference. For example, do you remember Jerome's battle with the desires of the flesh? He deprived himself of food, sleep and warmth. He attempted to win the battle over the flesh with the flesh. He was attempting to crucify the *psuche* life by using the *psuche* life. We can win this battle over short time frames, but ultimately, it will always be lost, resulting in failure and frustration. We are called to kill the *psuche* life, under the headship of the flesh, with the *zoe* life, under the headship of our Lord and Savior. In Him, and only in Him, lies the victory. It is for this reason that spirit-filled, victorious Christians should never glory over triumphs, because we never won it, but rather the Captain of Salvation won the victory. It is only ours, manifest by faith; for, we are saved by faith and not of our works lest any man should boast. (Eph 2:8-9) Therefore, Satan, the Great Deceiver, lies to the world, saying that the cure for the disease is to scratch the itch, but this only leads to greater damage to the soul. Meanwhile, The Way, The Truth and The *Zoe* Life offers us an unbelievable trade, peace for despair, joy for sorrow, health for disease, victory for defeat and life for death.

What does Jesus get out of the trade? He gets us. This is always His primary passion, to love the Lord His God and to love His neighbor as Himself. In a word, He is all about, reconciliation. His love is the greatest love the world has ever known. For this reason, we know that God not only loves us, but He is love! Thus, Jesus desired to reconcile us to God through Himself, by laying down His life and dying in our place; for, *"No one has greater love than this, that a man lay down his life for his friends."* (Joh 15:13) Praise and glory be His forever! This in turn, causes us to lay down our lives freely for the joy of the Lord that is set before us.

Therefore, the abundant life is for now. Nevertheless, the abundant life is not the fulfillment of our fleshly desires, because we observe that it was the *zoe* life that Jesus promised in greater abundance, and it is the *psuche* life that we must lose in order to obtain the abundant *zoe* life. This is the complete opposite of the health, wealth and prosperity teachers of our modern era. If they had not lost The Parable of the Cross, then they would never have fallen into this error and led so many sheep astray.

Now let us return to the trials of Jesus. When Pilate discovered that Jesus was a Galilean he sent Him to Herod, since *"He belonged to Herod's jurisdiction."* (Luk 23:7) Herod, then, *"greatly rejoiced ...because he had heard many things about Him. And he hoped to see some miracle done by Him."* (Luk 23:8) Albeit, after a great deal of questioning, Jesus stood silent, not acknowledging, or even responding at all to that great fox, king Herod. Because of this, Herod, attempting to save face, began *"humiliating Him [Jesus] with his guardsmen, and mocking Him by putting luxurious clothing around Him, [and then] Herod sent Him again to Pilate."* (Luk 23:11)

Herod was a despicable a man. Against the law of their day, he took his brother's wife, Herodias. She allowed her daughter to dance erotically before her husband and others. This was done in such an enticing manner that it caused him to offer as much as half of his Kingdom for the decadent passion she had stirred within him. He also feared and respected John the Baptizer, and yet, had his head delivered on a silver platter to his stepdaughter at the bequest of his depraved wife. This was not the model family, but rather, a family steeped in dissipation. Finally, he was especially fascinated with mysticism and desired to see miracles performed by this man, Jesus, whom he had heard so much about, and believed may have been John the Baptizer raised from the dead. (Luk 9:7) In spite of this, Herod still sought to kill Him on an earlier occasion. (Luk 13:31) Hence, that fox, Herod, was a depraved, intellectual man, whose passions and superstitions ruled over his heart and mind.

Herod asked Jesus to perform a miracle, and yet, he never repented of his ways. He looked at the holiness of God in the face and never felt any shame for his life, living an openly decadent, immoral life, even in the presence of the Holy One of God. He had no understanding that he stood naked before the Supreme Judge of the Earth. He believed that he was mocking of the King of the Jews, when, in reality, he was sealing his fate and mocking his own ignorance. He is a perfect illustration of people who profess to be wise and yet become fools. (Rom 1:21-22) He represents people today who have a superior intellect, and yet, will say things like, "*If God really exists, why doesn't He just show Himself to the world and then I will believe.*" Or, "*If Jesus is God, why doesn't He just come back and then I will believe?*" Or, silly questions like, "*If God created the world, then who created God?*" To all of these nonsensical questions, I believe we should respond as Jesus did, by saying nothing. At that moment, you will find that these naysayers will then despise you and your King, and begin to mock you and your faith in Messiah.

It is also unfortunate that a similar mindset has crept within the body of modern Christendom. Many of us have lost a healthy, reverent fear of the Lord and His punishments. Instead of comprehending a balance between Almighty's grace and His judgments, many only appear to focus upon the loving-kindness of our "*Abba, Father!*" (Rom 8:15) A great deal of this is because many believers still live in the flesh. Instead of choosing the abundant *zoe* life, they continue to abide in the abundant *psuche* life. This is precisely what Herod had done. He continued to fulfill his opulent desires, despite believing Jesus could perform miracles and John the Baptizer was a prophet from God. Notice, as well, that this man with so little morality believed in God, but he was not changed by God. Notice that this man wished to have Jesus, the magician in his mind, perform a show for him, but had no desire to see God's true miracle of a changed life performed within himself. He did not hate his *psuche* life but loves his *psuche* life. Because of this, he was the antithesis of John 12:25. He is a man who loved his *psuche* life and lost his *zoe* life, both in this life, and in the life to come. It is also fascinating that the world sees people like Herod as being richly fulfilled, but God's estimation is quite different, saying, *"Because you say, I am rich and increased with goods and have need of nothing ...[you] do not know that you are wretched and miserable and poor and blind and naked."* (Rev 3:17)

Furthermore, he is a mystical, spiritual man who has none of the marks of a holy, reverent life. He did not attend the synagogue of his day or read the scriptures, but he believed in God, and yet, had no boundaries that came with that belief. He is the epitome of the spiritual man without the Logos of God. He is the average American citizen and many unregenerate souls who claim Christianity today. For this reason, Lord makes it clear that first, we must repent, and then, He regenerates us. Since repentance precedes regeneration, it is necessary to know we need repentance. Because of this, we need the prevenient grace of the Spirit of God to convict us and cure our blindness, before we can see the Messiah standing right before our eyes.

Although Pilate was a ruthless, notorious and politically pragmatic politician, he looked so much better than the loathsome King Herod. At least Pilate was able to control his passions to some extent. He also had some degree dignity in the presence of the Lord of Glory and at least Pilate attempted to do the right thing, even though political expediency ultimately won the day.

Herod represents two things for us. First, he is the person you are witnessing to who has no desire to change his life. Therefore, we must pray that the Holy Spirit opens his eyes. Until that time, we should follow the Lord's admonition and *"not give that which is holy to the dogs"*. (Mat 7:6) He also represents who we were and what we are when we are so easily led astray from the moorings of the Holy Writ. For this reason, your life should be securely *"built upon the foundation of the apostles and prophets, [and] Jesus Christ Himself being the chief cornerstone.*" (Eph 2:20) Accordingly, I adjure you to keep the scriptures close to your heart and remain in them, lest you become deceived and "*tossed to and fro and carried about by every wind of doctrine, in the dishonesty of men, in cunning craftiness, to the wiles of deceit.*" (Eph 4:14)

Messiah would not acquiesce to Herod's desire for a magician's dog and pony show, and after growing tired of mocking and humiliating the Lord of Glory, he sent Him back to Pilate. Then, the ever politically pragmatic Pilate declared the Holy One of Israel innocent of all crimes, and yet, he still chose to punish Him with the brutally torturous cat o' nine tails, in order to appease the bitter wrath of Messiah's detractors, with the ultimate objective in mind to release Him, if He survived. However, nothing short of death would placate their vehement obsession for His blood. Choosing between good and evil is also similar to this, in that, we only have two choices, either we choose the headship of God or Satan. In our mind, we attempt to find a middle ground that will allow us to fulfill the desires of our sensual passions and still claim our innocence, but this is impossible, because God has made the choice mutually exclusive. It is as clear as black and white. With the primary purpose in view, to clear ourselves of the blame of sin, we attempt to rationalize our choices by mixing vain philosophies with the pure Word of God. Like the Gnostics of old, this is nothing more than "*giving heed to seducing spirits and doctrines of demons*", which taken to its ultimate conclusion results in a "*fall[ing] away from the faith*". (1Ti 4:1) However, The Way, The Truth, and The *Zoe* Life "*did not come to send peace*" in these circumstances, "*but a sword*" (Mat 10:34), "*the sword of the Spirit, which is the word of God*" (Eph 6:17), His Word of truth (Joh 17:17), which carries "*authority and power*" over the unclean spirits. (Luk 4:36)

> *For the Word of God is living and powerful and sharper than any two-edged sword, piercing even to the dividing apart of soul and spirit, and of the joints and marrow, and is a discerner of the thoughts and intents of the heart. (Heb 4:12 MKJV)*

Therefore, we should make no mistake about this, because there is no middle ground between sin and holiness and no grey reconciliation between good and evil. Sin is our Judas, the enemy that comes with all the deceitfulness of a friend, but in reality, it is a stalking lion waiting for an "*opportune time*" (Luk 4:13); crouching at the door, desiring to have you and to rule over you; but God has instructed us not to compromise with it but to rule over it. (Gen 4:7) Can there truly be any concession with the one who *"prowls around like a roaring lion"* (1Pe 5:8), who *"comes **only** to steal and kill and destroy"*? (Joh 10:10) Do not be deceived or deceive yourself Child of God, when you allow sin to enter the council chamber of your heart and intellectualize it, it will remain until it achieves its full desire, which is not to give you the abundant life, but rather to steal, kill and destroy your life. **You** are its desire. It desires to have you. God desires you as well, with a jealous and a fervent desire. Neither party will share you. However, the great Deceiver wishes to kill your *zoe* life by offering the deceitful food of desirable delicacies (Pro 23:3), which, in reality, are tasty morsels of death and disease that temporarily satisfy the appetites of your *psuche* life. Alternatively, the God of Light wishes to give you health and His life-giving spirit, which opens your eyes to the allusions of the shadows on the wall of the cave, which should in turn, give us the determination to mortify the *psuche* life of the flesh.

This is the greatest battle of history; it is our Armageddon. Yet how can we ever expect to win a battle against so great a foe? It is the battle of our lives, fought multiple times every single day for the ruler-ship of our hearts. Yeshua Our Righteousness admonishes, *"How long will you put off going in to take possession of the land, which the LORD, the God of your fathers, has given you?"* (Jos 18:3) How, Lord, can we ever expect to win the victory over the Goliath of our flesh? How can we say to that mountain of our ego, get up and be cast into the sea? Nevertheless, the Word of God promises, what is impossible with man is possible with God (Mat 19:26) and *"the battle is the LORD's"*; thus, He will give the victory into our hands. (1Sa 17:47) Yet how can we expect to win a battle with no armor or weapons? To which, the Lord says to fortify yourself daily with *"the full armor of God"* (Eph 6:13), girded with the belt of truth, the shield of faith *"and the sword of the Spirit, which is the Word of God, praying always with all prayer and supplication in the Spirit."* (Eph 6:13-18)

How could Pilate have withstood so great an enemy? He knew the spotless Lamb of God was innocent of all accusations, so he attempted to take a firm stand and set Him free. However, he stood on the shifting sands of relative truth; and when the tempest began to beat violently against the house of political expediency *"it fell, and great was the fall of it."* (Mat 7:27)

Now, after Jesus is brought back to Pilate, Pilate says to the Pharisees,

You brought me this man as one who was misleading the people. And after examining him before you, behold, I did not find this man guilty of any of your charges against him. Neither did Herod… Look, nothing deserving death has been done by him. I will therefore punish and release him. (Luk 23:14-16 ESV)

Notice how firmly he attempts to stand on the truth that Jesus is innocent, yet at the end of his statement is the compromise of that integrity, in an attempt to find a middle ground of concession with the bitter, acrimonious blood lust of the Pharisees. Notice also his self-contradiction. He said Jesus is innocent, and yet he will punish and then release Him. This is always the result of attempting to live in the nonsensical parallel universe of relative truth. People who hold to this worldview are walking contradictions. They are like a man attempting to stand firmly upon the shifting sands beside the pulsating waves of the sea. How can anyone ever expect to make a stand upon those sands? For, the sea will wash the sand away from under your feet. The truth is, no one actually believes in the relativity of truth. At some point, they will attempt to make a universal declaration they believe is true across all periods and all cultures, and so with their words they condemn themselves. (Mat 12:37) Here Pilate condemns himself, because he told the Pharisees that Jesus was innocent and then punished him severely anyways. In like manner Herod, found Messiah blameless, and yet he punished Him and then returned Him to Pilate. If the man was innocent, then why punish Him? This did not make sense in Pilate's case, except that he attempted to find a compromise that would appease the vehement passions of the fleshly Pharisees and the objective truth that the man was guiltless. As I stated earlier, there can be no middle ground of concession between the temporal fulfillment of sin and the truth of God; they are mutually exclusive choices. There is no fellowship between righteousness and lawlessness, no partnership between lightness and darkness and no agreement between Christ and Belial. (2Co 6:14-15)

Then, continuing to search for a way out of this dilemma, Pilate offered the people a compromise saying, *"But you have a custom that I should release one to you at the Passover. Then do you desire that I release to you the king of the Jews?"* (Joh 18:39) It is during this time in your trial, the Lord will speak to you in a still small voice to remind you to do the right thing. Likewise, we take note with Pilate that his wife sent him a message as the Pharisees begin to arouse the passions of the people. So *"as he was sitting down on the judgment seat, his wife sent to him, saying, 'Have nothing to do with that just man, for today because of Him I have suffered many things in a dream.'"* (Mat 27:19) In the meantime, *"the chief priests and elders persuaded the crowd that they should ask for Barabbas."* (Mat 27:20)

In this, we have an ideal, analogous picture of how the carnal man attempts to obtain victory over the passions of the flesh. Pilate is the intellect built upon relative truth. The Pharisees are the strong holds and those besetting sins to which a person is susceptible. The tumults of the people are the pulsating passions of the flesh. In this scenario, sin will eventually win the day and have its desire, you. Despite the fact that all logic says to do the right thing, you will make the irrational choice of death over life. This is how sin always wins its victories, because to select it defies reason. Consider a few examples. Does it make sense for a man to destroy years of faithful marriage and wreck his family to scratch the itch of erotic desires for one evening? Does it make sense to gamble all of your earnings away? Does it make sense to get drunk with your family's money they needed for dinner, shoes or other needs? Does it truly make sense to hit a person because he offended you? Does it make sense to steal when you do not need that substance to live, but rather wish to fulfill desire and want? Does sin ever make sense? The answer quite plainly is, never.

Therein lies one of the greatest contradictions of all. Most non-believers consider themselves the most reasonably objective people on the earth and the religious people as the ones driven by subjective emotions; and yet, they are the ones that choose relative truths and sin over logic. Sin does not even make logical sense to the non-believer, but they do all they can to intellectualize their choices and their justification, using reason to make the unreasonable reasonable.

Most unbelievers will not be as forthright as Aldous Huxley was in his book *"Ends and Means"* when he openly attested to his hidden motives for rejecting the God of the Bible:

> *I had motives for not wanting the world to have a meaning; and consequently assumed that it had none, and was able without any difficulty to find satisfying reasons for this assumption. The philosopher who finds no meaning in the world is not concerned exclusively with a problem in pure metaphysics. He is also concerned to prove that there is no valid reason why he personally should not do as he wants to do. For myself, as no doubt for most*

*of my friends, **the philosophy of meaninglessness was essentially an instrument of liberation from a certain system of morality**. We objected to the morality **because it interfered with our sexual freedom**. The supporters of this system claimed that it embodied the meaning - the Christian meaning, they insisted - of the world. **There was one admirably simple method of confuting these people and justifying ourselves in our erotic revolt:** we would deny that the world had any meaning whatever.*

I must admit that I find this passage refreshingly straightforward. I rarely will find a non-believer who is willing to be so transparent and honest about the actual reason they choose to reject God. It has nothing to do with logic, as you will notice, but everything to do with searching for a method to justify their desires, in order to allow passions to rule. This is to choose the *psuche* life over the *zoe* life. This is what the world chooses when it denies God, and unfortunately, this also is the choice Christians make when they choose the flesh over the spirit. The difference, although, between the Christian and the world is that the Christian cannot continue to live in that sin, being guilt-ridden and convicted by the Holy Spirit, until he falls to his knees and begs for mercy for having made the irrational choice of sin death over *zoe* life.

Pilate, then, feebly responds to the ever-increasing violent cries of the people, "*Why? What evil has He done?*" (Mat 27:23) To which the passions of the flesh begin a pulsating, riotous shouting against the spiritual man crying out, "*Crucify, crucify Him!*" (Luk 23:21)

What chance did Pilate ever have to win the victory over his sin? He built his life upon relative truth. He firmly planted his feet in the air. Next to him stood one who had built His life upon the ever-lasting, foundational truth of God. Next to Pilate was a man who was the physical embodiment of that objective truth, God's immutable truth. Next to the wavering Pilate stood the unwavering Messiah whose face was set as a flint. Pilate's armor of relative truth, political pragmatism, and compromise were "*weighed in the balances and found wanting.*" (Dan 5:27) His shield of faithlessness was not able to "*extinguish all the flaming darts of the evil one.*" (Eph 6:16) However, next to him stood one who had won the battle in the Garden of Gethsemane. When He was crushed in the spirit, when He was in such torment that He thought He might die, when He sweat great drops of blood, He won the victory by "*praying at all times in the Spirit, with all prayer and supplication*" (Eph 6:18) and was then strengthened by God in order to endure the trial.

Pilate failed, but Jesus succeeded. Pilate had no faith, no truth and attempted to stand in his own strength. Jesus, the Captain of our Faith, never wavered, not even for one moment. Jesus, however, was fitted for the battle, wearing; the *"belt of truth"*, *"the breastplate of righteousness"*, *"the shield of faith"*, *"the helmet of salvation"* and carrying *"the sword of the Spirit"*; having been strengthened in the spirit by *"all prayer and supplication."* (Eph 6:14-18)

Which one are you? Do you stand in your own faith or the faith of God? Do you have your own mixture of truth or hold only to the truth of His Holy Word? Do you stand in your own strength or the strength of the Holy Spirit through prayer? One has succeeded and one has failed. So many Christians today live defeat lives because they have not fully submitted to these truths. They attempt to win the victory over the flesh with their own *psuche* life, but that can never be, because God will not share His glory with anyone; nor should He. The victory is to lay down that *psuche* life and to allow The Way, The Truth and The *Zoe* Life not only to be your Savior but your Lord.

chapter fifteen

WHO DIES?

Now, Pilate, you are left with only one of two choices; either the *psuche* man will die or the *zoe* man will die. The Omniscient Lord of All Creation has not hidden this picture from our eyes. It is quite apparent, in His Providence; He had the people choose between Barabbas and Jesus. Yeshua Our Salvation, likewise, forewarned the people, *"If another shall come in his own name, him you will receive."* (Joh 5:43) Thus, Almighty God had the people choose between the murderous robber Barabbas and the innocent Lamb of God, Jesus. So *"The governor ...said to them, Which of the two do you desire that I release to you? They said, Barabbas."* (Mat 27:21)

Note that Satan is the foremost counterfeiter of the ages, and those who follow him as the lord of their flesh are being made in his image. Hence, we should not be surprised to discover that Barabbas' name also carries with it the hidden meaning, *"son of the father."* This means that the people chose the murderous, counterfeit son of the father for the innocent, genuine Son. Despite this similarity, they could not be more opposite. Barabbas was about revolution, but Jesus was about revelation. Barabbas committed treason. Jesus spoke the truth. Barabbas was a traitor. Jesus was a trusted teacher. Barabbas was a notorious murderer. Jesus came to give life and give it more abundantly. Yet when Pilate asked the people whom they preferred, they said, *"Barabbas"*! When they were asked what to do with this man who spent His life caring for, teaching, and healing the people they said, *"Crucify Him!"* What a terrible irony! The counterfeit son of the father was preferred over the genuine Son. Furthermore, He was falsely accused and unjustly crucified for the very crimes that Barabbas had actually committed; namely, treason and sedition against the state.

This is the ultimate picture of our salvation and propitiation we receive in Yeshua; that He paid the high cost for our sins. Therefore, you and I, Barabbas, do not have to die for our sins.

However, The Parable of the Cross has another subtle message hidden within this same picture; we may not have to die for our sins, but we have to die to our sins. You see, this is your daily sacrifice, "to present your bodies [as] a living sacrifice, holy, pleasing to God." *(Rom 12:1) This is our reasonable service, and this is the* "good and pleasing and perfect will of God." *(Rom 12:2) Thus, Pilate, we are called to choose daily between the notorious Barabbas of our flesh desires or the pure and Holy Son of God. We can do it our way, as Barabbas had done, or choose God's way. Like Pilate, we only have one of two mutually exclusive choices. Unlike Pilate, we cannot avoid the choice. Someone must die; it is either Yeshua Our Righteousness or the Barabbas of our notorious sin nature. This is the lost message of The Parable of the Cross.*

chapter sixteen

PICKING UP THE CROSS

Jesus, Our Example in the Faith, as all exceptional teachers do, led the way, demonstrating how we should accept the Will of God and pick up the cross set before us. He never acknowledged the circumstances of His trial, but all along kept His eyes fixed upon God the Father. Pilate was flabbergasted when He did not answer these false charges, so he asked, "*You will not speak to me? Do you not know that I have authority to release you and authority to crucify you?*" To which the Captain of Our Faith, whose face was set as a flint, responded, "*You would have no authority over me at all **unless it had been given you from above**.*" (Joh 19:11)

Christian, do you truly believe in Almighty God? Do you actually believe He is All-Powerful? Do you honestly acknowledge Him as the Sovereign Lord of the Universe? Then why do you always look at the circumstances and wonder "*why me?*" The answer to "*why you*" is, it is your calling that you have to die to yourself. It is the only way to grow into the high calling of your faith. Therefore, we should glory in our tribulations. We should not look at the trial and acknowledge it as supreme over our circumstance, but rather, we should keep our eyes fixed on the Almighty God that allowed these incidents to occur, because we have been "*predestined to be conformed to the image of his Son.*" (Rom 8:29) For this reason, we can then say with confidence and trust in God that "*all things work together for good, for those who are called according to his purpose.*" (Rom 8:28)

After Jesus carried the cross, a Roman soldier took Simon the Cyrene from the crowd, and placed the cross upon his shoulders. Once again, in this picture, we see The Parable of the Cross. Jesus came as your example in the faith and now that you have been called from the dead, Lazarus, it is time to pick up your cross daily and walk as He had walked. However, if you look beside you, Yeshua, Your Salvation, is walking with you every step of the way. For we are told, "*though I walk through the valley of the shadow of death, I will fear no evil; for You are with me."* (Psa 23:4) Furthermore, He has promised, *"I will never leave you nor forsake you"* (Heb 13:5), and *"I am with you always, to the end of the age."* (Mat 28:20) Therefore, in that time of trial, look beside you at the Champion of your Faith and do not give credence to the trial. Simon the Cyrene despised the shame of the cross, but Jesus walked with him the entire way.

Yeshua says to us *"I have said these things to you, that in me you may have peace. In the world you will have tribulation. But take heart; I have overcome the world."* (Joh 16:33) In addition, John the Apostle tells us *"For everyone who has been born of God overcomes the world. And this is the victory that has overcome the world--our faith."* (1Jn 5:4)

> *You say you have faith in God, then do as Jesus admonishes when He cursed the fig tree, "HAVE FAITH IN GOD." (Mar 11:22) Trust in His wisdom, trust in His plan!*

chapter seventeen

ON CALVARY

Notice how the Sovereign God painted the final picture of the cross. There were three men who were convicted on Golgotha, the place of the skull, Jesus, a repentant thief and an unrepentant thief. They were not only being crucified with the Lord of Glory, but at first, they spent their last hours reviling Him (Mar 15:32), and so one of them said, *"Are you not the Christ? Save yourself and us!"* (Luk 23:39) Yet the other thief, who had a change of heart, rebuked him, saying,

> *... Do you not fear God, since you are in the same condemnation. And we indeed justly so, for we receive the due reward of our deeds, but this Man has done nothing amiss. And he said to Jesus, Lord, remember me when You come into Your kingdom. (Luk 23:40-42 MKJV)*

What a perfect picture of our spiritual condition. Since we were called from the cave of sin and death, we now have the Spirit of Christ residing within us. Nevertheless, we still have that old corruptible nature of sin that also resides within us. At first, the spiritual man was dead, held entirely under the bondage of our sin nature, but now our spirit has been made alive to the new *zoe* life and recognizes Jesus as both our Lord and Savior. The unrepentant thief despises and reviles the Lord of Glory; he is the *"carnal mind [which] is enmity against God."* (Rom 8:7) However, the repentant thief is the man, who has been enabled by the gift of Messiah's all sufficient sacrifice, to *"walk not after the flesh, but after the Spirit"*, in whom, there is now no condemnation in Christ Jesus. (Rom 8:1)

Responding to the repentant sinner, Jesus says, *"Truly I say to you, Today you shall be with Me in Paradise."* (Luk 23:43) How wonderful is it that even though we have to go to the cross, Christ, our strength, is right there beside us the entire time!

The Lost Parable of the Cross

This is The Parable of the Cross. Jesus told us, "If anyone desires to come after Me, let him deny himself and take up his cross and follow Me." *(Mat 16:24) He also said,* "I am the Way, the Truth, and the Life; no one comes to the Father but by Me." *(Joh 14:6) Thus, we are to* **deny ourselves,** *for this is* **the way,** *and we are to* **take up our cross,** *for this is* **the truth** *of our salvation and sanctification, and we are to* **follow Him,** *for this is* **the life** *and the only way to the Father. This is it; there is no other way, for the Lord of Glory says that no one comes to the Father but by [through] Him!*

chapter eighteen

THE LAST WORDS OF THE INNOCENT

First and last words are always the most important. Communication researchers have found that most people pay little attention to the words in the middle, but the first and the last words are recalled at a significantly higher rate. So, what were Jesus' last words?

His last words on the cross were, "*It is finished.*" (Joh 19:30) Meaning,

> ...**we have been sanctified through the offering of the body of Jesus Christ <u>once for all</u>**. *And every priest stands daily at his service, offering repeatedly the same sacrifices, which can never take away sins. But when* **Christ had offered <u>for all time a single sacrifice for sins</u>**, *he sat down at the right hand of God, (Heb 10:10-12 ESV)*

That was it. It was a single sacrifice through which we are saved, once and for all-time, by which, we are able to be sanctified before God. It is not our work that saved us, Lazarus. Neither, is it our work that sanctifies us, Simon the Cyrene.

His last words in the Gospel and before the ascension were:

> *All authority in heaven and on earth has been given to me. Go therefore and* **make disciples** *of all nations, baptizing them in the name of the Father and of the Son and of the Holy Spirit, teaching them to observe all that I have commanded you. And behold,* **I am with you always**, *to the end of the age. (Mat 28:18-20 ESV)*

His last words in the book of Acts were:

> *But you will receive power when the Holy Spirit has come upon you, and* **you will be my witnesses** *in Jerusalem and in all Judea and Samaria, and to the end of the earth. (Act 1:8 ESV)*

The Lost Parable of the Cross

This is The Great Commission of Christ, and this is the final lesson of The Parable of the Cross. Everyone comprehends that Yeshua called us to be witnesses so the Word of God will go forth to the ends of the earth. As I have already related, we are now the hands, feet and mouths of Christ to a lost world. However, lost to most believers is that we are not only called to become witnesses for their sake, but also, we are called to be witnesses for our own sake. Notice, that the word witness in the Greek is *"martyr"*, which is exactly what we are called to be in our lives. The hope of our high calling is to live the *zoe* life by putting the *psuche* life to death. We are assisted in that endeavor by witnessing the Gospel of Christ to a lost world. Jesus told us that the world would hate us because it first hated Him. (Joh 15:18) If the world does not hate you, at least at times, then you may not truly be a martyr for Christ. As bad as this may sound to your lower-self nature, it is the only way to your higher calling to become like Him. Christ unequivocally states, *"You **will** be hated by all **for My name's sake**, but **the one who underlines to the end will be saved**."* (Mat 10:22)

We must continually remind ourselves we are eternal beings, and the small amount of time we spend in this temporary life will determine our entire eternity.

For that reason, the very last words of the King of Kings and the Lord of Our Hearts in scriptures are:

> *Behold, I am coming soon, bringing my recompense with me, to repay everyone for what he has done. I am the Alpha and the Omega, the first and the last, the beginning and the end. ...I, Jesus, have sent my angel to testify to you about these things for the churches. I am the root and the descendant of David, the bright morning star ...Surely I am coming soon. (Rev 22:7-20 ESV)*

He is appearing more and more every day in our lives. I said at the beginning of this book that the Old Testament story began with life, and the New Testament story, likewise, begins with life, but our story begins with our death. Now, however, notice that where the Old Testament ended with the failure of mankind to bridge the gap to God and find life, the New Testament ends with the success of finding life through death. We find our life through the death of Jesus, and we find the sanctifying abundant *zoe* life through the death of our *psuche* life.

> *The Bright Morning Star is coming soon. He is coming more and more every day in our lives as we learn through The Parable of the*

Cross to lay down our lives. Our Joshua, The Lord of Hosts, The King of Kings and the Lord of Lords, The Alpha and the Omega has come to conquer the land, and He will not stop until it is thoroughly accomplished. Our All in All says He will repay us for becoming that vessel through which He worked. As a result, we must decrease, so He may increase. (Joh 3:30) Therefore, The First Born Among Many Sons repeats in His last discourse "I am coming soon." *What else can we say to you our Beloved Lord and Savior, but with opens arms, and open hearts* "Amen. Come, Lord Jesus!" *(Rev 22:20)*

THE FOUND PARABLE OF THE CROSS

Throughout this entire book, I have spoken of The Parable of the Cross and yet the name of the book is the Lost Parable of the Cross. This parable has never actually been missing, and yet it has been lost for so many years. It has always been as obvious as the nose on your face, and yet it has been hidden to our generation. Unlike Josiah who sought after God, and then found the Word of God hidden by the priests from his evil grandfather, the Bible is alive and well on most American shelves. Nevertheless, very much like the days of Josiah, the actual message has been perverted by that Great Perverter of All Things. The American Puritans followed after God's Word in order to find a new land that would be set as a city upon a hill, a light, a beacon for the lost and so the Lord of All blessed this country with unfathomable riches. Then, as in the Book of Judges, we forgot the Lord Our God, and followed what was right in our own eyes. Now, a Bible is in every house collecting dust, and we have been led astray, because the Word of God has been hidden under our noses. Thus, The Parable of the Cross that so many Bible believing Christians clearly understood throughout the centuries has, likewise, become hidden, lost and forgotten to a lost generation that has forgotten God and His Word.

We have fallen prey to our own fleshly desires, because we do not know the voice of our Lord. Evil-doers preaching health, wealth and prosperity to fulfill those fleshly passions have seduced us. We have fallen so far that we have been sending our sons and daughters through the fire just as evil Manasseh did during his reign. We have set up idols in our houses, churches and our hearts.

Therefore, Lazarus, now that you know the truth, and you are no longer a blind beggar in the bondage of sin; what will you do? When King Josiah found the truth, he acted immediately taking *"away **ALL***

302

the abominations from __ALL__ the territory that belonged to the people of Israel." (2Ch 34:33) Will you now pull down your idols and "*present your bodies as a living sacrifice, holy and acceptable to God*" (Rom 12:1), so you will "*not be conformed to this world, but be transformed by the renewal of your mind*" (Rom 12:2); and thereby fulfill your destiny to become "*conformed to the image of his Son*"? (Rom 8:29) On the other hand, will you be a forgetful hearer, who is not blessed in your doings but rather deceived in your heart? (Jas 1:23-25)

My hope is that this parable will no longer be lost but will be found, in us, and revealed to the nations. So that we all can say, we now "*know Him and the power of his resurrection*", and because we "*share His sufferings*", we are "*becoming like him in His death.*" (Php 3:10) Therefore, we proclaim to ourselves and to the world:

> *I have been crucified with Christ. It is no longer I who live, but Christ who lives in me. (Gal 2:20 MKJV)*

Then, The Parable of the Cross will no longer be lost but found, in us.

www.ingramcontent.com/pod-product-compliance
Lightning Source LLC
Chambersburg PA
CBHW071407090426
42737CB00011B/1388